Casebook Rhetoric

David Tedlock and Paul Jarvie

Casebook
Rhetoric SECOND EDITION

A Problem-Solving Approach to Composition

HOLT, RINEHART and WINSTON

New York Chicago San Francisco Philadelphia
Montreal Toronto London Sydney Tokyo
Mexico City Rio de Janeiro Madrid

Library of Congress Cataloging in Publication Data

Tedlock, David, 1951–
  Casebook rhetoric.

  Bibliography: p. 342
  Includes index.
  1. English language—Rhetoric. I. Jarvie, Paul,
1949–   . II. Title.
PE1408.T375 1985   808'.042   84-15868

ISBN 0-03-070719-6

Address correspondence to:
383 Madison Avenue
New York, NY 10017

CBS COLLEGE PUBLISHING
Holt, Rinehart and Winston
The Dryden Press
Saunders College Publishing

For Sandy and Sharon—
Again

David Tedlock, after ten years of teaching composition at Brown University, Rhode Island Junior College, Roger Williams College, the Harvard Business School, and Iowa State University, is now Copy Chief at DuVal Advertising, Tucson, Arizona.

Paul Jarvie, who has taught writing at Tufts University, the Harvard Business School, and Boston University's College of Basic Studies, is now a vice president at Forum Corporation, Boston, Massachusetts.

To The Instructor

Assuming for a moment that you're already familiar with the case approach and that your first question in reading this preface is, "What's different about the second edition?," our first answer is "Part III: Beyond Cases." It's true that Parts I and II offer eleven new cases as well as new or revised discussions of problem solving, revision, invention, organization, the use of examples, and the use of division and classification. It's true that many of the original cases, discussion questions, and assignments have been strengthened. But most importantly, Part III takes students where they must go: beyond self-contained cases to research and to a real search for the kinds of subjects and approaches to subjects that characterize successful writing.

Part III begins with a brief discussion of library as well as other kinds of research and includes ten research cases. It also offers guidance on writing about literature, visual experiences, current events, and popular culture. This part of the text concludes with a discussion of selected approaches to essay writing, specifically: the humorous essay, the "letter," the confessional, and the dialogue. Part I of the text, in teaching problem-solving and audience analysis techniques, uniquely prepares students for success in using these selected approaches. In sum, Part III suggests ways for student writers to use the skills taught in Parts I and II to complete writing assignments that go beyond self-contained cases.

Parts I and II of the text continue with their two-part approach to teaching writing. Part I emphasizes the writing process, while Part II discusses the traditional modes and methods of development. With the additional cases in Parts I, II, and III, the text now contains 67 cases and more than 200 specific writing assignments. We still define a "case" as a statement which describes a problem-centered, writing situation, but the "research cases" in Part III are not self-contained; each *requires* students to gather information independently.

These research cases retain three of the important features of the cases from Parts I and II: they establish a genuine purpose for writing, fulfill the writer's need to identify a particular audience to whom to write, and provide a context in which the writing can be done.

If you want your students to see that writing well is a practical necessity in many real life situations, and if you want your students to write with a greatly improved sense of purpose and audience, then *Casebook Rhetoric* may be an excellent text for you and your students. In general what's unique about teaching writing through the case approach is that you and your students share crucial details about each particular writing situation. In the cases in Parts I and II of the text, you and your students share precisely the same information about each particular writing situation. This precise sharing of information provides you with unique opportunities to concretely discuss and demonstrate steps or aspects of the writing process.

In the "Officer Fox" case in Chapter 2, for example, you can assign the case as out-of-class reading and then follow up with in-class freewriting based on the first suggested writing assignment "You are Patrol Captain William E. Barton. Write a report for the chief in which you persuade him the action you have taken is appropriate." After the students have finished freewriting you could choose to temporarily collect their work and read a few samples (randomly chosen and completely anonymous) aloud. Brief discussions of these sample student freewriting exercises can show the students the value of the practice itself.

Alternatively, problem solving can be taught in a particular case by asking students to define the problems in the case and then propose solutions. By using the blackboard to record responses, you can guide the class through a concrete demonstration of problem solving. A different approach, applying the principles of audience analysis, would be to identify and analyze potential readers in a particular case—each case provides students with potential audiences as well as some details about those audiences. There are many more ways, of course, to use the cases to demonstrate the writing process. Some of these are discussed in detail in the Instructor's Guide, which we encourage you to examine.

To Basic Writing Teachers

In basic writing courses, one of the blessings of the case approach is that many students will be especially attracted to the real life writing situations which the cases describe. Another special benefit may be that the cases in Parts I and II, in providing large quantities of information for student writers to work with, allow students to concentrate on basics such as a solid organization, quality content, clarity and coherence, and, of course, correctness. First edition users of the text who teach basic writing courses have been enthusiastic about its success. The improvements in Parts I and II, particularly in Chapters 1 and 2, should make the second edition even more useful in basic writing courses. Part III may go further than basic writers are ready to travel, but even so, many basic writing teachers may want to discuss and make at least one assignment from Part III. "The Case of the Plagiarized Paper" is just one good source for a useful class discussion and a valuable writing assignment.

To Freshman Composition Teachers

Nearly all students find the self-contained cases in Parts I and II of this text initially refreshing, but these cases are by nature ultimately limiting. Thus one option for using the text successfully is to alternate assignments between the self-contained cases in Parts I and II and the research cases or options in Part III. In a sixteen week course requiring 8–12 essays, for example, the assignments might be arranged as follows:

1–2 assignments from 1 or 2 cases from Chapters 1 and/or 2

1   assignment from a research case (e.g., a campus problem)

1–2 assignments from 1 or 2 cases from Chapters 3 and/or 4

1   assignment from a research case (e.g., a literary analysis)

1–2 assignments from 1 or 2 cases from Chapters 5 and/or 6

1–2 assignments from Part III: Additional Sources (e.g., current events or popular culture)

1   assignment from 1 or 2 cases from Chapters 7 and/or 8

1   assignment from Part III, Approaches to Subjects (e.g., use of persona)

Varying the assignments in this way will help maintain students' enthusiasm for the case approach while providing them with a sampling of the assignments from Part III, all of which stress invention and/or research.

To Teachers Using a Reader

Casebook Rhetoric can also be used effectively in coordination with a reader of your choice. This combination of texts works well: the cases offer excellent opportunities to teach the writing process while the readings offer excellent opportunities to analyze writing models. This process/models approach can also provide an effective variety of writing assignments. One approach would be to begin with two case assignments and thereafter alternate between case and reading based assignments. Another possibility, of course, is to alternate case and reading assignments from the beginning.

To Teachers of Advanced Composition Courses

For students in pre-professional freshman English programs or in advanced composition courses, the case approach can be a stimulating way to improve analytical and writing skills. These students often expect to write at least a few critical analyses of literature and to be given some challenging, open-ended assignments. Thus an instructor teaching such a class may want to begin the course with one or two assignments from Part I, add two more from Part II, and then move on to Part III for a number of assignments—the ten research cases create dozens of opportunities and the section, "Additional Approaches to Subjects," suggests five additional possibilities.

To All Writing Teachers

Casebook Rhetoric has been an effective text for many writing teachers. The second edition should be useful to a wider range of teachers of writing while still serving first edition users well. Thank you if you've tried the text in the past or are considering using it in the future. We believe that this is a good book but the magic is still up to you. We hope you have a few tricks up your sleeve, and we admire the thousands of writing teachers who continue grasping for the rabbit in the hat.

Acknowledgments

For this edition of the text I am especially grateful to Charlotte Smith, our developmental editor at Holt, who provided me with so much guidance and support. I am also thankful to Helen Ewald, Iowa State University, who commented on the prefatory material. And I thank all of our reviewers, those who commented on the first edition of the text as well as those who read the revisions to it included here.

DAVID TEDLOCK

Contents

Part III
Beyond Cases   **307**

Cases Listed by Topic

Business Decisions

College Life

Campus Organizations

Family and Personal Relationships

Literary Analyses

Politics

Social Issues

To The Student

If you haven't already expected us to tell you what a casebook is, you should. As a reader, one of your first questions should be, "What does the title tell me?" Technically, we define a case as a statement which describes a problem-centered writing situation. In other words, cases are narratives about people who have problems to solve. The problems involve rhetoric—the art and science of communicating effectively. You'll become a better writer by analyzing cases, solving writing problems, and learning about rhetoric. That's the purpose of this text—to help you become a better writer.

The cases in Parts I and II of this case are self-contained. Therefore, you should never create information you cannot find in the case or reasonably infer from it. You may draw conclusions and make assumptions, but you have to be ready to support those conclusions and defend those assumptions based on the material in the case. Parts I and II require you to focus exclusively on the case because writers always reach limits to the amount of information available to them. You can never know all there is to know about a specific subject before your deadline comes and you have to complete a written assignment.

Focusing on case facts in Parts I and II will also enable you to spend more time developing specific problem-solving, writing skills. In Part III of the text your instructor may assign you one or more research cases—cases that require you to go out and complete research before you write your assignment.

There are two other aspects of the cases and this text you should know about right now. One is that the information in the cases is *not* already organized for you. That's a realistic feature too. Whenever you gather information about a writing situation you have to organize that information yourself; it never comes prepackaged. Good writers are chefs, not microwave oven operators.

Another characteristic of this book you should know about involves the sample student writing in Part I. You may find various errors and weaknesses in this student writing. Always remember that these samples were selected neither as the best nor as the only possible responses to a case.

The student writing simply provides you and your instructor with one more way to discuss the principles upon which each chapter focuses.

Now you're ready to read your first chapter and your first case. As you work your way through the text, remember that it's intended to give you writing opportunities of many kinds, not servings of fast-food or steady diets of one kind of writing for one kind of audience about one kind of subject. At its best, writing always involves you in a variety of challenging contexts; one way to grow in the beginning is to ensure that not all of these contexts are of your own choosing. This text creates hundreds of beginnings; the endings are all up to you.

Casebook Rhetoric

Part I

A Problem-Solving Approach to Composition

Problem solving, like many other terms, means different things to different people. In a calculus class, you may think of problem solving as working on an equation until you come up with the right answer. Problem solving in composition, however, does *not* mean simply using a few formulas to come up with the one and only correct answer to a problem. When you write, you can always communicate effectively—solve your writing problem—in many different ways. As we use the term here, problem solving generally means systematically analyzing and solving real-life problems. Specifically, problem solving means deliberately defining and solving the *writing* problems you face.

In Chapter 1, you will read about how to analyze and solve typical problems you might face in real life. In "The Summer Sun Club" case, for example, Mike Morenberg has problems with an employee, an unhappy customer, and an unhappy employer. Mike must analyze and solve these problems. As you read "The Summer Sun Club," you will need to analyze Mike's problems and consider various solutions to them. Similarly, as you read and discuss other cases in this book, you will be analyzing and solving real-life problems.

Because you are reading a composition text, the cases in it also focus on different kinds of writing problems. Each problem-centered writing situation you read about will differ in various ways, but all the cases will involve you in the process of defining the problem and finding solutions (Chapter 1), inventing and organizing your material (Chapter 2), analyzing your audience (Chapter 3), and determining your purpose (Chapter 4).

Writing involves you in a process of making thousands, even tens of thousands of decisions. We think you can make those decisions more easily and effectively by taking a problem-solving approach to composition each time you write. With a problem-solving attitude you know that no matter how much difficulty you're having, if you learn enough about writing and apply what you know, you can solve any writing problem you face. You tell yourself, "This is a tough decision to make or I wouldn't be stuck. Why can't I make this decision? What is the problem I am trying to solve? Who is my audience? What is my purpose? How can I invent and develop material to solve the problem? What are the possible solutions?"

Once you begin to ask and answer these questions each time you write, you are ready to move on to Part Two of the text. Part Two teaches you about specific rhetorical modes and methods of development and gives you cases with which to practice them, but you can learn more about them when you get there. For now, let's get on with Chapter 1.

Analyzing the Problem and Finding Solutions

This chapter is designed to help you analyze and solve the writing problems you face. It's a simple idea: if you take the time to define a problem, to make sure you really know what you're up against, then you can more easily come up with an effective solution. So this chapter gives you guidelines and practice in problem solving. We begin by discussing how you can define problems and end by showing you how to analyze solutions.

Know the Facts

If you are going to think clearly about any problem, the first step you must take is to make sure you know the facts of the situation. And because so much information is usually available to you, you have to search for the key facts. One way to begin to do that is to ask yourself the six questions: **Who? What? When? Where? Why? How?**

Suppose you are driving down the interstate by yourself and your car stalls. You try to start it up again as you begin to coast, but the car won't start and you have to come to a stop in the breakdown lane. If you asked yourself the six questions above, you might conclude the following:

Who?	Myself only.
What?	My car stalled and won't start.
When?	It's 7:45 and my first class starts in an hour and fifteen minutes.
Where?	About five miles from school, and about a mile from the nearest exit. There's no gas station in sight and the

ten-foot-high, chain-link fence looks too tall for me to climb over.

Why?   I don't know.
How?   I don't know.

You haven't answered the "How?" and "Why?" questions yet, but it is important to do so before considering possible solutions. In defining any problem, you must always be careful to consider all the facts and to avoid coming to hasty conclusions. Suppose, for example, that your answer to the "How (am I stuck)?" question is this: It's sixty degrees below zero outside with the windchill factor; I can't even get out of the car for more than five minutes without practically freezing to death. Alternatively, suppose your answer to the "How?" question is this: It's a balmy 60 degrees outside, the sun is shining, and I'm on my way to take a final exam!

You may think that for these simple examples the solutions are simple as well as obvious—if it's sixty below outside you wait in your car for help; if it's warm enough outside and you have to take a final in a little over an hour, you either fix the car in a hurry or walk to the nearest exit and try to get a ride to school in a hurry. But even these solutions are not obvious to everyone: every year people literally freeze to death because they've left their cars in extremely cold weather and tried to walk somewhere for help.

Suppose, finally, that your answer to the "How?" question yields these facts: It's a pleasant sixty degrees outside and sunny. I'm on my way to class; fortunately, I don't have any assignments due or tests to take. Now you may be ready to define the "Why?" part of the problem: *why* has the car failed? Perhaps most of us would begin by looking at the gas gauge. Suppose it says you have three-quarters of a tank of gas. So you think, "The problem isn't gas." Or do you?

Be Careful in Making Assumptions

What assumption would you be making if you concluded, by looking at the gas gauge, that you were not out of gas? Of course, you'd be assuming that the gas gauge was accurate. Suppose, however, you also know two more facts about the situation. First, you can't remember when you filled the tank, but you know it's been a long time. Second, you seem to remember that every time you looked at the gas gauge the last few times you drove the car, it read three-quarters full.

Given these additional pieces of information, or even without them, you might not want to *assume* that the car has some gas. Assumptions can mislead you, especially when they are based on little or no evidence.

Since assumptions are often not based on facts, it's easy to make the wrong ones, ones that other people will disagree with because they can just as easily make different assumptions.

Take a Different Perspective

One way to avoid making weak assumptions is to look at the situation from another person's perspective or point of view. Suppose you get a mechanic out there on the freeway to help you. Is the mechanic going to assume you have gas in the car? Of course not. Even if you tell the mechanic that your gas gauge reads three-quarters full, he or she probably won't assume the gauge is accurate. All experienced mechanics have presumably had a call from a motorist who ran out of gas because the gauge was broken. Therefore, by taking a different perspective on the situation, in this case a mechanic's, you're less likely to make poor assumptions and weak inferences.

Make Strong Inferences

An inference is a conclusion you make based upon the key facts you have. When you make a conclusion based upon specific information, you're reasoning inductively. Suppose, then, that you consider these facts: car stopped for no apparent reason, gas gauge says three-quarters full, gas gauge has read three-quarters for quite some time, can't remember when I last filled up. Using these facts, you might infer or conclude that you can't be certain you have gas in the car.

To continue defining your problem, you'd have a couple of options at this point. You know you need proof, evidence, a key fact to show you've got gas. You could simply say, "The problem is that I know absolutely nothing about cars so I've got to get help." But suppose you really do want to make sure you have gas. You decide to get out, take the gas cap off, rock the car, and listen for the sound of gasoline sloshing around in the tank. You find you can't hear a thing. Now, can you be certain you're out of gas?

Consider the Amount and Value of Your Evidence

Whenever you accumulate information, you should consider its amount and value. Suppose that while you are squatting there on the freeway with your ear plastered to the mouth of the gas tank, semitruck trailers are roaring by at sixty-five m.p.h. and nearly blowing you and your car off the road. Not only can you not hear gas sloshing in the tank; you can't even hear yourself think!

On the other hand, suppose you *do* hear gas sloshing around and you can smell it, too. Now you have enough valuable evidence to enable you to infer that you have gas. To continue defining your problem, you have to keep searching for key facts.

You might try starting the car again, or you might look under the hood and check the radiator to see if the car is overheated. You might even know enough to take off the air filter and look down into the carburetor. If the carburetor is dry, you could deduce that the trouble is somewhere in between the gas tank and the carburetor. You reason deductively when you use a generalization (gas has to go from the tank to the carburetor to run the engine) and apply it to a specific situation (I've got gas in the tank but none in the carburetor) to draw a conclusion (something is wrong in between my carburetor and tank). Your conclusion might be more specific—either there is a plug in the line or my fuel pump is broken. (Or, if you know more about cars than we do, perhaps you can think of other possible causes of the problem.)

Now Analyze Possible Solutions

Consider what you've done so far. You have gathered key facts, avoided making poor assumptions, considered the amount and value of your evidence, and made some good inductive and deductive inferences. You've also learned that part of defining the problem involves looking for its cause.

In this example, you've defined the problem as follows: the car won't work because, evidently, the gas isn't making it from the tank to the carburetor. Once you've defined the problem, it's much easier to decide on a solution. Three solutions you might want to consider in this case are: trying to repair it yourself, waiting in the car until help comes, or walking until you reach a pay phone or gas station.

When analyzing possible solutions, you should again consider key facts, the problem's cause, and the costs and benefits of each possibility. If you tried to repair the car yourself, for example, you might save money and time, but you also might cause more damage to the car, ruin your clothes, and waste time accomplishing nothing. If you stay in the car until help comes, you might feel safer—you can lock the doors and roll up the windows—but you might wait for hours. If you walk to a gas station, you have to consider how long it will take you, whether you can find one, what the weather is like, and whether you want to risk getting hit by a car. Only a careful consideration of these costs and benefits, based on the key facts you know and the assumptions and inferences you can make, will guide you to the best possible solution.

Take a Problem-Solving Approach to Writing Situations

Now that you have read about how a problem-solving approach can be applied to a general problem in real life—having your car break down on the freeway—consider taking a problem-solving approach to a writing situation. In the case of "The Summer Sun Club," which immediately follows this section, Mike Morenberg has to write to his employer, Mr. Garston. If you were to define Mike's problem of writing to Mr. Garston, you could begin by determining the key facts of the case. Asking yourself the questions Who? What? When? Where? Why? and How?, you might say, "Mr. Garston is angry because a mother, Mrs. Stephens, criticized the Summer Sun Club when Mike did not immediately notify her about her son's accident."

As you consider Mike's problem and what he should do, you have to be careful in making assumptions. You may note, for example, that Mrs. Stephens is the daughter of someone who is important to Mr. Garston, but you cannot assume that Mike should therefore either resign or be fired. One way to avoid making poor assumptions is to look at the problem from different perspectives. What is Mrs. Stephens's view of the problem? What is Mr. Garston's? What is Mike's? You can even look at the problem from the viewpoint of one of Mike's assistants, Maxine Kramer.

Considering these perspectives should enable you to make some strong inferences about the problem. Mrs. Stephens's concern is understandable; Mr. Garston has a reason to be upset; yet Mike made his mistake (and perhaps Maxine made a mistake too) during difficult circumstances—a fight, a bloody nose, a ruined blouse, a screaming child. Given this analysis, what possible solutions does Mike have? Of course, he could write to Mr. Garston and simply tell him what happened. Or, he could try to explain to Mr. Garston *why* it happened. Yet another possibility would be for Mike to explain not only what happened and why but also to persuade Mr. Garston that the problem won't occur again, that the cause of the problem has been eliminated. Mike has to decide which possible solution would be best for him given the circumstances described in the case. As you read the case, see if you can define the problem even more specifically than we have here, and consider other possible solutions to the problems Mike faces.

Remember that, in both defining a problem and analyzing possible solutions, you should find the key facts, be careful in making assumptions, take different perspectives on the problem, and make inferences based upon the amount and quality of your evidence. When analyzing the problem, you should consider its cause; when analyzing solutions, consider their costs and benefits.

Keeping these guidelines in mind can help you make writing decisions. Of course, the more you know about writing, the more easily you can analyze and decide. When reading about the problem of having your car break down on the freeway, you may have thought, "That's how writing is for me sometimes—I get stuck and don't know what to do." If you're inexperienced in writing, then you may feel the way many people do when their car stops running. They open the hood, look down on that hopelessly confusing collection of plastic and metal, and give up. They can't repair the engine *not only* because they don't know what the parts are called or how they work *but also* because they don't even have the right tools to work with.

Of course, repairing a car and solving a writing problem are different. In their way, mechanics have to be creative; perhaps writers need a different, special kind of imagination. Another big difference is that while inexperienced mechanics may be able to pay a professional to solve their problems for them, most student writers have to solve their own.

Define Your Own Writing Problems

As a writer, one way to classify your writing problems would be to say there are two kinds: typical problems you know you personally have any time you write, and special problems that arise in a particular piece of writing.

You should already know what many of your own typical problems are. Ask yourself, right now, "What kinds of problems do I have when I write?" Make a list. You know what your common problems are, generally, both from your own experience as a writer and from what teachers have told you. Your list might include problems such as these: getting started, spelling, thinking of the best topic, coming up with enough information, avoiding grammatical mistakes, getting organized, and so on. Since your first step as a problem solver is to identify problems, begin right now. Make a list of the problems you know you usually have when you write.

If one of your problems is "getting started" or "having enough information," then read Chapter 2 before you write your next essay, letter, or memo. Chapter 2 can help you now because it suggests possible solutions to the problems of getting started, getting enough information, and getting organized. After you make your list, you should also read the introductions to each of the other chapters in this book. If any of these chapters seem to be about particular writing problems you know you always have, then read those chapters too, right now. Perhaps you'll find some solutions there.

Of course each time you write something new you'll also have problems connected with that particular piece of writing. You know from your own experience that discovering problems is just as difficult, or even more difficult, than finding solutions to them. In fact, no one who writes, including professional writers, discovers all the problems before the writing itself gets read by somebody else, by a reader. The difference between beginners and professionals, though, is that professionals are better at *being* that somebody else to begin with. Professional writers are the best problem solvers in writing because they can imagine what readers will think as they read. Here are some ways you can try to be that somebody else, the reader, and thereby detect writing problems before it's too late to solve them.

Write Ten Drafts

Why not write ten drafts? Most professional writers write several drafts—they write a draft or two or three, combine them or select one, and then revise that draft several times. Since you're not a professional writer, you should write more drafts than the pros, maybe nine or ten.

However many you write, the most important point to remember is this: you have to write a number of complete drafts to discover most of the basic writing problems you have and then solve them. A major mistake inexperienced writers make is planning to write just a couple of drafts and then feeling pressured because dozens of writing problems come up all at the same time. No one can solve six problems simultaneously. It's much better to solve problems one at a time, one *draft* at a time.

Of course there's a kind of law of diminishing returns here. If you actually wrote fifty drafts of an essay you probably wouldn't discover and solve many problems between draft number forty-nine and draft number fifty. Perhaps you wouldn't find *any* problems to solve, and certainly whatever improvements you did make might not be important enough to warrant writing a fiftieth draft. But ten drafts might be just what you need. Be honest with yourself about the writing process and don't expect to solve all your problems in two or three drafts. Professionals can't, so certainly you can't.

Give It Time

Probably the biggest mistake beginning writers make is in not allowing enough time to elapse *between* drafts. Often the *worst* time to reread your writing and look for problems is just after you've finished a complete draft. If, for example, you finish draft number three at one in the morning, then you probably can't expect to make major revisions at five after one. Instead, wait until the next morning, or better yet, wait a *couple of days*. The longer you wait, the better chance you'll have to read your own work the way someone else would and therefore discover problems in the writing.

Try putting twenty-four hours between each major block of time you devote to writing. That way each time you return to your work you will be more likely to see your writing with a fresh perspective. The best problem solvers, after all, are people who manage to look at a problem in a new way.

Read It Aloud

Writing ten drafts and giving yourself time to gain a fresh perspective will help you the most in detecting organizational and content problems in your writing. Reading your prose aloud will be most useful to you in helping you to discover other problems—particularly in style and correctness. In other words, reading aloud will help detect problems such as awkward or incoherent sentences as well as grammatical and spelling errors.

Reading your draft aloud just once may actually enable you to eliminate as many as half the grammatical and spelling errors you would have missed otherwise. As you read your work aloud, circle the phrases that sound awkward to you or are difficult to read smoothly. And if your spelling or punctuation looks wrong, then circle those potential problems and keep reading. When you've finished the entire essay, try to define the problems you have and find a solution to each one. And remember, if you make any changes, read the essay aloud *again* to make sure the new version sounds right.

Try A Tape Recording

Some inexperienced writers don't detect weaknesses in grammar or style by reading aloud. These writers get so involved in *reading* they can't pay sufficient attention to what they're *hearing*. In other words, they can't be a listener because they're still too busy being the writer. In this case, an effective way to become a reader of your own writing is to tape record yourself as you read aloud and then play back your recording as you read your written copy. Note any problem areas.

If you don't have a tape recorder and can't borrow one, ask someone else to do the reading aloud for you. Either way, as a problem solver you should be listening for places that don't sound right and watching for phrases, words, or punctuation that doesn't look right.

Use Your Finger

If you really have written several drafts, given yourself time between them, and listened to yourself reading aloud, then you've probably eliminated virtually all the problems you are capable of identifying and solving. Still, some writers find it necessary to take additional precautions to avoid grammatical and spelling errors. If you know you're a poor speller or have problems with grammar and punctuation, then try this proofreading procedure.

Take a blank piece of notebook paper or typing paper and place it directly underneath the line you are proofreading. As you read, use your index finger to point out every word and punctuation mark. Read aloud so that you make yourself say every word and punctuation mark that's really there on the page—even the best writers occasionally read in words they haven't actually written down. Using the paper and your finger as a guide, you may be able to detect a few errors you might have missed otherwise. Writers desperate to eliminate spelling errors can actually go one step further in detecting problems—they can read their writing backwards, from end to beginning. Of course, the writing doesn't make any sense this way, so all that's left for the writer to do is look at each individual word and determine whether it's spelled correctly. Sometimes writers with severe spelling problems can eliminate many errors this way.

Find A Reliable Reader

Even professional writers get advice from other writers before their intended readers finally read what's been written. This textbook, for example, was read and analyzed by several professionals before it finally arrived in your hands. You can legitimately adopt this same practice, but you must select a reliable reader.

First, use common sense. A surprising number of inexperienced writers decide to ask their best friends to be their reading consultants. That's not necessarily a good idea. Why? Because under such conditions it's difficult for friends to be honest with each other. In addition, your reading consultant should be a good writer. If you knew someone was a lousy mechanic, you wouldn't ask him or her to tune up your car. Use the same judgment in looking around for someone to help you tune up your writing.

Second, make sure your critics know who, as readers, they're supposed to be. Suppose, for example, that you take on the role of Mike Morenberg in the "Summer Sun Club" case and you write to Mr. Garston. When you take your memo to your critics, make sure they've read the case and know exactly who they are supposed to be—Mr. Garston. What you want them to tell you is not what *they* think of your writing but what Mr. Garston would think.

Finally, be honest. There's a difference between asking for someone's advice and asking someone to do your work for you. Some instructors may be willing to act as your critic. Many instructors will expect to read your final draft only, the one you turn in to be graded.

Summary

The emphasis in the last half of this chapter has been on ways to detect writing problems. The rest of the book emphasizes finding solutions. When you begin to write your first draft, however, it's probably best not to worry about problems at all. Chapter 2 begins by discussing ways you can get the first draft written.

The Summer Sun Club

THE PHONE CALL

Mike Morenberg was working on the payroll for the Summer Sun Club when the phone rang. Summer Sun, a program sponsored by the City Boys' Club, averaged an enrollment of ninety-five elementary schoolchildren every week. Mike and his staff of six or seven college students (called leaders) supervised the children from eight to four Monday through Friday, providing them with a wide range of recreational activities.

When the phone rang, Mike picked it up right away, wondering who was going to bother him this time. It seemed to Mike as if he never had a chance to sit down at his desk and do the paperwork he was supposed to do. There was always some kid, leader, or parent who needed attention.

It turned out the caller was Mr. Garston, director of the City Boys' Club and a stickler for details, specifics, and correctness. Mr. Garston was a deeply religious man who always wore a black or blue suit, a skinny necktie, and a white shirt.

Garston said, "Mike? I'm calling to check with you about a Tommy Stephens you had enrolled in Summer Sun last week. His mother's pretty upset. She says the boy drank all the milk in his thermos bottle *after* it had broken and was full of glass. She says you knew about it and didn't tell her. The family doctor says the boy seems to be all right, but Mrs. Stephens is pretty angry. Frankly, Mike, I'm disappointed in you. And of all the people to foul up with, you have to pick the grandson and daughter-in-law of the chairman of the board of First National Bank. You know Frank Stephens is one of the Boys' Club's biggest supporters, and he's a board member, too. What's going on up there?"

Mike felt his stomach tighten up as soon as he heard Mrs. Stephens's name mentioned. He told Garston he remembered the incident, or at least most of it. She had called him up, Mike said, to ask him why he hadn't called her as soon as he had heard about her son.

"And I told her I just forgot, or at least temporarily," Mike said. "And I apologized."

"Well, she says Tommy might have gotten seriously ill," Garston said. "The only reason she found out about it, she said, is that when she washed out his thermos bottle she found it full of broken glass, but the milk was gone. So she asked Tommy about it. He said he'd told one of your girls about it, Maxine it was, and he said that Maxine said it was okay as long as he hadn't swallowed any of the glass."

Mike said that Maxine had told him about it, but he would have to check back with her to get the exact details. He thought it was hard to believe the incident had taken place only a week ago.

Garston told him it was a serious matter, especially if Tommy Stephens was involved. He said Mike should have reported it to Mrs. Stephens and filled out an accident report form.

Mike thought Garston frequently sounded as if he were chewing on a dead cigar, but this time he sounded as if he had swallowed one.

Garston said, "I want a full report on my desk by tomorrow morning."

Mike managed to wedge in a "Yes, sir" before Garston hung up. He thought to himself that Garston never had liked the Summer Sun Club. It was too successful for Garston to like it since it was run out of a branch of the City Boys' Club and therefore Garston couldn't take credit for it directly. All his favorite programs were run out of the Central Branch where his office was located.

MAXINE

But Mike pushed these thoughts out of his mind and headed for the pool, where he knew he'd find Maxine Kramer supervising the rec swim. As he went down the hallway, he could smell the chlorine floating up the stairway from the pool area. The steps were covered with the water that dripped off the kids as they ran upstairs to buy a candy bar before toweling themselves dry.

Maxine was down in the pool, all right, supervising a game of blindman's bluff. When she saw Mike, she climbed out of the pool and pulled on a T-shirt that said SUMMER SUN'S NUMBER 1.

Mike told her about Garston. Maxine said she had told Mike about Tommy at lunchtime last Friday. "We were all sitting down having lunch at the park, and the kids were just beginning to get restless."

Mike was feeling worse all the time. At first he'd thought Maxine had forgotten to tell him about it, but then when Garston called, and even before that, when Mrs. Stephens had called yesterday, he had begun to wonder. Now he was sure Maxine had told him. She was his best leader. If she said she'd told him the whole thing, she had.

Maxine was watching his face and saying, "Remember? We were just finishing lunch, and I was telling you about Tommy when, oh, I know, something happened and you said, 'Okay,' and that was all."

Suddenly Mike said, "Was that when Paul Gonzales socked Larry Harrison in the nose?"

"Yeah, that was it," Maxine said. "And Allison Chambers got all upset because Larry's nose bled all over the place, including on her brand-new white blouse. The one her mother had just bought for her."

Allison had screamed and Mike had run over and found Larry gushing blood and Paul looking like he knew he was in big trouble and wished he hadn't done anything.

PAUL GONZALES

Mike frowned. He hadn't sent in a report on Paul yet because Paul was in trouble already, and Mike hated to put his name on another report, even if Garston wouldn't notice it or suggest he do anything about it. Paul's parents were divorced, and at age eight the kid had been arrested twice for shoplifting and once for stealing a bicycle. The city police had told his mother that she might try putting Paul in Summer Sun or some such program rather than leaving him at home all alone Monday through Friday in the summer.

THE REPORT

Mike went back upstairs and sat down at his desk. Even with the door closed he could smell the chlorine from the pool and hear the kids yelling.

At least, he thought, he knew now why he had forgotten about Tommy Stephens for a while. He sighed and looked at his watch. If he was going to get the report to Garston, he'd have to hurry. In half an hour the kids would be out of the pool, the gym, and the reading room, and it would be time for the end-of-the-day storytelling and the rounding up of swimming trunks, towels, tennis shoes, and lunch boxes. Then he'd just have time to proofread and edit the secretary's work so that she could retype it and send it down to Central Branch in the morning interoffice mailbag.

SUGGESTED DISCUSSION QUESTIONS

1. What are the essential facts Mike should include in his report?
2. What caused the problem Mike has?
3. What procedures or actions would have prevented this problem?
4. Should Mike's report include information about what action he will take in the future?
5. Should Mike write Mrs. Stephens a letter? What should it say?

SUGGESTED ASSIGNMENTS

1. You are Mike Morenberg. Write a report on the Tommy Stephens incident. (Audience: Mr. Garston)
2. You are Mike Morenberg. Write a letter to Mrs. Stephens about this incident.
3. You are Maxine Kramer. Mike has asked you to write a short report explaining your involvement in the Tommy Stephens incident. (Audience: Mike Morenberg and Mr. Garston)
4. You are Mike Morenberg. Recent events make you want to establish one or more new policies for you and your leaders to follow. In a memo to your staff, state the new policies and explain why and how each one is to be implemented.
5. You are Mike Morenberg. Your program has grown enough to enable you to hire another leader. You want prospective applicants to understand what the program is like, yet you cannot afford to take the time to fully explain Summer Sun to every interested applicant. Write an orientation paper suitable for new or prospective leaders of Summer Sun Club. (With your instructor's permission, you may want to write an orientation paper about a club, team, or committee on which you yourself have served.)
6. Write a short essay in which you define the problems Mike is experiencing in the Summer Sun Club and suggest possible solutions. Mike is your audience. He's told you about Summer Sun and asked for your advice.
7. Write a short essay in which you define one or more problems you have noticed and/or experienced at your past or present job. (Audience: a college student)

STUDENT RESPONSES

After you have completed assignment 3, read the following student responses that are based on the Summer Sun Club. For each sample, decide whether the student's response shows a complete definition of the problem as well as implementation of the most effective solution. Is the problem clearly identified? Is the solution appropriate?

(The following memos and letter appear in acceptable formats. Your instructor may ask you to use this or another form.)

SAMPLE RESPONSE A

TO: Mr. Garston, Director of Boys' Club
FROM: Mike Morenberg, Coordinator, Summer Sun Club
SUBJECT: Tommy Stephens Incident
DATE: August 14, 1979

The following is the information you requested concerning the handling of the Tommy Stephens case.

The Incident

During lunch last Friday, August 8, Maxine, a staff leader, was in the process of explaining to me what had happened to Tommy Stephens when my attention was diverted by a fight between Paul Gonzales and Larry Harrison.

(Accident report filed separately.)

The situation required my immediate attention because Larry's nose was bleeding heavily. The situation was further complicated when some of the blood got on Allison Chambers' new white blouse.

After straightening out this situation, I completely forgot what Maxine had told me about Tommy Stephens. I would have filled out an accident report on Tommy if I had remembered; perhaps Tommy was overshadowed by the urgency of the other situation.

Mrs. Stephens's Call

I did not remember the incident until Mrs. Stephens called me yesterday, August 13, to ask about it. I apologized, and told her that I had simply forgotten the whole thing.

My Insights into the Situation

With ninety-five children usually enrolled every week in the Summer Sun Club, and six to seven leaders on the staff, each leader must supervise an average of thirteen to sixteen children each day. In addition, I have reports, payroll, and other paperwork to complete. It seems I have nearly continuous interruptions that prevent me from expediently completing all of this work. For this reason, accident report forms, such as those concerning Paul Gonzales and Tommy Stephens, are delayed in getting turned in to the Central Office.

In Paul's situation, I hesitated to file a report because of his past record of troubles and my fear of what repercussions the report might have on him. I hated to see him punished by losing his membership in the Summer Sun Club.

Conclusion

The whole problem about Tommy Stephens, therefore, boils down to a loss of effective communication between myself and one of my leaders, Maxine. In a sense, the Tommy Stephens near-accident was fortunate since it forces us to establish a clear policy for handling any future mishaps. I would like to recommend that we:

1. Give all accident reports, however minor, top priority over other daily paperwork;

2. Establish a definite, limited time interval (no later than the next day) by which each accident must be reported; and

3. Establish a standard procedure for dealing with the parents of any child injured or endangered while participating in our program.

I have enclosed the draft of a letter of apology to Mrs. Stephens and, if it meets with your approval, I will mail it immediately. Further, I would like to make a follow-up call to Mrs. Stephens to make sure she is satisfied with our explanation. Finally, we will have a meeting of all staff members in the near future to approve or modify the recommendations given above.

August 14, 1979

Mrs. Margaret Stephens
1000 Second Avenue
Fictionalcity, NM 87111

Dear Mrs. Stephens:

I hope you'll accept this letter as a formal apology for my failure to deal promptly with Tommy's situation. I want to assure you that I take my responsibility for the children in our program seriously; the fact that I was not able to give Tommy my full attention was the result of unfortunate circumstances. As I explained to you during our phone conversation, a fight broke out while Tommy's leader was telling me about the broken thermos, and the urgency of the interruption caused me to forget everything else.

I feel fortunate that Tommy was not harmed, and I have taken steps to make certain this type of oversight doesn't happen again. The matter has been reported to my superior, and we will meet in the very near future to work out a prompt and complete procedure for dealing with future accidents.

I hope you will be convinced of our genuine concern for the children enrolled in the Summer Sun Club, and I further hope that Tommy will continue his participation in our group. If you would like to discuss Tommy's situation further or if you have any suggestions for improving our program, please feel free to call me at your convenience.

Sincerely,

Mike Morenberg
Coordinator
Summer Sun Club

SAMPLE RESPONSE B

TO: Mr. Garston, Director of Boys' Club
FROM: Mike Morenberg, Coordinator, Summer Sun Club
SUBJECT: Tommy Stephens's broken thermos
DATE: August 14, 1979

The Incident

On August 8, Tommy Stephens drank milk from his thermos and then noticed that it was full of broken glass. When he discovered this, Tommy reported the incident to his group leader, Maxine. At that time no accident report was filed and Mrs. Stephens was not notified. Tommy did not show any abnormal behavior after drinking the milk, so it was assumed he was all right.

My Acknowledgment

Maxine began to tell me about the incident at lunch, but a fight broke out between two boys and my attention was distracted. Because of this interruption I forgot about the incident, and neglected to call Mrs. Stephens. Maxine didn't have time to complete her explanation of Tommy's accident, and that might explain why I forgot to call Mrs. Stephens.

Mrs. Stephens's Reaction

I forgot about the thermos episode until Mrs. Stephens called and expressed her anger. She was upset with me for not reporting her son's accident to her. I apologized and explained that another emergency had kept me from dealing promptly with her son's case.

Conclusion

Because I neglected the case, Mrs. Stephens felt she should inform you of the lax procedure that was followed in my department. To rectify this situation, communication between myself and the leaders, as well as with the children's parents, will be stronger in the future. Accident reports will always be filed at once and the involved child's parents will immediately be notified by me or one of the program's leaders.

SUGGESTED ASSIGNMENTS

1. You are Maxine Kramer. Mike has drafted a memo to send to Mr. Garston (choose either Sample A or Sample B), and he has also drafted a letter to Mrs. Stephens (Sample A). Mike has asked you to comment on the effectiveness of what he has written. Write Mike a memo in which you evaluate his statement(s).

2. You are Mr. Garston. You have just received Mike's memo (Sample A or Sample B). Write Mike a response to his memo and his handling of the case in general. Remember that two of your many responsibilities are to correct employee error and to encourage useful and effective employee action.

The Last-Minute Incomplete

As Steve Gomez sat at his desk on the third floor of the English Department building, he wondered what to do. Since he couldn't decide, he looked again at the message he'd found on his desk. There was a drop slip, all neatly filled out and just waiting for his signature, next to the note. The note said:

Dear Mr. Gomez:

I was hoping that you would be willing to give me an Incomplete in English 099, Basic Writing. I want to be honest in my reason for asking for this. This semester it looks like I'll get bs in my other 4 course and an F in 099. Obviously this isn't going to be to good for my grade point. If you give me an Incomplet then I can make up the class next semester I will retake it. I know I shouldn't have done so poor in your class, but I can't help that now. I would be gratful if you could sign the form and I promose to work much harder next semester. Thanks alot. I know you tired to help me.

Sincerely,
Bill Alleton

BILL ALLETON

Steve recognized the handwriting before he saw the name at the bottom of the note. Bill was the student whose work was usually late, who turned in his assignments on pages that for some reason were partially torn in half, and who frequently didn't complete assignments or pay sufficient attention in class. A couple of times he'd missed class, a couple of times he'd come in late, and three times he'd come in and then fallen asleep.

Even so, Bill had plenty of ability. Whenever he tried to do an assignment (the course was supposed to teach students all those things about writing—grammar, punctuation, capitalization, organization—that they were expected to know before coming to college), he usually did fairly well. It was obvious to Steve, however, that for some reason Bill hated English and that his hatred of the subject was interfering with his learning it.

Steve thought about the things he'd tried to do with Bill. Maybe he hadn't tried very many. When he discovered that Bill was an expert on fishing, he'd assigned him an essay on that subject—two in fact. He'd also tried to set up extra individual conferences, but Bill had come to only one. He never explained why he hadn't come to class or a conference, and Steve had only asked once. Even then, he didn't get an answer.

Lately, though, Bill had started to change his attitude. He had recently written a paragraph entitled "English" in which he said he wished he'd taken the time to learn the grammar from the beginning of the course because now it was too late to learn everything.

Steve now was afraid that if he gave him an F instead of an incomplete, Bill would hate English even more and maybe not even make it through college because of that hatred. If the guy could just get motivated, Steve thought, he would do okay; he could possibly even get a B in 099 and go on to do well in the regular freshman English courses. But that would take a lot of motivation and hard work because there was so much that Bill needed to learn.

THE UNIVERSITY'S INCOMPLETE POLICY

Since Steve Gomez was new at the university, he decided to look up the policy on incompletes. Of course he understood in general that incompletes were temporary grades given to students who needed extra time to complete work in a course. He was thinking, however, that whatever he did would surely have to be within the guidelines the specific university policy set, even if he did have to bend those guidelines a little.

The policy stated two major points. While it indicated that incompletes were normally given when some unforeseen circumstance such as illness or a family crisis kept a student from being able to complete the work in a course, it also stated that an incomplete could not be given in lieu of an F in a course. An "I" could also not be given in cases in which the course was to be repeated.

DECIDING WHAT TO DO

Steve wished that Bill hadn't waited so long to figure out what was happening. The final exam period had ended that very day, and grades were due at the Registrar's Office in forty-eight hours. Steve thought that having Bill repeat the course would be a problem since Steve wasn't teaching it the next semester. He looked at his watch. It was five-thirty, time to go home. Grades were due so soon. Besides Bill's F, Steve was giving two others. The dormitories had closed half an hour ago and most of the students would already be at home by now. Steve knew that whatever he decided to do, he'd want to be able to explain it so that Bill would be sure to overcome his hatred of English.

Steve looked back down at the open bulletin on his desk. Below the policy for incompletes there was a section entitled "Allowed Course Repeats." He read the section. It explained that for a certain number of courses, to be specified by the degree-granting college, a student could, at his or her option, repeat a course. For any course repeated, only the higher of the two grades would be included in the calculation of the student's grade point average. The other course would, however, be listed on the student's transcript, along with the grade originally received.

SUGGESTED DISCUSSION QUESTIONS

1. Does Bill Alleton deserve an "I"? Why or why not?
2. What does Bill's letter tell you about Bill?
3. What decision should Steve make?
4. How can he explain that decision to Bill? To the other students receiving an F? To future students?

SUGGESTED ASSIGNMENTS

1. Define the problem in this case by:
   a. making a list of all its parts,
   b. drawing inferences,
   c. summarizing a and b in one sentence,
   d. and writing one or more paragraphs based on a–c.
2. You are a friend Steve has asked for advice. Write him a note or letter in which you define his problem and tell him how to solve it.
3. You are Steve Gomez. Write a letter to Bill Alleton in which you explain the problem and how you solved it.
4. Study the grading (incomplete) policy in your department or college. If you agree with the policy, write a brief essay justifying it. If not, draft a new policy with accompanying justifications.

The Westridge Apartments

From where you sit looking out your window you can see the trash in the yard. A lot of it catches in the weeds and uncut grass because the complex is on the edge of town and the wind blows across the fields right through the front yard.

Looking at the trash in the yard makes you think of the problem with the cockroaches. Although the building isn't that old, the roaches have gotten in, and it looks as if they plan on staying forever. You've tried having your own apartment sprayed, putting out roach traps, and asking other people in the building to spray, but nothing seems to help. In a week or two the roaches are back, crawling all over the kitchen and every place else.

Of course you could move, but moving is a lot of work, and besides, you like living here. The rent is reasonable, lower than you could find elsewhere, and you've gone to a lot of work to repair the apartment. Besides, it is close to the campus and has some extras such as free parking and larger rooms than most other apartments in the area.

It isn't that you haven't tried to get the landlord to do something. You've called more than once, but the landlord is just too busy, evidently, to get around to doing anything. The last time you talked to him, he indicated that he was willing to repair all the things wrong, and acknowledged that he should, but then nothing happened.

JACK STENNER, LANDLORD

Almost a year ago when you first met Mr. Stenner, he seemed like a better-than-average landlord. He told you if you ever had problems to give him a call and he'd take care of them right away. When a faucet needed repairing, Mr. Stenner came over that night, and when a drain got plugged, Mr. Stenner had a plumber there in an hour, but lately he's been neglecting the building.

The reason Mr. Stenner is neglecting the building seems to be that he has overextended himself. You know that he recently bought two other complexes, and he doesn't seem to have time to manage them all properly. A neighbor told you that Mr. Stenner is considering having someone in your building manage it or supervise it because he doesn't have the time to do so himself. But the neighbor didn't really know whether Mr. Stenner was serious or how much he'd thought about the situation.

The communication problem with Mr. Stenner has gotten worse recently because he's using a telephone-answering device. When you call you leave a message, but then Mr. Stenner never returns your call. A different neighbor just told you that he heard Mr. Stenner is buying yet another complex, so you know he'll be even busier than before.

THE APARTMENT

Your one-bedroom apartment rents for $185 a month, all utilities included. It is on the third floor of the building, which contains twelve units altogether. The building is solidly constructed, but it requires the same maintenance any building does. The landlord has a man come by and clean up once a week, but the man hasn't been by for the last two weeks and things are starting to get a little messy.

OTHER PROBLEMS

The complex has the usual problems, such as students who party too late at night for others to get their studying done, but it also has some special problems that bother you. Many students bicycle to and from campus, for example, and then leave their bikes locked up in the hallway at night. The bikes are chained to the stairwell banister and make it difficult for anybody to get up and down the stairs. Another problem is that some people in the building keep leaving the front door open at night. Besides letting all that cold air in, leaving the door ajar allowed somebody to steal three bicycles.

THE LETTER

Your mail today included the following form letter, addressed to you but obviously sent to everyone else who lives in the building.

Dear ———:
Recent increases in the cost of gas and electricity have forced me to raise everyone's rent. Beginning next month your rent will be $15 more than it is at the present time. (Next month your lease expires and will be automatically renewed at the new rate.)

This rent increase will bring the cost of these apartments more into line with comparable units in the university area. If you have looked elsewhere, I'm sure you know that even with the increase you are still paying relatively low rent here.

Incidentally, I'm looking for someone to supervise this building for me since I've gotten too busy to do so. The superintendent would be responsible for calling a repairman when necessary, for making sure that the building is cleaned regularly by our janitor, and for cutting the grass. In addition, the super would be expected to generally look after the place and to handle complaints. If you are interested, let me know. We can arrange a rent reduction that should make it worth your while.

Rereading the letter makes you think things over. You can't really afford the rent, even if it's still a good deal. The people in the building aren't going to like it, but they'll probably all stay. There isn't any place else to go. You all know each other, and everyone seems nice enough.

But then there are the problems. On top of everything else there is a terrible smell in the hallway. You suspect somebody needs to throw out a cat box—that's what it smells like, anyway—but pets aren't allowed in the complex. You wonder how much Mr. Stenner would be willing to pay someone to supervise the building.

SUGGESTED DISCUSSION QUESTIONS

1. What factors would determine whether you moved or stayed in the apartment complex described in the case?
2. Assuming you decided to stay, how could you solve the problems there?
3. Could you be more effective in writing to Jack or by calling him?
4. What kinds of details would help persuade Jack to do what you want?

SUGGESTED ASSIGNMENTS

1. Define the problem in this case by:
   a. making a list of all its parts,
   b. drawing inferences,
   c. summarizing a and b in one sentence,
   d. and writing one or more paragraphs based on a–c.
2. Write Jack Stenner and tell him to renew your lease. Persuade him to eliminate the apartment complex's problems, but do not apply for the position of building superintendent.
3. Write Jack Stenner a letter in which you apply for the position of building superintendent. Be as precise as possible concerning your proposals to solve the existing problems.
4. Write an essay entitled "The Perfect Landlord." Alternatively, write an essay entitled "The Perfect Resident Assistant," or write an article entitled "The Perfect Tenant."
5. Discuss Jack's problem as an investor and "absentee" landlord. What are the legal and ethical responsibilities of a landlord? (You might review the standard lease in your own apartment complex or one used in your town.)
6. Write an essay containing a set of rules appropriate for the apartment complex or dormitory in which you now live. Develop the essay by defining the potential problems and showing how your rules solve them.

Intercity Bus and the Angry Commuters

Outside the window was only a view of a timeworn, grimy brick building, yet Alexandria Conrad looked out with such concentration that her secretary, had she walked into the office at that moment, might have thought that Alexandria was trying to decipher an answer written there on the brick wall. As public transportation advisor to the Transportation Regulation Board, Alexandria's responsibilities included the development of policies and the interpretation of regulations governing all bus or transit companies that operated within the state.

With the energy crunch forcing up gas prices, people had begun to expect and demand commuter bus lines to be run between cities and suburbs. Various companies had begun to respond to this new demand, but problems were increasing at the same time. The companies operating the commuter services came directly to the Transportation Regulation Board (TRB) to get what they wanted. Once service began, however, it was difficult for the commuters to communicate with the TRB. In fact, one survey Alexandria had taken indicated that 95 percent of a group of commuters from the western part of the state knew neither that the TRB existed nor that certain regulations about scheduling and other matters were in effect to protect consumer interests. Thus one major purpose of creating Alexandria's position to begin with, she knew, was to provide the TRB with a staff person who could investigate and report consumer concerns to the board. The Intercity bus company was a good example of the kind of problem faced by Alexandria and the TRB.

INTERCITY

Intercity had originally run an airport taxi service between the state's largest city, Des Plaines, population 300,000, and Dammerville, a small city of 40,000 that was thirty-five miles away. Dammerville's prosperity was based on light industry and a well-known college, along with some state offices. Des Plaines, however, was the capital of the state and had an airport with national service. Consequently, there was considerable traffic between Dammerville and the Des Plaines airport. Intercity also stopped at two other major points in Des Plaines, both of them at the capitol complex—a group of buildings surrounding the capitol.

Although this small amount of passenger demand was constant, Intercity did not make a profit. One partner, Jerry Meinert, frequently drove one of Intercity's six vans; Intercity paid Meinert a salary as manager/driver that was about average for middle-class workers in the state. Meinert's partner,

Georgia Huxley, managed the office and was also paid an average salary from company funds. In 1978, however, Meinert retired and Huxley decided to terminate the company's service. She could not afford to buy Meinert's share of the company.

REGULATIONS

Georgia Huxley knew that terminating the service required the approval of the Transportation Regulation Board. The Board, which was composed of three members appointed by the governor, was empowered to enforce the following regulations:

1. People in the business of providing regularly scheduled bus service must have a state license (initial fee $400).
2. Vehicles used must be state-inspected (annual fee $5).
3. Certain insurance and safety guidelines must be met.
4. Specific schedules and fees must be approved.
5. Annual financial reports must be filed.
6. Transportation must be provided only at places and times stated in the schedule, and the passengers must be charged only the approved fares.
7. A minor change in schedule (less than two hours at any point) may be put into effect thirty days after it is filed with the Board and proper notice is given to customers.
8. A major change in schedule (more than two hours at any point) may be put into effect sixty days after it is filed with the Board.
9. All changes must be posted at depots or stopping points to allow customers a chance to protest the change.
10. Vehicles must be clearly identified and periodically checked for safety.

THE NEW INTERCITY

Georgia Huxley had to wait sixty days to terminate the Intercity service because the proposed schedule change was major. Dammerville's newspaper learned of the proposed termination and published an article about it. A storm of protest arose. How were business people and college faculty and staff to get to the airport? If renewed support was needed, the college administration said, then it would consider ways to encourage or require more faculty and staff members to take Intercity rather than a personal or college vehicle to Des Plaines. The State Department of Agriculture, which was located in Dammerville but also had offices in Des Plaines, offered to guarantee Intercity that the state would buy a certain number of transit

passes each month. The governor of the state was requiring each department to reduce its gasoline consumption. More employees would ride an
Intercity van to Des Plaines.

All of this was enough to make Huxley reconsider; two other events
actually persuaded her to try again. A driver for Intercity, Harrison Gufstasson, offered to buy into the company. At the same time, a woman working
in a state office building in Des Plaines asked Intercity to begin a regular
commuter service between Dammerville and Des Plaines. Gas was getting
so expensive, the woman said, that she was sure at least ten people in that
building would be willing to ride the bus for a reasonable fee. Gufstasson
and Huxley felt sure that with increased airport business, guaranteed pass
purchases by the agriculture department, and some commuter passengers,
Intercity's six vans could be used profitably. Gufstasson became Huxley's
partner and eagerly took over many of the company operations. Huxley remained in the office to supervise the secretary, act as a dispatcher, and
handle the bookkeeping.

GUFSTASSON

Thus Gufstasson came down to Alexandria's office, applied for a new
schedule with new stops for commuters, and was eager to commence new
services. Alexandria now recalled just how anxious Gufstasson had been.
All the paperwork had clearly frustrated him. When he'd had some difficulties with the schedules, Alexandria had sent him to Hal Steinhem at Public
Transit, a division of the state's transportation department. Since the TRB
was purely regulatory and largely concerned with the transportation of
freight and not people, the board had no expertise in schedule making.
Steinhem, on the other hand, had all kinds of firsthand experience.

Intercity's six vans would be used in the new schedule much as they
had been in the old airport route. One important difference was that now
the first two runs from Dammerville to Des Plaines began earlier, at 6:00
A.M. and 6:50 A.M. Vans also left Dammerville for Des Plaines at 9:50 A.M.,
12:00 noon, and 2:00 P.M. There were four pick-up points in Dammerville,
two more than in the past, yet Gufstasson had added little additional time
to the new schedule to pick up riders at those points. Also, Steinhem knew
that getting out of Des Plaines at four or five in the afternoon, when the
commuters were scheduled to head back to Dammerville, could take as
much as an extra fifteen minutes, yet Gufstasson had added only five minutes to the old "airport-run" schedule. Gufstasson said he was anxious to
get the routes going and didn't want to delay any by taking extra weeks to
time drives over and over again. Steinhem reported his opinions to the
TRB, but the board reviewed Gufstasson's proposed schedule and approved it, finding that, "the proposed service will promote the public convenience and necessity."

PROBLEMS

Yet no sooner had Gufstasson expanded the route than troubles began. Airport business was up, but rather than picking up a dozen commuters to begin with, Gufstasson only had three on one commuter run, six on the second one. The following month the ridership increased, and Intercity purchased two buses to cover the two morning and evening "commuter" runs between Dammerville and Des Plaines. But they were disappointed. Monthly commuter ridership went up from three to eight to fourteen on one run and from six to twelve to twenty-two on the second run, but Intercity was losing money, a few hundred dollars a month.

Since the buses held forty-one people and were not full, Gufstasson thought Intercity could pick up more passengers by adding stops to two towns between Dammerville and Des Plaines. The present run took about fifty minutes, he calculated, and stopping at the two towns would add about fifteen minutes. He began working out a new schedule with Steinhem. The new schedule was approved by the board on October 1 and the thirty-day waiting period began.

COMPLAINTS

By this time complaints about Intercity had begun to trickle into TRB from commuters. One passenger complained about speeding between stops. Four commuters complained that Intercity always failed to maintain its schedule. Two commuters complained that Intercity wasn't doing any advertising and that was why the company didn't attract any new customers.

MORE COMPLAINTS

On October 24, Alexandria received a petition signed by twenty-two commuters who rode the second bus to Des Plaines. The commuters stated that:

—Intercity had distributed the new schedule (to commence November 1) just one week in advance; people deserved more notice than that.

—Intercity was not advertising enough and that was what they needed to do in order to get more commuters, not add two more stops.

—The stops at the two other towns would add more than the supposed fifteen minutes, perhaps as much as forty minutes, and would make the commute to Des Plaines unreasonable.

—Intercity wasn't coming anywhere close to meeting the present schedule, so how could it possibly add more stops?

At the same time, Alexandria's office got innumerable individual complaints about Intercity. The complaints were about speeding, driver inattention, drivers who didn't know the schedule, drivers who didn't know how to operate the bus, delays due to waiting for airport riders to have their luggage loaded, gross and continual failure to observe the schedule, and an unsafe schedule because the new route would travel on a state road, not the interstate.

In a phone call to Gufstasson, Alexandria learned that Intercity felt it was doing its best. It was losing money; it was having to train new drivers as experienced drivers were resigning because of low pay; the passengers were exaggerating their complaints—which were contradictory anyway—and Intercity couldn't afford more advertising.

Harry acknowledged that passengers had been handed new schedules only a week before the change, but he said he'd warned them earlier, in person, when he himself drove the bus on the commuter run one day. He also said that Intercity had posted the schedule at their office at the airport. He didn't know what else he was supposed to do. Intercity had no depots. Where was he supposed to post the schedule? Intercity picked commuters up and dropped them off at designated street corners and in front of certain office buildings. Sometimes the bus did run behind schedule, but the driver just couldn't help it. Traffic slowed him down or extra customers rode the bus or airport passengers with lots of luggage required special attention.

THE TRANSPORTATION REGULATION BOARD

The board asked Alexandria for her recommendation about what action, if any, should be taken in regard to Intercity. The board was expected to make a finding that Gufstasson's new schedule would promote the public convenience and necessity, yet there were numerous complaints about that schedule and about service in general. Among actions that the board could take were:

—to hold an informal hearing designed to air grievances and to allow Intercity to respond to them,
—to hold a formal hearing in which charges against Intercity were presented by Alexandria and the board took action,
—to suspend the new schedule,
—to issue an order forcing Intercity to change its schedule,
—to issue an order forcing Intercity to change its fares, or
—to revoke Intercity's license.

THE RECOMMENDATION

In considering which of the above courses of action she would recommend the board take, Alexandria reviewed some other information available to her. She knew that no other transit company could or would take over Intercity's service, even if Intercity terminated all services, as one commuter said it had threatened to do. She also knew that commuters were angry about the new schedule and seemed ready to quit the service if it was imposed. At the same time, she was puzzled over the contradictions between Gufstasson's accounts and those of the commuters. If the commuters were so dissatisfied, why was ridership steadily increasing? Gufstasson conceded that in one more month the commuter runs should begin to make a small profit. She looked at the grimy brick wall and thought of how she would begin her report.

SUGGESTED DISCUSSION QUESTIONS

1. What is the responsibility of the TRB?
2. In fulfilling this responsibility, how important is it to the TRB (and the state government it represents) to help Intercity continue its service?
3. How important are the commuters' needs and interests in TRB's fulfillment of its responsibility?
4. How do the accounts of Intercity and the commuters differ?
5. Are there any regulations that Alexandria can definitely conclude Intercity has violated?
6. What various courses of action can Alexandria take?

SUGGESTED ASSIGNMENTS

1. You are Alexandria Conrad. Write a report about Intercity to the TRB. Tell the TRB what action, if any, you think it should take.
2. You are Alexandria Conrad. Write a letter to Harry Gufstasson. Explain what action you have recommended the TRB take.
3. You are Alexandria Conrad. Suppose you persuade the TRB to hold a formal or an informal hearing about Intercity's service.
   a. Write a letter to the commuters and persuade them to come.
   b. Write a letter to Gufstasson and Huxley and explain your action.
4. Suppose you are an angry commuter who has recently spoken frankly and honestly with Alexandria Conrad. Write a letter to her and the TRB. Persuade the board to disallow Intercity's addition of two stops.

Robert Kelly, Sales Representative

As Dick Johnston sat at his desk Monday morning he considered the action he should take in regard to one of his sales representatives, Robert Kelly.

Johnston was district sales manager, textbook division, for Brown, Livingston, and Smith, Inc., a publishing house.

Brown, Livingston, and Smith did considerable business in both textbooks and trade books, but the textbook division was considered the backbone of the company. The trade division was smaller, and high discounting and fierce competition made profits small and growth nearly impossible.

Kelly had joined the firm three years ago, after graduating from a well-known New England college with a degree in psychology. He was married but had no children. His wife, Maureen, was enrolled in an advanced degree program at a local university.

During the first few months with the company Kelly seemed to perform exceptionally well. He reported in promptly, showed the capacity for perfection in his paperwork, and seemed to be increasing sales. At one university, for example, he secured several large orders from professors who had heretofore shown little or no interest in Brown, Livingston, and Smith textbooks. Dick had spoken with one bookstore manager who referred to Kelly as "a bright young guy who is much easier to work with than his predecessor."

Despite his early promise, Kelly had a disappointing sales record. In his first year with the company, sales dropped from $735K to $650K. While some of the drop in sales might be attributed to the inevitable loss of contacts when a new salesperson took over, Johnston was, of course, unhappy with the results. This sales record, along with a recent occurrence, had prompted Johnston to investigate Kelly's performance.

Dick had his first misgivings when he called a college store in the central part of the state to check with Kelly about a special order that was exceptionally large. Kelly had indicated that he planned to spend three or four days at the store during the week, yet when Johnston called on Tuesday, Kelly hadn't arrived. After leaving a message that got no response, Johnston called again on Friday. Kelly had never shown up. The next week when he was reached, Kelly explained he'd been sick and had forgotten to call in.

This incident prompted Dick's research.

He called the textbook buyer at one bookstore that Kelly's records indicated he visited twice each year. The buyer replied he had never met Kelly. He said, "As far as I know, no reps from Brown, Livingston, and Smith have been here in the last three years. But maybe I missed the guy or something."

Johnston also checked Kelly's reports about Los Altos State University. Kelly indicated that he had spoken to six professors and visited both the local college bookstores. He reportedly spent four days on campus. Johnston called all six professors, but managed to reach only four of them. Two reported they had never seen Kelly. Kelly's expense account indicated that he had taken all six to lunch.

Finally, Johnston checked Regina State University. He spoke to the manager at the local college store. The manager, Al Jackson, had been Johnston's friend for twenty years. Jackson said that Kelly had taken the tradebook buyer and a secretary out to lunch a couple of times, but their textbook buyer had declined the invitation because he was too busy. Dick trusted Al Jackson's judgment. He asked him what he thought of Kelly. Jackson said, "Well Dick, I think Bob's a nice young guy, and I know every-body around here likes him all right, but he spends more time talking than he does working. I guess you know he's trying to get into law school here. Bill told me that he spent most of the day yesterday talking to some people over at the law school. I guess his grades aren't quite good enough, and he wants them to give him the "benefit of the doubt."

Last Friday Kelly checked in and came to see Johnston. Dick showed him the results of his calls. Kelly admitted that he had made some mis-takes, but said he did his best not to. About the lunches at Regina State he explained that it was important to keep in the good graces of everybody in the bookstore, not just the textbook buyer. When questioned about the drop in sales, he argued that Brown, Livingston, and Smith had dropped three of its most important titles. He said, "It isn't my fault. We're just not picking up the hot titles the way the other houses are." Johnston pointed out that other sales representatives had pretty much managed to maintain sales. Kelly said that he had more competition than anyone else did. He felt he was already doing his best under difficult circumstances, but said he would try to do better.

When Johnston arrived at work the following Monday, the sales figures for the past year were on his desk. Kelly's sales had dropped to 590K. A note from the vice-president for sales was attached to the sales report. The vice-president wanted something done immediately.

DISCUSSION QUESTIONS

1. What is Kelly doing wrong on the job?
2. Why?
3. What courses of action does Dick Johnston have?
4. What should Dick Johnston do?

SUGGESTED ASSIGNMENTS

1. You are Dick Johnston. Decide what to do about Kelly. Write a letter to Kelly explaining your decision.
2. You are Dick Johnston. Decide what to do about Kelly. Write a letter to the vice-president of sales. Explain the situation.
3. You are Dick Johnston. Write an evaluation of Kelly's work to be placed in his personnel file.

Your Full-Time District Attorney

Michael Maretti fought off his feeling of panic and considered what to do first. As the newly appointed manager of Judith Peterson's campaign for re-election as district attorney, Maretti wondered how things could possibly be worse. And the election was just four weeks away.

There was so much to be done. On a notepad Maretti listed the problems Peterson herself had outlined for him and those he had discovered in the two days since he'd been running the campaign.

1. The 400 yard signs Peterson had ordered had been misprinted. Only 200 of the signs would be useable. And none of these had been stapled together and mounted on a stake so they could be placed in someone's yard.

2. Of twenty large roadside-type signs Peterson had planned to put up, only three had been painted and erected. Seven places for the signs on private property (a legal requirement) had been found, but Peterson said she wanted ten other signs up somewhere.

3. Peterson's opponent, Mack Durham, had recently spent approximately $2,000 in newspaper advertising during the past six weeks. These advertisements had been positively oriented, publicizing Durham's track record as a trial attorney and former assistant district attorney. So far, Peterson had spent $150 on advertisements; she had no new ads planned or placed.

4. Although Peterson assured Maretti that dozens of people had volunteered to help her in her campaign for reelection, these potential campaign workers were completely unorganized—thus far, few of them had actually been asked to do anything.

5. Peterson planned the customary postcard campaign, but it was going nowhere. Voting lists were supposed to be circulated among volunteers who read the lists and wrote postcards to all the people whose names they recognized as likely supporters: "Dear John: Please be sure to vote for Judith Peterson, your Lincoln District Attorney, on November 4. —Jackie." But of the eighteen lists, only six were already in circulation, and little had been done with those. It wasn't too late, however, since the cards were generally mailed out just a few days before the election.

6. The budget was a disaster. The campaign treasurer, Linda Lorzella, reported to Maretti that the fund showed a balance of $1,800, but Maretti had been told by key Lincoln Democratic Strategist Jack Reynolds that Peterson would need at least $5,000 to finish the race, more if Durham continued or escalated his media campaign, thus far the most intensive

in the history of the area. Moreover, Maretti's search through the fat file of miscellaneous paperwork Peterson had given him indicated that the fund had unpaid bills of at least $500. Finally, Maretti had heard through a friend of a friend that Durham's campaign manager planned even more newspaper advertising in the future, as well as some radio spots.

Thus the campaign's upcoming costs and the small balance of $1,300 troubled Maretti most heavily just then. Peterson had told him to spend whatever was necessary—she would reimburse the campaign fund personally. But Maretti didn't want to be responsible for putting the fund five thousand dollars or more in the red. What's more, it wasn't good politics—much better, Maretti had been told by Lincoln Democrats, to have lots of supporters helping Peterson pay the bills.

Maretti shook his head. He wanted to ask somebody, "How did things ever get so screwed up?" But he knew some of the answers already.

THE FUND RAISER

In late August of that year Judith Peterson had held her initial fund raiser—a beer, wine, and cheese party—at the First Presbyterian Church in Lincoln. The fund raiser, Maretti knew, was not especially well attended, but it had raised $1,100. In addition, the Petersons themselves had contributed $1,000 to the fund, but at the time both Judith and her husband Ralph recognized the need to raise more money—approximately three thousand dollars more would do, they thought.

Ralph Peterson taught psychology at the local university and had previously managed Judith's campaign (four years earlier) when she had first run for public office—for district attorney. Of course Ralph knew another fund raiser was needed, and so he planned to hold one just two weeks later, after the fall semester had begun and more of Judith's supporters were back in town. Ralph also planned, as he had in the previous campaign, to manage all the grunt work of the campaign: the postcard preparation and circulation, the yard-sign printing and posting, the leafleting door-to-door of materials that promoted Judith's record in office. As for the advertising, Ralph planned to leave that to Judith herself and to the nominal chair of the reelection committee, Jack Ostenkowski. Ostenkowski, a professor of commuter science, was to function as the sounding board for Judith's own advertising ideas, with Judith herself getting the advertisements delivered to the two city and three county newspapers. As in the past, two or three other friends of the Petersons would be consulted if necessary.

Thus the Petersons believed, at the end of August, that Judith's campaign, though off to a slow start financially, looked good. Judith was the incumbent. She had won her election on the promise that she would work for her district on a strictly full-time basis—she would not practice privately on the side. And Judith had done a good job in office; the Petersons had literally hundreds of contacts in the district. Durham, on the other hand, was a political newcomer. True, he was doing quite a bit of advertising early on in the race, and he did have lots of trial experience. But the job was mostly administrative, not trial-oriented, and so far Durham didn't seem at all likely to win. Ostenkowski had proclaimed, "We could do nothing between now and election day, Judith, and you'd still win."

TROUBLE BEGINS

On September 2, Ralph, complaining of chest pains, went to see his doctor. When he came home, he told Judith some frightening news—the chest pains were a danger signal; the doctor said by-pass surgery was required immediately. Less than two weeks later, Ralph was resting at home and feeling all right. Meanwhile, Judith ignored her campaign and concentrated on her roles as mother of two high school boys, part-time nurse to her ailing husband, and full-time district attorney. Nothing really got done on the campaign in September, but Ralph planned to get back to work on it come October, and Ostenkowski gave counsel and reassurance that there was no rush.

Judith agreed with Ralph that October would be soon enough to get around to the heavy-duty part of the campaign work—it would have to be. In late September, however, complications involving Ralph's surgery arose. He was rehospitalized for a week, then told to rest in bed indefinitely. Finally, with just four weeks left until election day, the Petersons realized that Ralph wouldn't be able to work at all on the campaign and that Judith would simply have to find someone else to manage it. Ostenkowski didn't have the time and wasn't suitable for anything other than reassurance that nothing need be done. Enter Michael Maretti, a colleague of Ralph's at the University. Maretti was teaching a full load, but he was willing to step in and work overtime on the campaign when it counted. Maretti was inexperienced politically, but he was energetic and able. With just four weeks to go, the Petersons felt grateful to have Michael volunteer.

ESCALATION

The second day on the job gave Michael his first taste of negative campaign tactics. That evening a new Mack Durham advertisement appeared in the *Lincoln Trader,* a shopper circular distributed to every household in the Lincoln area for free. The advertisement featured a large photograph of Durham and this text:

Dear Judith:

I've talked to hundreds of voters these past few weeks, and they've asked me why you plea bargain felonies down to simple misdemeanors. Why criminals are set free with hardly a hand slap.

And why, Judith, have you made mistakes that have allowed some criminals to go scott-free? People want to know why you're soft on crime and hard on businessmen who can't get you to prosecute bad check cases. Why do you keep promising to work full-time when all you do is let criminals go free full-time? Are you willing to answer these crucial questions, or am I going to have to tell the voters the truth?

The voters want to know what your record in office is really like.

Sincerely,

Mack Durham

Vote for Mack Durham, a tough man for a man's job.

Michael was inexperienced in politics, but he could read between the lines of this advertisement, and he had a gut feeling that a lot more negative advertising was on the way. He felt certain Peterson would have to counter it with considerable advertising of her own. But advertising was expensive and not especially easy to write well. What should be written, anyway? Michael considered what he knew about the district, the constituents, the district attorney's job, Peterson's performance, and Durham's likely approach.

THE DISTRICT

The district included all of Lincoln County and a small portion of adjacent Melrose County. The county seat, Lincoln, comprised fifty thousand of the district's approximately ninety-five thousand inhabitants. Lincoln, where the University was located, was largely a middle-class, white-collar city with a well-educated, politically moderate constituency. The rest of the district, however, was largely rural, although the town of Vaugn was fairly good-sized with a population of ten thousand. Traditionally Lincoln was primarily Democratic with an extremely high voter turnout while the rest of the district was strongly Republican but only average in voter turnout.

In short, nearly two-thirds of the people who actually voted lived in or just outside Lincoln, where Peterson's support was strongest. Durham, on the other hand, was a popular city attorney in Vaugn.

THE OFFICE OF DISTRICT ATTORNEY

The district attorney had a staff of two secretaries, three full-time assistant district attorneys, and three part-time district attorneys. The major portion of the district attorney's work consisted of managing the criminal caseload for the district. In other words, the district attorney was responsible for prosecuting anyone charged with a crime anywhere in the district—everything from speeding tickets to murders. The district attorney was also responsible for giving legal counsel to the Lincoln District Board of Supervisors and for representing Lincoln District in any legal matters. If, for example, someone sued the district because a district dump truck had crashed into that person's car and caused serious personal injury, then the district attorney would defend the district (and the truck driver) in the lawsuit. The district attorney also gave legal advice to approximately thirty-five district agencies—to the Rape Crisis Center, the Lincoln District Hospital, etc.

POLITICAL HISTORY

Two key political precedents had been established eight years before Judith Peterson had first run for office. First, a woman had been elected district attorney. Second, Rebecca Krantz, a young attorney at the time and now a consultant in Washington, D.C., had won election to the office on the promise that she would not carry on a private practice. Her opponent made no such promise—no attorney ever had until then. The voters, evidently, liked the idea, for they elected Rebecca Krantz as their first female district attorney and then reelected her four years later. During these eight years Krantz actually worked for less than what an attorney's full-time pay would most likely be—the position didn't necessarily demand full-time work—and the district couldn't afford to pay her a full-time salary. Krantz, however, made the position officially full-time by simply declaring she would do no other legal work.

Judith had spent four years working as a part-time assistant to Krantz. In her first campaign she ran on Krantz's platform—promising to work full-time. And just as previous Republican challengers had declared, Peterson's opponent declared that the job need not be full-time. He said he could carry on his private practice as well. This approach was perfectly legal as long as the district attorney accepted no criminal cases in his or her private practice and as long as he or she was careful to avoid any potential or actual conflicts of interest. In fact, many other districts in the state had only part-time

D.A.'s. In Lincoln District, however, the voters evidently wanted a full-time district attorney—Peterson won her race by a narrow margin.

MACK DURHAM

Durham was like his Republican predecessors in that he too was evidently unwilling to promise to do the job full-time. Meanwhile, however, an important change had taken place. As the district had grown, so had the demands placed on the district attorney's position. And so four years ago the District Supervisors had officially made the position full-time and given the D.A. a full-time salary. Now that the position was full-time, Durham would either have to give up his private law practice or persuade the supervisors to change the position back to part-time status.

Maretti reviewed Durham's advertising over the last several weeks and saw that Durham was promising to save the taxpayers money by cutting back the D.A.'s salary as well as the salaries of the assistants. Durham's campaign slogan, "A tough man for a man's job," was another indicator, of course, of how Durham planned to win.

Durham was evidently a popular man in Vaugn, his hometown. He was active in the Baptist church, a member of the Rotary and the Vaugn Chamber of Commerce, and a good public speaker, though his bald head and unattractive face were certainly liabilities in public appearances. Durham's campaign was being managed by his son, Ronald Durham, a young attorney who had just joined his father's law practice.

MARETTI'S OTHER DISCOVERIES

Michael was most disappointed by how little help he could expect to get from Lincoln District Democratic Headquarters. He had talked with several Central Committee members there and had discovered that nearly all the ready-made Democratic volunteers were fully committed to other district races. In fact, the prevailing attitude at headquarters was that while Judith deserved some kind of support given what had happened to Ralph, she had also mismanaged her own campaign and would just have to find her own workers. There just weren't any extra volunteers to go around.

On the positive side, Michael had gotten a list from Judith of about two hundred people she thought would be willing to donate time and/or money to the campaign. These people, Michael knew, were an amalgam of colleagues of Ralph's and Judith's, related legal professionals, members of the Petersons' church, personal friends of the Petersons, and some others Michael knew not how to classify. Most of them were middle-class professionals or business people; all of them would be sympathetic and supportive, Judith said. Michael knew, on the other hand, that nearly all of them would also be likely to be pretty busy, especially now that classes were well under way at the university.

DISCUSSION QUESTIONS

1. In what ways can Maretti use letters or reports to eliminate problems in the Peterson campaign?
2. To whom should Maretti write?
3. What should he ask them for?
4. How can Maretti persuade them to give him what he wants?
5. What factors might cause his readers not to act?

SUGGESTED WRITING ASSIGNMENTS

1. You are Michael Maretti. Write a letter to Rebecca Krantz (suppose you've called her and haven't been able to reach her—she's always in conference) and persuade her to give you whatever kind of help you think would be useful.
2. You are Michael Maretti. Write a letter to be sent to the two hundred people Judith listed as likely supporters and contributors of time and money.
3. Suppose Michael has given you all this information and asked you for your advice. Write him a report in which you specify what course of action you think he should take.
4. Write some advertisements for Judith Peterson's campaign. Suppose that you've been told the campaign can afford to buy a space in the paper about three by five inches in size.

Chapter 2

Inventing and Organizing the Material

Inventing and organizing material is at the heart of the writing process. All writers go through this process, this series of steps, when they write. The *most effective* writers know what the steps are and what choices can be made in completing them.

The order in which these steps are completed may vary from one writer to another or from one writing situation to another. For the sake of clarity, this chapter presents just one possible sequence of steps in the writing process. Keep in mind that many of these steps may be repeated or may go on simultaneously. Remember, too, that while some writers complete many of the steps in their minds, others may need to write everything out on paper.

Selecting and Limiting a Subject

Of course inventing material involves you in the process of selecting something about which to write. In general, you select and limit your subject based on what interests you and on what your audience wants and needs to know. Sometimes you will be given a highly specific subject; other times you will have to determine what subject would be appropriate for your writing situation. In either case, the usual advice given student writers—you may have already heard it—is to define your subject specifically so that it fits the length of your essay. The subject of a single paragraph obviously should be narrower in scope than the subject of a book. Any writer would need more space to discuss the pros and cons of marriage than to describe what someone should do on his or her first date, or even more specifically, to describe what it is like to say good night on a first date.

Suppose you decide to write an article on solar energy for the local newspaper, and its editor generously provides you with enough space to write a thousand words. The general subject, solar energy, needs to be more limited. Most readers would be bored by the generalities that any writer would be forced to make if writing about solar energy in one thousand words. One way to limit this subject would be to discuss uses of solar energy: to produce electricity, to distill alcohol, to heat water or buildings. If solar heating of buildings is selected as the specific subject, it might be possible to discuss the heating of either residential or commercial buildings. Furthermore, you might be able to limit your subject to the feasibility of using solar heating in homes in your town.

At this point, you might have to find material on your subject before you can make any more decisions about how to limit it. Here you can see one example of how the steps in the writing process can be interconnected: as you limit your subject, you can decide what material you need to find; as you find material, you can decide how to limit your subject.

Aside from matching the depth and breadth of your subject to the length of your essay, you should also remember that writers usually write most effectively about what they know and like best—what they are committed to. Before you finish your essay and tell yourself, *"That* was a boring subject," remember that if the audience is appropriate, there is no such thing as a boring subject; there are only writers who make a subject boring. So let's suppose you keep these guidelines in mind, analyze the writing situation, and come up with an appropriate subject. How do you invent useful material about it?

Inventing Material About Your Subject

All writers, beginner or advanced, amateur or professional, experience the problem of invention. We sit down, look at the blank page, and think, "How am I ever going to dream up the material for this one?" Here are six different ways you can find or invent material about your subject. If you practice using each one, you will have more choices available when you have to decide how to gather the material that will make up an essay.

Let It Germinate

Good writers don't just work on their writing when, pencil or pen in hand, they sit at a desk. Instead, they think about the subject and what they want to say about it at other times as well. As they take a shower, drive to work, walk to class, or sometimes even when they should be paying attention to something else, they search for and think about the seeds, the ideas that will make their essay grow. Seeds don't sprout unless watered; even then, germination time may take a couple of weeks or more. Subjects don't usually come to writers with fully or even partially developed ideas; it takes a lot of thought to invent them. If you have ever tried to "get yourself in the mood to write," or to "psyche yourself up," or if you have ever done something like sharpen eighteen pencils before beginning, then you have allowed yourself at least a small amount of germination time.

Successful writers avoid the frustration of sitting at a desk and staring at a blank page by thinking about the subject long enough beforehand to let some ideas about it germinate. If you have to write, but haven't allowed time for germination, then be patient with yourself. It may take you more time to get going than it does other writers. Most of us have known at least one student writer who sat next to us in class and bragged about having written an entire essay in an hour and gotten a good grade on it. Even if that student wasn't exaggerating, what he or she probably never tells anyone is that days or even weeks of worry and thought about the subject may have gone into that essay before it was ever written.

Try 5 W's and an H

Remember that Chapter 1 already reviewed one way you can develop material. Ask yourself these questions: **Who? What? When? Where? Why? How?** To generate more than just a one-sentence answer (Richard Weathers did it in the bedroom with a shotgun because his wife poisoned his dogs or let his son poison them), try looking at all the different relationships that are created by this set of questions.

Suppose, for example, that you were writing a letter to your local newspaper in which you argued that the legal drinking age should be lowered to eighteen. If you looked at the relationship between **Who?** and **Why?**, you might generate the argument that eighteen-year-olds should be allowed to drink *because* they're old enough to vote and get married. If you looked at the relationship between **Who?** and **Where?**, you might invent the argument that since eighteen-year-olds are obtaining alcohol and drinking it in cars and parks anyway, it would be better to let them drink in bars and restaurants where there is some control over every drinker's behavior. Answering the 5 W's and the H and looking at the relationships between the different questions is one way to get something written down to begin with.

Try Acting It Out

Remember that most writing situations are similar to the cases in this book: that is, they involve people in conflict, people in need of communicating with one another. So, by yourself or with a group of students, act out the writing situation, the case.

In the "University Bookstore" case at the end of this chapter, there seem to be a number of conflicts between students, faculty, administrators, and the bookstore. You could act out these conflicts. Have someone pose as a faculty member, someone else pose as a student representative, and so on. Try to really be these people. Say what you think they would say. When you're finished, write down what happened. Or as you go along, have someone take notes. Once you have dramatized a writing situation, you should have some good material to use in your essay.

Borrow Someone's Ear

Another way to get started writing is to ask your friend, spouse, roommate, or fellow student to "lend me your ear." Tell this person about the writing assignment, why it is a problem for you, and what you plan to do. Tell him or her everything that comes to mind about the situation and the assignment. If you have different ideas about what you might say about the subject, try them out on your listener. Encourage your listener to ask questions that make you talk and think about the assignment.

Many professional writers do the same thing. They talk with friends and colleagues as a way of generating and testing ideas. At some point, they decide they've talked enough and they are ready to write. When you reach this point, when you get some ideas you want to put down on paper, do it. If you've asked the right person, borrowed the right ear, he or she won't mind if you rush off and start writing.

Make A List

List making involves writing down everything you can think of about a subject without thinking whether you can really use it or how it is related to your other information. The idea is to loosen up your thinking and make a list of whatever comes to mind. If you get stuck, reread the list. What's already on it will probably lead you to other information or ideas to write down.

Successful list making requires you to avoid editing. Editing includes simple tasks such as looking up the spelling of a word in the dictionary and more complex ones like revising a sentence for improved emphasis or rewriting a paragraph for better coherence. When you're in the invention stage of the writing process, you want to avoid editing. Your goal here is to produce material, lots of it, not get bogged down trying to write the final draft of the essay, or even the first draft. So don't edit, and your brainstorming session should produce some fertile material rather than a long, dry spell.

Try Freewriting

Freewriting is similar to list making. First, decide on the general subject you want to write about. Your choices are limitless. You could decide, for example, to write on "What Subject I Should Choose for This Assignment" or "The Softball Diamond Controversy in Trinidad," or "What's Wrong with This Paragraph?" In other words, you can use freewriting either as a problem-solving technique or as a way to generate ideas and information.

Once you've determined your subject, decide on the specific amount of time you will write. Five minutes should be the minimum; ten or fifteen minutes probably work best. The last rule of freewriting is this: once you begin, you must keep writing words and sentences until time is up. You cannot allow yourself time to stop and look at what you've written or at the remaining blank page. You must keep writing continuously.

If you get stuck and can't think of anything to say, then write "I can't think of anything to say" over and over again until you *do* think of something to say. As is true of list making, the goal of freewriting is to free up your thinking, your imagination. Therefore, when freewriting you should not be concerned with correctness—in fact, it's okay to make lots of errors when you are generating material. You can always eliminate the errors later on.

Developing Supporting Ideas and a Thesis

Whatever method or methods of invention you use, once you've started gathering material for your essay, you will probably find that the information and the ideas fall into groups. Suppose you are Captain Barton and you are writing a report to the Chief of Police about Officer Fox (the "Officer Fox" case is included in this chapter, but you need not read it now). The following information could be placed in a group:

The dispatcher reported a silent alarm at Best Drug.
Officer Fox responded with [red] lights on.

Fox saw three men outside Best Drug; he recognized one man as
Mr. Best.

Mr. Best was pointing excitedly at the other two men.

The other two men ran when they saw Fox.

Of course this material is all related because it is about what Officer Fox
must have thought when responding to the silent alarm.

Most writers seem to go through this process of inventing material
and grouping it together as they develop ideas to support their thesis. In
the "Officer Fox" case, Captain Barton might almost automatically create
the following groups or topics: Fox's response when he first arrived on
the scene, Fox's arrest of Mr. Cooper, and Cooper's state of mind at the
time. Since Barton is an experienced professional, he would recognize
these key topics early.

At other times writers may not be so experienced or the writing
problem may be much more complex. Here's one technique commonly
used, in one form or another, by experienced writers who are faced with
the problem of organizing particularly large and/or complex quantities of
information.

First, these writers realize that their first job is to *gather* sufficient information, *not* to organize it. Thus initially they concentrate their energies
on gathering all available data. Once they have the information available
(as you do in the cases in Parts I and II of the text), then the next step is
to concentrate on combing through the data to determine what's relevant
to the problems and their possible solutions.

For the sake of an example here, suppose the writer is Gary Locolo
in the "Gra-Y" case at the end of this chapter. As Gary sorts through the
material he has on hand, he reaches a point at which he is ready to select
pertinent details. Using the technique suggested here, Gary writes each
relevant detail on a *separate* three-by-five-inch notecard or he lists details
on sheets of paper, leaving two blank lines between entries.

Here's a sample sheet of notebook paper Gary might produce when
working with some of the case facts under the case heading "The
Twenty-Dollar Membership Fee":

At second meeting boys should bring in application form with minimum $5 payment.

Boys pay a $20 membership fee.

Leaders used own judgment in hardship cases.

Every box of candy sold earned the boy 45¢ toward his membership fee.

Some boys sold candy even after their fees were paid.

Many boys didn't sell enough candy to pay the fee.

Accounts not paid in full were billed by the YMCA.

Once Gary has listed what seem to be the most relevant details *for the entire case,* he gets out a pair of scissors (since he's used notebook paper and not three-by-five-inch cards) and snips up his pages so that each piece of information appears on a separate slip. Then, using a large conference table or some other large table top, Gary spreads out the slips of paper. As he does so, he places related information in groups. Using this technique, Gary may eventually end up with about ten to fifteen groups of information. Some pieces of information may seem to belong to more than one group; others may not seem to belong anywhere. At least temporarily Gary can stick the disconnected information into a group and label it "miscellaneous." For the sake of convenience, Gary can also make copies of some pieces of information so he can put that information in more than one group at the same time.

Finally, Gary can sort through each of his groups one by one. Here's an example of one group of information Gary might be considering:

Al Kunnert suggested they cancel the second campout.

The boys paid $2 to attend the campout.

The campouts cost the program $3 per boy.

The campouts were popular but a lot of work.

Skip Winehart had suggested not having an activity every weekend.

Gary's next step would be to look for problems, solutions, and con-clusions. Two problems above appear to be that the campouts don't pay for themselves and that they're popular but a lot of work. Using this same process for each group of information, Gary should be able to break down what might seem like a complex set of problems into smaller prob-lems much more easily analyzed one by one.

All writers go through the kind of process described above; many writers may do most or all of this work in their minds while others may shuffle slips of paper around on a table top. This technique may be par-ticularly useful to you if you are confronted with a complex problem or large quantities of information. Placing related information into groups helps every writer invent the ideas that will support the thesis.

The thesis is the main idea or point that controls the essay. Your sup-porting ideas are the points or assertions you want to make that develop your thesis. As we use it here, a supporting idea is a *sentence* that relates the material about a single group of information you have put together. If you were to convert your supporting idea and the related material into a paragraph, the idea would become the paragraph's topic sentence—the controlling idea of the paragraph. The material would become the con-crete detail, support, explanation, or evidence that would develop that idea. If you thought of constructing a paragraph as a kind of equation, it might look like this:

$$\text{material} \begin{cases} \text{explanation} \\ \text{specifics} \\ \text{concrete detail} \\ \text{evidence} \\ \text{support} \end{cases} + \text{a controlling idea} = \text{potential paragraph}$$

As you come up with supporting ideas, you develop your thesis, the point of your entire essay. In writing an essay based on the "Kennicott College" case in this chapter, one student writer listed the following ideas:

Developing other places for the students to go will cut down on stu-dent drinking.

Many problems could be solved by the addition of resident assistants on each floor in the dorms.

Because closing the Tavern isn't a good solution but operating it at present is a problem, we must search for other solutions.

Recently there have been increased problems of excessive drinking at the Tavern, in individual rooms, by underage students, and in general.

Many problems could be solved by a few simple changes in the operation of the Tavern.

These ideas led the student writer to the tentative thesis that "With some changes, those concerned can be assured that students are getting a safe and complete education."

Since a sentence contains a subject and a comment about that subject (a verb or predicate), it is important that you be able to state your thesis and supporting ideas as single sentences. The subject of the sentence that states the thesis, for example, is the subject of the essay. The comment you make about the subject should complete your sentence and help you to make sure there is some point to your essay. If you can write your thesis and supporting ideas as single sentences, then you can be sure you have some control over the material you've invented.

Sequencing the Supporting Ideas and the Thesis

Whatever steps you go through when inventing material for your essay, the basic ingredients in effective writing are a well-defined subject, a clearly stated thesis, and a set of supporting ideas with relevant evidence. Once you have invented all this material, you are ready to organize it. In general, two of the next writing decisions you will then face involve sequencing ideas and writing paragraphs.

Of course anytime you have a number of ideas to support your thesis, you have to decide what order to put them in. Because this arrangement determines the order in which the paragraphs are written, it can be called the paragraph sequence. The paragraph sequence may be predetermined by the type of writing an essay involves. As you will read in Chapter 4, one way to classify writing is to say that it either describes, narrates, explains, or persuades. While Chapter 5 will give you more information about paragraph sequences in description and narration and Chapter 8 will discuss persuasion, you can review the basics of paragraph sequence here.

If you are telling a story or narrating an event, you will probably use a chronological sequence: that is, you will arrange your paragraphs according to the time of the event each paragraph is about. You will probably tell about the bank holdup, for example, before you describe the negotiations over the hostages or the capture of the bank robber. If you are describing a process, such as "How to collect Lincoln-head pennies," then you will be selecting a paragraph sequence according to the order in which the steps in the process must or should be completed. While narration (storytelling) and process analysis (telling "how to") usually offer almost ready-made paragraph sequences, describing, explaining, and persuading do not.

Aside from the chronological sequence mentioned above, you generally have two basic options for sequencing your ideas: the diminishing sequence and the expanding sequence. The diminishing sequence, or the "inverted pyramid," is the form newspaper writers frequently use. If you select this sequence, then the thesis is stated in the first paragraph, the most important ideas in the following paragraphs, and the least important ideas in the final paragraphs. As a newspaper reader, you experience this kind of sequence whenever you reach the bottom of a front-page article and it says, "turn to A-19," and you don't bother to. You don't turn to A-19 because you have already learned the most important ideas, and you don't care to read the least important ones. Journalists use the diminishing sequence because it is convenient for readers who want to read the newspaper quickly but not completely.

You may want to use the diminishing sequence when writing a final exam in a limited period of time. Doing so will help you make sure you state the thesis and many, if not all, of the most important ideas. In most writing situations, however, the expanding sentence is the better choice. It allows the writer to develop the thesis on a paragraph-by-paragraph basis so that the thesis is not fully stated until the conclusion. It encourages the reader to complete the entire essay because the essay gathers strength as the thesis develops.

In any essay the writer must always have a purpose in placing one paragraph after another. The reader assumes that any two adjacent paragraphs must be related. The writer must therefore show the reader how the paragraphs are interrelated, why they have been placed one after another in the essay, and what the purpose is of that placement. If your purpose in sequencing is clear to the reader, then your thesis will develop clearly and smoothly from one paragraph to the next. Here are some questions you can ask yourself as a guide to determining whether your paragraph sequence coherently develops your thesis:

Does the essay develop step-by-step, without big gaps between supporting ideas?
Are closely related supporting ideas placed next to each other?
Does the essay continually develop in *one* direction?

(The essay doesn't double back to a topic covered several paragraphs before or keep promising, "This topic will be covered in greater detail later on.")

Do the supporting ideas sufficiently interconnect so that the reader can follow the logical development of the thesis?

In the essay mentioned earlier about the drinking problem at Kennicott College, the student wanted to develop the thesis, "With some changes, those concerned can be assured that students are getting a safe and complete education." The student planned to develop this thesis by arranging the supporting ideas in the following sequence:

A. Recently there have been increased problems of excessive drinking at the Tavern, in individual rooms, by underage students, and in general.

B. Because closing the Tavern isn't a good solution but operating it at present is a problem, we must search for another solution.

C. Many problems could be solved by a few simple changes in the operation of the Tavern.

D. Many other problems could be solved by the addition of resident assistants in each of the dorms.

E. Developing other places for the students to go will also cut down on student drinking.

F. With these changes, all those concerned can be assured that students are getting a safe and complete education, not attending a wild, crazy party.

By reading the outline of a paragraph sequence such as this one, you should be able to trace the development of an essay's thesis. Here the student begins by outlining the problems, then rejects one possible solution, and finally proposes some solutions that lead to the conclusion. After you read the next section on paragraphing, you may want to turn to Sample Essay B at the end of the "Kennicott College" case and see how this student writer turned the above outline of a paragraph sequence into an essay.

Paragraphing

Although some writers have completed entire books that discuss the paragraph, we are limited here to a brief discussion of three major aspects of it: its material, its internal structure, and its connection with other paragraphs. In other words, we will explain what goes into a paragraph, how the supporting idea and evidence should be organized, and how one paragraph can be connected with another.

The Supporting Idea and Evidence

In paragraphing, as in all writing, the most essential writing unit is the sentence. The sentence is the basic writing unit because it enables you to state a grammatically complete thought; it enables you to focus on a subject and express an idea about that subject. By writing one sentence after another about the same subject, you can develop one idea about that subject. Suppose, however, that as you developed one idea after another in support of your thesis, you never once indented and began a new paragraph. Suppose you just wrote one solid paragraph of five hundred words. Doing so would present two problems to any reader.

The solid left-hand margin would discourage any reader on sight; the constant reading of many sentences in a row would exhaust any reader. In fact, the readers would probably look for natural breaks in the text so as to rest their eyes and their minds. Those natural breaks would come between supporting ideas. When writers indent and begin a new paragraph, they forewarn the reader that the essay is moving from one supporting idea to the next. If an essay were just one long paragraph, any reader could be misled or become confused because of not realizing that the writer was finished with one idea and beginning a new one. To allow eyes to rest and to guide the reader as the thesis is developed, the writer should begin a new paragraph each time a new supporting idea is introduced.

Remember that a supporting idea controls all the sentences in a paragraph. If you actually write down a supporting idea in the paragraph, it could be called the paragraph's topic sentence. Most student writers are told to explicitly state the supporting idea—write a topic sentence—for each paragraph they write. These writers are given this advice because it is a simple way to encourage them to write well-organized paragraphs.

You should know, however, that some professional writers use supporting ideas that are only implied by the paragraph. In other words, a good writer can clearly communicate a paragraph's central point without actually stating it as one particular sentence in the paragraph. You may want to write paragraphs with topic sentences—explicitly stated supporting ideas—or you may want to imply the paragraph's central point. Using topic sentences may make you feel more self-assured because you can explicitly tell your reader the point of each paragraph. Whichever choice you make, always remember that the purpose of a paragraph is to use a group of sentences to explain, support, or develop one point or central idea you want to make.

The effectiveness of a paragraph depends as much upon the quality of its material as it does upon the clear statement of a main idea. Good material includes vivid, concrete detail, and specific rather than general information. While you can learn more about developing good material by reading Part Two of the text, here are three examples of weak and strengthened material:

(little detail)	There were a lot of people in the dorm room.
(concrete, vivid detail)	That single dorm room contained only a desk and a bed, yet seventeen people had managed to wedge themselves into it so that they covered the floor, desk, bed, and even had to lean out of the closet.
(generalization)	Mr. Cooper was obviously upset.
(specific evidence)	His sister's ex-husband was wanted on an out-of-state warrant for failure to pay child support. Mr. Cooper, a local businessman, was certainly not used to being tackled.
	Mr. Cooper was also not used to being cuffed, frisked, and made to sit in the back of a police car.
	Mr. Cooper refused to listen to Fox's apology or Best's explanation.
(generalization)	Officer Fox has a good record.
(specific evidence)	Lieutenant Ingram, Fox's supervisor, thinks highly of him.
	According to Ingram, the other officers respect Fox.
	Fox was recently promoted.
	Although Fox has been on the force five years, he has only one other charge against him, and this was dropped.

If you always use specific evidence, and concrete, vivid detail to develop your supporting ideas, your reader can better understand those ideas and how they support your thesis. A clearly stated supporting idea and concrete material are the basic ingredients of any good paragraph, but the way these ingredients are put together determines how successful the paragraph will be.

Paragraph Unity and Coherence

Two more terms—unity and coherence—are important to understand when you are faced with any paragraph-writing problems. As you have already read, the first "acid test" of a paragraph is whether it is unified, whether all its material supports, explains, or develops a single idea. If you read one of your own paragraphs and can say that all its material explains the paragraph's supporting idea, then you can be sure the paragraph is unified. The paragraph is held together as a unit by a central idea. The following paragraph is unified by the idea, "Your paragraph has coherence when the sentences are interconnected so as to smoothly and clearly develop a central idea."

Paragraph coherence, the way we use the term here, means what you would probably expect it to mean. *Cohere* means "to stick together." Your paragraph sticks together when each sentence develops smoothly and logically from the one that comes before it. In other words, your paragraph has coherence when the sentences are interconnected so as to develop smoothly and clearly a central idea.

Here's one way to check on your paragraph coherence. First, recopy your paragraph on a separate sheet of paper. List each sentence separately and be sure to leave a blank space between each sentence. Next, take out a pair of scissors and snip up your paragraph so that each sentence is listed on a separate slip of paper. Now scramble your sentences and then arrange them in the best possible order. You can also ask another writer to try ordering your sentences. Is only one good sequence of sentences possible? If not, you probably have weak paragraph coherence.

Below are three different paragraphs in which the sentences have been listed separately and then scrambled. Try putting each paragraph back together again. Compare your results with someone else's. Are your sentences sequenced the same way? If a paragraph has good coherence, its sentences will fit together in just one way.

PARAGRAPH A

A. Also, she said she hoped to expand the volunteer program.

B. Before choosing an assistant, I outlined the aspects of my job that I wanted the assistant to help me with.

C. She felt certain she could handle all the scheduling and training of volunteers—probably could even improve the volunteer program.

D. I decided my assistant would recruit, schedule, and train volunteers.

E. Erica expressed an interest in assisting me with these particular areas of responsibility.

F. This assistant would also be "head trouble-shooter" in charge of the daily inflow of kids, which would require that the assistant direct the volunteers in handling the tours, lecture demonstrations, and noon meals.

PARAGRAPH B

A. You can see the old farmers in the corner of the local fast-food restaurant on weekend mornings.

B. He is talking now, every wrinkle on his face changing somehow as he glances out the window.

C. In bib overalls faded almost white, plaid shirts frayed at the cuffs, and soiled seed caps, one or two from businesses that don't exist anymore, they sit and talk.

D. If you listen hard, you can hear the others, but the big one with the thinning hair and strong nose speaks the loudest as he sips his coffee.

E. "I still say there's going to be a corn blight this year."

PARAGRAPH C

A. But then, of course, she falls, and the falling proves the law of gravity and the maxim that cats always land on their feet—all four of hers hit me squarely in the stomach when she hits the earth at Mach 1.

B. At three in the morning, mice in the attic are an entertainment for sleepless souls.

C. Then the cat joins the act as she tries to prove that cats are spiders too.

D. First there's all that suspense about what those sounds could be.

E. She can cling, she thinks, to the ceiling with her paws, and race along upside down.

F. And then, the mystery solved, there's little else to do that late at night but listen to them scamper above, between the rafters, and across the attic side of the acoustical ceiling tile.

As you analyze the sentence sequences for these three paragraphs, note what words or phrases help you decide on the best sequence. Note, too, what words could be changed to make the sentences fit together better. What other devices help these sentences fit together?

Paragraph Transitions

Just as the sentences in a paragraph should only fit together in a particular order, so should the paragraphs of an essay fit together in just one sequence. In addition to arranging paragraphs in a logical order, paragraph transitions are one device you can use to make sure your paragraphs interconnect with one another.

Paragraph transitions enable you to maintain coherence as you develop your thesis from one paragraph to the next. A paragraph transition is a word, phrase, or sentence that connects the supporting idea of two adjacent paragraphs. Paragraph transitions are bridges between paragraphs. They are signposts that make sure the reader follows the essay from one idea to the next. When two supporting ideas in your paragraph sequence are closely related, a paragraph transition may be unnecessary. When the essay moves from one major section to another, a paragraph transition can provide a crucial link in the development of your thesis.

One way to check your paragraph sequence and your need for paragraph transitions is to cut up your essay into individual paragraphs and to scramble those paragraphs. If you asked another writer to put those paragraphs in the right order, would he or she see your signposts and rearrange your paragraphs as you've planned?

Introducing

Some essays simply begin at the beginning: that is, the first paragraph is based on the first supporting idea in the expanding sequence. As the reader reads each paragraph, he or she gradually becomes aware of the thesis. Frequently, however, writers begin by introducing the readers to their thesis. The length of the introduction varies according to the length of the essay, the complexity of the subject and thesis, and the writer's relationship with the reader. A short essay and a simple thesis can certainly be introduced in a single brief paragraph. A complex thesis and an essay of several pages might require a two-paragraph introduction. Your relationship with your reader also helps determine your introduction's length. You can be brief in your introduction if the reader is friendly and well known; a hostile, unknown reader requires more serious attention.

Whether your introduction consists of one short paragraph or two long ones, you should be aware of three problems facing the reader at the beginning of your essay. The reader's first problem is not knowing the subject of the essay. The title, if there is one, will help define the subject, but no writer can rely upon the title to clearly define the subject. People interpret titles in different ways. Therefore, the introduction should connect the reader with the particular way you have defined the subject. Moreover, the introduction should make the reader receptive to that subject. In other words, the reader should feel willing to listen to what you have to say. If you have completed a thorough audience analysis (See Chapter 2), then you should be able to make the reader receptive to the subject you have selected.

Another problem the reader faces is not knowing the writer's thesis. People are curious about what is going to happen to them whenever they are about to try a new experience. Reading your essay is a new experience for your audience. One way to satisfy their curiosity is to generally or tentatively explain your thesis. Ideally, you will tell them enough so that they know generally what to expect, but not everything; that way they still have something to look forward to.

As a part of being curious, of wanting to know what is going to happen in your essay, readers often want a sense of how it is organized. A third problem for the reader, then, is not knowing how your essay will develop, or in what direction it's going. One way to solve this problem is to state generally how your essay is organized. How much you need to "forecast" the essay's organization is, once again, determined by the complexity of your subject and thesis and by your relationship with the reader.

Besides all these basics, readers have another demand they place on the writer: the writing should be interesting. A good introduction does more than define the subject, state the thesis and, possibly, indicate how the essay is organized. A *good* introduction grabs the reader's attention or at least makes the reader interested enough to read on. Read the introductory paragraphs of the two essays that follow the "Kennicott College" case at the end of this chapter. What are the strengths and weaknesses of those introductions? Have the writers worked hard enough for the readers?

Because introductions require much effort on the writer's part (to make it easy for the reader), some writers complete all the paragraphs in the expanding sequence before writing an introduction. On the other hand, some writers complete a rough draft of their introduction before writing anything else because they want to have a place to start from, a foundation to build on. Whenever you choose to write your introduction, you can expect it to be one of the most difficult and time-consuming parts of your statement to complete. That's because you and the reader are beginning a new experience together. Introductions are hard work, but remember this: the harder you work as a writer, the more you will have to offer to the reader.

Concluding

When readers reach the end of an essay, they expect some kind of conclusion. If your essay is several paragraphs long, then a summary of your major ideas helps refresh the reader's memory about what you had to say. Since readers pay the most attention at the beginning and at the ending of your essay, some kind of restatement of your thesis is important in the conclusion. However, a conclusion would seem flat if you simply repeated your thesis as you stated it in your introduction. A particularly revealing quotation, a provocative question, or an analogy are just three possibilities for turning a dull summary into a refreshing conclusion. When you read the two sample student essays that follow the "Kennicott College" case, ask yourself whether the last paragraph merely summarizes or truly concludes each essay.

Summary

You have seen that inventing your material and organizing your essay is a challenging, complicated part of the writing process. And like the entire writing process itself, inventing and organizing is cyclical—during one stage you may return to an earlier stage or jump forward to an advanced one.

The stages of the writing process can be identified in many different ways, but generally include inventing, writing, and organizing material; revising a particular draft; and editing and proofreading that draft for final copy. The invention stage involves you in selecting a subject as well as in gathering information and ideas about that subject. The material development stage involves you in writing bits and pieces of an essay (or entire, separate drafts of an essay) until you have most or all of a particular draft you want to revise (material development may require three "drafts" or thirty). The revision stage involves you in constantly improving your single draft until you are certain you have solved all its problems in organization and content (another three to thirty drafts). The editing/proofreading stage involves you in the process of making your essay graceful and attractive in style as well as grammatically and mechanically 100 percent correct (perhaps another three to thirty drafts).

Some successful writers write with incredible slowness as they submit each sentence to the torture test of ten to fifty revisions before the next sentence is written. Most successful writers probably spread their problem solving out: they view the different stages in the writing process as different opportunities to create, construct, revise, refine, and correct a particular piece of writing.

Kennicott College

As President Samantha Wolfe sat at her desk, she considered the problem of whether to close the college-owned and operated tavern. The Tavern was located in the Student Union Building and had recently been damaged during a student disturbance. But then, she realized, a dormitory had also been damaged, and perhaps the problem was larger than that of what to do about the Tavern.

Whatever President Wolfe decided would have to be explained to the students, to their parents, and to interested alumni, not to mention to the Board of Regents. She was fairly certain that the students were opposed to the closing of the Tavern, but she wasn't sure what action parents, alumni, and the Board might support.

THE COLLEGE

Kennicott College was a small liberal arts college located on the New England seacoast. Although the college certainly had no national or even regional reputation, it was financially secure and attractive in appearance. Located right on the coast, it covered almost two miles of private beach.

The faculty was respectable, though not especially well known, and was particularly friendly toward its twelve hundred students. Two or three special studies programs, such as an artists exchange program with a Parisian art school, and one or two special admissions policies helped keep up admissions.

One of the special admissions policies allowed two or three dozen high school juniors to enter Kennicott a year early. After a year at Kennicott most high schools retroactively awarded their students a diploma. These students could then complete college in just three more years. These early-admission students, however, were part of the problem.

DRINKING IN THE DORMS

The college was located in a rural area between two small towns. The only package liquor store—Stetson's—was located ten miles up the road on the edge of Ely, one of the towns. There were a few bars in Ely and in Canton, the other nearby town, but fishermen and dockworkers, not students, filled the bars.

Many students drove up the road to Stetson's to buy package liquor, and sometimes they drove elsewhere to drink it; other times they drank it on the way back to or in the dorms. Drinking in the dorms was technically permitted only at parties organized and recognized by each dorm's governing officer and the office of student housing. Parties were officially confined to the large recreational rooms located on each floor of each of the four dormitories.

In practice, many students drank in their own rooms and had parties there, large and small. Parties were popular at Kennicott, so popular that most students could find some party or other to go to every night. Some students partied every night of the week. Beer was always available, and usually so were wine and the usual assortment of hard liquors. If students got involved in other forms of getting high, college officials didn't talk about it, and no one asked.

THE TAVERN

The Tavern at Kennicott College was originally opened to provide students with a place to relax and have a drink when no parties were scheduled. Only beer and wine were served, as was the case with sponsored dorm parties. The Tavern was located in a basement, had a pleasant atmosphere, largely because it was dark and filled with oak and leather furniture, and was owned and operated by the college itself. Students could begin drinking at four, but by eleven (twelve on Friday and Saturday nights) the place was closed and the students went back to the dorms or to the few apartments near campus.

One of the problems associated with the Tavern became most noticeable at closing time. It was well known that on any night of the week, especially on Friday and Saturday, students could be seen leaving the bar feet first. Their friends would carry them back to the dorms and put them to bed.

THE BOARD OF REGENTS

The Board of Regents was composed of a cross section of business people and professionals from the surrounding area. President Wolfe knew of only one member who had a special interest in the alcohol-on-campus issue: Robert Stetson. Not only was Stetson the owner and manager of Stetson's Liquors, he was also the father of Terese and Robert Jay Stetson, aged nineteen and seventeen, who were both students at Kennicott. Although they lived at home, President Wolfe knew that both of them were actively involved in many campus social activities.

THE STUDENT DISTURBANCE

What had happened the weekend before brought the whole problem to the attention of both the president and the entire college. After the Tavern closed the previous Friday night, a large group of students had continued their party in a dorm room. Evidently the party had been orderly enough until about one in the morning, when the students had run out of liquor.

As the story was reported in the campus newspaper Monday, the next thing that happened was word began to spread that someone had hidden two cases of beer in the floor's refrigerator. (Each floor of eighty students shared two large refrigerators, one per wing.) Some male students reportedly raced off to the refrigerators, only to find both empty, of beer anyway. At that point somebody suggested the party-goers get even by throwing the refrigerator out the window. They tried, but found that the refrigerator didn't fit very well, so the entire window, casing and all, ended up with the refrigerator on a sidewalk three floors below. Damage was estimated at $1,575.

THE CONCERNED PARENTS

Even before this most recent occurrence the president had received a few letters from concerned parents. These parents had seventeen-year-olds, and even one sixteen-year-old, attending Kennicott under the special admissions policy. The parents said their children had reported considerable drinking in the dorms, both of soft and hard liquor. The parents pointed out that under the state's eighteen-year-old drinking law their children were very much too young to be involved. Yet the college seemed to condone, even encourage, drinking in rooms, at parties, anywhere, everywhere, anytime, it seemed, except perhaps in the classroom during the daytime.

THE BOARD MEETING

At the last board meeting President Wolfe had discussed the problem of alcohol on campus with her fellow board members. Few were in favor of shutting down the Tavern and eliminating drinking in the dormitories. Some wanted to know more about the problem. Why weren't students satisfied with a party or two once a week in the recreational rooms? Color TV and plush furniture filled these rooms and surely made them as comfortable as, if not more comfortable than, most people's living rooms. Weren't these rooms the ideal place for parties? Would it be possible to limit party size in some way? Why did there have to be any big parties at all?

THE OFFICE OF STUDENT HOUSING

The Office of Student Housing included just one administrator (the director) and two secretaries. Students were assigned dorm rooms in the usual ways in one of the college's four small dormitories. One student, a junior or a senior, was in charge of organizing parties in each dorm, in coordination with The Office of Student Housing.

SUGGESTED DISCUSSION QUESTIONS

1. What is the problem President Wolfe faces?
2. What actions can President Wolfe take?
3. Suppose you are a student at Kennicott. How can you influence President Wolfe's action?
4. What should be done about the Tavern?
5. What should be done about drinking in the dorms?
6. What should be done about the sixteen-year-old students? The seventeen-year-olds?

SUGGESTED ASSIGNMENTS

1. You are a student at Kennicott College. Write a letter to President Wolfe in which you argue what she should and/or should not do.

2. You are a student at Kennicott College. Write a letter to Robert Stetson in which you persuade him to use his influence on the Board to help solve the problem.

3. You are editor-in-chief of Kennicott's student newspaper. Write an editorial in which you argue for solutions to the problems as you see them.

4. Write an essay in which you argue whether there is a drinking problem on your campus. (Audience: the readers of the campus newspaper)

STUDENT RESPONSES

The following student responses are based on "Kennicott College." Student A wrote to President Wolfe; Student B wrote a letter to the editor of the campus newspaper. As you read each sample student response, ask yourself the following questions:

> Does the writer clearly state a thesis?
> Are the paragraphs arranged in a logical order?
> Does each paragraph focus on one main point the writer wants to make?
> Does each paragraph contain specific, concrete detail to support and develop the paragraph's main idea?
> Does each main idea support the thesis?
> What other material could the writer include?
> Is any unnecessary information included?

Your instructor may have other suggestions about how you can analyze these two writing samples.

SAMPLE RESPONSE A

Dear President Wolfe:

1. As a senior at Kennicott College, I was concerned when I heard rumors recently hinting that the Tavern might be closed down permanently. That prospect is very disturbing to me and a number of other students who frequent the Tavern. We enjoy the Tavern's pleasant atmosphere and feel it is a good place to go in order to relax and socialize. While we realize the position the disturbance last weekend places you in, we also feel there are more effective alternatives to the problem than closing the Tavern.

2. In order to evaluate the situation involving the Tavern properly, I feel we must also touch on other aspects of the drinking problem here at Kennicott. First of all, it's no big secret that the minors on campus have access to liquor. In fact, many of them have been going to the Tavern and are served there. Secondly, drinking in the rooms is a problem that only gained attention after the episode last weekend. Although extensive damage, like the $1,575 bill quoted by the campus newspaper, isn't common, a major part of the vandalism seems to take place during these

"spontaneous parties." Thirdly—and the problem I'm most concerned about—is the Tavern. It has been the site of alcohol abuse in the past, and since it has already sustained damage, some feel it should be closed. I plan to deal with this and all the other problems in the proposal that I've worked out. My recommendation is as follows: the college should place all underage students on the same floors in their respective male/female dormitories, and drinking in dorm rooms should only be allowed when fewer than four people are present or the resident of the room has in his possession a signed party form dated at least twenty-four hours in advance. The Tavern should be allowed to continue its operation, although a new series of measures should be enforced in conjunction with its operation.

3. The first point in my proposal requires the consolidation of all the younger students at Kennicott on the same floors. If this is done, the college still can't prevent underage students from mingling with the upperclassmen and getting hold of liquor, but at least it will reduce some of the peer pressure to which younger students are so susceptible. Because of this pressure, they often end up drinking when they don't really want to.

4. There is another positive aspect of this proposal that is unrelated to the drinking problem. It is that segregation of younger students will ease their transition into college life. The adjustment to life in a college setting is hard for most students, especially younger ones. Besides, the average sixteen-year-old lacks the maturity of his older classmates, so his adjustment to college may be more difficult. Therefore, if he is placed in a more familiar atmosphere with kids his own age, it stands to reason that the shared experience eases the transition for everyone.

5. My second recommendation is to allow groups of fewer than four people to drink in their rooms. Since the present alcohol policy prohibiting drinking in the rooms isn't enforced, it would be preferable to allow some drinking with better controls. Allowing larger groups to drink in their rooms on weekends might not be a bad idea provided they have a signed party permit. This permit should contain such information as the date of the party, the room it will be held in, and when the form was filled out. It should also be signed by both sets of neighbors (unless for some valid reason confirmed by the R.A. one was unavailable) and by the floor's resident assistant. This precaution would help eliminate spontaneous parties being carried from the Tavern or other parties into the dorm rooms since the form must be filled out at least twenty-four hours in advance. I can see where this wouldn't be a very popular measure, but I feel it is necessary to promote a more serious, scholarly atmosphere in the dormitories. While the use of a party policy doesn't actually come out and say anything against room parties, the red tape should serve to discourage students from having them. Thus the threat of vandalism instigated by alcohol abuse will be somewhat reduced.

6. My third proposition includes letting the Tavern remain open, but also involves a series of measures designed to reduce some of the problems there. The first measure is to initiate a more effective carding system at the door. Identification card checkers should be instructed to look at the picture and description on each card more closely. I've heard of some schools that even offer rewards of up to $50 to employees finding fake or misrepresentative IDs. This seems to work extremely well in curbing the number of minors getting into the bars.

7. Another reason for leaving the bar open is that closing it will encourage students to go to Ely or Canton for social drinking. It is common for couples to go to the Tavern on dates, and since Ely and Canton contain the nearest taverns, many students would be inclined to go there if the Tavern closed down. Because it is harder for students to get to these towns, closing the Tavern might reduce the numbers in the bars. Those that would still go, however, would create an even larger problem.

They would force Kennicott to deal with the problem of drinking *and* driving. The consequences of this combination could be deadly. Because of this, I feel the Tavern should remain open.

8. In addition to the above proposals, fines for excessive rowdiness could be instituted. They would have to be strictly adhered to, however, because it is the certainty of punishment, not the severity, that deters students. If severe penalties were established for vandalism and disorderly conduct, students might think twice before getting drunk.

9. Something else that could be done in conjunction with the alcohol policy is to look into alternate forms of recreation. Kennicott offers very little in the way of recreation, so students make drinking their favorite pastime. The college's isolation from metropolitan nightlife creates problems for most students, since few have cars up here. It is inconvenient for them to leave the campus for entertainment. Therefore, I feel it would be wise for Kennicott to investigate the possibility of utilizing its beach to a greater extent and possibly even opening up a roller-skating rink, bowling alley, or discotheque. Any one of these would provide students with an alternative to the standard Friday or Saturday night drunk. It would also be an attractive feature for high-schoolers considering coming to college here. Thus it would seem to be a worthwhile project for the college.

10. As a student of Kennicott, I feel my proposals are in the best interest of the college. I hope you'll consider them carefully, especially the recommendations pertaining to the Tavern. I've enjoyed my time here at Kennicott, but I believe the quality of campus life could be improved by making some adjustments in the alcohol policy.

SAMPLE RESPONSE B

Editor:

1. Each and every day the students of Kennicott College abuse alcohol. Recently there have been increased problems of excessive drinking at the Tavern, partying in individual rooms, drinking by underage students, and general misuse of alcoholic beverages. Increased concern for the students' welfare has forced us to search for solutions to these problems. I feel that a change in the operation of the Tavern, an addition of resident assistants, and a new recreation center will help resolve these problems.

2. One possible solution would be to close the Tavern entirely. This idea is absolutely ridiculous. The closing of the Tavern would force students to find other places to drink. Many students would spend a great deal of time driving to neighboring towns to purchase and consume alcohol. Therefore, closing the Tavern would in turn increase dangers by causing people to drive after drinking. That would be unsafe for students and others who travel these roads. Closing the Tavern might also force students to party in their rooms, which is already a problem. Since closing the Tavern doesn't seem to offer a good solution and there is a problem as the Tavern is presently run, we must search for another solution to the problem.

3. I feel many problems could be solved by a few simple changes in the present operation of the Tavern. The Tavern should be open for shorter hours, should require proper identification for admittance, and should provide some form of live entertainment. If the Tavern was open fewer hours there would be less time for students to drink, and hopefully they wouldn't drink so much. It would be sensible for the Tavern to open at a later time, say after dinner, around six-thirty or seven o'clock. This would be especially important on weekday evenings since students

have classes the next morning. It presently appears that the Tavern does little or no checking of identification for admittance. This seems somewhat logical since the Tavern is operated for students of legal drinking age, but it's not right. The Tavern should begin checking for proper identification since this will help keep out underage students. This change is a necessity for all concerned. Another change should be the addition of some form of live entertainment in the Tavern. The addition of live entertainment would make the Tavern more of a social place than a place to drink. In turn, people would spend less time drinking. Obviously there would be some cost involved, but this cost could be kept low by providing small-time entertainment and by giving the students themselves a chance to show their talents. Adding live entertainment, requiring identification, and staying open fewer hours could significantly straighten out the problems of alcohol abuse we are having at the Tavern.

4. Many problems could be solved by the addition of resident assistants in the dorms. At present there is no one in charge. Because there are no resident assistants, there is no one to see that the rules are followed. There is definitely a need for some change. I propose that the college hire one resident assistant for every forty to fifty students. The cost of employing these resident assistants would be minimal because they would be older students whose pay would be nothing more than room and board. The job of the resident would be a big one. Not only would they help solve problems in the dorms, but they would also learn about leadership and responsibility. The resident assistant's major job would be to see that the dorm rules, as set up by dorm government, are followed. This would involve making sure that students do not drink in the dorms at times other than dorm government-sponsored parties, that underage students do not drink, and that the general rules are enforced. The addition of resident assistants would create a big change in the abusive use of alcohol. Underage students would not drink because they would be watched over. General consumption of alcohol in the dorms would decrease. There would be fewer parties in the rooms, and such parties would not be so wild. Hopefully, the addition of resident assistants would eliminate problems such as the one that happened recently, when $1,575 worth of damage was done when some students got rowdy and threw a refrigerator out of a third-floor window. Obviously, the addition of resident assistants cannot solve all the problems, but it would definitely put some control over the problem, and a little control is better than none whatever, as is the present case.

5. Another problem is with students who have nowhere to go except to the Tavern. These students have the TV room and lounge, but other than that they have very little besides their own room. The town itself doesn't offer any means of entertainment for the students because it is so small. I feel that developing other places for the students to go will cut down on student drinking.

6. By building a small recreation center, the college could offer something more to the student. Such a center could offer games such as pinball and billiards. The center would pay for itself because the machines would cost money to run. This recreation center would give the underage students someplace to go and would give other students a choice of what to do during their free evenings. The establishment of this recreation center would decrease the number of students going to the Tavern and road-tripping to nearby towns.

7. Another idea might be to build athletic facilities. This would be a very costly project, but it would be a valuable investment in the long run. It would give students more options and encourage them to do something healthy for themselves.

8. The abuse of alcohol has been a problem on campuses around the nation for years and years. No one has found a total answer to the problem, but I believe the

few simple suggestions I have made will greatly decrease the problem of alcohol abuse on the Kennicott College campus.

9. By diminishing some of the Tavern's hours, placing resident assistants in the dorms, and offering students new forms of recreation, we will hopefully decrease the abuse of alcohol on this particular college campus. It may only be a start, but these suggestions are definitely a step in the right direction. With these few changes, all those concerned can be assured that the students are getting a safe and complete education instead of a wild and crazy party.

University Bookstore

For the last three weeks you've been working on a special investigative committee at the university. The committee has been assigned the task of finding out how the university's bookstore could give better service to students and faculty. The committee, which is composed of six students and six faculty members, was formed because general campus opinion was that the bookstore was frequently out of textbooks required for courses, didn't order enough of them, made students wait in line for up to an hour during registration in order to buy books, promised to order extra copies of textbooks and never did, and frequently told students that the seventy-five dollars worth of textbooks they had purchased the previous semester were now nearly worthless.

The committee has been gathering information from various sources across the campus. All faculty members were mailed a brief questionnaire about bookstore services. The questionnaire asked about book ordering, follow-up on out-of-stock orders, and general services. A space for written comments was also provided. Fifty-one percent of the faculty responded. Because the student body was too large to survey individually, the committee set up a table in the student union and encouraged students to discuss the bookstore with committee members or to drop off written comments.

You have been assigned the task of organizing the information gathered from various sources for a report. The report will be directed primarily to the administration since it is responsible for the bookstore operation. A special edition of the student newspaper will publish the report.

THE UNIVERSITY

The university is a large public facility with a moderately good academic and athletic reputation and a growing student population. Two years ago the enrollment was 17,500 FTE (full-time-equivalency) students, but now the figure is 21,575. Since the university is not located in a large city, the university community is dependent upon the university-owned bookstore, along with three privately operated stores, to provide it with its necessary textbooks and supplies.

THE COMMITTEE'S INFORMATION

Here is a condensed form of the information the committee was able to obtain through its preliminary investigation into the bookstore problem:

1. The faculty said that the bookstore frequently (as opposed to never, seldom, often, or always) failed to notify faculty members when a book was out of print or out of stock.

2. Students complained that the bookstore never bought back enough of their books even though these texts were required for courses taught every semester.

3. Forty percent of the bookstore's backstock area had been eliminated recently when one building was demolished and part of another was converted to office space.

4. A French instructor reported that the bookstore repeatedly promised that three textbooks would be put on the shelf immediately, and then, when the term was one-third over, she was suddenly told the texts were unavailable from the publisher.

5. The new bookstore manager, Marty Lewis (second year), has a degree in agronomy and has worked as assistant manager for two years.

6. Presently, the bookstore has 5,000 square feet of selling space, the same amount it had in 1965 when annual gross sales were only 20 percent of the current amount.

7. The bookstore said it could not buy back students' books until the faculty got their book orders in.

8. A university bookstore in Canada, similar to the University Bookstore, had increased its efficiency in ordering and shelving books by 40 percent by use of a computer-inventory and sales-control system.

9. Fifty-seven percent of the faculty said that the bookstore asked for book orders weeks before it was practical to turn them in.

10. The bookstore no longer granted discounts to faculty members.

11. The student union building in which the bookstore was located was already overcrowded.

12. Marty Lewis, whom you interviewed, said that over 40 percent of the faculty ordered their books late.

13. Students often had to go to all four bookstores to buy their books.

14. The administration was opposed to hiring any more employees to work in the bookstore.

15. The previous bookstore manager had allowed a tremendous overstock in textbooks to build up.

16. These textbooks were out-of-date and could not be returned to the publisher.

17. Two faculty members had reportedly ordered their books from a drug-store/newsstand and had been pleased by the service.

18. It was common knowledge that the bowling and billiards department in the student union wanted to expand its operation.

19. It was common knowledge that three other bookstores or stationery stores in town ordered required books for courses.

20. Marty Lewis said the University Bookstore's lease on the present cash registers would expire by the end of the semester.

21. None of the bookstores that sold textbooks informed the other book-stores about titles and quantities ordered.

22. The university-operated bookstore refused to order more than 60–75 percent of the books needed for courses because the other stores sold so many texts.

23. The department chairpersons polled (67 percent responding) said that their departments were slow in deciding which teachers should teach which courses because the administration required that teaching assignments be based on registration figures (actual) and not projected needs.

SUGGESTED DISCUSSION QUESTIONS

1. How can you reduce these twenty-three items to a few groups of ideas and facts?
2. Which items are clearly related?
3. What conclusions can you make about each group of related information?
4. Who will the audience for your report include?
5. What are the students' problems?
6. What are the bookstore's problems?
7. What are the faculty's problems?
8. What additional information should the committee acquire?

SUGGESTED ASSIGNMENTS

1. Write the report by:
   a. grouping related information;
   b. drawing conclusions;
   c. stating your conclusions as sentences; and
   d. using the information and your conclusions as a basis for your report.

2. Write a report in which you identify and analyze any problems that you face, as a student, in buying books and supplies at your college bookstore. (Audience: the bookstore manager)

Apartments Unlimited

Bob Sullivan, a recent college graduate, was the newest and youngest employee in the office, but Helen Ewell respected his work and his opinion. Ewell was owner and manager of Apartments Unlimited, a property management company owning or managing nearly five hundred units in Albuquerque, New Mexico.

Bob worked primarily in the office handling tenant complaints and tenant communication in general. He did a variety of office tasks and occasionally showed apartments if no one else happened to be available. Ewell had hired Bob in part, she said, because her own increasing involvement in a condominium development left her without sufficient time to handle office details and communication.

Just before she left on her Christmas vacation to Mexico City, Ewell had given Bob a new assignment: decide what to do about informing tenants about upcoming rent increases.

ALBUQUERQUE

By far the largest city in New Mexico, Albuquerque (1980 population 300,000) was growing rapidly. Located right in the heart of the sun belt, Albuquerque's sources of economic strength included Sandia Laboratory, Kirtland Air Force Base, the University of New Mexico, and light industry represented by firms such as GTE, Singer, Levi-Strauss, etc.

In the late sixties and early seventies apartment construction had failed to keep up with rapidly increasing demand. The result was a tight rental market, the growth and prospering of management companies such as Apartments Unlimited, and an unprecedented surge in housing construction.

By the late 1970s, apartment complexes, large and small, nearly filled previously undeveloped sections of the city's northeast quadrant. And by 1980 rental property supply actually exceeded demand. Now, in heavily developed areas of the city along, for example, Louisiana or Montgomery Boulevards, "For Rent" signs were constantly on display. Tenants could afford some selectivity in choosing where to live and how much rent to pay, and rent increases trickled down to the bare minimum required to keep up with rising costs.

APARTMENTS UNLIMITED

Helen Ewell had built up her business during the sixties and seventies boom; now she was doing well enough, though she planned no new construction or acquisition of rental property. Ewell's tenancy rate was approximately 85 percent, 5 percent higher than the citywide average as reported by the Albuquerque Realtor's Association, and well above the 75 percent rate she estimated as her break-even point.*

Still, Ewell felt she could not afford to become lackadaisical or overconfident. It was true that Albuquerque would surely continue to grow at a higher than average rate, and that high interest rates turned many prospective home buyers into renters. It was also true, however, that a couple of larger property management firms were just beginning or completing huge rental complexes, and countless small investors continued to build despite high interest rates. Ewell felt that her tenancy rate was satisfactory, but she would have been pleased to increase it; her 1981 figure of 85 percent was the lowest in her business's history.

THE UNITS

Nearly all of Ewell's units were located in the northeast section of town, where the most rapid housing growth had occurred. Some of the units were near the University, which now had a student enrollment of over twenty thousand. Apartment Unlimited's tenants included nearly every kind of typical Albuquerque resident: government worker, student, teacher, business person, factory worker, researcher, etc.

Most of the units—367—were leased on a six-month basis with the leases renewed on September 1 and March 1. Rents ranged from $145 for a completely furnished, all-utilities-paid efficiency to $395 for a three-bedroom deluxe unit, but the vast majority of units fell in between the two extremes. Some of the complexes were large and had on-site managers; others were as small as duplexes.

Ewell believed her better-than-average tenancy rate was due to three factors. First, she always tried hard to maintain communication with tenants, to learn of any upcoming vacancy as soon as possible, and to fill the vacancy quickly through advertising and on-the-spot showing to interested parties. Second, she raised rents only when truly necessary. Her rentals were neither bargains nor ripoffs; they were just fair, average for the market. Third, she tried to please her tenants by maintaining the property well and by responding to complaints as quickly as possible—twenty-seven of her complexes had resident managers.

---

*The "tenancy rate" is determined by calculating the percentage of rent actually paid on a unit during a year compared to the amounts of revenue the unit would produce if rent were paid in full for twelve months.

1982

By late 1981, however, even Apartments Unlimited began to be affected by the nationwide recession. Late and uncollected rents went up significantly, and although vacant apartments were rented nearly as soon as before, Ewell's staff reported that more and more prospective renters were concerned with price—"*How much* is the rent?" people would anxiously ask.

MARCH 1

Just before Christmas Ewell reviewed present costs and began to prepare new leases. As usual, costs had gone up: property taxes, electricity, and water had all risen. New rent increases were in order. Ewell carefully calculated all the increases herself. They ranged from a mere five dollars in some cases to as much as forty dollars a month in extreme instances. The average increase was twenty dollars. A few apartments, because the rent was already high, because the unit was difficult to rent, or because an elderly person on a fixed income lived there, warranted no increases. However, the vast majority of the tenants, some 90 percent, got an increase.

An even higher number of tenants, roughly 95 percent, Ewell thought were worth keeping. The other 5 percent, because of a variety of problems such as unpaid rent or severe damage done to a unit, needed to be dealt with differently and individually. Ewell compiled a list of both types of tenants, renewals and nonrenewals. She also made a list of increases to be made in the new leases.

When she had gathered this information, she went to Bob Sullivan with the information. "What should we do," Helen asked Bob, "about announcing these increases? I was never any good at English in high school, and I did my best to stay away from it in college."

BOB'S REVIEW

Bob knew that tenants were required to give the standard one-month notice if they were not planning on renewing their leases. Many tenants, of course, knew much sooner than one month in advance that they would be leaving, but sometimes they didn't let Apartments Unlimited know.

In the past, leases had been sent out just about two months in advance (just after the first of the year, and just after July 4th). Bob knew that the new leases were accompanied by some kind of cover letter explaining any increases and directing the tenant to sign the lease and return one copy to the office.

Although the office was now equipped with a word processor that would easily enable a secretary to send out individually typed letters, Bob's check of the correspondence file rewarded him with only a poor quality copy of the previous letter sent out. Obviously this letter had been typed once and then run off on the office copy machine, with the blanks filled in according to whom the letter was sent (see Exhibit A).

EXHIBIT A
APARTMENTS UNLIMITED
"a roof over your head"

July 5, 1981

Dear tenant:

Here is your new lease. Please sign both copies and return the original to us in the enclosed stamped envelope.

Your rent as of September 1, 1981, will be _____, an increase of _____. The increase was necessary because of increases in property tax, water, and electricity.

If you are not going to renew your lease, please let us know so that we can begin looking for a new tenant.

Please let me know if you have any questions or if there is any way we can continue to serve you.

Sincerely,

Helen Ewell

HE/dpt _____

SUGGESTED DISCUSSION QUESTIONS

1. How will most tenants respond to an announcement of an increase in rent?
2. Can Helen Ewell's previous letter to tenants be improved?
3. What kind of letter should go out to tenants this year?
4. What potential problems should this letter try to avoid or solve?

SUGGESTED ASSIGNMENTS

1. You are Bob Sullivan. Write a memo to Helen. Tell her what you think the letters to the tenants should accomplish. Discuss both renewals and nonrenewals.
2. You are Bob Sullivan. Write a letter to be sent to tenants whose leases will not be renewed.
3. You are Bob Sullivan. Write a letter to be sent to tenants whose leases will be renewed with a rent increase.

4. You are Bob Sullivan. Write a new letter to renewal tenants. Provide Helen with an accompanying explanation of how you've changed her letter and/or why you've written yours the way you have.

Officer Fox

Patrol Captain William E. Barton works in the City Police Department. The department's 100 officers serve a city with a population of 75,000, most of whom are middle and upper class. The city, which contains some light industry of a largely technical nature, is governed by a council and a city manager. Under the chief of police, who reports to the city manager, are the assistant chief of police, detective and patrol captains, shift lieutenants, detectives, shift sergeants, and patrol officers. As the patrol captain, Barton has the power to investigate and discipline the officers in the patrol section and is responsible for their actions. Captain Barton is accountable directly to the assistant chief and the chief of police. Within Captain Barton's disciplinary powers are the following:

1. Recommend to the chief that an individual be discharged.
2. Recommend to the chief that an individual be suspended from duty without pay for five days or more.
3. Suspend an officer from duty without pay for up to four days.
4. Serve the officer with a letter of reprimand, with a copy placed in that officer's personnel folder.
5. Give the officer a verbal reprimand with no record of the reprimand placed in that officer's personnel folder.
6. Clear the officer of the complaint with a letter stating so, placed in the officer's personnel folder.

MONDAY MORNING

In the middle of Monday morning, Captain Barton received a memo from the chief of police. The memo (shown below) instructed the captain to investigate a complaint against Patrol Officer Fox. After reading the memo, the captain followed standard police procedure, which meant interviewing Lieutenant Swift (Officer Fox's shift commander), Mr. Cooper, Mr. Best, Officer Fox, and Dispatch Supervisor Sergeant James M. Wesson. After these interviews were transcribed, Captain Barton sat down, read them over, and prepared to write his report. Here is the material with which Captain Barton had to work:

OFFICE MEMORANDUM

TO: Patrol Captain William E. Barton
FROM: Chief of Police Albert P. Davis
DATE: Monday Morning
SUBJECT:
    I received the attached letter today and feel that it deserves your immediate and direct attention.
    I am also aware that copies of this letter have been sent to the members of the Council, the City Manager, and the City Attorney by the complainant. The City Manager has already asked that I report to him next Monday.
    By no later than Wednesday I want a written report about this incident, your conclusions, and the action taken by you.

COOPER'S LETTER*

Saturday Night

Chief of Police
Police Department,
City Hall,
128 Center Street

Dear Sir:
    As you may know, I have been a businessman in this town for the past ten years. During that time, I have had a high regard for the police of our city.
    I now regret to inform you that my feelings, for at least a part of the department, have greatly changed.
    Last Saturday night I was knocked to the ground and jumped on by one of those men in blue. He then cuffed my hands behind my back, yanked me up, and threw me against his car.
    I was searched and things were removed from my pockets. Afterward, I was thrown into a caged patrol car and hauled over to the front of Best Drug Store where the officer pulled me from the car and told me it had all been a mistake.
    I have never been so roughed up in all my life, and all he could say was, "I am sorry." That's not enough! I want him *fired*!
    Mr. Best saw this entire incident and the officer involved was #68 Ronald A. Fox.

Sincerely,

D.B. Cooper
Cooper Finance Company
Suite #727
Northwest Airlines Building

*As is standard procedure, a copy of this letter has been placed in the officer's personnel file.

INTERVIEW WITH LIEUTENANT INGRAM S. SWIFT (Shift Commander 3 P.M. to 11 P.M.)

W.B.	I've got a complaint on Officer Ronald Fox. How long has he been here?
I.S.	Ronald Fox has been with the department for five and one-half years and on my shift for the last two years.
W.B.	Any complaints?
I.S.	Yes, two. About a year ago we booked this guy for drunk and disorderly. The guy said that Fox hit him in the face, but I couldn't see any marks and the guy didn't push the charges. Then six months ago Fox arrested a guy escaping from the scene of a burglary out at the City golf course. The guy had a car full of clubs and finally abandoned the car and took off on foot. Later he said Fox beat him up when he was arresting him out on the green for the sixteenth hole I think it was.
W.B.	What happened?
I.S.	Well, we checked the guy out, and he didn't have any broken bones or bruises. No witnesses. Fox said he resisted arrest and he had to wrestle with the guy for ten minutes just to get the cuffs on him.
W.B.	Anything else?
I.S.	No. The guy had two priors on burglary and he dropped the charges against Fox after he talked to his attorney.
W.B.	What area does Officer Fox work?
I.S.	He doesn't work an area. He got a promotion up to a utility car about three months ago and works as a backup car for the north three areas.
W.B.	How does he get along with the other officers?
I.S.	Super. Most of the guys look to him for help and he is always there when they need him. I feel that Ron would make a fine sergeant some day.
W.B.	Do you know of any problems Officer Fox may have had at Best Drug Saturday night? Were you there or did he say anything to you?
I.S.	No, but I heard some of the guys talking about a guy that was wanted some place getting away from Ron. Do you want me to talk to him?
W.B.	No, the chief gave this one to me personally. I want to talk to some other people first; then I'll talk to Officer Fox. In the meantime, don't say anything to him. Who worked as dispatcher last Saturday evening?
I.S.	Well, I believe it was Kate Smith, but you might check with her supervisor, Sergeant Wesson.
W.B.	OK. I'll get back with you later.

INTERVIEW WITH COMPLAINANT, D. B. COOPER

W.B.	I have been asked by the chief to look into your complaint and I have read your letter. Can you start at the very beginning and go over what happened for me?
D.C.	What do you plan to do about it?
W.B.	Nothing until I've got the full story.
D.C.	Well, I was talking to my brother-in-law in front of Best Drug and I guess we were getting a little loud. Anyway, the owner came out and was standing there for just a bit when this patrol car came screaming around the corner of the mall and came right at us. Jess, my brother-in-law, took off running across the parking lot toward those apartment houses west of the mall. I took off after him and the officer chased me down.

W.B.	Why did you run?
D.C.	Well, Jess just got here from out of state and he told me he was behind in his child support payments and a warrant had been issued for his arrest. That's what we were arguing about. I wanted him to turn himself in. Anyway, when he saw the police car he must have panicked and I was trying to stop him. That's when the officer jumped on me from behind and knocked me down. I was yelling at him that he had the wrong guy, but he didn't listen. He slugged me in the back of the head a couple of times and kneed me in the kidneys real hard. I was just lying there on the ground trying not to get hurt anymore. Then he jerked me up from the ground and slammed me against his car and forced me to bend over the hood. He was not listening to me and was pulling stuff out of my pockets. He then pushed me into the back seat of his car. All the time I was trying to tell him it was the other guy he wanted, but he wouldn't listen. He just wouldn't listen. By this time there were police cars all over.
W.B.	What happened next?
D.C.	He drove back to the drugstore and got out of the car. He and the store owner talked and went inside for a while. He came back out in a little bit and got in the front seat while I sat in the back and he asked me why I had run when he drove up. I explained to him and he let me out. He took the cuffs off and told me it was all a mistake on his part. He said he thought I was an armed robber or something, and now he had learned it was all a mistake.
W.B.	Anything else you want to add?
D.C.	I want you to know I am really upset. I've never been so upset over anything in my life and I feel the officer used far too much force.
W.B.	What time did all this happen?
D.C.	Well, it wasn't dark yet, so I guess it was about eight-thirty.
W.B.	Saturday evening?
D.C.	That's right.
W.B.	That's all for now, but I'm sure the chief or I will be getting back to you.

INTERVIEW WITH CANTON B. BEST

W.B.	What can you tell me about what happened here in front of the store Saturday night about eight-thirty? Do you remember it?
C.B.	You bet I do. I heard these two guys arguing right over there. I couldn't hear what they were saying in here, but when I got outside I heard the one guy, you know, Doug Cooper, say, "Give yourself up. It's the only way." The other guy I've never seen before and he was protesting and saying the police wouldn't give him a fair shake. Cooper told him, if the police have a warrant, running will only make things worse. This was when the police car came around the corner with the red lights on. The guy started running over toward those apartments and Cooper went after him. I was jumping up and down and pointing at them and the officer chased them. The officer must not have known Cooper because he ran him down instead of the other guy.
W.B.	Did you see the actual apprehension of Mr. Cooper?
C.B.	No, the officer's car was blocking part of my view while they were on the ground, but I saw him grab Cooper from behind and fall down with him. When I saw them next, Cooper was standing up by the hood of the car.

	After they drove over here, I told the officer the other guy was the one who was wanted. I told him what I had heard. He said he was coming to my store because of our armed robbery alarm going off, so we checked it and it was. I guess it must have malfunctioned again, or something.
W.B.	Does that happen often?
C.B.	No, not really. It has a couple of mornings when I have opened up, though.
W.B.	What happened next?
C.B.	The officer went out to the car and talked to Cooper for a short while and then let him go. That officer sure felt bad. He tried to explain to Cooper what had happened but he wouldn't listen. Cooper was so mad he wouldn't even listen to me. He just stomped off.
W.B.	Thanks, I think that will be all for now.

INTERVIEW WITH PATROL OFFICER RONALD A. FOX

W.B.	Officer Fox, the chief has asked me to investigate a complaint from a Douglas Cooper about your actions of last Saturday evening. I'd like to hear from you what happened.
R.F.	Well, where should I start?
W.B.	How about with why you went to that location.
R.F.	Okay. At about eight-thirty I heard a silent robbery alarm call go out to the Area #6 car from Best Drug. I was in the mall parking lot, but on the other side of the building at that time. As I came around the corner, with my lights on, I saw these three guys standing near the doors to Best Drug. One of the men I knew was Mr. Best. They all looked at me about the time I saw them and two started running west through the lot. Mr. Best was jumping up and down with excitement and pointing at them. I chased them to the edge of the lot, jumped out, and ran down the one closest to me. That turned out to be Mr. Cooper. At the time I grabbed him, he tripped and I went over him. When we quit rolling he was face down and I controlled him with my knee while I cuffed him. He was screaming about the other guy and yanking around quite a bit. I had already radioed that two guys were fleeing and the Area #6 car was west of us. I searched him and put him in the back seat. I radioed a description of the other guy and drove back to the drugstore.

Mr. Best told me I had the wrong guy and what he had heard in front of the store. I asked about his alarm and he said it was not going off. I told him that it was and that is why I had come in with my lights on. We went and checked and it was going off and none of his people had set it off. I went out and talked to Mr. Cooper and then released him. He was really mad and I should have known he would beef me. He just wouldn't listen to me. He wouldn't even listen to Mr. Best when he tried to explain for me. |
| W.B. | Do you have anything you wish to add? |
| R.F. | No, I really do not. I just wish he would have let me explain at the time and it would have made things much simpler. |

INTERVIEW WITH DISPATCH SUPERVISOR SGT. JAMES M. WESSON

W.B.	Do you have the transcript from the tapes from last Saturday night that I called you about?

J.W.   Yes, we just took off the traffic pertaining to that call.
W.B.   Thanks.

Transcript

Time	Car	Message
2028	526	Silent alarm, Best Drug, Jefferson Mall, has not reset.
2028	503	I'm in the back lot, Jefferson Mall, responding.
2028	526	E.T.A. Two minutes 503.
2029	503	I've got two white males running from the front of the building westbound.
2029	503	Out on foot.
2030	526	I'm in the area west of Best Drug. Ron's got one by the apartments. Checking west.
2032	503	The other suspect has got on a brown jacket, blue jeans, and glasses. I'm en route to Best Drug with one.
2036	503	(526) Terry, did you find the other guy?
2036	526	No. Nothing.
2036	503	There was no robbery. It was a false alarm, but that other guy is wanted on warrant from out of state. I'm releasing the one I've got.
2039	503	Radio, disregard alarm at Best Drug. Owner will reset. False alarm.

SUGGESTED DISCUSSION QUESTIONS

1. What caused the problem in this case?
2. Exactly what is Mr. Cooper's complaint?
3. Did Officer Fox respond properly by pursuing Mr. Cooper?
4. Did Officer Fox respond properly in arresting Mr. Cooper?
5. What evidence do you have to show that Fox's actions were or were not correct?
6. In what ways does the testimony of the interviewees differ?
7. In what ways is the testimony of the interviewees similar?
8. What does the transcript of the dispatch recording tell you?

SUGGESTED ASSIGNMENTS

You are enrolled in Political Science 399, The Sociology of Police Work, Crime, and Violence. On the first day of class your instructor gives you the case and your choice of the following assignments.

1. You are Patrol Captain William E. Barton.
   a. Write a report for the chief of the relevant facts about the incident, your conclusions, and the action you have taken.
   b. Write a letter for the officer's file. The letter should explain your investigation and the action you have taken.

2. You are Chief of Police Albert P. Davis.

   a. Assume you have received Patrol Captain Barton's report. Write a letter to D. B. Cooper in which you explain the Police Department's response to his complaint.

   b. Assume you have received Patrol Captain Barton's report. Write a letter to members of the city council, the city manager, and the city attorney. The letter should explain the Department's response to D. B. Cooper's complaint.

3. You are on a citizen's advisory board of the City Police Department. The chief of police has asked the board members for their opinions, both about the process by which this complaint has been handled and about the action you would take if you were Patrol Captain Barton. Write the chief a letter in which you analyze the case and tell him what you would have done.

Harrison College

Walking back to the dorm from your part-time job, you slow down and take your first real look at Harrison College in a long time. It's midwinter of your sophomore year, and, until today, you felt you knew Harrison as well as anybody. Today your boss, Joe Goodman, gave you your next assignment.

Goodman is Director of Public Information at Harrison. He's about thirty-five, articulate, and demanding. You enjoy working in his office because he tries to see to it that you really learn something from each assignment.

Since your internship began in September, you've written two reports, a brochure, and about a dozen letters to newspapers, politicians, and so on, on behalf of the office. You have done your share of filing, phone answering, and grunt-work, but you feel that the internship has been quite valuable.

THE NEW ASSIGNMENT

This new assignment represents a new challenge. Joe told you this afternoon that it was all straightforward enough. Surprisingly enough, Harrison's information booklet for prospective students hadn't been updated since 1972. It was still a good booklet, but things had *changed* since 1972. Joe said Admissions felt that prospective students needed something more up-to-date—something that didn't smack of the 1960s quite so much.

As you and Joe examined the cover of the old brochure, you felt you knew just what he meant. The cover showed two pictures, with the word *harrison* in bold, lowercase letters cutting diagonally across. In one picture was a male student, with shoulder-length hair and a full beard, playing a twelve-string guitar in front of the Harrison statue on Fraternity Row. The other picture showed a young professor animatedly lecturing his students as they sat on the Quadrangle on a sunny afternoon.

Things really *had* changed, you realized, as you compared the students pictured with the way people dressed and acted around campus now. Joe pointed out that the change was more than the way people looked and acted. The whole spirit of school was different now. Students were into politics and activism then—lots of causes. Now, most of the students were interested in learning what they needed to know to get good jobs. They were interested in success.

You listened and felt that updating the brochure would be good. Joe was going to have new pictures taken, and all you had to do was rewrite some pages of copy to reflect what Harrison was really like in the 1980s.

"People who are thinking of coming here really aren't interested in this stuff any more," said Joe, pointing to the old brochure. "Write to *appeal* to them; let them know Harrison's their kind of place."

Joe gave you a copy of the old brochure and a file of Harrison information, and you left. Heading back to your room, you began to get your thoughts in order. What was Harrison, or any other college for that matter, really like these days? How was college today different from going to school eight or ten years ago? You hoped the information Joe had given you, plus your own knowledge of college life, would help you to handle the assignment well. In any case, you were supposed to have a revision of the first two pages of the brochure ready to hand in by the end of the week. You reached your room, sat down at your desk, and opened the brochure.

———————

Page One

Harrison College: The Emphasis Is on *GROWTH*

Founded in 1856, Harrison has always been a haven for the independent. Since Jacob Harrison founded the college as an act of protest against the policies of the area's powerful sectarian universities, Harrison has always attracted students who aren't afraid to question the system.

At Harrison, you'll find that the emphasis is not on success for its own sake. Rather, the emphasis is on *personal* achievement and growth. We pride ourselves on the fact that many of our students go on to graduate school and pursue careers as scholars, educators, lawyers, and so on. But we're equally proud of students who leave college to succeed in other ways: our alumni and alumnae number among them two Pulitzer Prize-winning authors, a painter of international repute, a well-known sculptor, and several well-known musicians.

The point is this: at Harrison, the *individual* is our concern. And our concern brings with it a toleration for dissent. We respect our students' right to speak out, and they respect each other's right to disagree.

Harrison has several active political groups on campus. These include a Libertarian Party group and political clubs such as the Young Democrats and the Young Republicans.

The college's belief is that such extracurricular activity, while it should not interfere with formal academic studies, is a necessary part of our students' education.

Page Two

What's Harrison Really Like?

We thought you'd like to know what it feels like to be at Harrison from a student's point of view. So we interviewed a sampling of people on the Quadrangle during a typical day. Here are some of their reactions to the question: What is Harrison really like?

"It's exciting. You learn about *people,* mostly. No one tells you what to do— you can even plan your own course of study. I feel like I'm learning to be a better person."

—Becky Perogovitch, sophomore

"Controversy, that's the word. Somebody's always getting worked up about sexism, racism, the way people in this country aren't getting a fair shake. That's really what I'm learning about here—about politics and how to make things better."

—Rita Simpson, junior

"I came here because people told me that it's not a pressure place. I mean, people never get on you to get A's and get into some big grad school. The pressure *is* on you, but it's pressure to be yourself, grow, and get in touch with your role as a human being."

—Lee Farris, senior

FILE MATERIALS FROM JOE GOODMAN

ITEM ONE

Admissions Applications Excerpts
Data from Admissions Office; compiled Fall 1980

Question4a: How can a Harrison educator further your personal and career aims?

Student A: Harrison has a good reputation and good professors, particularly in chemistry and economics. I feel a degree from Harrison will help me get into a good professional or medical school.
Student B: It's simple, really. I want to get a good job when I get out of college, and I feel that Harrison's reputation will help me do it.
Student C: I have two reasons for choosing Harrison. First, it is known as a top school for prelaw students. Second, my older friends tell me that Harrison is not a "factory," and that I will be treated like a person here.
Student D: My brother went to Harrison back in the 1960s, and he tells me that it's a *liberal* kind of place—that they let you be yourself there. At the same time, I want to go to a school with a good reputation, as my goal is to attend a top business school after college.

ITEM TWO

Harrison College, Vital Statistics, 1971–1981

	1981	1971
No. of Students	5,600	7,800
Freshmen	1,190	1,800
Sophomores	1,350	1,900
Juniors	1,405	1,800
Seniors	1,455	1,700
No. of Full-time Faculty	280	325

PROGRAMS OF STUDY

	1981	1971
Liberal Arts (all fields)	20%	40%
Ind. Study in Liberal Arts (plan your own major)	5%*	15%
Prelaw	15%	10%
Premed	25%	20%
Business	35%	15%

*Plan your own major discontinued for classes after 1981.

Students going to graduate school:

	1981	1971
Liberal Arts	15%	35%
Professional Schools	45%	20%
Other	5%	5%

ITEM THREE

Student Activities and Services Ranked in Order of Popularity
Source: Student Union Polls

1970
Student Forum
Psychological Counseling
Monthly Rock Concerts
Campus Mixers
Football Games

1980
Fraternity/Sorority Activities
Job Placement Services
Preprofessional Clubs
Campus Disco Club
Football Games

1970
Campus Weekly (Newspaper)
Job Placement Services
Draft Counseling
Fraternity/Sorority Activities
Annual Homecoming Weekend

1980
Basketball Games
Career Counseling Services
Psychological Counseling
Annual Homecoming Weekend
Campus Religious Services

ITEM FOUR

Faculty Opinion Survey

Question: We are in the process of updating Harrison's information booklet for prospective students and would appreciate your comments on the types of students Harrison attracts and what we should tell students about Harrison. All comments are confidential.

[Here Joe has included three sample responses. In pencil he's written parenthetical comments.]

SAMPLE A (Probably 28–35% of our faculty think this way.)
In talking to students we should emphasize Harrison's personal approach to education. In appealing to them we should get away from the current and ever-so-popular theme "we can get you a job" and get back to our real concern for self-discovery and growth through a strong, broad educational background.

SAMPLE B (about 40% fall into this category)
Simply emphasize the curriculum and the value of a Harrison education. If we must be so damned practical, let's at least wait until the student has attended for a year and had a chance to make some decisions on his or her own. In other words, let's not be job-oriented at the expense of the Harrison tradition.

SAMPLE C (about 25%, but a vocal minority)
Let's be more practical and emphasize the fact that we can offer students a fine preparation, on the undergraduate level, for a career in business or any profession. We're both personal and professional. These students want professional careers. Let's tell them that we can prepare them for one.

SUGGESTED DISCUSSION QUESTIONS

1. What kind of student does the present information booklet appeal to?
2. What kind of student presently attends Harrison College?
3. What are the differences, if any, between the two?
4. In what ways have student interests changed? Why?
5. What does a prospective student need and want to learn when he or she reads about a college or university?
6. What should the booklet's purpose be?

SUGGESTED ASSIGNMENTS

1. Using the data from the file, rewrite the first page of the brochure to appeal to students who are likely to be interested in coming to Harrison today.
2. Prepare a one-page analysis of the new audience for the brochure (the incoming freshmen of the 1980s) to show to Joe Goodman. Be sure to outline: (1) the attitudes, career aims, and expectations of the incoming students as far as you can tell from the file data, (2) how these attitudes, aims, and expectations differ from those expressed or implied in the brochure.
3. As you're at work on the brochure, Goodman brings you a letter from an alumna, class of '71. She has recently visited the college and reports that she was "bewildered" by the changes that have taken place. "The old spirit of activism is gone, replaced by the mechanical desire to succeed," she says. "Now Harrison is part of the system. You've sold out, just like anyplace else."

Goodman asks you to draft a reply to show to him since you're working on the brochure and have been thinking about how the college has changed. He wants you to describe the changes in the college *and* the student body, and respond to the charge that the college has "sold out."

If you feel the alumna is wrong, write the letter Goodman has asked you to write; be as specific as you can, using the information in the case. If you agree with the alumna, write to Goodman, describing the changes and showing that the college has changed for the worse since the brochure was written.

The Redondo GRA-Y

On November 1, 1973, Gary Locolo and Marc Knoll sat in their office and stared at each other.

"So Winehart wants the report ready for the board members on Monday," Gary said. "And we're supposed to be ready by Monday evening to give an oral report to them, too, if they decide they want one."

"Meanwhile," Marc said, "Gra-Y is running in the red and we have to decide what to do."

SKIP WINEHART

Redondo was a fast-growing city of some three hundred thousand people, located in central Arizona. In 1969 the YMCA Board of Directors had hired a new President of the YMCA of Redondo. One of Jacob "Skip" Winehart's first moves had been to stabilize the Y's financial situation through a fund-raising drive. Next, Winehart had acquired a federal grant to support programs run out of the inner-city Y in downtown Redondo. In addition, he had instituted the policy that all programs run out of the branch Y were expected to be self-supporting. The branch would provide the basic facilities—pool, locker room, gym, meeting rooms—but costs incurred by any program had to be earned by it.

In two years Winehart's hard-driving approach stabilized the Y's budget. At the same time, Winehart began to hire the kinds of full- and part-time workers who could renovate the Y's program. Gary Locolo was one of Winehart's protégés. Locolo, a sophomore in college, began working for the branch Y as a desk clerk and night supervisor. In 1971 Winehart initiated the first Gra-Y program to appear in Redondo in ten years. He hired Gary to run it.

THE HISTORY OF GRA-Y

Gra-Y was the YMCA's organized grade school boys' club. Boys in grades four to six met with their leader once a week for one hour immediately after school and once on Saturday morning for one to three hours. The Gra-Y after-school meeting emphasized some kind of recreation—playing football or softball—but also included a brief business meeting and a short story, told by the leader in two or three minutes, that ended with a simple, clear moral. The weekend activity was frequently a game of football, basketball, or softball between two Gra-Y's. The boys got to go up into the mountains (two hours away) on an overnight campout twice a year.

The common YMCA practice was to hire college students as leaders. After an organizational meeting in which the Gra-Y supervisor showed the new leader the basics and introduced the boys to the leader and to Gra-Y, the rest was up to the leader. Leaders were expected to serve as models for the boys, big brothers who were admired, trusted, even loved. A single Gra-Y could contain as many as twenty boys, but fifteen was thought to be the optimal number. Gra-Y's with fewer than ten boys could make sports participation awkward, particularly if two or three boys missed the same meeting. In theory, a Gra-Y with fewer than ten boys would be disbanded for organizational and economic reasons.

GARY LOCOLO

Winehart's choice of Gary to introduce the sports-oriented Gra-Y to Re-dondo was a wise one. Two promising-looking elementary schools in a well-to-do housing development were chosen as test schools, and within weeks Gary had a thriving Gra-Y at each one, with fifteen or more devoted boys regularly attending after-school meetings and on weekends. The campouts were particularly popular and had been responsible for part of the boys' initial attraction to the club.

Perhaps because these schools were located in middle-class neigh-borhoods, the parents readily paid the five-dollar registration fee. A few weeks later when they were billed for the remaining fifteen dollars (the total charge per boy was twenty dollars per year), a high percentage paid im-mediately. A canned peanut sale later in the year more than covered the unpaid memberships.

Gary enjoyed the work. When Winehart offered him a raise and the job of Gra-Y Director for the next year (1972), he readily accepted. The pro-gram was expanded to include four leaders, with each leader responsible for three Gra-Y's. In 1972, then, there were twelve Gra-Y's in Redondo. The increased number of schools made football and other tournaments possi-ble, as well as large events like the year-end picnic called "Gold Rush Days."

Gary's best leader that year was Marc Knoll. Marc acted as a kind of unofficial assistant director and got along well with Gary since they were close friends. Skip Winehart was pleased with the program, but he was now further removed from it. Skip had hired Al Kunnert, a former employee of his from a Texas YMCA, as Director of the Branch YMCA out of which the Gra-Y operated. Fortunately, Kunnert got along well with Gary and Marc. Essentially he helped out on occasion, but let them do whatever they wanted. Gary and Marc now rarely saw Winehart.

Not all the Gra-Y's reached optimum size in 1972. Some of the larger Gra-Y's helped make up for the smaller ones, but by the end of the year, even with the candy sale, only 142 memberships were paid in full (the goal had been 180—15 boys × 12 Gra-Y's). While Gra-Y hadn't paid for itself as Winehart normally expected each program to do (a deficit of $470), he said repeatedly that he was pleased by its growth. Al Kunnert was too. Two of the twelve members of the Branch YMCA Board had sons in Gra-Y, and they happily reported to Kunnert that their sons were enthusiastic about the program, especially about the overnight campouts.

Late in the summer of 1973, Winehart challenged Locolo and Knoll to expand the Gra-Y program to the fullest extent possible. The only off-limits areas were the inner city and the west mesa; boys and girls in those areas were served by other programs that were federally funded. Even so, that left thirty-seven elementary schools for Gary and Marc to work with. They began the process of calling school principals to see which ones would grant them permission both to enter the schools to describe the program to the boys and to meet on the school grounds after school and on weekends. Despite repeated attempts to persuade them, five principals refused—it was within their power to do so. Two schools were ruled out because they were located on the air force base, where many programs were already available to elementary school boys.

LEADERS

Leaders were paid fifteen dollars a week as follows: three dollars for each hour-long, weekday-afternoon, after-school Gra-Y club meeting ($3 × each of three school meetings = $9); three dollars for the Saturday-morning activities for the three schools, averaging two hours per Saturday; and three dollars for each weekly, hour-long leaders' meeting. Thus the leaders got paid fifteen dollars to work about seven hours a week. Each leader had to have his own car and pay for his own gas to and from each school and weekend activity. Each campout involved additional hours, from Friday at 3:00 P.M. to Saturday noon. Each leader had signed a contract that specified the duties to be performed. It was commonly understood that leaders worked for the experience and/or to contribute to the community, not for the money.

THE LEADERS' MEETINGS

The purpose of the weekly leaders' meeting was threefold. First, the meeting was used to plan weekend activities. With thirty schools' and ten leaders' schedules to consider, careful planning of weekend activities was required. Second, the meeting was used to continue the training of the leaders. For example, at one meeting Skip Winheart spoke about the purpose and goals of the YMCA. At another, a cardiologist taught a minicourse on CPR. Finally, the meetings were used to discuss and help solve problems the leaders encountered and to share their experiences and successes.

THE TWENTY-DOLLAR MEMBERSHIP FEE

The twenty-dollar membership fee was collected as follows. At the first club meeting, boys were handed application forms for parents to fill in. The boys were told that all boys must bring at least five dollars (cash or check) to the next (the second) meeting. At the second meeting boys attending for the second time without the five-dollar deposit were sent home. Boys attending for the first time had another week to pay the deposit. Leaders were told to use their own judgment in hardship or unusual cases. Some parents sent the full twenty dollars with their boys to the second meeting. Most, however, sent five dollars; thus their sons still owed fifteen dollars. A few weeks later, the candy sale was held. This year chocolate was sold.

For every box of chocolate sold, a boy earned forty-five cents toward paying off his membership. Thus a boy paying the five-dollar deposit and still owing fifteen dollars would need to sell thirty-four boxes of chocolate to be paid in full. Some boys whose memberships were already paid in full sold candy to help other boys in their club. A few boys sold more boxes of candy than required to pay their memberships in full. They too were then helping pay off other boys' memberships. Many boys did not sell enough candy to pay off their memberships.

After the candy sale, all accounts were credited accordingly. If a boy's membership was still not paid in full, the branch YMCA would bill his parents, by mail, for the balance.

THE BUDGET

Marc felt that their originally projected budget, approved by the Board only after much argument, was what had gotten them in trouble. It had been extremely optimistic.

Gary disagreed. He felt that the budget was perfectly reasonable at the time but that many unforeseen problems had arisen.

Marc put his finger on the Peanut Sales line and said, "Just look at this. This is what screwed us up, or at least it sure helped a lot. Kunnert helped out with that." Al Kunnert had ordered chocolate candy for the boys to sell when Marc and Gary had asked for peanuts. Kunnert had not consulted them about his change. The previous year the peanuts had sold extremely well, sold out in fact.

"We didn't find out about the change," Mark said, "until the truck pulled up and the guy started putting cases of chocolate candy all over the place."

"I know, I know," Gary said.

All thirty schools had sold only 143 cases (1716 individual boxes). And the manufacturer had cut the profit per box by a nickel, so Gra-Y boys only earned $766.80." (See Exhibit Two.)

"We were supposed to sell 300 cases easily, and make $1800," Gary said. "I'm telling you, people didn't like that chocolate."

"And some of the leaders didn't talk it up the way they were supposed to, not like we did last year, and some kids—the ones who owed the money mostly—just didn't sell very well. I mean there were kids who only sold two or three boxes. That chocolate was terrible!"

Marc agreed. But the question was, what were they going to do?

OPTIONS

The two young men looked over their desks and discussed the problems. Gary half-jokingly offered to quit. That would save them a lot of money. Besides, the job had him worn out. Organizing weekend activities; supervising the leaders and meeting with them; meeting with Al, Skip, and the Board; filling in for absent leaders; and preparing brochures, payroll, and membership lists seemed like too much work even for the two of them. Marc agreed. When the overnight campouts were counted, for which either Marc or Gary had to go along to supervise, cook, and guide the leaders, both of them were working thirty to fifty hours per week. And their grades were starting to show it.

Al Kunnert had suggested they cancel the second campout. Marc and Gary wondered how they could. "We promised those kids two campouts and we've only given them one," they both said. "How can we just cancel the one we've got planned for the spring?" The campouts were popular but a lot of work.

Skip Winehart had suggested not having an activity every weekend. That would save Gary and Marc a little time and effort and enable them to pay the leaders less. If activities were held only every other weekend as Winehart suggested, the program could save quite a bit of money.

Marc thought, however, that once the boys got into the habit of coming every weekend, they expected to. He said the previous year, when each leader was allowed a weekend off after the campout, the boys complained and were disappointed.

"But Gary pointed out that a few board members had complained about Gra-Y keeping the boys too busy by meeting every weekend."

Marc looked angry. "Isn't that the way Kunnert and Winehart did it in Texas—having them meet every week?"

"Yeah." Gary shuffled some papers and said, "I talked to Kunnert about eliminating the Jefferson and Monroe Gra-Y's."

Marc said, "Well, it's November 1. The principals there never did give us much of a chance to organize. I substituted for Constantinopolis out there at Monroe. You know how painful it is to meet with just four kids?"

Kunnert had said he wanted the Monroe and Jefferson Gra-Y's to continue to meet, but Gary and Marc were sure they could directly go to Winehart about closing those Gra-Y's. They were just never going to make it. Eliminating them would save some money and time. Moreover, the Jefferson boys didn't meet on the school grounds because the principal wouldn't let them. They had to meet at a park near Bullfinch Elementary. The schools dismissed students at the same time so the two Gra-Y's could be combined to form one good Gra-Y. Monroe, however, was near no other school.

That brought up the whole issue of what was happening to the budget. Winehart had told Gary the Board seemed to be most concerned with cost.

THE BUDGET THREAT

Gary and Marc were particularly worried about the Gra-Y budget because they'd had to fight so hard for its approval in the beginning. At first Winehart had actually turned them down, saying their projected enrollment was too optimistic and their own salaries were too high. Then Gary met with the Board. He argued their position, Winehart finally grudgingly gave his approval, and so did the majority of the members of the Board. At the same time, however, Winehart said that if the program began to run a serious deficit, then Marc would lose his job.

But Gary and Marc felt the program was a big success, even with the deficit. Still they were concerned about their grades in college. Clearly, some way to reduce the workload was needed.

ANOTHER CANDY SALE

Al Kunnert reassured Gary and Marc about the financial situation in a general way by suggesting they could have another candy sale in the spring. The Y had lots of chocolate it was anxious to get rid of, Kunnert said, and another sale would bring in some more money. Then, he said, he could send out another set of statements, having deducted forty-five cents from the amount due for every box of dollar candy a boy had sold.

Gary wasn't convinced that many parents would pay in the spring if they hadn't paid already. He didn't have any figures on it, and the Branch didn't really have the kinds of records they could check to find out exactly, but he generally remembered from last year that the spring billing hadn't been very successful. Some checks would come in, Gary admitted, but it would be maybe a third of what they got after the billing that followed the first candy sale, and even that billing had only brought in about seventy-five checks for various amounts.

The problem with being a nonprofit organization, Marc believed, especially one founded on brotherly love, was that the Y wasn't supposed to really go out and sell people, and they weren't supposed to really try hard to collect bills, either.

Gary agreed. They had set up the rule that no boy could attend Gra-Y after the organizational meeting unless his parents sent him back with the five dollars, a down payment on the twenty-dollar annual fee. But when some parents called in and said they couldn't afford the five dollars because they'd have to send more later, Kunnert told Gary and Marc that it was okay. The YMCA was here to serve everyone, he said. Let the kids stay. Even Winehart said the Y had to make exceptions to its rules.

THE LEADERS

Another option Gary and Marc considered was to review the performance of the leaders and fire one or two of them. If they eliminated a couple of leaders, Marc argued, they could reassign Guillermo, one of their best leaders, and one or two others. Besides, a couple of other leaders were complaining about the pay, and they wanted another Gra-Y. They'd even settle for a three-dollar-a-week raise, since some of the weekend activities would overlap.

The two leaders who were undoubtedly not equal to the rest were Henry Scheville and Peter Constantinopolis. Scheville had already missed three weekday Gra-Y meetings, including one he failed to notify Gary or Marc about. He had also been unable to attend a campout. Two parents had even called in and complained about him. Rather than play football with the six boys who had attended one week's meeting, Scheville had packed the boys in his car and taken them to the Dairy Queen. The parents complained because, they said, he had made all the boys promise not to tell their parents he'd bought them all ice cream and hamburgers. The parents said he'd said maybe they'd go someplace different next week.

When Gary checked with Henry about the trip to the Dairy Queen, Henry admitted he'd taken them there rather than having the regular meeting, but denied the rest of it, saying the boys had misunderstood him. Marc reminded Gary that Kunnert had personally recommended Scheville.

Peter Constantinopolis was different. Gary had observed Peter during two Gra-Y meetings and found him to be unenthusiastic and uninspiring. The boys seemed indifferent toward him, and his schools' memberships, three of the more promising schools originally, were dropping off. In addition, Peter couldn't seem to get the details of weekend plans right. On one occasion, for example, his school had failed to show up for a football game, and he had really botched the job of collecting campout fees.

"Besides that," Marc said, "I overheard Constantinopolis tell one of the lifeguards here that he was moving to Los Angeles in December and transferring to UCLA. Then when I casually asked him about it, he denied it."

"When I interviewed him I remember he sort of stumbled on that 'We have to ask each leader to make a full-year commitment to the program, can you do that?' question."

One of the Gra-Y cardinal rules, however, was never to change leaders at a school because the boys got so attached to one person.

EXHIBIT ONE
1973–74 PROJECTED GRA-Y BUDGET

REVENUE

450 memberships at $20 per member	$ 9,000
(30 schools; average of 15 members per school)	

CAMPOUT FEE

$2 per boy; 10 boys per campout; 60 campouts	1,200
(projecting 66% attendance per campout)	
Candy Sale Added Income*	300
	Total $10,500

EXPENSES **

Gra-Y Director $65 a week × 35 weeks	$ 2,275
Assistant Director $55 a week × 35 weeks	1,925
Gra-Y Leaders (10 leaders) $15 a week × 28 weeks	4,200
Campout Costs—600 boys; $3 per boy	1,800
(includes gasoline, food, prizes, etc.)	
Equipment 10 each: footballs, basketballs, softballs, and bats	300
	Total $10,500

*From boys whose parents pay the full membership cost but are willing to sell to help Gra-Y pay for other boys' memberships.

**These expenses do not include printing costs for flyers and membership applications since the Branch normally includes these items in its operating expense budget.

EXHIBIT TWO
CURRENT GRA-Y BALANCE SHEET
November 1, 1973

REVENUE

386 memberships:	paid in full (226)	$ 4,520
	partially paid (170)	1,480
Campout Fees (approximately 300 boys)		600
Candy Sales*		166

Total $ 6,766

EXPENSES

Gra-Y Director	$ 780
Assistant Director	660
Gra-Y Leaders (10 leaders; average 8 weeks)**	1,200
Campout Costs (food, gasoline)	900
Equipment	375

Total $ 3,915

*Some boys, whose memberships were already paid in full, sold candy to help pay the memberships of other, less fortunate boys.
**The initial Gra-Y club meetings were held during September; leaders were getting paid at varying times.

EXHIBIT THREE
ENROLLMENT BY GRA-Y

as of November 1

	School	Leader	Paid in Full	Partially Paid	Total Attending
1.	Washington	Guillermo	8	4	13*
2.	Adams	Guillermo	11	3	13
3.	Quincy	Guillermo	9	9	17
4.	Jefferson	Constantinopolis	3	2	5
5.	Monroe	Constantinopolis	4	2	6
6.	Madison	Smith	12	4	16
7.	Whittier	Smith	9	2	11
8.	Polk	Queen	7	12	20
9.	McKinley	Queen	6	4	10
10.	Taft	Queen	7	6	13
11.	Johnson	Jakes	8	7	15
12.	Lincoln	Smith	5	12	16
13.	Hoover	Mondragon	10	4	13
14.	Eisenhower	Mondragon	7	9	14
15.	Truman	Mondragon	11	4	15

*Some schools had a boy attending who was new or who was not required to pay. Some schools had a boy who had paid his membership in part or in full but was no longer attending Gra-Y.

EXHIBIT THREE *(continued)*
ENROLLMENT BY GRA-Y

School	Leader	Paid in Full	Partially Paid	Total Attending
16. Kennedy	Hill	10	6	16
17. Fillmore	Scheville	8	4	12
18. La Cienega	Scheville	7	9	16
19. Mesquite	Scheville	4	9	13
20. La Grande	Hill	13	4	14
21. El Paso	Hill	5	5	10
22. Marquette	Jakes	8	4	12
23. Roosevelt	Jakes	14	0	14
24. Taylor	Constantinopolis	6	4	9
25. Scott	Sayers	8	8	15
26. Jackson	Sayers	5	9	13
27. Alexander	Sayers	6	6	12
28. Bullfinch	Blye	5	5	9
29. Tomasita	Blye	7	3	10
30. Del Norte	Blye	3	11	14
		226	170	386

DISCUSSION QUESTIONS

1. What are the different problems Gary and Marc face?
2. What are some solutions to those problems?
3. Who must be persuaded that these solutions are the best ones?
4. What changes in the program would you recommend?

SUGGESTED ASSIGNMENTS

1. You are Gary or Marc. Write a formal report about the program. Propose solutions to any problems you foresee.
2. You are Gary or Marc. Write a letter to the parents. Inform them of any changes you are making in the program.
3. You are Gary or Marc. Based on all this experience, write a report in which you propose how the programs should be run next year. Explain any changes you would make.
4. You are Gary or Marc. Write a memo to the leaders explaining all changes you are making in the program.
5. You are one of the leaders. Write a memo to Gary and Marc persuading them to make or not make certain changes in the program.

Chapter 3

Analyzing the Audience

Whenever we write, we are writing for an audience, a reader. If you are taking notes during a lecture, you are writing for yourself—at a later time, you will read the notes. If you are writing a letter to the editor of a city newspaper, your potential audience is everyone who reads that newspaper. Taking the time to analyze your audience will make your writing much more effective. Audience analysis includes:

—knowing the types of possible audiences,
—identifying your particular audience,
—making conclusions about the audience's characteristics,
—determining how these characteristics are relevant to your writing,
—generating readers' questions.

Effective writers always consider what the audience wants and needs to know. A writer's audience analysis determines the way the thesis, the point the writer wants to make, is expressed. However, honest writers always state what they think and believe. They never change the heart of the thesis itself simply to agree with or please the reader.

Identifying the Audience

As a writer, one of the first choices you have to make is to decide to or for whom you are writing. Since there are an infinite number of possibilities, writers find it helpful to classify the basic types of audiences. One way to define audiences is to assess how much we know about them (and in turn, how much they know about us). Envision a complete spectrum of possible audiences. At one end of the spectrum the audience is one specific person whom we know the most about; at the other end is the most general audience, the one about whom we know the least.

Suppose you are writing in a diary, which you keep hidden in your room, a diary no one but you will ever read. Since you are its sole reader, the diary is written for the most specific audience possible. At the opposite extreme, suppose you put a note in a bottle and throw it into the ocean. In this instance you are writing to a completely unknown, general audience. Or, to take the example to the greatest extreme, we could say that the United States is "writing" to an utterly unknown, general audience when it sends a satellite in search of life forms beyond our solar system.

Of course most of our writing does not involve keeping diaries or putting notes in bottles. Even so, one useful way to begin audience analysis is to classify readers as two types—specific and general. In personal writing, you write to a specific audience when you write a letter to your parents, a note to your roommate, a card to a friend. You write to a general audience when you complain to a government agency, give Ann Landers advice for her readers, or tell a company what you think of its product.

In most college classes, you will usually write to a general audience. You may be told that your readers are the students in your class, or you may be writing for any student attending your college or university or even for any student or instructor at *any* college or university in the United States. In a first-year English course, the students in your class would probably make up a very general, nontechnical audience because many different experiences, backgrounds, interests, and college careers would be represented. In a senior-level course, Quantum Mechanics 495, for example, your audience would be more specific, and technical.

You may be thinking that in a college composition course you know who your audience is—the instructor—but that is not exactly true. Your instructor reads your writing, but the instructor's goal is not to make you write to him or her; it is to teach you how to effectively communicate with your chosen audience. Each of the cases in this book gives you a specific or general audience to whom to write. In effect, your instructor tries to become that audience in order to evaluate your work fairly and objectively.

As you will see in the examples given below, deciding who your reader is and analyzing that reader can make a big difference in how you express the point you want to make. One of the first questions you should ask yourself as you prepare to write, then, is "To whom am I writing?" In some college classes the answer may not always be clear. If you do not know whether you are expected to write to a specific audience or for a general college audience, then ask. Make sure you know who your audience is. Decide whether you have a general or a specific reader that you need to keep in mind. Then use the guidelines below to analyze that audience.

Analyzing a General Audience

Analyzing a general audience can be difficult because you have to generalize about your reader's characteristics. Here are some questions you can ask yourself as a guide in generalizing about the general reader.

How Will My Audience React to My Subject and Thesis?
Interested? Some subjects, such as death, sex, and violence, usually create some audience interest, at least initially. Other subjects may not be so intrinsically interesting. What is important to remember is that your own enthusiasm (or lack of it) about a subject will affect your reader.

Emotionally involved? Some subjects, such as "abortion on demand," may guarantee an emotional reaction from part or all of your audience. Other subjects, such as "jogging as a way to improve your health," are more neutral.

Just as you consider the audience's interest and emotional involvement in your subject, you need to consider the audience's interest in the point you want to make and whether they will react to it emotionally. The thesis "We all deserve to be rich," for example, would probably catch the attention of readers who wished they were wealthier. The thesis "Women have been proven to be anatomically inferior to men," might well spark an emotional reaction in the readers of *Playboy* or *Ms.* magazines (though that reaction might vary).

How Intelligent and Well Educated Is My Audience?
The intelligence and education of your audience can make a difference in the words you choose, the complexity of the sentences and paragraphs you write, and the overall approach you take. If you are writing an article for a newsletter sent to graduates of the Harvard Law School, for example, you can be certain that your audience is well educated, and you can make some generalizations about its level of intelligence. If, on the other hand, you are writing an article to be read by corn growers, you cannot be sure about your audience's educational background. Some may have advanced degrees while others may not have finished high school. Also, while many would no doubt be extremely intelligent businesspeople, others might be only average in intelligence.

What Does My Audience Know about the Subject?
Unless you have some specific information about your audience, you have to assume that they just know an average amount about your subject. Of course, deciding what an "average amount" is can be difficult. Suppose you are trying to persuade the listeners to your radio broadcasts that a recent change from classical music to news was best for the station and for its listeners. Your explanation is to be published in a program guide that the station sends out to hundreds of listeners on the station's mailing list. What do these people know about the subject? Is it possible that some of them have not even noticed the change? Those that have will certainly not automatically understand the reasons for the change. On the other hand, since these people do listen to the station, they will know what its music format is like and even what certain programs are like. Determining what the audience already knows helps you answer the next question.

What Does My Audience Want and Need to Know about the Subject?
Once you have decided what your readers know, you can decide what to tell them. That does not necessarily mean you only tell them what they do not know. One way to begin is to tell them something they already know and then develop your essay from there.

What Does My Audience Know about My Thesis?
The answer here is always NOTHING! Remember that your readers never know what your central idea is until you tell them.

An Example of General Audience Analysis

Suppose there is a nuclear power plant near your campus. You are on the staff of the college newspaper and you decide to write an article about the power plant and about nuclear power in general. After some investigation, you decide that your thesis will argue that the local nuclear power plant is safe. Given this writing situation and this thesis, you might come up with the kind of audience analysis completed below.

How Will My Audience React to My Subject and Thesis?
Nuclear power is of interest to many people; it is also a subject that many people feel strongly about. Therefore, I can depend on many readers, at least initially, to be interested in my article. I must, however, be careful how I discuss the issues. (Just last week there was a No-Nukes demonstration on campus.) If, for example, I immediately argue that we absolutely have to have nuclear power, then my readers may not believe me when I argue that our nuclear power plant is safe.

How Intelligent and Well Educated Is My Audience?
In general, newspaper readers vary in intelligence and education so the writing must be neither too complex nor too simple. Of course, the readers of my college newspaper are better educated than average newspaper readers! Since we do not have a college of engineering, I will not be writing to nuclear engineers, but no doubt some of my readers (physics professors, for example) will understand the technical aspects of nuclear power. Therefore, I will have to explain everything fully, but I need to do so in a way that will not offend or bore my more knowledgeable readers.

What Does My Audience Need and Want to Know about the Subject?
People probably need to know more about how nuclear power plants work. Two major issues seem to be whether we actually need nuclear power and whether the plants are safe. Some people may want to know whether a Three-Mile Island-type accident could happen here.

Generating Readers' Questions

Another way to analyze the audience is to ask yourself what questions your readers would be likely to ask as they read what you have written. Given the writing situation discussed above, here is a list of questions you might expect a campus audience to ask about a local nuclear power plant:

Is the plant really safe?
Could we have an accident here similar to Three-Mile Island?
Why was the plant located here?
Do we need it?
Is there anything that can or should be done to make the plant safer?
Who decides whether it is safe?
What makes it dangerous?
What is the China Syndrome?
Why don't we just use solar energy and turn off all the nuclear plants?
Why are so many nuclear plants built?

One way to measure the effectiveness of your writing is to ask yourself whether you have answered the kinds of questions your audience is likely to ask.

You can see how completing an audience analysis can guide you in a writing situation in which you have a general, unknown audience. An audience analysis guides you in deciding what to include and what to leave out, what to say, and how to say it. You can use these guidelines for general audiences, and you can also use them, along with some more specific steps, when writing to a specific reader.

Analyzing a Specific Audience

Suppose you are Mike Morenberg in the case "The Summer Sun Club," which is included in Chapter 1. (You may want to review that case before reading on, but it isn't necessary.) In that case Mike has to write a report to Mr. Garston. Mr. Garston is an example of a specific reader.

If you were Mike in this writing situation, one question you would have to answer would be "What do I need to recognize about my specific reader?" One way to answer this question would be to list Mr. Garston's specific characteristics and then to determine how these characteristics are relevant to your writing situation. Here is the kind of list you could make:

> *Specific Characteristics*
> stickler for details, specifics, correctness
> deeply religious
> wears black suits, skinny ties, white shirts
> sounded as if he had swallowed a cigar
> did not like Summer Sun Club
> particularly concerned about the Stephenses
> Director of Boys' Club

Next, you could make some inferences about this information (see Chapter 1 on making inferences). Here are some inferences that one student made about Mr. Garston:

Specific Characteristics	*Inferences*
stickler for details, specifics, correctness	report must be exact, correct
deeply religious	old-fashioned morals
wears black suits, skinny ties, white shirts	old-fashioned dresser
sounded like he had swallowed a cigar	angry, expects an explanation
did not like Summer Sun Club	may be extra critical of report
particularly concerned about the Stephenses	need to reassure him about them
Director of Boys' Club	knows what Summer Sun Club is like

Consider how these inferences are relevant to this writing situation. Suppose you begin with "old-fashioned morals and old-fashioned dresser." Are these sound inferences? Maybe not. Are they relevant to the way you would write the report? Probably not. This example should show you two guidelines about analyzing your audience. First, everything you know about your reader may not be relevant to your writing situation. Second, you have to be careful not to draw false inferences.

On the other hand, you can see how some of the other inferences are important to you when you write the report. First, you know that Mr. Garston expects the report to be exact, specific, and correct. You could also conclude that because he may be extra critical of it, you should be extra careful in writing it. Since he sounds angry, you should probably be conciliatory—try to calm him down and make peace—and since he is concerned about the Stephens family, you should try to reassure him about them.

Generating Readers' Questions

Another way to analyze your readers is to decide what kinds of questions they may ask after reading what you've written. In "The Summer Sun Club," for example, you could make up a list of specific questions that Mr. Garston would be likely to have in mind as he reads the report. Here is a list of questions that one student thought Mr. Garston would ask:

Why did you forget to tell Mrs. Stephens about Tommy?
Why didn't you fill out a report of some type?
Are you sure Maxine did the right thing?
Will this kind of thing happen again?
What will you do to prevent it?
Why didn't you think this was a serious problem?
What will Mrs. Stephens think about the Boys' Club?
What will Frank Stephens think?

You will communicate effectively with your audience partly or largely according to whether you have answered all the questions the audience has in mind.

Summary

So far you have read about specific and general readers. Practice in writing to both will make you more effective in writing to either one. Since you can communicate more effectively by anticipating what your audience wants, it's important to take the time to identify and analyze that audience. These questions can guide you in audience analysis:

How will my audience react to my subject and thesis?
How intelligent and well educated is my audience?
What does my audience know about the subject?
What does my audience need and want to know about the subject?

Another way to keep your audience in mind is to make up a list of questions you expect them to ask about your subject and thesis. In *addition* to the questions listed above, you can write more effectively to a specific, known audience by carefully making inferences about that audience's characteristics and by relating these inferences to your subject and thesis.

Professor Abromowitz and the Unexpected D

You are a senior this fall semester at Bell State University. Last spring you took Economics 450 under Professor Abromowitz. You got a B on the midterm, and a B− on the one paper you had to write. Your paper was entitled "The Economics of Monopoly: A Capitalistic Board Game of the Depression." You thought you did all right on the final exam, but it was pretty tough. You thought you did very well on the short-answer part and on two of the three essay questions, but you felt at the time your last essay could have been a lot better. Still, you thought you did well enough on the final. The problem is that when you received your grades for the spring semester your grade in Economics 450 was a D.

This past summer you were home working and you could see no point in getting upset about the grade since you were pretty sure it must have been a mistake. You considered writing to Professor Abromowitz, but you weren't sure of his address, and you didn't like the idea of having to write. So you waited until the fall term to solve the problem. When you got back to school, you decided, you could go to see Professor Abromowitz and, of course, persuade him to change the grade.

Going to see Professor Abromowitz in person would have its advantages, you thought, because you weren't sure he'd remember you very well if you just wrote to him. Econ 450 was required for all economics majors, so the class was fairly large. Professor Abromowitz wasn't good at remembering names, either, though twice he'd recognized you on campus and said hello. He hadn't however, called you by name.

THE DEPARTMENT OF ECONOMICS

Since the professor wasn't in his office when you started looking for him, you went into the department office to ask the secretary where to find him. She explained that he was taking a one-year leave of absence to study abroad. He was spending the year in London. You remembered that he was interested in the economic impact of socialism on the upper class.

Although you told the secretary about your problem with the grade, she wasn't much help. She did say that two other students had been asking where the professor was because of their grades, but she also said she couldn't help any of you because she had no copy of the grade sheet, didn't know where the final exam papers were, and couldn't help anyway unless the department chairperson or Professor Abromowitz himself told her to.

The secretary suggested that you check with the registrar to make sure the computer had not made a mistake. She also said you could write Professor Abromowitz in England and ask him about your grade. His address, as she gave it to you, was: Professor Morton C. Abromowitz, 254 Abbey Street, London, England.

THE REGISTRAR

All of this is upsetting, of course, especially when the registrar told you that the grade sheet with Professor Abromowitz's signature clearly shows your grade as a D. Finding that out makes you think back over the course to decide how you could possibly have gotten a D. Professor Abromowitz never said exactly what percentage of your final grade would be determined by the final exam, and you never asked. All you can remember is that he said the final exam would count more than either the midterm or the paper.

Meanwhile, your instructor in Economics 451 is urging you to drop 451 and take 450. Since you got a D in 450, you have to retake it because a grade of C or better is required. Your instructor in 451 says you have to get this issue resolved in a hurry so you can get into the right course and graduate on time.

SUGGESTED DISCUSSION QUESTIONS

1. What are the problems in this case?
2. What communication gap(s) produced the problem?
3. As Professor Abromowitz's former student, what should you do? Why?
4. What grade did you deserve, minimally, in the course?

SUGGESTED ASSIGNMENTS

1. Suppose you decide to write to Professor Abromowitz.

   a. State whether Professor Abromowitz is a specific or a general reader.

   b. Write out answers to all questions you should ask yourself about any reader.

   c. What special characteristics, as a reader, does Professor Abromowitz have? List each characteristic separately.

   d. For each characteristic you can identify, state whether and how that characteristic is relevant to your writing situation.

   e. List some of the major questions that you believe will occur to Professor Abromowitz as he reads your letter.

2. Select a writing situation in which you are asking a specific person for something (your parents for money, an out-of-state friend for a favor, a relative for some information about summer jobs).

   a. State who your audience is; state your subject.

   b. Write out answers to the questions you should ask yourself about any reader.

   c. List your readers' characteristics.

   d. For each characteristic, state whether and how that characteristic is relevant to your writing situation.

   e. List some of the questions that may occur to your readers as they read your letter.

SAMPLE STUDENT RESPONSES

Here are two student letters based upon the Professor Abromowitz case. Given your own audience analysis, decide which of the two better recognizes Professor Abromowitz's perspective. Given your readers' questions, decide which one tells Professor Abromowitz everything he needs to know. You may want to analyze the two letters in other ways that may occur to you.

> **SAMPLE RESPONSE A**

Dear Professor Abromowitz:

(1) Chances are you probably won't remember me, but my name is Bill Brown and I was part of your Economics 450 class last year. I apologize for disturbing you on your leave but after checking with your secretary and the registrar, it appears to me that you are the only way of solving my dilemma. It is important to me to have what I believe was a mistake on my grade sheet corrected as soon as possible. Despite

the fact that I received B's on two out of three major criteria for evaluation, I received a D as a final grade in your course.

(2) As I recall, the basis for grading in your Economics 450 class last spring consisted of three major grades. There were midterm and final exams as well as a required paper. As your records should show, I received a B on my midterm exam and a B− on my paper entitled "The Economics of Monopoly: A Capitalistic Board Game of the Depression." Although I cannot be sure of my performance on the final exam, I feel confident that I did not do poorly enough on it to constitute a D as my final grade. I realize you indicated the final would be weighed more heavily than both the midterm and the paper but even if I did as poorly as a D on the final I feel I still deserve a C for the course.

(3) Assuming the grade was an error of some kind, I first talked with your department secretary, who said she had no record of the grades. But she suggested that I go to the registrar to check if it was an error on his part. All the registrar would tell me was that you clearly marked my grade as a D on the grade sheet.

(4) If it was an error or not, please send a response as soon as possible. Because I am an economics major, I need at least a C in Econ 450 to be able to go on to 451 and fulfill my requirements. I hope you will understand my situation and reply quickly. I appreciate your help.

SAMPLE RESPONSE B

Dear Professor Abromowitz:

(1) Last spring I took Econ 450 and you were my instructor. I felt that I had done fairly well, receiving a B on the midterm and a B− on the assigned essay. Although I didn't know what I got on the final, I felt confident that I would receive a passing grade, but when I received my final grades this summer I found an unexpected D beside Econ 450.

(2) When I returned to school this fall, I immediately went **to** your office and discovered that you had gone on leave. I described my situation to your secretary and she said that she would like to help but that she didn't know where the grade sheets were. She told me the best thing to do was to check with the registrar's office. When I went there, the only thing they could tell me was that my grade was clearly marked as a D. I went back to your secretary and she suggested that I write to you directly.

(3) I was curious as to the background of my poor grade so I took her advice and wrote this letter. I am wondering if it possible that when transposing grades to file cards my grade got mixed up with someone else's. The only way I know of to check this would be to go over the grade sheet, recalculate my grade, and check it against the grade I received.

(4) The problem is that we don't know the location of the grade sheet or how you calculated the grades. I am hoping that if you have the grade sheet with you, you would recheck my grade—Mary M. Enard, 443-596-005—and see if the correct grade has been given me. If the grade sheet is here, would you kindly notify your secretary of its location and explain the grade-calculating procedure so that a check might be run to verify my grade.

(5) I need to establish my grade situation as soon as possible so that I may enroll in the proper course. I had planned on taking Econ 451, but I must have at least a C in Econ 450 before I can enroll in this course.

(6) I know that you will be concerned about my situation and I appreciate your help in clearing up this matter. I hope that your leave proves to be beneficial to you. Thank you once again.

SUGGESTED ASSIGNMENTS

1. Write an essay in which you compare and contrast the two student letters in terms of each one's application of audience analysis. (Your audience is other members of your class.)

2. Suppose you are a friend of either Bill or Mary. Write him or her a note in which you suggest ways the letter to Professor Abromowitz could be improved. (Assume you've been given all the information in the case.)

Marcia Johnson

Marcia Johnson sat alone in her room overlooking Commonwealth Avenue. She watched the traffic snarls, the buses coming and going, and the students rushing back and forth to the dorm. She was trying to review her situation and decide on her next move.

Marcia had just come from a meeting with Peter Wallace, instructor in biology and premedical advisor. Wallace's news had not been good. Marcia's grades did not seem strong enough, he said, to allow much hope that she would be accepted by a medical school. Her grade-point average was fair, but 60 percent of her freshman and sophomore grades were C's, and in that 60 percent were clustered most of her important premed courses.

"It's only the second semester of your sophomore year," Wallace had said. "Your record here at the university is not bad. You can easily change your major and do very well after you leave here in two years."

Wallace added that it was his definite opinion that Marcia should get out of premed now.

THE JOHNSON FAMILY

Marcia was the oldest of the three children of Dr. Samuel Johnson, a prominent surgeon. Dr. Johnson, chief of surgery at City Hospital and professor of surgery at the medical school, was the son of a heavy machinery operator. He had worked hard to get through his four years as an undergraduate and his four years at a major medical school, from which he graduated with distinction. He had once run the Boston Marathon (twenty-six miles) in under three hours, at age forty-seven. He prided himself on having brought his children up to believe that there was no such thing as failure.

It was no secret to Marcia's family and friends that her father wanted her to go to medical school. He had given several parties for her after her graduation from high school and at one had had the guests toast her as "the next Dr. Johnson." He was liberal in his financial and moral support and had tried to convince his daughter of the need to make her own decisions. Generally, he and Marcia got along well, and she considered him an even-tempered and reasonable father.

MARCIA'S CAREER

For Marcia, the news from her advisor was not unexpected. She felt that she was a dutiful daughter, and she had been working hard in her studies. She'd always assumed she was going to become an M.D., but lately her view of herself had begun to change. For example, she had received high praise for a biomedical engineering paper she'd written this year (she'd taken the course as an elective), and more than one of her instructors had pointed out that math and physics were her strong points. In fact, most of the A's and B's she had received at her university were in these subjects. Also, she had found it easier to concentrate on math, physics, and engineering courses. All in all, although she was a little scared at the change in her attitude, she was pleased to think that she was getting a clearer idea of what she wanted to do with her life.

Last week Marcia had written to Susan Wilson, her closest high school friend and a premed student at a different university, outlining her feelings:

> I really think I have more ability as an engineer or physicist than as a doctor or biologist—and besides, I like working with machines and numbers a lot better than I ever thought I would. But I'm not sure that getting out of premed is the best thing to do because you know Dad's going to be mad as hell—did I tell you he got me a summer job at the hospital???—and I don't have any idea how to tell him so he'll understand.

SUGGESTED DISCUSSION QUESTIONS

1. What are Marcia's problems?
2. What should Marcia do? Why?

3. How will Marcia's father react to what she tells him?

4. How much does Marcia's father know about how she is doing?

5. What kind of father is he?

SUGGESTED ASSIGNMENTS

1. You are Marcia Johnson. Write your father a letter in which you explain your situation, but first:

   a. Write out answers to the general questions you should ask yourself about any reader.

   b. What special characteristics, as a reader, does Dr. Johnson have? (List each characteristic separately.)

   c. For each characteristic you can identify, state how that trait is relevant to your writing situation.

   d. List the questions you believe your father (Dr. Johnson) will have in mind as he reads your letter.

2. Select a writing situation in which you have to tell your reader something unexpected (your parents about your sudden marriage, your roommate that you are moving out, your boyfriend, girlfriend, lover, or spouse that you aren't going to see him or her anymore).

   a. Identify your reader.

   b. Write out answers to the general questions you should ask yourself about any reader.

   c. List your readers' characteristics.

   d. State whether and how these characteristics are relevant to your writing situation.

   e. List the questions you believe your readers will have in mind as they read your letter.

3. Assume you are Susan Wilson, Marcia's friend. Complete an audience analysis for Marcia and write her a letter telling her what you think she should do.

4. Write an essay to any student who has read about the Marcia Johnson case. State what you think Marcia should do, and why. Complete an audience analysis for a general, unknown reader.

5. Analyze the factors that should (or, in reality, *do*) go into a student's choice of a major. Don't restrict yourself to your own decision: "I chose art education because I've always liked to draw . . ." Make your analysis useful to readers of the brochure provided for those interested in attending your college or university.

6. Write an essay suitable for a family magazine. Discuss the parents' role in decisions such as a student's choice of college, major, future occupation, and so forth.

The Big Bike-A-Thon

The bike-a-thon is finally over, and you've just read the article that Mary Robert was nice enough to include in *The Journal,* a major newspaper:

YMCA BIKE-A-THON A BIG SUCCESS
(Your name) and Don McDonald announced in the park at the end of the bike-a-thon that the project was a big success. Pledges totaled $9,450, which was more than enough needed to begin construction of an outdoor jogging track and a playing field the Y has wanted for years.

You are thinking, among other things, that Mary's been a big help to you through the whole thing.

When the director of the family YMCA asked you to organize and direct a fund-raising drive for the track, you were surprised. You work only part-time for the Y. You knew it would be a lot of work, and you weren't sure you could do it.

The director said, "You like bicycling. Try a bike-a-thon. And don't be too disappointed if you don't make much money. Anything will be a big help."

A bike-a-thon, you learned, involves getting people to bicycle for ten or twenty miles—or for as many miles as they can—and asking these bikers to convince someone else to donate money for each mile ridden. You yourself rode twenty miles, for example, and people pledged a certain amount per mile. One big tall man you called on took one look at you and said, "If you go the whole twenty miles, I'll contribute a buck a mile. If you don't, I'll call an ambulance for you."

The money came from roughly two thousand people and was earned by over a hundred bikers. The bikers were as young as six years old and as old as eighty-five. There was a group of about fifty people who assisted in setting up the bike route, helping direct traffic, and organizing the picnic afterward.

Mary Roberts agreed to publish two articles to help generate interest in the event. Her husband, Bob, the principal of a local school, and their two children, Jack and Phyllis, completed the entire twenty miles right along with you.

The Roberts family wasn't the only special help you got. You realize now that you never would have been able to do it without the help of two other people. One was Bill Phillips. Bill owns and operates The Bike Outlet. He contributed a couple of extra bikes and helped plan and organize the event. He planned the route, and when three bicycles broke down during the event, Bill repaired them on the spot.

You also got lots of help from an unexpected source: a local gas station operator. When Don McDonald heard about the bike-a-thon, he offered to help you organize it. There was a time when you weren't sure whether you or Don was really directing the bike-a-thon. He contacted a lot of people who rode their bikes. The picnic afterward was his idea.

You thought all this over because the Y director just came by and said to you, "Your work's not over yet, you know. The Y always thanks people, in writing, when it gets a lot of help like this. You know who you need to thank and what you need to thank them for. Don't worry about postage. We're nonprofit, and maybe we can send some of it bulk rate."

While you're thinking over what the director just said, he sticks his head back in the door and says, "Hey, maybe you can do this again next year."

SUGGESTED DISCUSSION QUESTIONS

1. What does the writing situation in this case involve?
2. Do you have to write over 2,000 letters?
3. Would it be better just to make some phone calls?
4. How else could you thank the people?
5. Who are your potential readers?
6. What is important to recognize about them?

SUGGESTED ASSIGNMENTS

1. Audience Analysis:
   a. In one paragraph, define your audience problem.
   b. Summarize the paragraph in a single sentence.
   c. Identify all your potential readers.
   d. Complete an audience analysis for each reader or group of readers you identify.
2. Write a short statement explaining how you would communicate to each group by letter, phone, or newspaper article. (Your classmates are your audience.)
3. Write a letter to one or all of the audiences you have identified.
4. Invent a writing situation in which you are thanking someone for help given you.
   a. State your subject and identify your audience.
   b. Complete an audience analysis.
   c. Write a letter to that audience.

Pets? Forget It, Sorry

Assistant manager Marilyn Button and her boss, Dan Kenner, disagreed on exactly what pet policy Property Management Incorporated should adopt.

Kenner said, "You're probably going to argue with me, but I think PMI should go to a no-pets policy. We're meeting with Hickman next week to discuss it, so be ready."

Kenner, Button knew, always encouraged her to state her own opinion, so she carefully considered what policy she should recommend.

MARV HICKMAN

Marv Hickman, formerly a big businessman in Normal and now a real estate developer in the Chicago area, was PMI's silent partner, its near sole owner. Three years earlier, when Hickman had become heavily involved in a Chicago real estate development, he had hired Kenner to manage PMI. PMI owned or managed nearly three hundred apartments, duplexes, or houses in Normal, a medium-sized college town. At present, PMI's pet policy was fairly complex. First, no pets were allowed in any of PMI's two-hundred-plus apartments. In the remaining eighty or so rentals, PMI allowed *one* pet (a dog or a cat, for example) in twenty-eight of the duplexes. But even in these twenty-eight units the pet had to measure twenty inches or less in height. In these units a pet deposit equal to one month's rent was required.

THE PET POLICY EXPLAINED

The reasons for the present policy were straightforward. To begin with, no pets were allowed in the apartment complexes, because if one tenant could have one, then every tenant would want one, Hickman once said, and "then the place would turn into a zoo, and smell like one, too."

Each of the twenty-eight duplexes in which small pets were allowed was a luxurious unit with a small, partially fenced-in yard and patio. The rent, relatively high for Normal at $375 a month, assured a certain quality of tenant. Then, too, only couples without children were allowed to rent these units. Thus Hickman had said he could see no harm in a cat or small dog living there too, inside, of course. True, the dog or cat might damage the carpet or draperies, but the rental and pet deposits combined totaled $750; $750 would cover considerable damage.

Larger dogs, however, were simply not allowed. Hickman and Kenner both felt that the larger animals would do more damage inside, would be more likely to misbehave, and simply weren't suitable for the modest size of the two bedroom units and their small yards.

Kenner, however, now told Button he wanted to refuse pets altogether, though of course he said present tenants would not be forced to either move out or get rid of their pets. Kenner explained his reasoning this way: first, the rule seemed arbitrary and caused ill-will with prospective tenants, and second, the rule was costing PMI money.

"Just last week," Kenner said, "I showed a guy one of the duplexes, and then he argued that his labrador retriever would be a lot less risky than some high-strung cockapoo. And he said his lab would make less noise, too."

"Then just last month," he reminded Button, "that lady's dog ruined the entire carpet. The replacement cost was $800 and I'm still planning on taking her to small claims to get back the fifty dollars that wasn't covered by the security and pet deposits." Since the woman had moved out of town, moreover, collecting the fifty dollars seemed unlikely. Kenner was still surprised that a little ten-pound dog could do so much damage to anything.

Kenner said he'd had plenty of bad experiences in his five years in rentals before he signed on with PMI. Dogs ruined carpets, tore up yards, and made neighbors angry by urinating and defecating on their property. One unit Kenner managed years ago had been left infested with fleas; another unit's carpet had to be completely replaced. Then, too, some prospective tenants were severely allergic to dogs and/or cats. These people really couldn't rent a unit that had been previously rented to a pet owner—the dander remaining on the ceilings and walls simply required too much effort to get it all washed off.

Button acknowledged all these problems, but she asked Kenner, "Have we really had any serious problems in the duplexes as a result of renting to pet owners?"

"Not yet," Kenner said, "but why wait?" Kenner felt that excluding pet owners would have no effect on the tenancy rate at PMI—the percentage of time the duplexes were rented.

Button wondered aloud whether PMI might gain extra goodwill by renting to pet owners. Hickman-Dawson Realty was right next door, and though the two firms weren't financially connected, Hickman was majority owner of both; at times PMI referred interested tenants to Hickman-Dawson when they decided to look into buying a house. Neither Kenner nor Button had any idea what percentage of referrals resulted in sales, but both agreed surely they'd helped H-D sell a few houses.

Kenner, however, thought the number of pet-owning tenants likely to buy a house would be extremely small. Button argued that maybe pet owners would be much more likely to buy a home—after all, 95 percent of the rentals in Normal specified No Pets Allowed.

"And besides," Button said, "what do we say to pet owners, just, 'Sorry, No Pets Allowed?' At least now we have an out—we can say we do allow them in those twenty-eight duplexes."

"All right," Kenner finally said. "You write your memo to Hickman and I'll write mine."

DISCUSSION QUESTIONS

1. Does Hickman expect to receive a memo about PMI's pet policy?
2. How will Hickman react to a memo recommending "no pets allowed?"
3. How will Hickman react to a memo recommending that the present policy be maintained?
4. What questions will Hickman have about *any* recommendation regarding the pet policy?

SUGGESTED ASSIGNMENTS

1. You are Dan Kenner or Marilyn Button. Write Marv Hickman and recommend a particular pet policy for PMI.
2. You are Dan Kenner or Marilyn Button. Suppose Hickman agrees with your policy recommendation. For the sake of clarity, you decide to write out the policy. Along with it write a memo to employees who work for PMI. Explain the policy to them so they can answer questions from tenants.
3. Suppose Marv Hickman sells the twenty-eight duplexes to your employer. Suddenly you are in charge of these units. Establish your own pet policy and write a letter to your tenants explaining your policy.

Job Interview Success

In the summer of 1982, Rick Ronaldson, an assistant professor in State University's School of Business Administration, was wondering about offering a consulting service to students and community members.

A teacher of management communication, Ronaldson had come to State University two years before. He was an experienced teacher with special training in the use of videotape recording equipment to improve students' managerial communication skills.

The course Ronaldson taught, Business Administration 383: Management Communication, focused on the oral and written skills needed for a student to succeed in an entry-level managerial position. Ronaldson believed that a couple of the teaching techniques he used in the course would also be useful to prepare students for job interviewing. Specifically, what he had in mind was giving students mock job interviews, videotaping them, and playing them back so the students could see where improvement was needed. Ronaldson believed that carefully planned, realistic mock job interviews, videotaped and discussed with the students, would make most students much more successful in getting a good job. However, Ronaldson's course did not include job search materials and wasn't designed to. Thus,

Ronaldson began looking around the University to see what courses and services were available to students.

BACKGROUND

With nearly twenty thousand students, State University offered a wide variety of degree programs. The major colleges were Arts and Sciences, Engineering, and Agriculture. The College of Arts and Sciences offered its 5400 undergraduates job assistance through the Career Development Office. Career Development offered these services: aptitude and interest testing, job-search guidance, assistance in writing resumes and job-application letters, and practice job interviews with a guidance counselor. There was no charge for any of these services. According to Ray Jackman, Director of Career Development, well over half the College's students received guidance of one sort or another. Mainly, Jackman said, students were concerned with the basics: resume and application letters. Only a few were intersted in practicing mock job interviews.

The colleges of engineering and agriculture offered similar services, but their placement officers, Doug Hedberg and Steve Martone, made no mention of providing mock job interviews when Ronaldson called and asked. Hedberg, from the College of Engineering, commented, "Our students get offered so many interviews that they don't worry about doing a bad job on the first two or three." Martone's complaint was that too many students waited until the last semester to even begin work on a resume. By then, most of the good jobs were taken. Agriculture, Martone reported, was getting very tight as a job market, and many applicants really had to work hard to get any job at all.

THE DEPARTMENT OF ENGLISH

The Department of English offered a course, Professional and Business Writing, in which resume and job application letter writing was taught. However, Ronaldson's friend Rebecca Moore reported that job interviewing techniques were really not taught in the course, and were certainly not practiced. "I'm the only one who includes a mock job interview in the course," Rebecca reported. "And students almost unanimously praise it highly. Many say it's the best part of the course. But then often they don't say that until after the interview is over." Beforehand, lots of students dreaded the interview, Rebecca reported.

THE SERVICE

What Ronaldson had in mind was a job search/job interview service for which students would have to pay. It would include the following:

    —a one-hour lecture on the job search
    —a one-hour lecture on the resume and application letter

—a one-hour session on the job interview

—a 20-minute mock job interview, videotaped and then replayed and discussed with the student

—practice *giving* a job interview, to gain an understanding of the role and problems of the interviewer

—a 15-page packet of materials, including sample resumes, application and follow-up letters, and an annotated list of helpful books on the job-search process

The way Ronaldson planned it, JOB INTERVIEW SUCCESS would work like this:

1. Students would attend all three sessions at the Student Union.

2. After a brief sales pitch, Ronaldson would collect the $35 fee, hand out the packet of materials, and begin the lecture on the job search.

3. After the first session students would write their resumes, write a 300-word description of a real job for which they would like to apply, and write a job application letter.

4. At the second session, Ronaldson would discuss the job interview, give a couple of on-the-spot sample interviews, with discussion, and have students sign up for their videotaping session.

5. After the second session, students would prepare to be interviewed. They would also prepare to interview another student, who had handed over to them the job description, resume, and application letter that student had completed for a job.

6. At the agreed-upon time, each participant would meet back at the Student Union with his or her partner and Ronaldson. One participant would interview the other; then the two would reverse roles. Meanwhile, Ronaldson would videotape the interviews, take notes, and then, finally, play them back and discuss them with the participants.

Ronaldson knew that in the four and one-half hours or so each participant would spend in lecture or practice, it would be impossible to promise any real evaluation of the resumes or job-application letters themselves. Resume and application-letter consulting could literally take all day, time Ronaldson couldn't afford to give, except upon special request, and then only at the rate of thirty-five dollars per hour.

What Ronaldson thought he could guarantee, however, was that each student would have a much improved job interview performance. All the other time spent was simply necessary to create the high quality materials required to make the interview realistic and successful.

THE COMMUNITY

Though he had no way of judging, Ronaldson thought he might also attract some clients from the surrounding community. Advertising, even in the

University's small town (population 50,000) newspaper, was expensive. Allowing for a minimum expense for some kind of publicity, however, in addition to room rental, equipment rental, and materials reproduction, Ronaldson calculated he needed ten fully paid participants to break even on costs. If he were to be paid for his time, which he calculated to be worth thirty-five dollars an hour, then he estimated that he needed an enrollment of forty-five participants to break even. More participants would, of course, gradually increase his hourly return, but he doubted whether he could handle more than forty-five and still keep up with all his other work.

OTHER COMPETITION

There was virtually no other competition for Ronaldson in town or nearby. Many printers advertised resume-writing services, but Ronaldson found these really consisted only of setting into type and printing resumes on recommended paper. The services provided no editorial or proofreading help.

OPINIONS, OPINIONS

Ronaldson called the various placement officers back and asked them what they thought of his idea for a job-search-and-success session. Jackman at A and S said he didn't mind if Ronaldson offered the service, but he felt that students could get virtually the same thing at A and S. "But then you know how some people are," Jackman said. "They don't think they're getting something good unless they have to pay for it." Hedberg said he thought engineering students had so many job interviews that they just weren't worried about anything but the basic resume and application letter. Martone said he thought anything that would help agriculture students get a job was a good idea, and maybe they could even refer a few students, very informally, to Ronaldson. All three, however, said that of course they could allow no advertising of this service in their offices.

YES, NO, MAYBE SO

Ronaldson was left unsure what to do. Half out of curiosity he wanted to try the sessions just to see if they would sell. He also admitted to himself that he would be happy to make an extra thousand dollars, if it came to that. And in his own department, he knew that many professors regularly did consulting work for additional pay. But how could he sell the service to students? He learned by contacting the Office of Admissions that without any special use of his position in the University he could acquire a list of seniors, including addresses. But would it be better to advertise in the city or school paper, to hand out fliers, or what? Or would students be at all interested?

DISCUSSION QUESTIONS

1. Suppose you are Ronaldson's graduate student. How will he react if you tell him J.I.S. will not be successful? How will he react if you propose changes in J.I.S.?

2. Would a program similar to J.I.S. be successful in your community? Why or why not?

3. What changes in J.I.S. would make it more successful?

4. What features of J.I.S. are most attractive?

SUGGESTED ASSIGNMENTS

1. You are a graduate student working on an independent study with Rick Ronaldson. Ronaldson has given you all the information about his consulting service, Job Interview Success. He's asked you to analyze the data and to write him a report in which you argue whether students would pay for the service.

   Use the material in the case to support your argument. Remember, Ronaldson has told you to be honest: "If you think this thing's a dog," he said, "then let me know. But give me reasons."

2. You are an undergraduate student Ronaldson has hired part-time to help promote Job Interview Success. Write a sales letter, to be mailed out to prospective customers. Sell them on the value of the program. To secure a place, interested students need to send in a $10 deposit to Job Interview Success, 1212 North Lincoln Avenue, Collegeville, 02134. Or they can drop by Ronaldson's office, 375 Mitchener Hall.

3. Suppose J.I.S. were available on your campus. Write a report in which you argue whether the program would be successful. Address your report to the head of the English Department or to a particular professor of your choice.

WDL AM-FM Radio

In the spring of 1978, the National Public Radio Network announced to its member stations, including WDL AM-FM, that it was planning a morning news program that would be available to stations in the fall of 1979. National Public Radio is a nonprofit organization of public radio stations. NPR produces and distributes programs used by more than two hundred stations nationwide. Each station has complete discretion as to whether to use any particular program. NPR activities are financed primarily with federal funds.

Most of the NPR stations welcomed the announcement because these stations believed that a morning network news and public affairs program was a needed complement to NPR's "All Things Considered." "All Things Considered" was an evening radio news program that offered the most extensive report and analysis of national and international news and features available on American radio.

THE MORNING EDITION

In the fall of 1979, NPR announced that the new program, entitled "Morning Edition," would be available to WDL in hour-long segments from 5:00 A.M. until 10:00 A.M., Monday through Friday, starting November 5th. NPR also made pilot (audition) samples of the new program available to all stations. Each hour-long segment contained headline news on the half-hour followed by news features. Each hour the program was rebroadcast with updated news followed by the same news features.

WDL AM-FM had been airing "All Things Considered" for many years and was pleased with it. The show had won every major journalistic award in the radio field and had proven to be an audience booster for the two WDL stations. Thus, as Jerry Fathers, station manager, and Benson Woo, program manager, listened to the "Morning Edition" sample tapes, they judged, on the basis of what they heard and on NPR's track record in news programs, that "Morning Edition" would make a fine addition to the AM and FM schedules at WDL. No programs were simulcast on the two stations. "All Things Considered" was broadcast on both, but at different times. Thus Fathers and Woo had the same thing in mind for "Morning Edition." As it turned out, however, the addition of the new program created some problems.

THE HISTORY OF WDL AM-FM

WDL AM-FM were two of many public university-owned and -operated stations across the nation. WDL-AM began broadcasting in 1921, WDL-FM in 1949. The stations were dependent on state tax revenues for about 80 percent of their operating funds, with the balance coming in the form of grants and gifts from a variety of sources. WDL-AM operated only during daylight hours, but because of its power and dial frequency, it could be heard throughout the state. Since its beginning, the station had carried a heavy schedule of market news and agricultural programs. In recent years, the programming trend at WDL-AM had been toward an increase in public affairs and other talk programs with a corresponding decrease in music programming.

WDL-FM was licensed to operate on a full-time basis and could easily be heard by listeners within a seventy-mile radius of its transmitter. While the station did broadcast some talk programming, its primary emphasis was on arts and performance materials, primarily classical music and jazz. Although State University, which was located in the central United States, owned WDL, Fathers and Woo felt they had complete authority to run the station without fear of administrative interference.

WDL-FM

The decision to add "Morning Edition" to the FM program schedule was an easy one since WDL-FM had previously not been operating before 6:00 A.M. By adding "Morning Edition," WDL-FM could simply come on the air an hour earlier and thereby establish itself that much sooner each day. It was true that WDL-FM aired a somewhat similar, locally produced program from 6:00–7:00 A.M. Monday through Friday, but Fathers and Woo saw no harm in offering both. Most people who got up at 5:00 A.M. would not listen to the six-to-seven show; listeners who got up at 6:00 A.M. had obviously missed "Morning Edition." Besides, most or all of the material in the two shows was different anyway.

WDL-AM

The AM situation was a bit different. Although both Fathers and Woo had felt that AM should continue its policy of moving away from its early morning emphasis on classical music, in the past the station had simply not had the resources to offer more news-oriented programs on AM. Then the NPR program became available. It was rebroadcast every hour with updated news. With the coming of "Morning Edition," Fathers and Woo thought it good planning to add the program to the schedule.

Under ideal conditions, the new program would probably have fit best between 7:00 A.M. and 9:00 A.M. Unfortunately, WDL-AM was licensed to operate only during daylight hours. It could not broadcast earlier than 7:30 or 7:45 some winter months. On the other hand, it could broadcast as early as 5:30 or 5:45 during summer months. Fathers and Woo felt that a news program like "Morning Edition" should be a reliable source of information in the sense that the program should be available to listeners every weekday of the year at the same time. Therefore, they decided to schedule the new program to run from 8:00 A.M. to 10:00 A.M. That scheduling would couple "Morning Edition" with the station's own production called "This Morning." "This Morning," which was a news and call-out talk show, ran from ten to noon. Thus Fathers and Woo believed WDL-AM would have a very solid news and information presence during the entire morning. In the afternoon, the various news and information programs were broken up by a classical music concert from 2:00–3:30.

THE MUSIC SHOP

The scheduling of "Morning Edition" from eight to ten meant that the eight-to-ten segment of the station's "Music Shop" program would no longer be broadcast. The "Music Shop," a classical music "wake-up" program, had run from sign-on to 10:00 A.M. on WDL for nearly fifty years—probably the longest-running concert music program in the U.S. Fathers and Woo were a little nervous about tampering with such a long-time favorite. However, they believed that enough classical music was available, *in better fidelity,* from the various FM stations around the state. They also believed that the policy of converting the AM station to a primarily informational outlet was sound and should proceed. And of course they believed in "Morning Edition." So on November 5th, the "Music Shop" ran from sign-on to 8:00 A.M., and "Morning Edition" ran from eight to ten.

THE COMPLAINTS

No sooner had AM begun to broadcast "Morning Edition," however, than the letters started coming in. The first week there were twenty-five of them. Some of the letters were from rural areas and from listeners located "between" the signals of FM classical music stations: that is, the listeners could not receive FM signals adequately, so WDL-AM was their only source of concert music by radio. Many listeners said they had been enjoying the "Music Shop" for a great many years and had "grown up" with the program. A variety of occupational groups were represented. Several lawyers wrote to the station as did a few farmers. It seemed that the types of individuals writing closely paralleled what the station believed its audience characteristics to be: that is, rural or small-town dwellers with above-average education and an interest in the arts. The following three letters are representative of those received by the station:

I am really mad at you guys!!!! What are you doing to us out here in the hinterlands who HUNGER for decent musical programs? The one big joy in the morning around here was to turn on the "Music Shop" and listen to something DECENT. It is relatively rare these days and what you have substituted for that, from 8–10, is TERRIBLE, UNBELIEVABLY ROTTEN, and it makes morning irritating instead of soothing and pleasant.

PLEASE!!!!!!! Please get back to music. I gave it a yeoman's try this morning and the pits was Firestone Theatre. Come ONNNNNNNNN, we want good music here, not THAT JUNK, which one can hear on any other station on the radio these days. It is not funny, it is SAD.

I am not alone. I speak for the yearning millions out here who want something better. Good Music. How about it???????

> Sadly and sincerely,
>
> Terrance McCue
> P.S. My state representative's going
> to hear about this and so is the
> Governor!

First off I wish to say how much I enjoy your radio station. I live 100 miles west of Dullis and my thirst for classical music is satisfied only by radio stations such as yours. I am a farmer and listen very diligently to all of your morning and afternoon concerts on my tractor radio.

But now I have a gripe—why in heaven's name did you change your programming in the morning to include that news program? Shows of that sort are a dime a dozen. So please go back to your previous programming. Maybe I am alone in thinking this way but I would hazard a guess that I am not.

Anyhow, thank you for all the beautiful hours you have given me, and I will look forward to many more.

> Sincerely yours,
>
> Michael Kent

I was very sad to see "Music Shop" cut back on its broadcast programming. Here's one vote for restoring the schedule. No complaints about the quality of the morning NPR programming. It's just that the people in charge there should understand the uniqueness of your program and its historic contribution and tradition.

Everywhere one goes in this country, one finds fewer indications of regional uniqueness. Everything from mass media giants to corporate magnates regulate and routinize everything. I was reminded of this on a recent trip to South Carolina. The signs, newspapers, fast-food services, it was all the same as back home, so precious little of the regional uniqueness that is our heritage. We're being slick-faced away by the big guys!

In this regard, your full programming was a RARE and REFRESHING experience. We had our own quality gem giving us what no one else would. Thus I vote NO for the new change in programming to this thing sometimes referred to as "progress." What in all creation will it take for the powers in control there to understand this? We CAN be different, and we should.

Sincerely,

Karen D. Webb

SUGGESTED DISCUSSION QUESTIONS

1. What is the relationship between NPR and WDL?
2. On whom does WDL depend for financial support?
3. Why did Jerry Fathers and Benson Woo decide to add "Morning Edition" to the FM station?
4. Why did Jerry Fathers and Benson Woo decide to add "Morning Edition" to the AM station?
5. What should they do about the letters of complaint?
6. How representative are the people who are complaining?
7. What arguments against "Morning Edition" do the letter writers make?

SUGGESTED ASSIGNMENTS

You are Benson Woo. Jerry has asked you to complete one or more of the following assignments.

1. Write a letter to each of the three people whose letters of complaint are included in this case.
2. Write a memo to Jerry Fathers in which you argue whether WDL should change its recent programming decision due to the complaints received.
3. Write a letter to be included in the next monthly issue of the WDL program guide. In the letter, explain WDL's recent programming changes.
4. Write a statement to be broadcast. Either justify the change and apologize for it or justify the return to the original programming (or some modificaiton of it).

Chapter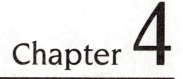

Determining the Purpose

At any one point in your life you probably have some personal goals you want to reach. You may want to save enough money to buy a Pontiac Trans Am, to write well enough to get at least a B in English, or to study enough to end the term with a certain grade-point average. Some of your goals are short term, some long term; all of them give your life direction and purpose. Establishing goals gives you a reason for putting $200 a month into savings, for rewriting your English paper three times, for studying twenty-five hours a week. Working toward various goals in life gives you a sense of purpose. The people you communicate with can understand you better if you have a sense of purpose in your life.

The same is true in writing. Your writing will be more easily understood if it has a clear purpose. Therefore, one of the most basic ways you can avoid or solve writing problems is to determine your purpose. Effective writing always has some purpose to it, a goal or goals that the reader knows the writer is working to reach. The purpose of this chapter is to show you how to use goal setting to write more effectively. Asking yourself questions about the purpose of your writing can help you to determine not only what overall form your writing should take, but also what your purpose is in writing a paragraph, a sentence, or even a single word.

The Purpose of the Essay, Letter, Memo, or Report

One way to determine your purpose is to ask whether you want your statement to describe, narrate, explain, or persuade. Suppose you are driving down the Interstate, it's a sunny day, the traffic is light, and you are fifteen minutes late for a final exam. You are late because before you got in the car to go to school you had to fix a flat tire. Now you decide to make up the time by driving seventy, but as you come around a corner on the Interstate you get caught in a speed trap. An officer gives you a speeding ticket before you can say a thing; you have the right to appeal the citation in traffic court.

That night, in a letter to a friend, you tell what happened. Your letter describes the incident as it happened; it tells the story. As you write the letter, you realize that you want your friend to know exactly what it was like to get that ticket. Once you have your goal in mind, you can use what you know about describing and narrating (see Chapter 5) to reach that goal and write a good letter.

Your purpose could change if you pick up the phone and call a friend who also drives to school. If you know that your friend drives over the speed limit, you might want to warn him or her about the speed trap. So you explain in great detail where it is and how to avoid it. Suppose that once you hang up, your father, mother, spouse, or roommate comes in, holding your speeding ticket in hand, and says, "How'd you get this?" Now you might want to explain your actions so your listener can understand them. (For some guidelines on developing an explanation, see Chapters 6 and 7.)

Finally, suppose you appeal your ticket to the traffic court judge. Here you argue whether you should have to pay a fine. You try to persuade the judge not to fine you. Your purpose is to reduce or avoid the penalty for speeding. (For some guidelines on persuasion, see Chapter 8).

The Appropriate Writing Situation

It is important to make sure that your purpose in writing is appropriate for your writing situation. If you write to a friend and *argue* that you should not have gotten the ticket, is your purpose appropriate? Your friend may just think, "Why argue with me? *I* didn't give you the ticket and I can't waive the fine, either." Suppose when you pulled over and the officer walked up to your window, you began to *explain*, "Officer, I had a flat and I'm fifteen minutes late for my final exam . . ." Would an explanation be appropriate here? It might be, but the officer might just take the position that, "Radar indicates you were doing seventy, so you get a ticket for doing seventy." In these two instances, an argument or explanation might not be appropriate for the situation.

Similarly, if you simply tell the traffic court judge what happened—

"I was late to my final exam because I had to change a tire and then I hit a speed trap, Your Honor, and this officer gave me a ticket even though I tried to explain why I was going seventy"—you are not focusing on your purpose, which is to *persuade* the judge to waive the fine and to make the ticket only a warning. By focusing on your purpose, you may realize what you said to the officer is probably irrelevant as far as the judge is concerned. Instead, perhaps in addition to briefly mentioning your reason for speeding, you should tell the judge whether you have ever been cited before or been in an accident. This kind of information might persuade the judge to waive the fine.

In summary, one way to determine your purpose is to analyze each writing situation and ask yourself the broad, general question, "Is the goal of this statement to describe, narrate, explain, or persuade?"

Purpose and Audience Analysis

A similar way to determine your purpose is to ask yourself what effect you want your statement to have on your reader. In the discussion that follows, these general questions about the reader are explained. At the same time, some sample answers are given based on this writing situation: Suppose you are the head of a sky-diving team and have been asked to write an article on sky diving for the local newspaper.

What Do I Want the Reader to Feel or Imagine?

If you are describing or telling about an incident, your purpose may partly or largely be determined by what you want the reader to be able to imagine. If you are writing a feature article about sky diving, you may want the reader to be able to imagine what it feels like to get dressed, put on the parachute, climb in the plane, take off, and jump out. Obviously you would want the reader to be able to imagine what it is like to fall to earth.

What Do I Want the Reader to Know?

In writing any statement you should have a purpose for including each piece of information and every idea. You may decide that part of your purpose in writing about sky diving, for example, is to tell the reader some basic facts such as where it can be done, how much practice it takes, and how high the plane is when people jump out. In this example, part of your purpose might be to inform the reader about an exciting but not widely understood sport.

What Do I Want the Reader to Think or Conclude?
Of course your thesis focuses your statement on a single point you want to make. Your supporting ideas enable the reader to make conclusions that develop and clarify your thesis. If you want the reader to make certain conclusions, then you must include the material that will lead to those conclusions. If part of your purpose is to make the reader conclude that sky diving is not dangerous, for example, then you need to include information on safety procedures and perhaps statistics on the number of deaths and on the probability of accident.

What Do I Want the Reader to be Able to Do?
You may want the reader to be able to do certain things after reading your statement. You may, for example, want the reader to be able to look elsewhere for more information, so you include references. Your purpose might also be to instruct readers on the basics of sky diving so they will know, if not how to do it without professional help, at least where to go for lessons, how much the lessons cost, and what it takes to become a sky diver.

What Do I Want the Reader to Do?
You may want the reader to take some particular action or hold some particular belief. If you are employed at a sky-diving school as an instructor, for example, perhaps the goal of your article is to persuade readers to sign up for lessons. If you are writing a pamphlet for a prolife group, your goal might be to make your readers believe that abortion is immoral. If you are writing about a political candidate, your goal might be to get the readers to go out and vote for that person.

The point here is simple: your ultimate goal or goals in any writing situation determine your thesis and what you should include to develop it.

The Purpose of a Paragraph

If you consider the various goals of the sky-diving article, you can see that while its ultimate goal might be to persuade people to try sky diving, the way to reach that goal might be through others: to enable the reader to imagine what it feels like, know what the facts are (how it is done), conclude that it is safe and exciting, be able to get in touch with you, and decide to do so. Since a statement can have a set of related goals, different paragraphs within that statement can have different purposes. Therefore, each time you write a paragraph, you can ask yourself this question:

What is the goal of this paragraph? It may be that the paragraph is designed to describe, narrate, explain, or persuade. Or it may be that the paragraph is intended to communicate a feeling or sensation, knowledge, conclusions, ability, or to create action.

You can also analyze the purpose of a paragraph in *organizational* terms. As you read in Chapter 2, a paragraph is a group of sentences that develops a single idea (a topic sentence) in a coherent manner. Yet certain paragraphs have special organizational *purposes* in any statement. In a lengthy essay, for example, you may write one or more paragraphs as an introduction and one or more paragraphs as your conclusion. You may even have a short paragraph or two in between central sections of your essay. These paragraphs' sole purposes may be to make transitions from one major topic to another. Introductory, transitional, or concluding paragraphs should be written with their special organizational goals or purposes in mind. Of course other paragraphs are written to express ideas that develop your thesis. Take time to ask yourself what is the organizational purpose of each paragraph. By asking yourself this question you may be able to write more quickly and effectively because you are setting an organizational goal for that paragraph to achieve.

One way to determine the organizational purpose of each paragraph you write is to complete the statement: The purpose of this paragraph is to . . .

> introduce the essay,
> develop an idea to support the thesis,
> interconnect two major sections,
> conclude the essay.

If you are writing introductory, transitional, or concluding paragraphs, you can apply what you know about them (see Chapter 2) to write more effectively. If you are developing a supportive idea, then you should be able to further determine your purpose by completing the following statement: "This paragraph develops or supports my thesis by . . ." Remember: if any paragraph does not clearly support your thesis, then that paragraph has no purpose—it does not belong in your essay.

Asking yourself about your purpose in writing each paragraph can help you to write more effectively. In general, determining the purpose of a paragraph can make it easier for you to decide whether the paragraph is effective. Specifically, you may want to think about purpose most carefully for paragraphs that seem to be especially difficult to write. Perhaps you will find that your problem is that you are trying to describe a situation instead of explaining it, or that you are trying to interconnect two parts of your essay that don't fit together, so the interconnecting paragraph doesn't fit together either. Whatever the situation, you will write more effectively if you keep purpose in mind on a *paragraph-by-paragraph* basis.

The Purpose of the Sentence

Of course the basic unit of all prose is the sentence, so you may also want to think about your purpose on a *sentence-by-sentence* level. Grammatically, sentences are generally classified as simple, compound, complex, and compound-complex. The composition of a sentence can vary tremendously according to its inclusion of prepositional phrases, relative clauses, participial phrases, parallel structures, dependent clauses, independent clauses, absolutes, appositives, noun substitutes, and restrictive and nonrestrictive clauses. Sentence structure variety is so great, in fact, that there is not enough space here to discuss sentence composition in terms of purpose.

You may, however, find it useful to think of a sentence's purpose in terms of that sentence's organizational relationship to the paragraph. In organizational terms, sentences within a paragraph are generally designed to:

> imply or explicitly state the paragraph's central idea (topic sentence),
> include evidence to support and develop the central idea,
> provide paragraph coherence by showing the interconnections between evidence and central idea, or
> interconnect adjacent paragraphs with a paragraph transition.

Sentences tend to tear and break when writers try to make them do too much, or leave gaps between ideas and information when writers make them do too little. Therefore, you should ask yourself your purpose when a particular sentence seems to be "wrong" or to create a problem.

Tone and the Words you Choose

The purpose of your statement can also be communicated in terms of your tone. Your tone in writing is the attitude that your words, phrases, and sentences convey. Your tone may be hostile, friendly, serious, humorous, detached, intimate; the whole range of human emotions can be conveyed in your tone. In most academic writing, you will probably want to convey an impersonal, serious tone. In other situations, when you are writing personal or business letters, for example, your tone may vary considerably from one statement to the next. In each writing situation, you will want to consider the tone of your statement in relationship to your purpose or goal in writing.

Of course you must analyze your audience when determining your tone. You must be careful about your diction (word choice) because just a few words can do much to determine your tone. In "The Place Department Store," the case that follows the conclusion of this chapter, Grace Montgomery must write a report to Pat McMurphy, the personnel manager. Grace is in a difficult position, as you will see when you read the case. Right now, consider the following sample paragraphs from memos written by different students. Look for key words and phrases that communicate the tone of the memo, and therefore indicate its purpose.

1. I enjoy my job very much and take pride in my work. I feel I am guilty of nothing but trying to do the best possible job I can. Ryan is very enjoyable to work with and does things the best possible way to promote goodwill at "The Hotel Place."

2. The violations I was confronted with were failing to give receipts twice, failing to record each sale on the terminal, and of having recorded nonexistent sales. As the receipt tape showed, I had not failed to record any sales. The other two charges stem from problems of ability to carry out store policy and still run an efficient business.

3. The violations of store policy unintentionally carried out by me were the direct result of instructions and methods conveyed to me by my supervisor, Ryan White.

4. I have always felt that I've been an honest employee and a hard worker. I might have violated store policy, but it was because I was trying to cover up the inadequate job of another employee (Ryan White).

5. Since becoming an employee of The Place Department Store, I have strived to become a better sales representative. That effort involved learning from Ryan White the best methods of operating the store. I assumed that Ryan knew the best method of operation since he had been here for many years. Thus, I went along with his way of doing things and assumed they were right.

Writer 1 seems to have a positive, friendly attitude while writer 2's tone sounds cold and formal. In example 3, the writer is very direct, perhaps to the point of seeming pointed, abrupt. Sample 4 shows internal variation as the tone ranges from defensive to accusative. Lastly, the tone of 5 seems reasonable, calm.

Summary

By setting goals for your words, sentences, paragraphs, and for the entire essay, you can write more effectively. You can determine your purpose by asking yourself whether you need to describe, narrate (Chapter 5), explain (Chapters 6 and 7), or persuade (Chapter 8). This question may lead you to asking yourself how you should develop your thesis. Is your purpose to judge, define, classify, compare, contrast, illustrate, show cause and effect, or describe a process (Chapters 6 and 7)? You can also determine your purpose in organizational terms (Chapter 2). In establishing writing goals, you must consider your audience and make sure that your choices are appropriate for the writing situation you face.

The Place Department Store (A)

When Grace Montgomery got her job at The Place, she was fairly pleased about it. She was put right into the manager's training program, and the personnel manager, Pat McMurphy, told her she had a bright future at The Place.

"We're happy to have sales representatives like you who've figured out what they want to do with their lives," Pat said.

Grace planned to go into retail sales as a career. After three years of college she was tired of books and eager to get out into the real world. She planned to obtain her degree in business administration by going to night school for two or three years. Meanwhile, she thought, she'd be gaining invaluable work experience and building up seniority at The Place.

THE HOTEL PLACE

The trouble was the position they'd given her to start with. The Hotel Place was located in a large downtown office building/hotel. Years ago, when a magazine and sundries store in the hotel lobby had gone out of business, The Place Department Store had leased the space and opened up its own magazine, stationery, tobacco, candy, and sundries store.

This little store was nicknamed The Hotel Place, since it served the hotel's guests as well as the people who maintained offices in the building. It was treated like a special department of the main store. The Hotel Place was managed by a middle-aged man named Ryan White. Ryan had managed the store since it opened. He had only one assistant, Grace, and just one cash register. On days when either Ryan or Grace was off, the main store sent over a floater—a salesperson not assigned to any particular department—to fill in. Thus at times Grace ran the store, and she was unofficially called the assistant manager.

Grace's job entailed running the register and helping Ryan order merchandise from the main store. Ryan was an agreeable man who laughed a lot and was well liked by the hotel customers. But Grace realized he was determined not to change anything he did, and it didn't take her long after she got the job to see that there was room for improvement in the store's operation.

THE NEW COMPUTER TERMINAL

One of the biggest problems came up when The Place converted all its departments to a computer-terminal cash-register system. Ryan couldn't seem to learn how to use the machine efficiently, even for simple tasks like selling a newspaper or a can of Coke. And the new terminal actually took longer than the old register to complete such transactions.

The Hotel Place often had "rushes" in which forty or fifty business executives or secretaries or hotel patrons would come in and buy *The Wall Street Journal* or a pack of cigarettes. At these times no single cashier could keep up with the business, even on the old register. Ryan's solution to this problem (even before the new terminal was installed) was to have the cashier make change out of a cardboard match box and then ring up two or three dollars' worth of sales for Department 65, Newspapers/Candy all at once. This procedure was in violation, however, of The Place policy, which stated that "individual purchases must be rung up individually. Under no circumstances will employees put two or more separate customers' purchases on the same receipt."

ISSUING RECEIPTS

Another problem arose with issuing receipts to customers. The policy stated that "each customer must be *handed* a receipt for his or her purchase." When secretaries bought a paper, however, they just laughed when Grace tried to hand over the receipt. It was not uncommon, Grace noticed on her first day of work, for twenty or thirty receipts to pile up on the counter. Then, after a while, Ryan would throw them away.

When Grace asked Ryan about the change box, he said that personnel and security knew about it, didn't like it, but agreed he had to have it. With the new terminal, however, and because of Ryan's inability to run it efficiently, Grace found that sometimes when she came back from her coffee break there would be five or six dollars' worth of change in the box, much more than there had been under the old system. And Ryan would be standing there talking to a customer and relaxing, now that the rush was over.

What's more, Ryan had mentioned a couple of times that when he closed out at the end of the day and totaled up the cash, the count would be two or more dollars over most of the time. Just two weeks before, when the old register had been in use, Grace and Ryan had gone a week without going over or falling short.

THE FIFTH WEEK

After another week with the terminal—Grace's fifth week at The Hotel Place—Ryan seemed to be getting worse, if anything, and Grace was beginning to wonder what do do. Then the whole thing seemed to explode in her face.

Grace came back from her break one morning to find Ryan further behind than usual. There was at least ten dollars worth of change lying all over the counter, some of it covered up by receipts that were scattered everywhere. And no sooner did Ryan go back to his office than another few customers drifted into the store. It was all Grace could do to sweep the receipts off the counter, ring seven dollars worth of change into the terminal, and wait on the next customer.

Of the next several customers, Grace recognized a couple who always bought *The New York Times,* but there were a few people who seemed new to her. These all purchased one or more items, including such things as magazines, paperback books, or deodorant. Between serving two customers she managed to get five more dollars' worth of sales rung into the machine, and felt proud of herself for being able to handle the customers so fast and still clear the mess on the counter that Ryan had left behind. She even was deft enough to make change out of the box once to save time.

THE STORE DETECTIVE

After that, things happened fast. A big, red-faced man in a wrinkled double-knit suit stepped behind the counter and said, "I'm from security, come with me, please," and Ryan suddenly appeared, looking grim and taking over the job of running the register.

In Ryan's office the store detective explained that Grace was in serious trouble for violating store policy. She had failed to give receipts twice, failed to record each sale on the terminal, and had recorded nonexistent sales. Her customers had not been real customers, he said, but "shoppers"—individuals hired and trained to observe and report on the actions of cashiers.

Grace denied any wrongdoing, and the store detective nastily said, "I can prove it to you. I'll pull the tape on the machine. I don't know if you're going to lose your job over this. That isn't for me to say. But you have violated store policy. That's a fact."

The receipt tape showed that Grace had not, in fact, failed to record any sales. Evidently she'd recorded some sales so rapidly that the shoppers hadn't seen them. As for the receipts, she could only say she had placed them on the counter next to the purchases as was the habit she had acquired from Ryan. But the store detective said she was still in violation on all counts since she had recorded large sales in Department 65 when nothing in that department cost over a dollar. He also told her that the change box was in violation of store policy.

"But that box is Ryan's idea," Grace said. "I'm not the store manager here. Ryan told me you said it was all right."

The red-faced man said stubbornly, "It's a violation of store policy. A copy of my report will go into your permanent file as soon as Pat Mc-Murphy's read it. You can go back out there now. I have to talk to Ryan."

RYAN'S REACTION

Grace reluctantly went back out to relieve Ryan. He said, "Ah, Grace, you have to be careful to always give the customers a receipt. I always do unless it's just for a newspaper."

Grace noticed, after Ryan went back to his office, that the change box was gone. At this point she reached under the counter for the phone and called Pat McMurphy to tell her what happened.

McMurphy said, "I'm sending a floater down there within the hour. I want you to come up here and write out a full report of what happened. And don't worry about your file. If your report makes sense to me, the security department's report will never make it past my desk."

SUGGESTED DISCUSSION QUESTIONS

1. What are the problems that Grace must solve?
2. Who will her audience be?
3. What will be the purpose of Grace's report? (Be specific.)
4. Is there anything Grace should leave out of her report?
5. What should Grace include?
6. What is Grace's goal in writing the report? (Be specific.)

SUGGESTED ASSIGNMENTS

1. You are Grace Montgomery. Write a paragraph for yourself in which you state your report's purpose. Write your report.
2. You are a co-worker of Grace's. She's just told you what happened. Write her a note in which you state what the purpose of her report should be.

STUDENT RESPONSES

Using your statement of purpose based on assignment 1, analyze the following sample student responses. What is each author's purpose? Is it the same as yours? Does the author achieve the desired goal? Why? Why not?

SAMPLE RESPONSE A

TO: Pat McMurphy
FROM: Grace Montgomery
SUBJECT: Store Policies
DATE: May 19, 1979

(1) When I first started working here, you told me about store policy. I was told that each purchase must be rung up individually and that each customer must be handed his or her receipt. When I began working with Ryan White, however, I was told to disregard these instructions.

(2) Ryan had a system worked out for handling the large groups of people who would come in for newspapers; we would make change out of a cardboard box. Later, when things settled down, we'd ring up the money under Dept. 65, Newspapers/Candy. I asked Ryan about store policy, and he said personnel and security knew about the change box. He said you didn't like the arrangement but agreed it was necessary.

(3) I decided that if you and security knew about the change box, it must be OK. Recently, though, things have been getting out of hand. When I've come back from my break, Ryan has had $5 or $6 in change lying around instead of the usual $2 or $3. I assumed he didn't like the computer terminal and was waiting for me to ring up the money.

(4) This morning when I returned from my break Ryan had at least $10 in change lying on the counter, and receipts were piled all over. When Ryan went back to his office, I tried clearing the counter as usual.

(5) I first cleared the receipts off the counter and then rang $7 worth of change into the register. Some customers came and bought a few things, and as I rang up their items I got another $5 of the newspaper money into the register. At one point, I made change out of the box to save a little time.

(6) The next thing I knew, a man from security said he wanted to talk to me in Ryan's office, so Ryan took over. The store detective said I had violated store policies and could lose my job. He said that I had failed to give receipts and record each sale, and also that I had recorded nonexistent sales.

(7) I explained that I was only doing what Ryan had told me to do. He pulled the receipt tape and found that I had recorded each sale, so that charge was dropped. As for the receipts, I had set them on the counter next to the purchases just as Ryan does. The security man said I was still in violation of store policy, though, because of the large sales I'd rung up in Dept. 65 and because of the change box. I told him this was Ryan's method, but he still blamed me.

(8) When I went back to the register, Ryan told me to give receipts with everything except newspapers. Then, when he went to his office, I noticed the change box was gone. At this point I decided to call you.

(9) I'd like to repeat that I questioned Ryan from the start about the conflict between his way of doing things and store policy. He assured me that he knew best; consequently, if I am guilty of anything, I am guilty only of following the instructions of my immediate superior. I want to do a good job for "The Place," and I would greatly appreciate your consideration in this matter. Thank you.

SAMPLE RESPONSE B

TO: Pat McMurphy, Personnel Manager
FROM: Grace Montgomery
SUBJECT: Alleged Policy Violations
DATE: May 19, 1979

(1) I was informed by security this morning that I was in serious trouble for violating store policy. I was accused of failing to give receipts to two customers, failing to record each sale on the terminal, and recording nonexistent sales. However, I felt I was guilty of nothing more than trying to do the best job possible for The Place Department Store.

(2) I did not fail to give receipts to the customers. I placed the receipts on the counter next to each purchase, a habit I picked up from Ryan White. I couldn't put the receipts in sacks because small items such as newspapers, magazines, and paperback books don't require sacks. If I handed receipts to customers along with their change, they would be inconvenienced by having to handle too many small items at once. In addition, when a secretary bought a newspaper, he or she just laughed when I tried to hand over the receipt. The customers seldom wanted receipts, so they usually left them on the counter. On my first day of work I noticed twenty or thirty receipts piled on the counter. Then, after a while, Ryan threw them away. I concluded that placing receipts next to purchases was the best thing to do.

(3) However, store policy states that "Each customer must be handed a receipt for his or her purchases." This policy is good for the security of the store, but it is not practical enough to be carried out at our branch, since customers buy only a few small items and almost never want receipts. Therefore, I feel I have not violated this rule.

(4) The second violation I was accused of was failing to record each sale on the terminal. As the receipt tape showed, I recorded each sale on the terminal; I merely recorded some so fast that the shoppers didn't have time to see them. The receipt tape is positive proof that I performed my duty as instructed.

(5) Finally, I was accused of recording nonexistent sales. The store detective said I had recorded large sales in Department 65 when nothing in that department costs over a dollar. Therefore, he concluded that I had recorded nonexistent sales. The real problem, however, stems from the change box used by Ryan.

(6) As you probably know, "The Hotel Place" often has rushes when many business people, secretaries, and hotel patrons come in to buy copies of *The Wall Street Journal* and other newspapers or packs of cigarettes. At these times no single cashier can keep up with the business, even on the old register. The problem became worse after installation of the terminal cash register, because Ryan can't use the new machine efficiently. Ryan's solution to the problem is to have the cashier make change out of a change box and then ring up two or three dollars' worth of sales for Department 65. I realized that the change box violated store policy and asked Ryan about it. He said that personnel and security knew about it and didn't like it but agreed that he had to have it. So, I was accused of having recorded nonexistent sales because I followed my supervisor's instructions and methods of running the business.

(7) As an employee of "The Place," I have worked hard to become a better sales representative. I felt that this involved learning from Ryan the best methods of operating the store. For this reason, I went along with his way of doing things and assumed they were right. Furthermore, as Ryan was my supervisor, I assumed that I should follow his instructions.

(8) In conclusion, I did not fail to give receipts to customers, I did not fail to record each sale, and it was not within my power to eliminate the use of the change box. I hope you will agree that I was guilty of nothing but trying to do the best possible job. I would like to build a career at The Place Department Store, but it seems impossible to do so with a file containing misleading information.

ADDITIONAL SUGGESTED ASSIGNMENTS

1. You are Pat McMurphy. Based on Grace's report (see student response A or B), write her a letter explaining what you intend to do about the situation and why.

2. You are Grace's friend. She has told you about the situation and asked you to read her report (student response A or B) and tell her what you think of it. Although you want to discuss the report with her in person, Grace's work schedule and yours don't allow you to. Write her a letter in which you state how her report is effective and how it could be made more effective.

Too Much Financial Aid?

Janet Shaw stood outside her apartment and stared at the letter she had just received. Unless she could persuade the financial aid office otherwise, the letter meant that she couldn't afford to go to school the following term. She didn't know what she was going to do.

The letter explained that in accordance with the agreement Janet had signed last August, her loan for the second semester would be reduced by $1,025. The university had reduced her loan by $1,025 because she had been working as a university employee; $1,025 was the amount she had earned thus far. She would still receive $300 as a grant for the second semester.

Janet was shocked. When she had first applied for financial aid, the university had sent her some forms to fill out and sign. They'd offered her an option: a $600 grant for the year, a part-time job (work-study she supposed) earning her approximately $1,800, and a $1,400 loan; or, a $600 grant and a $3,200 loan if she rejected the job offer.

To Janet the choice was obvious. She was transferring to the university in the first place because she couldn't afford to borrow the money for the high tuition at the small college she had previously attended. Her parents were broke; they could have barely afforded, with a family of eight, to have her live at home, even if there had been a college within commuting distance. But even by going to the public university, Janet would have considerable expenses. The university had no dormitory space available for sophomores, so Janet faced the extra expense of sharing an apartment with someone.

In short, Janet needed as much money as she could get. She chose the second option ($600 grant and $3,200 loan) thinking that if she got a part-time job when the semester began, she would have enough, if she was lucky, to pay tuition and rent, and to buy food, clothes, and books.

When she arrived in town, she found that just about the only part-time jobs available to students were in retail sales, service stations, or restaurants. All these jobs paid only the minimum wage. Then she got lucky, or so she thought anyway. She learned about a job at the Alumni Association Theater Center. The job paid a dollar more an hour than anything she'd seen up until then, was right on campus, which was helpful since she didn't have a car, and she liked the work. Although her paychecks came from the university, the job was not a work-study position, and it had never occurred to Janet that she might be breaking her agreement.

The letter she held in her hand explained that her agreement limited the total help available to her, aside from the grant, to $3,200. Her loan would be reduced according to how much she earned from the university. Thus far she had earned approximately $1,025. She had already been loaned $1,600. That left her with $575. If she continued to work, the university would be unable to lend her any money the second semester; the additional $1,025 she would earn would considerably exceed the $575 she had left. The letter implied that she was lucky they wouldn't ask her to return some of the money.

After some searching, Janet found her copy of the agreement. It simply stated the amount of the grant and the terms of the loan. She searched through other papers she had initially received. A careful reading revealed the following statement located at the bottom of one of the pages: "An applicant accepting a grant/loan thereby agrees not to accept the unversity's offer of employment in, for example, a work-study position."

Janet quickly considered her options. She hated to quit her job because the pay was good, and so were the hours. She knew her folks couldn't help. So far as she knew, there were no other loans available, and she didn't know where to look anyway. The university's loan was at an unbelievably low 3 percent interest rate. She couldn't cut expenses further because she was already having to spend more than planned and had been trying to cut back.

The letter ended, "If you have any questions, or if we can be of assistance, let us know." This isn't my fault, Janet thought. I didn't think of every possible interpretation of the agreement. She felt like writing back to say, "Just tell me how I can change your mind." The university was so big and the town was so small it seemed as if there wasn't any good place to look for a job. And she didn't understand how they could claim she was getting too much financial aid. How could you give someone too much help in getting a college education?

SUGGESTED DISCUSSION QUESTIONS

1. Does Janet have any hope of persuading the university not to terminate the loan?
2. Why should the university not terminate her loan?
3. What means of persuasion can she use?
4. What was the communication problem between her and the university?
5. What would Janet's purpose(s) be in writing to the financial aid office?

SUGGESTED ASSIGNMENTS

1. You are Janet Shaw. Write to the financial office.
2. You are a friend of Janet's. She has told you about her problem and asked what you think she should say in writing to the financial aid office. Write Janet a note in which you explain what you think her purpose in writing should be.
3. Investigate financial-aid granting procedures at your own institution. Could the problem Janet Shaw faces occur? Why or why not? Prepare a report about your school's financial aid department based on your investigation.

Living Together, Living Apart

Mary Iron would never know how she'd managed to get involved, but now the only solution seemed to be either to do the work or tell her friends Henry and Judy to get a lawyer, or maybe two lawyers. But they didn't want a lawyer, they said, because lawyers were expensive and their finances were already in bad shape because of the separation. Besides, they'd both told her (at different times, of course, since they weren't speaking to each other) they weren't getting a divorce. They had never been married to begin with.

Mary knew enough about the situation to know they had been serious about each other at the start. Judy had moved into Henry's apartment six weeks after they met. Henry and Judy used one checking account, paying their bills out of it and enjoying their two incomes by jointly buying new things for the apartment. They decided they would try living together first and then get married later. Mary was not at all sure she approved; in fact, she thought they should get married. But at first they seemed so happy together it was difficult for Mary to feel that her friends were doing something wrong.

THE PROBLEMS

In the long run, the relationship between Henry and Judy had developed problems. Henry was Jewish; Judy was Catholic. Henry liked classical music and steak. Judy liked old-fashioned rock 'n' roll and Mexican food. Henry smoked; Judy didn't. Henry liked to watch sports on television; Judy liked to play them.

They tried to find things in common, but there just didn't seem to be any. Then Judy's shift at the hospital was changed. She'd been working in X-ray, from eight to five, Monday through Friday, but her boss said they had to have another technician from five to midnight and Judy had the least seniority.

Henry worked eight to five. By the time Judy came home at 12:30, Henry was ready to go to sleep. They hardly saw each other, and though they argued less, the time alone made them realize they'd made a mistake. Judy found a small apartment of her own and moved out, first just taking her clothes. Then the argument came. Judy came back to get the rest of what she thought was hers. She and Henry couldn't agree, however, what to do with the checking account, the savings account, or all the things they'd brought together. They argued and argued and ended up not speaking to each other. That's when they asked Mary to help them. She had long been a good friend to both Judy and Henry; in fact, she had been the one to introduce them.

THE MONEY, THE CAR, AND THE REST OF IT

As far as Mary could piece it together, one of the major arguments had been about the car. Henry owned a 1977 Monte Carlo. Judy had always paid the repair bills on it (six months' worth) because she usually drove it more than Henry, who took the bus to work. Judy bought all the gas, she said, to compensate Henry for the car's depreciation. They had agreed all this was fair enough, but then a week before Judy moved out she had a major tune-up and some other work done on the car. The cost was $384.73. She charged the bill on her own credit card. Now, she thought, Henry should pay her the entire amount since she wasn't going to use the car ever again. Henry thought he shouldn't pay anything. Her use of the car, he said, caused the need for the repairs.

They also disagreed about the checking and savings accounts. They split the money in the checking account because Judy had just written herself a check for her half of it. The savings account, however, was a different matter. Whatever had been put into it was from Judy's paycheck; she said

Henry had never saved any money on his own. Henry argued otherwise, saying Judy was the one who moved out so she shouldn't have the $467.35 they had saved together. He had gone to the bank, cleared out the savings account, and put the money into a new account in his own name.

They also disagreed about the stereo. They had bought a stereo out of their common checking account. The amount was $587.94. Henry said Judy could have the stereo if she would pay him his half. Judy said she couldn't afford a stereo when she had to buy a car. She wanted Henry to pay half the amount to her and keep the stereo. Henry said he couldn't afford to.

The color television was another problem. Judy had taken it with her when she moved out because, she said, she and Henry had purchased it largely with a gift from her mother. The TV had cost $325 and the gift was $300. Henry said the gift had been to both of them and, besides, Judy never watched television and he didn't want to miss any of the games on weekends.

Their microwave oven was yet another problem. Henry had charged it on a credit card. Judy had taken the oven but Henry still owed $189 on it. He said he didn't give a damn about the oven but repeated how much he missed having the television.

The biggest problem, however, was probably the puppy. The Irish Setter puppy was what they argued about the most. After living together for three months, they bought an Irish Setter puppy for $150. Henry liked the dog but said Judy was much more attached to it than he was. He said she should probably take the puppy. Besides, it had been her idea to get the puppy to begin with.

Judy agreed that she cared more about the puppy; she had always been the one to take it to the vet for shots and to feed and groom it. But the problem was that she hadn't had much time to look for an apartment when she decided to move out and the apartment she had taken came with a lease that did not allow pets. Later, she talked to her new landlord, and he agreed she could have a pet if she put up the (outrageous, Judy said) sum of $300 as security against any damages incurred by the puppy.

A SETTLEMENT

Both Henry and Judy told Mary that the more they discussed these issues the more they argued. They were depressed about their failure to make their relationship work and they were upset about all the complications in ending it. They just wanted an impartial third party to mediate a settlement since living together was out of the question.

So they asked Mary for help as a concerned friend. Mary was a sophomore in college and was majoring in psychology. Neither Henry nor Judy wanted legal advice; they just wanted someone with plain common sense.

If that person happened to have a little background in psychology, so much the better.

Henry said, "I just want something that says "I, Henry Rothman, and I, Judy McQuillan, agree to the terms set forth in this document."

"That's what I want," Judy agreed. "A written agreement on how we have to split things up."

They told Mary they'd pay her for her work. They said they both trusted Mary and didn't want to have to tell all their problems to a stranger.

SUGGESTED DISCUSSION QUESTIONS

1. Is there anyone at fault in this case?
2. Does it matter whether one party or the other is at fault?
3. Should Mary try to help her friends?
4. What should Mary do if she decides Judy and Henry were immoral in living together?
5. What is their biggest problem?

SUGGESTED ASSIGNMENTS

1. You are Mary Iron. Write a letter to Henry and Judy in which you explain why you are or are not going to write a settlement for them.
2. You are Mary Iron. Write a settlement for Henry and Judy. As a part of your settlement report entitled *Rationale*, present the reasons for your various decisions. Your purpose in the rationale statement will be to convince Henry and Judy that you have been unbiased, logical, and thorough in considering both sides of the issue.
3. Write an article for the school newspaper or the graduate student's association magazine at your college. Using the case as an anonymous "case study," show how students who live together might avoid the kind of problem faced by Henry and Judy.

The Lukewarm Recommendation

It's the spring of your junior year, and you're applying for a summer job as a marketing assistant with Delta Components, Inc., a major electronics company in the Midwest. Your ultimate goal is to make it to a top business school, and you feel that a summer's worth of experience with Delta will be a major step in getting there.

As a management student at State University, you've done well, and you feel that you should have an inside track on getting the job. At least you *did* feel this way until this morning, when you went over to the Student Placement Office and read a copy of the letter of recommendation that Jay Sterling, your marketing professor, had written for you. The letter concluded this way:

> To sum up, I feel that this candidate should be a better than adequate marketing assistant for you this summer.
> While not the *best* student I've ever had, this candidate is certainly not the worst, and will probably fill the job fairly well.
> I should add that this candidate seems to have more potential than performance at college would indicate.

Sterling had signed the letter, and it was sent to Delta last week. Obviously, there is no possibility of recalling it now.

JAY STERLING

The tone of the letter surprises you because you've taken two courses with Sterling in the past (Basic and Intermediate Marketing), and he's given you A's in both. His comments on your work have generally been enthusiastic, too, and he agreed readily to write you the recommendation. He even said he thought you had a great chance of getting the job.

Of course, you don't really know Sterling personally all that well. But he has degrees from a major business school; he's authored several books on marketing and market research, and, frankly, you'd counted on a good recommendation from him to help get you into a top-flight business school.

Nevertheless, you don't find Sterling too easy a person to get along with and you do know that his frankness and occasional sarcasm in the classroom turn some people off.

THE DELTA JOB

Your primary concern is to get the job at Delta. You have had other letters of reference sent to them, of course—from another professor and from a previous employer. You know that both of these letters are highly positive, and you're sure that your good grades will help. But Sterling is widely known—a big gun—and a less than enthusiastic recommendation from him could be the kiss of death at Delta.

The real shocker, of course, is that in every contact you've had with him so far, Sterling has been favorable and enthusiastic. He knows your name, calls on you in class, and nods when you pass in the hall. The thought strikes you that perhaps he got mixed up and wrote the letter with some other student in mind. But, you reflect, that is not really a possibility.

It would be easiest just to do nothing about his letter and hope for the best, but the tone of the letter has gotten under your skin. Even if it's too late to save the situation at Delta, it might be wise, you think, to have the copy withdrawn from your permanent file at Placement Services. That might save some grief next year when you will be applying to graduate school. Still, it would be interesting to know what went through Sterling's mind, if only to learn how to act differently in the future. Clearly, you conclude, you've got to do something.

STERLING'S OFFICE

You call Sterling at his office, but the department secretary tells you that he's out of town until next week, and is coming in then only to pick up his mail. So you decide to drop him a note, expressing your concern and asking for more information. However, as you begin to write, you realize you really need to be very careful. You are still enrolled in an advanced marketing seminar with Sterling, and you don't want to jeopardize your position any further with a hasty letter.

GRADES AND COMMENTS

You decide to look at the facts again before writing. Here is a summary of your grades in Sterling's courses, and a sample of his comments on your papers and exams:

Intro to Marketing	Midterm:	89	
	Paper	A	
	Final	77	
	Grade	A−	
Intermediate Marketing	Midterm:	91	
	Paper	A−	
	Final	90	
	Grade	A	
Marketing in Technological Environments	1st paper	B	
(Advanced Seminar presently enrolled in)	Midterm:	85	

Introduction to Marketing—Final Exam
  Super job on question 1, but you based question 2 on the wrong figures (good analysis, nonetheless). I'm giving you an A− in the course, despite this so-so exam, because your paper on IBM was so good.

Comment on Intermediate Marketing—Final Exam
  Good job—very perceptive look at the influence of foreign competition on the "Big 3" automakers. Next time, though, avoid the Watson book. It's been out of date for years now.

Comment on First Paper, Advanced Seminar
  Not up to your usual standards, though your analysis of Digital's *history* is very good. You really leave out the whole issue of the *home* computer market, however, and that seems critical to me. Let's talk this over *before* the follow-up paper in April.

(Note: You had tried to see Sterling to talk this paper over, but you couldn't seem to catch him.)

SUGGESTED DISCUSSION QUESTIONS

1. What is the actual problem you wish to solve?
2. Given the information in the case, what makes Sterling's comments negative?
3. What would you have expected him to say?
4. What should be your goals, in general, in dealing with Sterling?
5. What, exactly, do you want to accomplish in writing to Sterling?

SUGGESTED ASSIGNMENTS

1. Write a one- or two-page letter to Sterling asking him to reconsider the recommendation. Tell him why you feel his judgment is inaccurate, and state the judgment you feel he should have made in your case. Use evidence to back up your argument. As you write, consider your audience carefully. Remember that you are still a student in Sterling's seminar and the grade for that course is very important for your future plans.

2. You contact Sterling by phone, and he expresses surprise at your reaction to the letter. He says it's stronger than most of the letters he's written over the last few years. You don't get to say much because he has to rush off. You decide to drop him a short note explaining why you feel the letter will hurt your chances at Delta and asking him to reconsider his wording, tone, and so on.

3. You see Sterling when he comes to the office to pick up his mail, and you explain to him how you feel about the letter. He's surprised at your reaction but feels the letter is accurate and must stand as is. He is adamant on the subject.

   You decide to withdraw the copy of the letter from your file at Placement Services, but you discover that their policy is to notify the writer if a letter of recommendation is withdrawn. You feel that a form letter announcing that you're withdrawing Sterling's letter will make your relationship with him even worse and may hurt your chances of receiving a decent grade in his seminar. You decide to write to him directly and explain your reasons for withdrawing the letter from your file at Placement Services.

Bookstore Manager or Campaign Manager?

Dave Roberts, manager of Collegiate Bookstore, considered what to do about Annette Bisbee's request for a leave of absence. Annette wanted to take an eight-week unpaid leave of absence to become the manager of Lee Butler's campaign for election to the State Senate.

There was virtually no precedent to consider when making a decision about Annette's request. Dave had only had two requests for leaves of absence in Collegiate's seven years of operation. In one case a seriously ill part-time student employee had taken six weeks off to recover from pneumonia and try to catch up on his course work. In the other case a part-time employee had become pregnant. Dave had granted her request for a three-month leave because it came during the summer months when the store was much less busy and Dave routinely reduced his part-time staff anyway.

Annette, however, was a full-time employee. Moreover, the eight weeks she wanted to take off came during the worst possible time—from September 10 through November 5. During this time the store would be experiencing its fall rush, at least until late September, that is. Annette, as the stationery and gifts department manager, was responsible for having in stock all the standard supplies students bought at the beginning of a school year—everything from spiral notebooks to mechanical pencils. She was also responsible for overseeing all gift-related items—greeting cards, t-shirts, jackets, etc. During fall and spring school openings, Annette also helped oversee the work of the temporary cashiers the store hired.

COLLEGIATE BOOKSTORE

Located just across the street from central campus, Collegiate was one of three bookstores in town serving students at State University. The University-owned store was the largest. Collegiate sales were approximately 50 percent of the University store. The third store, Aram's Drugstore, did about half of Collegiate's volume.

Collegiate's staff consisted of Dave Roberts, manager and part owner, and five other full-time employees. There were supervisors in textbooks, tradebooks/special-order books, and supplies/gifts. One employee worked full-time as a cashier and one worked in receiving. The part-time or full-time/temporary staff ranged from eight to twenty-five, depending on the time of year.

Roberts wanted to keep Bisbee because she was a fine employee, but the timing of her leave was terrible as far as he was concerned. Annette pointed out that all of the merchandise for which she was responsible was on hand, but she admitted freely that fall was the most hectic time of year and she always did play an important part in overseeing the work of the temporary cashiers.

Roberts didn't care one way or the other about the upcoming State Senate race. As far as he was concerned, two good candidates were running. But he did worry over creating a precedent if he granted Annette's request. How many others would ask for time off? Then, too, he wondered whether Annette might end up leaving the store anyway, if she went to work on the campaign. Perhaps she'd get some kind of job down in the Capitol

Complex—she was a political science major at State, with just a few courses left before graduation.

On the other hand, Roberts was also aware that if he said no, Annette might just resign. She said Lee Butler had offered her the campaign manager's job as a full-time, paid position. Perhaps even if Annette knew there was no job in the Capitol Complex for her she might take the campaign manager's job just for the experience and worry about getting a new, post-election job later on.

BISBEE'S WORK

Bisbee had been with Collegiate for just over two years, first as a part-time employee, and during the last year and a half as a full-time supervisor. In June and July Bisbee had worked after hours, Roberts knew, on Butler's campaign. In August she'd worked even more hours on the campaign, and Roberts could see that she was pushing herself to the limit, yet her work at the store was still acceptable. Roberts admired her energy and her interest in politics. But he also felt that in eight weeks he could make a lot of progress toward training a replacement for Annette. It was also true, however, that during the peak four weeks of rush he would have no extra time for training.

Annette had been honest and realistic about the demands of running a political campaign. She said flatly that running the campaign would demand about sixty hours per week of her time, and she wouldn't have time to do anything else—not even come by the store and help on weekends.

VACATION

During the first week in August Annette had taken some of her vacation time to work on the campaign. She would be returning to the store for the remainder of August. However, Dave Roberts had scheduled his own vacation to begin the second week of August, and he knew Annette needed an answer as soon as she returned to work. Moreover, Dave wanted to write something about his decision regarding her request, just in case at some point he decided to write a policy statement about leaves.

DISCUSSION QUESTIONS

1. What should Dave Roberts do? Why?
2. Suppose you are Dave Roberts. What is your purpose in writing Annette?
3. Suppose you are Annette and you decide to write Dave Roberts. What could your various purposes be?
4. What is the purpose of a policy statement?

SUGGESTED ASSIGNMENTS

1. You are Dave Roberts. Write a memo to Annette. Explain your decision in such a way that she will decide to continue working full-time at the store.

2. You are Dave Roberts. Write a policy statement about leaves of absence. Make sure the policy allows for whatever action you decide to take in Annette's case.

3. You are Annette Bisbee. Write a memo to Dave Roberts in which you persuade him to give you the eight-week leave of absence. Remember that you'll have no time to even drop by the store for a chat.

The College Rock Concert

It all began when Cole Davis, Professor of Music at Southwestern University, died in an airplane crash. Alice Sontag and Miles Guest were both former students of Professor Davis. Alice, a senior and student senator at Southwestern, knew that Miles would want to hear the news, so she called him long distance. She remembered that Miles, who was her long-time friend, thought Davis was an exceptional music teacher. Miles was now leader of a pop and rock group called PEACE.

Miles and Alice talked about Davis for quite a while. Then Miles asked how things in general were going at Southwestern. Alice said fine, except the music department still didn't have the auditorium or music hall the university had promised it three years ago. There just wasn't any money to build it.

That was when Miles got the idea for the benefit rock concert. He offered to bring his group, PEACE, to the campus for a benefit concert if the university would construct the auditorium and name it Davis Music Hall.

PEACE

Considering the recent popularity PEACE had experienced, Miles's offer was impressive. After cutting two hit singles, "Next Time's Too Late" and "Before the Night Begins," PEACE had released their first album. It had sold over a million copies and acquired a golden record for the group. The second album was currently on the best-seller pop-rock chart at number five. It was sure to earn another golden record. In fact, the group had just finished a cross-country tour that was so successful that PEACE was leaving for Europe in a month.

Alice could hardly believe that PEACE would be willing to come to Southwestern for a benefit concert. She felt certain that they would be an instant sellout.

"It'll be super," Alice said. She suggested charging twenty dollars a ticket and filling the basketball field house. The house seated five thousand. After parking fees and concession profits, PEACE could probably present the university with a check for $75,000, perhaps even $100,000. If the ticket outlets, ushers, and everybody else worked for free, Alice said, surely the university could start construction of the music hall with that much of a down payment.

Miles laughed and said he would talk to Jim LaSalle, the group's agent.

THE STUDENT SENATE

Alice tentatively presented the plan for the benefit concert to the Student Senate two days later. After explaining the concert's purpose—to create funds for a Cole Davis Music Hall—she explained the offer as it had been made to her by PEACE's agent, Jim LaSalle.

"Jim LaSalle says PEACE will not play at a benefit concert for which regular admission is charged. He's worried about setting a precedent, and he says they've finished all their concerts in the States this year anyway. Moreover, some of the band members are opposed to another 'typical concert.' They just got off the road and they're tired. What PEACE *will* do is perform a free concert on the university Green. We estimate the Green can hold 15,000 people. The weather we've been having this fall would be perfect. They'll play on and off for three hours or more on a Saturday. LaSalle said PEACE could donate 100 signed copies of their latest album, *Traces*. We could auction them off. We could also pass the hat and charge for parking."

After much debate and excitement, the Student Senate voted to extend an invitation to PEACE under the conditions that LaSalle demanded. Southwestern's 20,200 students would ensure a good turnout. Though the university was located in a small town of 40,000, a nearby city of 500,000 would no doubt produce additional concert goers. PEACE was so well known, the Senators argued, that thousands would come to hear them play.

As the Student Senate planned it, the concert would raise money in a variety of ways. First, volunteers would collect a $3-per-car parking fee at all lots. There were 1,350 spaces for student commuters, 1,500 for faculty and staff, and 4,050 for resident students. Parking for the Saturday concert would not be allowed in residence hall lots, but the 3,200 spaces at the football stadium would be used. Thus a total of 6,050 spaces were available, earning $18,000+ in parking fees.

Student volunteers would also ask each concert goer to contribute at least $3 to the benefit concert. These volunteers would be strategically located at parking lot entrances and sidewalks leading to the main campus. Contributors would be handed a PEACE badge to wear. Since some people might contribute more than $3, the Senate estimated earnings of $30,000 in concert contributions.

PEACE albums would be sold on the day of the concert at the special benefit price of $10 each. The Senate hoped to sell 500 albums and make $1,000 in profit. One hundred signed albums would be auctioned off before the concert. Bidding would begin at $20 an album. The Senate estimated that total album sales would cover concert costs.

Lastly, a numer of concession stands would be set up to sell food and drink. With ten to fifteen thousand people attending the concert, it seemed reasonable for the Senate to expect the concessionaires to gross a dollar a person for food and drink. Since the concession stands would also be run by volunteers, the Senate estimated that a profit of $2,500 might be made. In total, the concert was expected to make at least a $50,000 profit, more if the crowd was larger than ten thousand.

THE ADMINISTRATION

The administration rejected the Senate plan for a number of reasons. Alberto Cordova, Dean of Students, had the responsibility of explaining the decision to the Student Senate. There were, Mr. Cordova said, numerous problems. Alan Mogul, head of the physical plant, expressed opposition because of the impact that ten thousand weekend concert goers would have on the campus. The grass, trees, and shrubs on the Green would be damaged, the trash problem would be enormous, the parking lots would be a mess, and the Senate had mentioned nothing about toilet facilities. Judith Cort, registrar, pointed out that in fact some special classes met on campus on Saturday. A concert might very well make it impossible for those students to attend class, not to mention faculty and staff not being able to find a place to park.

Police Chief Theimann of the local police department expressed concern about traffic and crowd control. He supposed, however, that these problems could be handled in much the same manner as were the football game crowds. The stadium seated 27,000 people.

President Sears personally met with the Student Senate the next day to discuss the proposed concert. The university, he said, would be glad to honor such a fine faculty member as Davis had been. Moreover, he said his vice-president for business affairs assured him that a minimum of $50,000 would be sufficient to commence construction of the long-delayed concert hall. Some funds already on hand, increased student fees, and a long-term mortgage would finance the rest.

However, President Sears added that the kind of attitude and behavior encouraged by a "free" outdoor concert, the inevitable parking conflicts, the difficulty in establishing restroom facilities and concessions, and the difficulty in collecting contributions all seemed to make an outdoor concert on the Green undesirable.

Nonetheless, the university was willing to help in the presentation of a concert in the football stadium. President Sears pointed out that the established parking, eating, drinking, seating, and restroom facilities would make holding the concert there much more practical. The university hoped the Senate would be able to adjust its plans and hold the concert at the stadium. Because of its natural turf, impressive landscaping, and tasteful Southwestern architecture, the stadium was often pointed out with pride by university officials.

ALICE

The Senators were disappointed by the university's response, but most of them admitted that a stadium concert would certainly be an easier and surer way to raise the desired amount of money. Alice was asked to call Miles Guest and persuade him and PEACE to perform in the stadium.

Miles said, "Just imagine how Professor Davis would react to the idea." He felt that a serious benefit concert couldn't be held in a football stadium. It just wasn't what PEACE wanted to do. Still, Miles could see why the university would want it that way. However, LaSalle had reminded Miles that PEACE's contract did not allow the group to accept any engagements that LaSalle did not approve.

LASALLE

Alice called LaSalle. He argued that PEACE could benefit from a free concert on campus—all that architecture, the openness, the naturalness. It went with PEACE's mellow style of music. He even said he had begun the planning of TV coverage and a live album. But a football stadium would ruin all that. The concert would not seem "free." It would seem like crass commercialism—"Fans in the bleachers eating hot dogs as the band plays on the fifty-yard line," LaSalle shouted at her. "That's no benefit concert. That's a travesty."

LaSalle added that he'd had an expert check out the Green's capacity. The expert said the Senate was underestimating its capacity. A better estimate was that they could squeeze 25,000 people in there if PEACE were placed on the steps of the Administration Building. LaSalle said that if PEACE were allowed to set up the stage and sound equipment for a live recording of the concert, they would donate five hundred PEACE albums. PEACE would also pay all expenses for security and for clean-up afterward. Nearby buildings on the central campus had restroom facilities on the first floor. Extra portable toilets could be brought in. LaSalle said, "Doesn't that city of yours realize what this concert will bring in? Ten or fifteen thousand people from out of town can spend a lot of money in one day!"

Alice hung up the phone. The Student Senate wanted her next report by the end of the week. LaSalle had said time was getting short and they had two weeks to decide. Because of her personal connection with Miles Guest, Alice was expected to make the final recommendation about how the concert should be planned. The Senate would then forward the report to the president and his administration.

SUGGESTED DISCUSSION QUESTIONS

1. What are the conflicts in this case?
2. How can they be resolved?
3. What is each group concerned about?
4. Whom does Alice need to persuade?

SUGGESTED ASSIGNMENTS

1. Assume you are a reporter for the college newspaper. You've covered the PEACE rock concert story by interviewing and attending various meetings. Write an inside account about it.
2. You are Alice Sontag. Should you try to persuade LaSalle to change his mind or should you persuade the university administration to change its mind? Make your decision and write a persuasive report to the appropriate audience.
3. Suppose the administration agrees to allow PEACE to hold the concert on the college Green, provided the student senate gets 5,000 advance "ticket" sales. As head of the Concert Committee, write an open letter for publication in the campus newspaper in which you persuade students to buy "tickets" in advance to ensure that the PEACE concert will be held.

Part II
Rhetorical Modes and Methods of Development

Part One of the text gives instruction and practice in the definition of problems and the invention of solutions, in audience analysis, in determination of purpose, and in organization. We believe that all effective writers use these skills each time they write. Part Two, on the other hand, gives instruction and practice in rhetorical modes and methods of development, a variety of techniques that writers may or may not use each time they write. Only a careful analysis of the writing situation can lead to the right decision about which rhetorical mode and what method or methods of development to use.

As you read these chapters, remember that, as in Part One, each case is placed in a particular chapter not because that is the only way the case could or should be used by instructors and students, but because certain cases seem to us to provide the best practice for each chapter's instructional material.

Chapter 5

Description and Narration

Describing and narrating are natural activities that all of us are highly experienced in doing. Imagine how many times you have described one friend to another, or told an amusing story about yourself or someone else, and you will see just how much practice you have already had in describing and narrating.

Although we all have the basic ability to describe and narrate, doing so *in writing* can be difficult. Communicating through speech can be easier than communicating in writing for at least two reasons. First, we all do much more speaking than writing. Second, when speaking, we have a "live" audience. If something we are saying is not having the desired effect, the audience shows us right away through facial expressions, body language, or tone of voice. As our audience responds to us, we have the chance to clarify, add detail, change the subject—to continually make whatever changes are necessary to communicate effectively. Moreover, our own facial expressions, body language, and tone of voice can help make the description or narration effective.

Written descriptions and narrations are, of course, much more fixed and limited. Every word is vital because once it is down on the page and the essay is completed, those words must do all the work. These differences between speaking and writing make it important for every writer of description and narration to consider certain guidelines while still depending on his or her experience as a speaker. Three basic guidelines discussed below are: selecting significant details, making the writing come alive, and structuring the description or narration.

Selecting Significant Details

One key to effective descriptions and narrations is the careful selection of the details to be included. When we are speaking, we tend to relax and describe or narrate easily and naturally. But when writing, some people try to compensate for the absence of a live audience by including in their writing every minute detail, every single action that took place. These writers try to make their writing effective by indiscriminately including much more detail than they would if they were speaking. The problem is this: especially in writing, only the *most significant* details should be included.

You can see how important (and natural) such selection is if you consider discussing a day in your own life. If you could really tell about *everything* that happened to you yesterday—every thought, action, conversation, even every heartbeat—your narration would fill volumes. But these volumes would be filled, mostly, with detail that is not really significant. Like most of us, however, if you spoke or wrote about yesterday you would automatically describe the day much more briefly. You would choose only the most significant things that happened, such as meeting a friend for lunch, taking an exam, finishing an art project, or getting an unexpected check in the mail.

Only the writer can determine what details are most significant. The writer bases that decision on what the thesis of the essay is going to be. In short, your thesis determines, in general, what details should be included. Every detail should help to show why "The car accident made me realize I'm a coward," or "The funeral made me feel what my grandmother really meant to me," or "The Kute Kitty signs show how disgusting these massage parlors are."

Making Your Descriptions and Narrations Come Alive

Once you have selected the details you want to use in a description or narration, you have to consider how to phrase them so that the reader can get the most out of what you have written. Again, some writers allow the fact that they are *writing* and not *speaking* to change the way they might otherwise describe events. Essentially, your natural speech is the best language you can use to write effective descriptions and narrations. Hardly anyone, however, goes around speaking so dramatically that he or she can simply write down those spoken words and expect them to come alive on paper. Therefore, you should use your natural speech as a starting place for lively writing, but you can enrich this writing by following the following four guidelines.

Use Concrete Details

Readers have five senses. Make your readers see, hear, touch, taste, and smell what is happening. Let them use all five senses when they read what you have written. Writers seldom forget to describe what something looks like, but they often forget the other four senses. Describe what the noise probably *sounded* like as the arsonist sloshed gasoline over the walls. Tell what the spray can *felt* like in the vandal's hand as he sprayed red paint over the signs. Describe what the arsenic would or would not have *tasted* like when the Russian wolfhounds gobbled down the meat. Tell what a room *smells* like after someone has died in it.

When you're writing your first two or three drafts, don't be afraid to write too much. Good writers *always* write too much to begin with. If the assignment calls for 500 words, good writers may write 1,000. If the assignment calls for 2,000 words, they may write 3,000. Then they go back and start weeding out the weakest prose—it's a little like thinning a row of young lettuce or pruning a young tree. Only the healthiest, sturdiest stalks or limbs—or *language*—should remain. If you end up throwing out so much weak prose that you're short on words, that's okay. The amount of description you can produce should be infinite, really, so there should always be plenty more to imagine if you allow yourself enough time to let your imagination go to work.

Use Active Verbs

Active verbs do just that—they carry action. Writers who use active verbs say:

The team won the game.	(Not: The game was won by the team.)
Someone murdered the woman in cold blood.	(Not: The woman was murdered in cold blood.)
An arsonist burned down three buildings.	(Not: Three buildings were burned down by an arsonist.)
The city of Farlee provides plenty of excitement.	(Not: The city of Farlee is exciting.)

Use Powerful Verbs

Besides using action verbs, look for the verbs that tell the reader something about the quality of the action as well as the simple fact that the action took place.

Writers who use powerful verbs say:

The car slammed into the wall.	(Not: The car hit the wall.)
The dogs greedily gobbled down the meat.	(Not: The dogs ate the meat.)

Consider the Context and Occasion

Of course it is possible to write so vividly that you end up with language that sounds so flowery, so exaggerated that it is inappropriate for the writing situation. First, remember to try reading aloud what you've written. If your prose doesn't sound conversational, it may seem unnatural to the reader. Then, too, the purpose of a particular piece of writing is also a good guide to your use of vivid details and language. If the purely objective reporting of facts is your goal, then your words should seem factual and unemotional. If, on the other hand, your goal is to make your readers so angry they'll write their U.S. Senators, then much more vivid language may be necessary.

As you select the appropriate details and consider ways to make your language lively, you must also structure your description or narration.

Structuring the Description or Narration

Structuring a description or narration means imposing some order on your paragraph or essay. Your thesis, the sharp focus, the dominant, unified impression you want to achieve, should provide you with an overall sense of structure. However, once you have decided on what that thesis, that central point, will be, how do you go about ordering a description or narration on a sentence-by-sentence or paragraph-by-paragraph basis?

Structure Descriptive Writing Spatially

A description should move in an orderly way over the scene, object, or person it describes. The structure in a description is essentially *spatial*; that is, it moves in space from top to bottom, side to side, inside to outside, far to near, and so on.

Suppose, for example, you are describing Yankee Stadium on opening day. You might start with the scene down on the field, then work upward to the stands and finally move into the upper reaches of the crowd. If you wanted to describe your new car, you might move from the front to the back or from the inside to the outside. If you are describing a murdered woman as she lies on her bed (as you might in "The Water Bed Murder Mystery" case included in this chapter), you might begin with her feet, move up to her bloody dress, and end with a hand drooping over the edge of the bed.

Which way you move depends on the point of view you take. If you are looking at Yankee Stadium from the perspective of the pitcher, you would probably begin on the field and move up into the stands. If your perspective was that of a spectator from China, on the other hand, you might begin with the surrounding crowd and then move outward and downward to the field.

Your thesis serves as a good guide when you are deciding which perspective to take and in which direction to move. For instance, your thesis could lead you to begin a description of a close friend by describing his or her unique physical features, not by routinely beginning at the top of the head and ending with the shoes. Or, if the point of description is to show that a woman was murdered without warning, without her having the faintest idea she was about to be killed, then you might begin with a description of the quietness and neatness of the room she was in and end with the look of surprise on her face. On the other hand, first describing the shotgun shells on the floor, then the pink water trickling out the door, and finally the woman's bloody body would emphasize the violence of the scene, not the point that the death was unexpected.

Whatever the writing situation, any description must have a structure. That structure will generally be one of the spatial ones we have discussed here. Always remember that the thesis or point of your essay or paragraph, not mere formulas, should guide you in choosing a perspective and a direction for your description.

Structure Narrative Writing Temporally

Choosing an effective structure for your narration is equally important. We all love a good joke or a horror movie, and half the secret of our enjoyment is in its structure: the punch line comes just at the right moment; the door to the haunted house slams shut when we least expect it; the monster leaps out when we thought everyone was safe.

Written narratives are effective the same way jokes and movies are. Timing is crucial. You can build the same effectiveness into those narrations by consciously choosing structures for them. Since stories, by nature, are a sequence of events that occur in time, they are structured temporally.

Many stories are arranged in chronological order. They begin with what happened first and end with what happened last. More sophisticated narratives may begin in the middle or at the end of the action and then go back in time to explain the sequence of events that led up to what was first described. All of us have read or heard stories that begin with a shot being fired, a battle being fought, a murder being committed, or a building burning down. Writers who begin this way are telling the audience one highly significant or most interesting part of their narrations first and using this part to "hook" the audience and get them to read the rest.

The structure you choose will vary according to the purpose of your narrative. A witness in a courtroom would probably tell about a car accident in a straightforward, chronological account. The audience—the jury—would need to know the facts in the exact order in which the witness observed them. On the other hand, a popular magazine writer telling the same story in a paragraph or essay might want to begin with the sickening crunch of metal against metal, the sound of shattering glass, or perhaps with the last-minute, desperate trip to the hospital.

Just as in descriptive writing, any narration must have a structure. That structure gives the events a sequence in time. Though you may choose to rearrange the order of some events for a particular effect, the audience should still be able to determine the basic chronology of the events by reading your narration. The purpose of your narration—to inform, to excite, to dramatize—is a good guide to choosing how the paragraph or essay should be structured.

Summary

Writers make their descriptions and narrations effective by: selecting significant details; using vivid, concrete, active language; and, generally, by structuring the descriptions spatially and the narratives temporally. Of course any writing that includes narration may very well include description. The reverse is also true. Moreover, although description and narration can both be used as pure modes of writing—that is, by themselves as ways of writing an entire essay—many writing situations call for a combination of these two modes with other rhetorical modes and methods of development. Only a careful analysis of a writing situation—the problem, the audience, and the purpose—will tell you which rhetorical modes and methods to use and how to use them effectively. Other rhetorical modes and methods of development are discussed in the chapters following this one.

The City of Farlee

Susan Norris, Personnel Director of Rayon Corporation, looked impatiently across the table at her boss, Glenn Udall, the Vice-President for Production and Operation.

Glenn was saying that the personnel department had to do a better job of informing and attracting employees to Rayon. The company was growing fast and it was hard to get the best. "I went all the way out to California to interview the kind of computer programmers, systems analysts, and engineers we want—those people out there are fed up with high taxes, polluted air, and gasoline shortages—but you know how few we lured away . . ."

"But you already told me all this," Susan said. "You took the company's literature with you, didn't you?" She held up a couple of brochures. "We're paying highly competitive salaries, the taxes are relatively low here, and it's a great place to live. What more do they want?"

"I don't know, exactly," Glenn said. "They're impressed by the salary and the talk about taxes, but the other stuff doesn't interest them much. Somehow we're just not convincing them, enough of them, to move. One engineer with five years' experience said, 'You know, it's a long way from L. A. to Farlee,' and he wasn't talking about moving expenses."

ARLENE FRANCON

When Arlene came into Susan's office, Susan gave her the company's brochure about the city of Farlee and told her to look it over and see what, if anything, she thought was wrong with it. She told Arlene that prospective employees didn't realize that the state's taxes were low and that the state always balanced the budget.

Arlene was a student majoring in sociology who had just begun working at Rayon for the summer. She'd taken the job because she thought it would be good experience and because Rayon was located in her home town. She was living with her parents and saving her money for next year's college expenses.

THE BROCHURE

When Arlene got back to her desk, she carefully read the brochure; then she wondered what to do next. In general, the brochure seemed to her to have plenty of information in it about the city of Farlee. A representative section of the brochure looked like this:

City History

The city of Farlee was incorporated in 1852, but really got its start back in 1809 when Colonel Albert M. Farlee, an army man with experience in the War of 1812, settled on four sections of land that he bought from the U.S. government. The colonel began ranching initially, then built a general store and other buildings as he sold land to those who moved into the area. The town, which he named after his grandfather, grew slowly until 1857 when the railroad went through. Today Farlee's population is 45,867.

As Arlene read the rest of the brochure, she gave up analyzing the prose and just skimmed the paragraphs. Since many paragraphs were just lists of information, she began jotting down the information they included. Her notes looked like this:

—a major city with national airlines service just 10 miles away
—a rose festival is held every fall
—3 full-service banks (assets listed)
—4 savings and loans (assets listed)
—3 local radio stations
—reception of 5 (1 public) television stations
—two miles of Interstate 99
—one airport for private and chartered air service
—20 parks, 680 acres total
—highly efficient police and fire departments
—three major shopping centers, including a modern mall
—more than adequate number of doctors, lawyers, and other professionals
—a major state university within commuting distance
—120 miles of paved streets
—public water and electric supply
—serviced by Greyhound and Transcontinental bus companies
—one of the oldest towns in the state
—30.7 inches of rain a year (average)
—32.4 inches of snow a year (average)
—average temperatures, by the month, listed
—a well-respected school system

When Arlene finished listing the information, she went back to see Susan. She told her that she agreed. There was lots of information in the brochure. Arlene wasn't sure why people didn't move to Farlee. "Farlee is such a great place to live," she said.

Susan sighed and suggested that Arlene talk to Glenn about it.

When Arlene called Glenn she asked him what it was the people wanted to know that the brochure didn't tell them. Had they asked him anything?

Glenn said, "Nothing special. They understood the positions that were open, all right—they're professionals, they know about the work they do—but they didn't seem so excited about Farlee."

"But it's such a great place to live," Arlene repeated.

"I know it, and you know it," Glenn said. "But they just didn't seem to get that idea, even after reading the brochure. It's an awfully damn dull brochure."

When Arlene hung up, she looked again at the brochure. She had to admit the information listed was dull, but what should she do?

SUGGESTED DISCUSSION QUESTIONS

1. What does the information in the case tell you about Farlee?
2. What doesn't it tell you?
3. How would you feel about moving there?
4. What should Arlene do to improve the brochure?
5. Does the brochure need more facts about Farlee? More details?

SUGGESTED ASSIGNMENTS

1. You are Arlene Francon. Write a memo to Susan in which you describe the problem with the brochure.
2. You are Arlene Francon. Write an addition to or replacement for the brochure. Within reason (don't say Farlee has the world's greatest amusement park), invent additional material that will make Farlee come alive in writing. Try to enable the reader to vividly imagine what it is like to live and work in Farlee.
3. Write a factual brochure for your own hometown. (You may want to do research.)
4. Write a description of your hometown for someone moving to it. Assume this family already has a brochure that includes the same basic facts about your town as are given for the city of Farlee.

The Water Bed Murder Mystery

Kenney Katz went out on assignment for the *City News*. His boss told him a murder had been reported at 383 New York Avenue. "Cover it," he said.

A lady had called in and reported two police cars and an ambulance on the scene. "You ought to send someone out," she said. "It's just awful."

When Kenney arrived, the ambulance was gone. One police cruiser was still there. An old woman sat weeping on the front steps.

"Excuse me, ma'am," Kenney said. "What happened here?"

"They say Richard done it, but I don't believe it," she said, not weeping now, but sounding angry and aggrieved. "Just because he wasn't at work when they called don't mean he done it. He's a good boy."

"Did what?"

"Killed her." She began weeping again. Kenney asked her who she was. She was Mrs. Weathers, Richard's mother. After spending the morning at a meeting of the Retired Persons Association, she'd come home and found the police already there.

She began weeping again. Kenney went on inside the house without knocking; the door was open.

Water was trickling down the stairs. Pink water. A policeman sat on the living room couch, taking notes. A policewoman was standing in the center of the room and saying, "That wraps it up as far as we're concerned. The detectives'll be here in ten minutes." She stopped abruptly when she saw Kenney, then said, "Who are you?"

"Kenney Katz. *City News.* What happened here?"

"It's hard to tell, exactly," the policewoman said. "There's two dead dogs out back. And there's a very dead lady upstairs."

"What's all the water?" Kenney said, looking at the stairs.

"Water bed," the policeman muttered. The policewoman said Kenney could go up and look, but she went with him and told him not to touch anything.

It was a woman about forty-five, maybe 5 feet 6, overweight, blond hair, brown dress. She'd been lying on the bed. Otherwise the room was neat and clean—it looked like a bedroom set from a department store window—but the woman and the bed were a mess.

"What tore things up like this?" Kenney asked the policewoman.

"Shotgun," she said. "We found it in the backyard. Evidently the murderer reloaded both barrels and fired them a number of times," the policewoman added. "The shells are over there on the floor." She pointed.

"Why?" Kenney asked.

"Good question," the policewoman said. "Are you ready to go back downstairs?"

Kenney went out to look at the dogs. They were Russian wolfhounds, weighing about 150 pounds each, he guessed. The dogs lay on their sides on the ground. Their bodies were frozen in grotesque positions. They were gray, scraggly, ugly dogs.

"Probably poisoned," Kenney said under his breath.

He spotted a woman looking over the wall into the yard.

"Excuse me, ma'am," he said. "Do you live around here?"

"I'm Mrs. Beel. Susan Beel. Yes, I live here. Those dogs are dead, aren't they?"

"Yes, ma'am."

"Thank God, I didn't do it but I'm glad they're dead. Better off than alive, if you want my opinion. Two huge dogs like that, chained up all the time, howling so nobody could sleep. That man, Richard I think his name was, would come out and wrestle with them, but he never once let them off the chains."

She looked at the yard and sniffed. "Or cleaned up after them, either. A few people called the city to complain, but nothing ever happened."

Kenney noticed the backyard was pretty smelly all right. He asked her whether she'd been home that day. She said she'd heard somebody hollering, and then later she'd heard a bunch of blasts coming from the house. She didn't know how many. A bunch of them. She wasn't the one who called the police. She didn't know what a gun sounded like.

Kenney checked a few other neighbors' houses to get more information for his story. At one of them he found Anita Squire. She was sixteen and had just gotten home from school. Kenney was distracted by the swimming suit she answered the door in. She explained she was on her way out back to work on her tan.

She knew a little about the Weathers's. Weathers and his wife, Harriett, lived there, she said. And the mother. It was Richard's mother. They didn't have any kids at home. They had three that were old enough to be on their own. The only one that ever came home was Robert, and that was just to cause trouble. Kenney asked what kind of trouble. Anita just said, "All kinds. I think maybe Harriett hated those dogs. She never came out in the backyard. When she left the house, she always went through the front door. She really dead?"

"Very," Kenney said. "And so are the dogs."

Kenney found one more neighbor, William Baskin, who knew a few things about what had happened.

"When I left for work this morning, I saw Weathers leaving, too. When I come home from work, I talked to my wife, who said she heard shots at three-thirty-five. She said to herself, "If that's a murder, somebody'll want to know what the time was.' Course she wasn't serious. I tell her she's watchin' too much television.

"The Weathers's were good folks, I thought, except for those dogs. Ugliest dogs I ever saw and yowlin' all the time. Bark big enough to make the house shake, it seemed like."

"Who do you think did it?" Kenney asked.

"I don't know. It's hard to believe Richard could've shot his wife or that she would've poisoned the dogs. They have a kid, son, named Robert, that's pretty wild. One night they wouldn't lend him some money to go into business for himself, so he drove their car through the garage. Nearly killed both dogs."

By now Kenney was tired. He went back to the Weathers's house to check with the detectives. Richard Weathers was being questioned and would probably be arrested shortly. He had left work on a delivery about the time of the murder. The dogs had been killed with rat poison, probably, sometime after Weathers had left for work. The shotgun belonged to Weathers, and it had lots of fingerprints on it, though they were not necessarily all his. They'd learned from Weathers that his son, Robert, was in town. According to Weathers, Robert had threatened to kill the dogs unless his father loaned him $15,000. Weathers had told Harriett they couldn't afford it and had told Robert to go to a bank if he needed money for an honest business enterprise. Harriett argued with him, saying that they could take a second mortgage on the house. Robert's business deal sounded okay, she said. Weathers had not wanted to lend his son the money.

"That's all I've got right now," Lieutenant Holt said. "We haven't picked up Robert Weathers yet, but we will as soon as we find him."

Kenney went back to the *News* and checked in with his boss. He told him it would make a great front-page story. "Bizarre Dog Poisoning and Water Bed Murder a Mystery" Kenney proposed.

His boss, David Hart, said, "You got a lot to learn. We've already gone to press. Write it up for the morning edition."

Since Kenney was inexperienced, he showed his first draft to Hart. Hart's reaction was, "How can anybody make murder so dull?" He ripped the page in half and threw it in the wastebasket.

"Don't just give me the bare facts! It's the details, the human interest, in addition to the basic facts. People want to be able to feel as if they're there. Have it ready in a couple of hours."

After Hart left, Kenney retrieved his story from the wastebasket:

Police said Mrs. Harriett Weathers was murdered today as she lay in her water bed. Police found two poisoned Russian wolfhounds behind the house. Mrs. Weathers, neighbors say, hated the dogs. Her husband, Richard, is being held for questioning. Their son, Robert, is also being sought for questioning, but police have been unable to locate him.

Two hours, Kenney thought. He sat down and looked at some notes he'd taken:
Second interview with Mrs. Rudolph Weathers (Richard's mother):

—Richard Weathers owns a television sales and service retail store in Eastgate Mall Shopping Center.
—Weathers and his wife have lived in this four-bedroom house for twenty years, since moving to the city in 1960.

—Mr. Rudolph Weathers died five years ago in a coal-mining accident in West Virginia. She moved in with her son and daughter-in-law six months later.

—Robert Weathers, her grandson, needed a loan to enter into a partnership in the construction and operation of some hamburger chain restaurant—she couldn't remember which one—McDonald's, Burger King, Hardee's, Wendy's—one of those.

—Weathers's assistant said Weathers had left the office for just fifteen minutes.

Telephone follow-up interview with Lieutenant Holt:

—Weathers's occupation confirmed.

—Robert Weathers, according to his father, never got a chance to tell him all the details because Mrs. Harriett Weathers screamed she didn't want to know about it.

—Robert Weathers's whereabouts unknown; they had some ideas about where to look.

Kenney thought back over all the time he'd spent at 383 New York Avenue and in the neighborhood. Of course he hadn't written down every little thing he'd seen. Now, he wondered, what was he supposed to do?

SUGGESTED DISCUSSION QUESTIONS

1. What kinds of details would be of interest to the reader of an article about this story?

2. In what ways can Kenney describe the situation without accusing anyone of the murder?

3. What different perspectives can Kenney take to dramatize the story?

4. In what ways could Kenney sequence the events of his story?

SUGGESTED ASSIGNMENTS

1. You are in your first college journalism course. On the first day of class your instructor gives you this case and tells you that you are Kenney Katz. Assume *City News* serves the populace of the largest metropolitan area in your state or the one nearest you. Concentrate both on selecting the key facts and on using concrete, vivid detail in a well-structured article. Assume your article will appear on the front page and continue on another page or pages. The point of the assignment, your instructor says, is not to ask you to apply journalistic principles—you haven't learned any of those yet. The purpose of the assignment is to assess your ability to select significant details, use your language effectively, and organize your material. Within reason, you can invent details you think Kenney would remember as he thought back over the day's

events. As Kenney thinks again about what the yard, the house, and the bedroom looked like, for example, you can invent details that will make the scene of the crime come alive for the reader.

2. Assume the above article is written for the Saturday morning paper. For Sunday's paper write a feature-length article to further explore the murder. Instead of breaking a front-page story, you are really digging into the case, providing a variety of perspectives, examining all possible motives, and so on.

Kute Kitty Massage Parlor

Alexis "Lex" Potter knew a good story was in the air when she heard about the first fire, so she went out to discover whether her instinct was once again to be proven trustworthy. Lex was not disappointed. On the corner of Locust and Vine, an inconspicuous spot on the edge of town, she found the Kute Kitty Massage Parlor, its windows broken out, its walls smoke-stained.

"Yes, I suspect arson," said the fire marshal, who was there when Lex arrived. That was about all he would say. At 1:47 P.M. the fire department had answered a phone call from the address. Susan Lamb, one of the women working there, had smelled smoke and then noticed the trash out back had caught fire and so had the rear wall of the building. No one was injured but the building, valued at $48,000, was a total loss.

Lex noticed two detectives from the police department poking around, investigating. They didn't have much to say either. Lex asked one of them, Detective Bronitsky, whether there might be a connection between the fire and the type of business.

"What do you mean?" he said. Lex asked whether he would feel the same way about the investigation if it had been a hardware store that caught fire. He said that massage parlors were licensed to operate by the city just as other businesses were. They also got the same treatment.

"Yes, but a *massage* parlor," Lex said. "Use your imagination. What do you suppose goes on in there?"

The detective gave her a sour look and went back to work. Lex gave up and headed for her car, but then she noticed the sign. The massage parlor's sign was lying in some weeds near her car. The sign, as Lex recalled from seeing it on her daily drive down Locust, had featured a kitten luxuriously stretched out on a velvet massage table. Now the sign was covered with a thin layer of red paint. The paint appeared to have been hastily applied with a spray can. When Lex called the fire marshal and the detectives over to look at the sign, she looked at the one detective and said, "Just like any other business?"

THE PINK PUSSYCAT

Two days later the Pink Pussycat, another massage parlor, this one just outside the city limits, also burned down. This time the fire department answered a call from an unidentified person who said he had been driving home when he noticed flames coming out of the parlor's windows. It was 2:49 A.M.

Lex was once again on the scene, as were the two detectives and the fire marshal. So was the county sheriff. It was too soon to call it arson, the fire marshal said, but arson was suspected. The police told Lex no, they didn't see any connection between the two fires. Not yet anyway. Then one of them found the sign. The Pink Pussycat's sign showed a woman loosely holding a pink towel over her otherwise naked body. The towel showed a pink cat lolling in a hot tub. The sign, sprayed over in red paint, had been broken in half and thrown into the bushes.

GAINSVILLE

Lex wondered who in Gainsville, a small city of fifty thousand located in a midwestern state, would be interested in burning down massage parlors and painting their signs red. As was true of most midwestern cities, Gainsville was thought to be fairly conservative, its population made up largely of family-oriented, religious people from a farming background.

Lex got a better idea of what might be happening the next night. Shortly after one in the morning she got a phone call. The caller said, "You Alexis Potter from the *Daily Times*? You've been investigating the massage parlor fires, right? We're burning the third one tonight. The Mellow Meow. More than massages goes on in those places and we're burning them down." The man hung up. Of course Lex knew that anonymous phone calls were far from being very trustworthy sources of information. Even so, she got dressed, called the fire department, and rushed off.

THE MELLOW MEOW

By the time Lex found the Mellow Meow, it was too late. The fire department had already put the fire out. It was the same story: a sexy sign was found covered with red paint. Suspected arson. At exactly 1:00 A.M. the fire department had received an anonymous call from a man. The fire marshall told Lex that tests had shown the other two fires were caused by arsonists. That made it pretty clear that the same would be true of this third one. The police said they didn't have any particular leads but were keeping the case open. The investigation would continue.

ARSONISTS

"Why did people set fires?" Lex asked the fire marhsal. He said one of the most obvious reasons was so the owner could collect insurance money; another reason was out of compulsion—pyromania. Of course sometimes in the big cities organized crime could be involved in setting fires to punish people, but he didn't think that was too likely in Gainsville.

Lex went home thinking about a feature story about the massage parlor fires. The police still maintained they had no evidence to show the parlors were used for anything other than massages.

SUE LAMB

The next day Lex called Sue Lamb, former masseuse at the Kute Kitty. Ms. Lamb was twenty-eight years old, had two children, ages three and eight, and had gone to school to learn her trade. She had just moved from Chicago to Gainsville four weeks ago.

Lex asked her what she would do without a job. Lamb said she was divorced, had little child support, and would have to move out of town and get another job elsewhere. It was ironic that she had lost her job, she said, because she had quit anyway. Lex asked why. At first Lamb wouldn't answer, but when Lex guaranteed her anonymity, she said there were two things about it she didn't like. Kute Kitty management allowed two teenage girls to work there—there was no law against it. Some men got ideas, Lamb said, and she wasn't at all sure a sixteen-year-old could handle men like that. Each masseuse worked in a separate room with the door closed. Lamb also said that she just plain knew that at least one woman working there was a prostitute. Lamb considered herself a professional masseuse and could not tolerate the atmosphere that a couple of the other women were creating.

Lex asked further questions, but Lamb refused to say much more. She was leaving town the next day, she'd already said too much, and it wasn't safe to say anything. Lamb did promise to suggest that one of her friends call Lex, but she refused to give Lex the name.

Surprisingly enough, later in the day Lex got a call from Lamb's friend. All Sherry would say was that she had not worked at Kute Kitty but a different parlor, that yes, teenagers worked there—and came there too, by God—and maybe a couple of women were prostitutes and maybe they weren't. After that, Sherry hung up abruptly.

Lex sighed, picked up the phone book, and started calling people. She managed to find five people who had worked in one of the parlors, but each person refused to make any comment whatsoever. Of course there was much, much more to be learned, but a story, the first story at least, had to be written now.

SUGGESTED DISCUSSION QUESTIONS

1. How could the arsonists be explained in this case?
2. What do you think the spray paint on the signs indicates?
3. What kind of article should Lex write up about the fires?
4. What facts does Lex have?
5. What details should Lex use?
6. What events should Lex describe? In what order?

SUGGESTED WRITING ASSIGNMENTS

Today is your first day of class in Journalism 101. Your instructor gives you this case and suggests one or more of the following assignments. Of course you don't know all the special tricks of the journalism trade. The purpose of the assignment is to assess your ability, at this point in time, to write vivid descriptions and clear narrations.

1. Write a short report in which you tell the basic facts about the three fires.
2. Write an enlarged story in which you report the facts while suggesting possible explanations.
3. Write a feature article about the fires. You may want to tell the story from the point of view of a potential arsonist, from your own point of view, or from the point of view, say, of someone who worked at one of the massage parlors and is now out of a job.

Howard Blues

As Editorial Assistant at Printall Publishers, Inc., part of Sheryl Gordon's job is to prepare press releases, statements, and promotional announcements for forthcoming books. The company has just astonished the publishing world by acquiring the rights to the *Autobiography of Howard Blues,* the story of a reclusive, eccentric millionaire. The book is coauthored by Alva White, the famous journalist, and is sure to be a blockbuster.

Sheryl Gordon's boss has just called her in to tell her that the company plans a spectacular press briefing the day after tomorrow to announce the acquisition, let the press ask White questions, and generally get people excited about the book. Part of the preparations include an information packet with brief biographies of White and Blues, a synopsis of the book, sample chapters, juicy tidbits, and so forth. "That's where you come in," says Sheryl's boss.

"We need a one-page biography of Blues—something the reporters can read in five minutes before they talk to White. It'll give them a chance to ask intelligent questions."

This doesn't bother Sheryl; she knows she can check back issues of newspapers and magazines and get just what she wants.

"Wait a minute," says her boss. "We've already got all the information. This is White's summary of Blues's life." He hands her a single sheet of paper. "But we don't want to use it as is. It sounds too crazy and disjointed. Take it and fix it up. Break it up into sections somehow . . . Give it some shape. You know what I mean."

Sheryl doesn't know exactly, but she takes the sheet anyhow.

OUTLINE OF THE LIFE OF HOWARD BLUES

© 1980 BY ALVA WHITE

1899:	Blues born to tenant farmers, Hudson, South Dakota.
1918:	returns from WWI an ace pilot; attends MIT, but leaves before graduation.
1920s:	instant millionaire as head of Blues Manufacturing Co., nation's largest oil-drilling supplier; invents and patents most effective drill bit ever devised—still in use 50 years later.
1930s:	invests in various airlines (TWA, PAN-AM), founds Blues Airline Co.; becomes the major force in U.S. aviation, according to *Wall St. Journal;* ends 2nd marriage, runs off with Rhonda Lavarona, the "it" girl of Hollywood.
1938:	warns U.S. government of threat in Europe; gears up Blues Industries for war; renews fortune twice over selling arms.
1940:	despite preoccupation with war, makes first venture into movies; buys Universal Studios, writes, directs, and (according to legend) acts in wildly successful westerns and detective stories. Pals around with Bogart, Orson Welles, John Wayne, other Hollywood biggies.
1941–45:	guides Blues Industries through WWII; receives Medal of Honor for contributions to war effort; sells Universal; moves in with actress Farah Russell. Marries her one month and divorces her the next.
1950s:	starts to buy up Las Vegas; last public appearance, with Frank Sinatra, in Vegas, 1958; invents and flies world's first full-size paper airplane; when U.S. government refuses to accept patent, Blues sells it to government of Paraguay for $5 million.
1960s:	Blues "empire" in full bloom; Blues interests own half of Las Vegas, controlling stock in 15 major U.S. corporations; Blues reported to be secret financier of Nixon's 1968 primary campaign; turns down offer to become ambassador to Mexico; lives in entire top floor of his own Desert Inn Hotel; last interview granted to Mike Wallace; Blues complains of chest pains, thinks aliens are out to get him.
1970s:	Blues a complete recluse; front men from Blues Industries are the only ones who see him; tries to buy Costa Rica; sells interests in airlines just before recession of '74—makes huge profit; regularly reported dead after move to Bahamas in '71; reportedly eats only natural foods, wears gloves to bed; calls Nixon right after resignation—but no report of conversation.

| 1980: | dies while airborne from Bahamas to Boston—reportedly on way to Massachusetts General Hospital for emergency heart surgery; last words: "I left it in my other suit"; body immediately cremated; reports persist that it was actually a Blues aide who was incinerated, that Blues is still alive in South America, being cloned. |

SUGGESTED DISCUSSION QUESTIONS

1. How would you describe Blues's life?
2. How could you summarize Blues's life?
3. Based on the brief outline given here, what conclusions can you make about Blues?
4. What would a single day in Blues's life have been like?
5. What kinds of details will readers be interested in?

SUGGESTED ASSIGNMENTS

1. You are Sheryl Gordon. Write a one-page biography for the reporters.
2. Rather than writing a brief biography about Blues's entire life, choose one incident mentioned in White's outline and tell a story about that incident. The story should represent some point you want to make about Blues's life in general. Assume this story will be released to the press and public as a sample of what they can look forward to in the book.
3. Suppose you are the book reviewer for the school newspaper and you have just read the Howard Blues book. Make the review simply an account of the life of Howard Blues in which you draw whatever conclusions seem to be appropriate.

Pie in the Face

As a sophomore, one of your big hopes for the year is to make it onto the school paper, the *University Register.* The paper is one of *the* big activities on campus. Even though you're not exactly sure what you want to do after college, you know that some experience of the kind the *Register* can offer could definitely give your career a big boost.

THE TRYOUT

Last night, you and about twenty other sophomores and freshmen (it seemed like about a hundred others, you thought) attended a meeting at the *Register*'s offices in the Student Union Building. You liked the way the offices looked—just like a newspaper office in an old movie, with hanging globe lights, lots of dust, and old gray metal desks. You also liked the busy-ness of the office; people were working to get the paper out even as the tryout was being discussed. You're aware that the *Register* is known to be one of the country's best collegiate newspapers, and you felt that this kind of professionalism must have something to do with the paper's success.

During the meeting, *Register* Editor-in-Chief Brad Thomas explained that the policy was to let any student try out for the paper. After the tryout, three people would be accepted provisionally, and probably two of those would actually make it onto the paper.

The "audition," Thomas said, was to be the same for everybody. Everyone was assigned to cover a speech the following night, he explained. Warner DeMarest from Consolidated Oil and Chemical was going to be on campus recruiting. He was scheduled to give a speech on business and the government's economic policy that night in Carey Hall. Applicants to the *Register* were expected to be there, take notes, and come here afterward to write their stories.

"What angle do you want us to cover?" asked the woman next to you. "I mean, there are a lot of ways to handle a story like that."

Thomas told the group to just go there and keep their eyes and ears open. The would-be reporters would get their "angle" when they got back to the *Register*'s offices. There was opposition to CO&C on campus, so the question-and-answer session—in fact, the whole meeting—was expected to be pretty lively.

THE MEETING

You arrived at Carey Hall at the last minute since you had to finish a couple of things for classes tomorrow. You had a hunch this was going to be a long night, so you wanted to clear the decks early.

Carey Hall was packed, but you managed to squeeze into a crowd of students at the rear. You noticed quite a few university police in the hall and remembered that DeMarest's visit had sparked a lot of protest from a cou-ple of campus groups—especially Clean Air/Clean Water and the Student Energy Coalition. In fact, the building in which DeMarest had been doing his recruiting had been picketed all day.

Consolidated Oil and Chemical, it seems, had a poor environmental re-cord in years past and was now seen by some as one of the big oil inter-ests, profiting at the expense of the little people. At least this was what you'd heard. The company obviously had its own side of the story; De-Marest would tell it tonight.

Promptly at 7:30, the dean of students got up to open the meeting. After a few remarks about the university's tradition of academic freedom and open expression of opinions, he introduced DeMarest. The reaction of the crowd, you noted, was fairly favorable, but with a noticeable mixture of hissing and booing.

DeMarest was a tall, lean man in his early fifties. You really couldn't see his face well from the back of the hall, but you did notice that he had salt-and-pepper hair, wore glasses, and was dressed conservatively. He stood up at the podium and began to speak, opening with a couple of witty remarks about the university (where, it turned out, he himself had been educated). He went on, good-naturedly referring to the demonstrations that had attended his recruiting efforts and echoing the dean's remarks about freedom of expression. Then he launched into his speech. He began by describing CO&C and its record and then turned to his industry's role in the national economy. As he got into his speech, you began to take notes.

But just then, you felt a stir in the crowd. You looked up from your notebook and saw several university police starting for the stage. You glanced at the stage in time to see a youngish man in jeans and a sweater running up behind DeMarest, who was absorbed in what he was saying. The man was holding something in his hand.

As the crowd grasped, the man came up behind DeMarest, reached around him, and thrust a big, white, fluffy pie squarely into the businessman's face. At that point, the meeting went crazy. The stage was immediately so full of police, officials, and spectators that you couldn't see what was going on. But from the noise and the sounds of struggling coming through the still-open mike, you knew that something wild was happening, and a few people up front were shouting.

THE AFTERMATH

As a would-be reporter, you felt embarrassed that you hadn't been in a position to see more. As you watched, the crowd on the stage thinned out, and both DeMarest and the pieman were gone. The dean came back to the podium. He apologized for the scene, said that DeMarest had agreed to come back and finish his speech "at a later date," and declared the meeting over.

People still were milling around the hall, just as you were. Everybody seemed a little stunned, and few really had a clear idea of what had happened. You decided that you had to get a story out of this somehow, despite your bad luck in being at the back of the hall. Almost everybody involved in the tryout, you reasoned, was probably already at the *Register*'s office right now, trying to scoop everybody else. Even so, perhaps if you looked into the incident in a little more depth, you'd be able to get something really good out of it. So you headed to the front of the hall and tried to find people who had really seen the incident. By good luck, you did find a few. Here are the notes you took.

1. *Mike Smith, university police*
   Says it's a "disgrace." Done by "some creep" probably from the energy coalition. Says DeMarest's suit was ruined—pie contained shaving cream, will stain the wool. Also D's glasses broken. Mike says this is exactly what the university is *not* supposed to be. "I took this job because I thought this was a place where people would act like thinking adults. If I'd wanted this kind of crap, I could've stayed with the city P.D."

2. *Susan James, junior, elementary education*
   Says she was sitting right in front row. The guy wasn't a student. She heard that Clean Air/Clean Water had *hired* a pie-thrower to come and "hit" DeMarest. She heard that CA/CW was going to take credit for the "hit" in a press release—"just like the IRA, I guess." Also says she saw D's glasses broken. But thinks she saw DeMarest slug the pieman, too. Doesn't know what to think. "After all, Consolidated is supposed to be a pretty piggy company, isn't it?" Said later—"Maybe this is one way of speaking for the people. I'm not sure."

3. *Bill Boston, senior, political science*
   Member of Clean Air/Clean Water. Said they didn't hire the pieman, but knows that he was a hired "hit" man. Feels this kind of thing is a risk DeMarest ought to be prepared to take. His company, Banks says, is "ripping people off, screwing up the environment—he deserves it. And he doesn't deserve the chance to get up in front of all of us. Consolidated's *actions* say all they need to say." Admits that DeMarest doesn't seem like a bad guy. But D. is the only symbol of his company, says Banks, just as the pie was a symbol of "the way we'll try to get back at that kind of company in the long run." "DeMarest got back at the pieman, too," added Banks. "Punched him right out—I saw it. So he's not exactly the innocent victim here, either."

4. *Sara Bett, assistant provost*
   Says this is "terrible—a violation of academic freedom." Believes that a university is useless without a free exchange of ideas—that events like this are threats to the whole institution, "to our whole way of life." Says she's not a big supporter of the oil companies, doesn't know much about Consolidated, but feels this is not the way to change things.

   At the *Register,* Thomas says that given the unexpected events, no particular "angle" is required.

SUGGESTED DISCUSSION QUESTIONS

1. How can you go about describing the general scene at Carey Hall?

2. How can you describe DeMarest and the pieman?

3. What facts do you have? What assumptions do you want to make?

4. Does DeMarest have the right to speak on campus without fear of attack?

5. What would readers most want to know about the incident?

6. What kinds of vivid detail can you use?

SUGGESTED ASSIGNMENTS

1. Write an objective narration/description of the meeting and its aftermath. Be sure you stick to the facts; label assumptions clearly so your reader will not be misled.

2. Write a "think piece" about the conflicting ideas that surfaced after the meeting. Briefly and factually describe the points of view you heard expressed. Remember, this is reporting; stick to the facts and clearly label opinions.

3. Write an editorial about what happened. Speaking for yourself, describe your own reaction and be sure to reply to points of view expressed in your notes that may be opposed to yours.

Northwoods Oil and Exploration

The first couple of weeks on the job were fairly uneventful for Kathy Fisher, but then came an assignment to a project already behind schedule.

"Tracy Pappas quit just last week," Dan Wentworth explained to Kathy, "and there's no time to do research on Bethel. The information has just got to be worked up into acceptable form. Our Vice-President for personnel wanted all this yesterday."

Bethel, Alaska, Dan went on to explain, was the site of a new area office for Northwoods Oil and Exploration. Because of Bethel's unattractive environment, the company was concerned about attracting the best present and new employees to work there. A major new oil contract in the area increased the importance of the Bethel office every week.

Dan explained that the company wanted to be sure all employees knew what they were getting into when they were assigned to any new location. Dan said the recruits might come from any of Northwood's ten regional offices in the United States or, for that matter, straight from any major college campus. Northwoods planned on hiring a full complement of staff members for the Bethel office—everything from secretaries and maintenance personnel to engineers and management teams.

Given this explanation from Dan, Kathy went back to her office to review the information that Tracy Pappas had gathered about Bethel. The information had evidently come directly from Bethel itself, perhaps from some sort of unofficial chamber of commerce.

1980 BETHEL INFORMATION

Bethel is located 420 miles west of Anchorage and 80 miles from the Bering Sea. It is 400 miles south of the Arctic Circle. Summer has frequent periods of wind and rain; lightweight jackets are worn most of the time. Seven months of the year the temperature averages below freezing—the coldest months to −30°F. With the addition of wind velocity, the chill factor can go as low as −70°F. There are nineteen inches of precipitation annually. Total snowfall during the winter months averages from 40 to 50 inches. Down parkas or fur parkas are essential winter wear.

Housing in the area is generally poor. Many do not have water lines or sewage. "Honey buckets" are used for human wastes with city disposal service. The running water system and sewer system is operational in two residential areas of the city. Most people have electricity. Housing in Bethel is of frame construction, and is small and has lower ceilings than are customary. The available housing includes furnished and unfurnished apartments, trailers, cabins, greezer-vans. Some sample prices:

1 bedroom apartment, no sewer/water is $175–300/mo.
1 bedroom furnished (BNC Apts.) is $410–525/mo.
1–2 bedroom house rental is $450–650/mo. (no sewer/water).

Electrical rates start out at $0.133 per kilowatt hour. Telephone service is supplied by General Telephone: monthly rate for a private line is $13.00.

There are no paved roads in or out of Bethel. The normal means of transportation is by air. Wien Air Alaska operates jet aircraft twice daily to/from Anchorage. The round-trip fare is $171.74, but group fares may reduce this fare to as little as $99.95 round trip.

There are only fourteen miles of road in Bethel. The downtown portion is mostly sand and dirt. One paved road runs from the main section of town to the airport. Bethel registers one vehicle per eleven residents. Taxicabs are abundant and the general fare is $1.50, but this is not for exclusive use, as the taxi may make two to six stops for other passengers before you reach your destination. Many people coming to Bethel may bring cars. If you bring a car it would be good to bring snowtires and a block heater or battery heater. The heaters are essential, as the engines will not start on cold mornings unless the oil has been warmed. The wear caused by weather, mud, dust, and sand often requires extra maintenance to keep vehicles operational. Cars can be used in the wintertime to drive on the frozen river to the nearby villages. However, cars are not a necessity. Many people rely on footpower most of the year. Walking is not rough if you are adequately clothed and booted. Many residents use bikes in the summer and snowmachines in the winter.

The three largest general stores handle groceries, hardware, clothing, and miscellaneous items. Prices in Bethel are the highest in the state. Many people order caselot food orders from Seattle, which come in the summer by barge. Some sample food prices:

Butter	2.99	½ gal. fresh milk	3.59
10 lb. flour	5.50	10 lb. sugar	4.49
Apples/lb.	1.19	Lettuce/lb.	.95
Hamburger/lb.	2.65	Bread, sandwich loaf	2.79
6-pack Coke	3.59	Family-size Tide	9.79

There is a Consortium Library run by the City of Bethel and the Kuskokwim Community College. The Bureau of Indian Affairs Agency also houses a good library. There are two elementary schools (enrollment 700) and one regional high school (enrollment 500). The First National Bank of Anchorage, Bethel Branch, offers all banking services.

Bethel has three main restaurants. Price of meals varies between eight and fourteen dollars for a dinner meal. The Kuskokwim Inn also has a sixty-nine-room hotel. Room prices are thirty to forty-six dollars for a single room. Also available locally is a pet shop, ice cream parlor/pool hall, bakery, laundromat, marina, lumber company, barber, and hairdresser. A veterinarian makes regular visits from Anchorage.

Bethel has a general hospital with forty-two beds. Its daily medical/dental Outpatient Clinic handles about twenty-nine thousand visits each year. Bethel is a second-class city with a Council/Mayor/City Manager form of government. There is no property tax. City sales tax is 2 percent. The Fire Department has one paid fireman and twenty volunteers.

The local radio and television station is affiliated with the Public Broadcasting System. The TV station also has access to satellite programming and televises National Network programs.

Job opportunities are abundant in Bethel. The usual maintenance, clerical, janitorial, and secretarial opportunities of any small town are available. There are nursing positions available at the Public Health Center, PHS Hospital, and Yukon-Kuskokwim Health Corporation. Accountants and professionals are needed in many of the federally funded programs.

The only big-game animals in the area are moose and caribou. They are found 100 miles upriver and hunting them requires an air-charter or river trip. Duck and goose are within easy boating or snowmachine distance of Bethel. A hunting license is necessary, and for a first-year resident the price is high. Local fishing is done with nets. Charter flights provide access to the rainbow, dolly varden, grayling, and pike fishing areas, where rod and reels can be used. Since these are clear-water streams, sport fishing is excellent. In Bethel you are allowed to "subsistence fish," which means that you can catch as many fish as you want for your personal food supply.

Social life in bush areas is largely what you make it. There are no entertaining establishments like those you would find in a large city. The people are friendly and outgoing, and there are many spontaneous get-togethers. Summer months are times for riverboat excursions and picnics.

Christmas is a time of snowmachine trips for a tree. Entertaining is usually informal and casual and often centers around outdoor activity. In summer, fishing is popular; in winter there are dogsled and snowmachine races, ice fishing, and cross-country skiing. The mosquitoes are abundant during the summer months under the best conditions. During moist summers their numbers and attacks are increased tenfold. This is no exaggeration. Believe it and bring plenty of bug repellant.

The slow seasons of the year for outdoor recreation are during river freeze-ups and break-ups, since travel on the tundra is impossible and most of the rivers and airstrips are unusable. The town experiences a carnival-type atmosphere during the time of break-up of the frozen river sometime after the middle of May. It is the official declaration that spring has arrived.

Suggested reading would be *Napaskiak,* by Wendall Oswalt, available by mail from the Moravian bookstore in Bethel. This book was written in the late fifties about a nearby Eskimo village and will give you an insight into the Eskimo environment. Another book of interest is *On the Edge of Nowhere* by Jimmy Huntington.

DISCUSSION QUESTIONS

1. What kind of information do people in the company need?

2. What are some of the weaknesses in the present information?

3. What are some details that could be added?

4. How could these details be organized?

SUGGESTED ASSIGNMENTS

1. You are Kathy Fisher. Dan has told you, "Write an informational brochure using the information you've got, for now. Don't worry about artwork or layout—once we get the text, we'll send this over to art and design and let them worry about that."

2. You are Kathy Fisher. Write the informational brochure described in assignment 1. Then write a memo to Dan explaining the essence of what you've done.

3. You are Kathy Fisher. When you go to lunch, you get into a conversation with Ken Denkels from the Vice-President's office, personnel. Ken seems to think that while the V-P is anxious to see the Bethel brochure (he's fuming about the delay, Ken says), Ken is sure the V-P would also be willing to consider improvements or changes in a future draft. Write a letter to Dan in which you argue whether you need any new information about Bethel in order to write a better brochure. If you need new information, specify exactly what it is you'd like to know and how you expect to find out.

Chapter 6

Methods of Development

Methods of development are ways of expanding and shaping your material as you invent and organize it (see Chapter 4). You develop the material by using different techniques for telling, describing, explaining, or persuading. The most commonly used methods of development involve writing about how a generalization can be illustrated (example); how something is done (process analysis); how people, objects, or ideas can be divided or categorized (division and classification); what a word or phrase means (definition); how two things are similar and/or different (comparison and contrast); and how some things make other things happen (cause and effect). These methods of development—example, process analysis, classification, definition, comparison and contrast, cause and effect—can actually be used in any writing mode, but they are described at this point in the book because they are usually taught to and used by student writers in connection with exposition and persuasion.

For the sake of clarity, each of these methods is discussed separately, as if each one could be the focus of a group of paragraphs or an entire essay. But most of the time your writing will include some combination of these methods. Therefore, the chapter explains the methods one by one and then concludes with a set of fifteen cases. In each of these cases, you must decide which methods of development would be most appropriate to use. In some situations your choices will be obvious; in others, the choices will not be. Finally, remember this: while you are choosing methods of development, you must also decide upon your purpose. If your purpose is to persuade, you may want to read Chapter 8 before completing your writing assignment.

EXAMPLE

One of the best ways for a writer to clarify and/or develop a main idea is to use an example. Sometimes it's easier to do a good job of giving examples when speaking rather than when writing. Imagine this conversation:

> "You know what gets me is how popular soap operas are becoming; they're taking over television to the point where that's all people watch."
> [The speaker delivers main idea.]
> "Yeah, I know. I know a guy who schedules his classes so that he never has to miss *General Hospital*."
> [The listener interprets the main idea.]
> "No. What I mean is that soaps are dominating programming. Look at all the soap operas on nighttime TV now."
> [The speaker clarifies the main idea.]
> "There aren't any soap operas on at night."
> [The listener simply disagrees and is unconvinced.]
> "Yes there are. Just think about it. *Dallas, Dynasty, Falcon Crest, Knots Landing*—the list goes on and on. All of them are soap operas."
> [These examples support and illustrate the speaker's main idea.]

Giving examples of what you mean when you make a point, then, is one of the best and easiest ways to develop your main idea. Of course your examples should be well chosen—they should truly illustrate what you mean. Using more than one example is important, too. It's a way of broadening the support for your main idea. A single example might seem to the reader to be a unique circumstance rather than your single, obvious proof of your general point or idea. To sum up: use examples that vividly support your main idea, and use more than one. By the way, *Emerald Point* and *For Love And Honor* are soap operas, too, depending on how one divides, classifies, and defines television programs. To learn about these three methods of development—division, classification, and definition—read on.

PROCESS ANALYSIS

Most of us don't stop to *analyze* a simple process such as changing a tire or making an omelette. We simply *do* them and get by very well. Even when you're dealing with basic processes like these, however, you'll find that an analysis of the process is essential to a clear explanation of it.

In addition, with most processes, especially complicated ones like tuning up an engine or programming a computer, a careful analysis will help you to perform the process more efficiently and effectively. When coaches run and rerun football films, for example, they are analyzing the *process* of each play. Their purposes are the same ones we've been discussing: to explain to their players what went wrong (and right) with the play and to improve performance.

At bottom, a process is simply a series of steps, actions, or events that lead to some specific results. The process of baking a cake results in something to eat while the process of transplanting a kidney results in a patient becoming healthier. Of course, technically complex processes like those in the sciences may be difficult to describe. The steps in these processes may be chemical changes, combinations of forces, and so on, and their results—changes in atomic structure, for example—may be less easy to pin down.

Writers may have one of two different purposes in completing a written process analysis. Writers may explain a process so the audience can do it—collect coins, construct a garage, write a paragraph. Or, writers may describe a process so the audience can *understand* how the process works—how political caucuses choose delegates, how Pepsi is bottled, how satellites are used to beam radio and television signals around the world. Regardless of the purpose, the first task the writer faces is to analyze the basic elements of the process, the steps, actions, or events that lead to a specific product, condition, or end state.

Divide the Process into Steps

The difficulty in explaining any process lies in identifying and sequencing what you consider the "steps" in the process to be. Imagine, for example, trying to write a description of the steps in the process of executing a perfect somersaulting dive from a 10-meter board. The dive appears to be one long, smooth tumble into the water, but experienced divers would tell you that the dive is actually a series of several specific actions or bodily movements. If you had to explain the dive to somebody else, or *teach* it, you would have to be aware of each of these steps and be able to describe them.

For most of us, of course, explaining a 10-meter dive is beyond reach. But let's look at a simpler process—changing a tire—for an illustration of how to divide a process into steps, and why such careful division, or analysis, of a process is important.

Step 1—Most of us find, by trial and error, that Step 1 is *not* jacking up the car. Instead, you remove the hubcap and loosen the lug nuts that hold the wheel on. You do this before jacking up the car because you need the weight of the car to hold the wheel in place and give you enough leverage to loosen the nuts.

This explanation of Step 1 raises two issues. First, it's important to get steps in the right order. It's also important to explain why one step comes before the other, especially in an example like this one in which many people would begin with the wrong step. Recipe books, the examples of process analysis most of us are familiar with, don't always give you the "why" behind each step. But your readers will be seeking understanding as well as "how-to," so you should explain the logic behind your steps when it is not already obvious.

Second, Step 1 shows that your process needs to be divided into *manageable* steps. We lumped taking off the hubcap and loosening the nuts into one step because neither action is very complex and both contribute to your preparation for jacking up the car. We could have made the removal of each nut a separate step, but that would have made the analysis unnecessarily repetitious and boring as well.

Step 2—Jack up the car. Here jacking up the car is a manageable step—that is, it forms a self-contained, clearly defined part of the tire-changing process. Realizing that not everyone knows how to use a bumper jack, and that some people are afraid of them, you might break this step down into substeps to make your explanation as precise and clear as possible. Your substeps might be:

Set up the jack.

Position it carefully and follow the instructions that came with the car.

Use the handle to jack the car up until the flat tire is 3 to 4 inches off the ground (you would explain that the 3 to 4 inches is necessary to allow the bigger, fully inflated spare to clear the ground).

Your judgment will tell you which possible steps can be lumped into one (loosening lug nuts) and which must be spelled out as substeps, like the jacking process or the 10-meter dive. But devote some thought to these divisions before you begin writing; dividing the process into these *manageable* steps is the key to a clear explanation.

With the points we made in steps 1 and 2 in mind, the rest of the process may be described more briefly:

Step 3—Remove the nuts and take the flat off the wheel.

Step 4—Place the spare on the wheel and hand-tighten the nuts. (Again, explain that leverage will make it easier to tighten the nuts fully when the car is on the ground, so you are only hand-tightening them here.)

Step 5—Lower the car to the ground.
Step 6—Tighten the nuts and replace the hubcap.

Once again, you should review the manageable steps you have devised and make sure they are arranged in an order that will seem logical to the reader. You can also check to make sure you have warned the reader about particularly important steps, such as not jacking the car up before loosening the nuts.

Introduce and Conclude the Process

The six steps above are the actual steps in the process, but a full explanation would also contain an *introduction*, a paragraph in which you would state the process being described, list any required tools, materials, and so on, and state the importance or significance of the process—tell why it is important. An effective process analysis essay should also include a *conclusion* indicating that all the steps in the process that have been explained and describing the finished product. The conclusion helps the reader because, like any other conclusion, it signals *closure* and because its view of the finished product helps the reader to check on the results.

Obviously, it's easier to describe simple processes you can actually carry out yourself than more abstract or complex processes like historical, economic, or scientific processes. But the basics of describing the process—the introduction, steps, and conclusion—remain the same. With more complex processes, of course, your introduction is even more important because you will be setting the stage with more complicated and difficult materials (the "ingredients" necessary to a nuclear explosion, for example). And your choice of steps will be all the more crucial since you will not be able to assume much understanding or ability to "fill in" on your reader's part.

Summary

Describing how to analyze a process is a process analysis in itself; here are the *crucial* steps in analyzing a process:

Step 1—*Introduction*
State what process you'll be describing, why it's important or significant (if this is not obvious to your reader), and what materials, tools,

and so forth the reader will need to complete it. If your process is more abstract, not something the reader can actually do, describe the materials, conditions, background, and such that lead up to the process, and were (or are) necessary for it.

Step 2—*Describe the Steps in the Process*

Make each step manageable—clearly defined, important enough to stand alone, but not so big the reader can't take it in at once. Be sure you have arranged the essay so that it describes the steps in the most logical, easiest-to-follow order. Explain the logic behind the order of your steps if it is not obvious to your reader.

Step 3—*Conclusion*

Let the reader know the process is concluded, that you've completed the final step. Describe the finished product or end state in which the process results (e.g., a recipe might produce a cake, a surgical procedure some specific improvement in the patient's health). Restate the importance or significance of the process.

DIVISION AND CLASSIFICATION

Division and classification are two closely related methods of development. "Division" means simply that—separating something into its parts. College administrators often divide college students into groups based on undergraduate or graduate status, year in school, sex, major, minor, place of residence (in-state or out-of-state; on-campus or off-campus; U.S. or foreign). These are all simple methods of dividing a whole into its parts.

Classification, on the other hand, involves identifying a genus or group to which something belongs based on its characteristics. Suppose, for example, that you have decided that *Knots Landing, Dallas, Dynasty,* and *Falcon Crest* are all soap operas, but you are equally certain that *Hill Street Blues* is not. How do you prove your point? First, you determine what characterizes soap operas—an on-going plot; a series of dramatic situations; a large cast of actors and actresses; entanglements involving love, sex, power, and wealth; and so on. Second, once your list of characteristics is complete, you test your classification. Do *Knots Landing* and the others test out as 100 percent soap operas? Does *Hill Street Blues* not match up? How? These are the questions you must answer whenever you classify.

Because classification will probably be more useful to you as a method of extended development than division would be, the rest of this section is devoted to a discussion of how to organize and develop classifications. Still, you may want to use the principle of division as a way to organize your own arguments in your introductory paragraph or as a way to begin analyzing a problem.

Developing a Classification

Like many patterns of thinking, classification is fairly simple when you're dealing with concrete objects that have clearly defined characteristics. You know that a mammal, for example, has certain specific characteristics you can use to test with. Classification is a much more demanding activity, however, when you're dealing with ideas, controversies, or people. For instance, it may be easy enough to describe the characteristics of a political liberal as you see them, and to fit one example (Edward Kennedy) into the class while excluding another (Ronald Reagan). However, convincing others, who may view the characteristics of a liberal differently, that Kennedy really is a liberal may be difficult. It certainly will be more difficult fitting your friends, relatives, and others whom you know well into any such abstract scheme. Most of us get only a stylized view of a public figure like Kennedy or Reagan. But we see *all* sides of those around us.

A paragraph or essay of classification, unless you're dealing with only the simplest, most obvious classes and examples, may also need to be an essay of persuasion. Your writing explains your view of the class and your reasons for assigning a certain example to the class. Since others are not necessarily going to share your views, your essay must *defend* these views just as you would defend any other kind of assertion.

When you classify, you should defend your assertion by anticipating and overcoming your reader's possible objections to your view of the class itself (i.e., your description of its identifying features or characteristics) and to your explanation of how the example you're discussing fits into the class. Let's begin with ways you can defend your view of the characteristics of the class from objections by others who view those characteristics differently. There are two common ways of defending the characteristics you have chosen to describe the class.

Include All Important Characteristics

First, be sure, as you describe the characteristics of the class, that you have not omitted any characteristics that other people would consider obvious (e.g., cold-bloodedness in a reptile). Of course, you may have *pur-*

posefully omitted a characteristic others would consider obvious on the grounds that it is not truly characteristic of the class. If so, be sure to show plainly *why* that characteristic is not relevant. For example, if you omit the characteristic "female" from the class of "nurses," you must make it clear that your view of the "nurses" has nothing to do with sex, that sex is a characteristic that has been added to the class "nurses" by a social system, not by logic.

Explain the Validity of All Characteristics

Similarly, if you *include* a characteristic that others will not find self-explanatory, be sure to explain its validity. For example, in describing the class of "adults," you might wish to include "over eighteen" as one of the characteristics. This characteristic could draw objections from those who believe that twenty-one is the age at which one becomes an adult. You could defend your assertion by discussion of the eighteen-year-old vote, the government's acceptance of eighteen-year-olds into the military, and so on, to show that eighteen, not twenty-one, marks the real beginning of adulthood. Remember, though, that you must defend your assertion in some way, and not *assume* that others would accept the age of eighteen as one of the characteristics of adulthood.

Your discussion of your example (the person, object, idea, and so on, that you want to fit into the class in question) has to be persuasive too. Here are two common ways of defending the way you have fit the example into the class you are discussing (i.e., the way you have matched the characteristics of the example with those you have already outlined for the class).

Apply the Characteristics Consistently

Once you have determined which characteristics are relevant, never alter the application of them. If you decide to classify students according to whether they are married, engaged, "going" with someone, or "dating around," then consider only those characteristics and no others. Don't get started and then decide, after classifying many students, that in some instances you also want to consider whether students are gay or straight. If you are classifying beds strictly according to size—twin, double, queen, king, and nonstandard sizes—then considerations of a bed's structure—

foam, box spring and mattress, flotation—are out unless you want to create a subclass.

Show That Potential Objections Are Invalid

You can anticipate objections to the fit between your example and the characteristics you have outlined. First, show that such objections are based on a misconception of the class and therefore do not really exclude the example from the class. Your younger brother or sister, for example, might not believe that the whale is a mammal, since whales live in the sea and look like fish. To convince him or her, you should show that, regardless of the whale's appearance or habitat (characteristic though they are of the class of "fish"), it meets the *true* test of the mammal class in such ways as breathing through lungs and bearing live young.

You can also defend the fit between your example and the characteristics of the class by showing that objections that might be raised are not *typical* of the way the example fits into the class. Obviously, this kind of defense will work primarily with people, ideas, and abstractions rather than with simple, concrete objects. Let's return to the idea of "adulthood" for example. Imagine that you and your friends are discussing adulthood, and you are trying to show that an eighteen-year-old can be an adult by using yourself at that age as an example. Imagine that one of the adult characteristics you've outlined is a sense of responsibility. Your friends might object that you're not responsible since you came in late six nights in a row, or dented the car once or twice over the last two years or more. You could anticipate these objections by admitting that not every single thing you do is "responsible," but that the general pattern of your actions *is* so. This defense is especially useful when discussing political or intellectual positions since few people, no matter how devoted to an ideology or philosophy, are ever totally consistent in their actions.

Summary

When you write about classification, ask yourself the following questions:

What Are the Characteristics of This Class?
Anticipate objections. Don't omit obvious characteristics without explaining why they are irrelevant or invalid. Don't add characteristics that are not obviously relevant without explaining their relevance for the reader.

How Does This Example Fit the Characteristics of the Class?
Anticipate objections; show that they do not really exclude the example from the class or that they are not typical of the way the example fits into the class generally.

DEFINITION

It's difficult to imagine how important it is to define words clearly and concisely. But if you recall how many times you've asked a friend or teacher, "What's that?" or "What do you mean?" you'll begin to see the need for clearly defined words.

The Logical Definition

There are many ways of defining objects, ideas, emotions, and so on, but most of these ways boil down to what is called a *logical definition*—a simple two-stage process. To create a logical definition, first you classify and then you differentiate.

First, *classify* the thing being defined. Tell what class or group of objects the thing being defined belongs to. For example, you could classify "orange" by saying that an orange is a *fruit*, but your classification would not be as precise as possible. Specifically, an orange is a *citrus fruit*.

Second, state the *differentia*, the characteristics that make the object or idea *different* from others in its class. An orange, for example, is different from other citrus fruits because it is orange in color, round, generally sweet, and very juicy. The importance of the differentia is that they exclude things that are similar to what you are defining (things in the same class), but not *exactly* like what you are defining (i.e., a grapefruit, rather than an orange).

It's easy to see how to make a logical definition when you consider physical objects such as a particular airplane, the Boeing 747, for example.

Classification: A jet aircraft
Differentia: Large bulbous nose, carries between two hundred and five hundred people, made by Boeing, pilots located on separate level from most passengers, bulge in nose where first-class passengers' lounge is located.

Usually there are many differentia. Your goal is to choose the most significant ones, that is, characteristics that most clearly differentiate the

747 from other jet aircraft. If you depend upon number of passengers carried to differentiate the 747, for example, then you won't be clearly excluding the DC-10, which in some instances carries more passengers than does the 747. On the other hand, a distinctive feature of the 747 is its large nose—the bulge in the fuselage that is due to the pilots' being located on a separate level along with the first-class lounge, an exclusive feature.

Remember, too, that your differentia should not exclude any 747s. If one of your differentia is "passenger aircraft," your definition would be too narrow because it would exclude any 747s that carry only freight.

The Extended Definition

The logical definition gives you a shape, or formula, to use in defining words. However, in situations in which you have to define abstract, controversial, or loaded words such as *liberal, conservative, radical,* and *fanatic,* the logical definition will not be enough. In cases like these, your definition needs a *defense,* as well as simple clarity. To define words that stand for complicated or controversial ideas effectively, you need an *extended definition.*

Many student writers are surprised when they are assigned a two- or three-page paper on definition, and it's easy to see why they might be. To most of us a "definition" is a short blurb in the dictionary, a logical definition fleshed out with examples of the way the word is used. It's true that dictionaries are structured this way, but their purpose is to give you *all* the current meanings of the word, not to explain one specific meaning of importance or to demonstrate which meaning of the word is more useful or appropriate than the others.

The writer's purpose in giving an extended definition of one word is usually different. The writer wants to take one difficult word standing, for example, for an idea, concept, political or economic issue, and define it—*as he or she sees it.* The writer of an extended definition has two goals: to define the object or the idea in question thoroughly, in much more detail than the dictionary would, and to *argue* that this view of the object or the idea is more nearly correct than any others the reader may know of.

This kind of definition is obviously more complex than the kind we find in the dictionary. Writers who define an object or idea in this way are usually grappling with significant and difficult questions, questions difficult for themselves, and sometimes for the world in general.

Perhaps you can see the value of an extended definition when you compare the dictionary definitions for words like *anger, fear,* or *love* to the reality you've felt and seen in your own life. Or compare even the finest dictionary's definitions of concepts like *nazism* or *laissez-faire* economics with your own knowledge and with extended definitions of those terms in history and economics texts.

The Development of an Extended Definition

A good deal of the writing you'll do over the next few years at college, and later on in your career, will involve definition. Some of this writing will involve extended definition—your view of what an idea, concept, or philosophy *really* is. Some students object, and rightly so, that a 500-word theme defining *racism* is a mere exercise, not something they'll be called upon to produce in real life. True. But definitions of such important words will be vital *parts* of almost all your speech and writing—from the proverbial letter to the editor, to reports for your boss, to explanations of the technicalities of your profession to others—whether customers, patients, or the general public.

Given the importance of the definition process, then, and the frequency with which you'll be defining difficult, controversial, or abstract words, let's look at an example of how an extended definition can be put together. This model has three basic steps.

1. Formulate a logical definition.
2. Show why your definition is better than other common definitions of the same word.
3. Support and develop your definition with evidence.

You should always begin with a logical definition. Your defense of your definition can be developed in many other ways, but the order given above is a simple and effective one to start with.

Let's put this model to use with a word that's familiar to all of us yet abstract and difficult to pin down: *professional*, or *professionalism*. Your first step is to look in the dictionary, where you'll find a professional defined as a "person" (classification) who: (1) takes money in return for the performance of a skilled job; (2) belongs to one of the recognized professions—a doctor or lawyer, for example; and (3) displays a dedication, loyalty, and skill in his or her job that puts him or her above others in the field. (Note that numbers 1, 2, and 3 are differentia).

Given this dictionary definition, consider what *you* think about the word. Perhaps you think the dictionary's third characteristic probably comes closest to the true meaning of *professional*, although it may not include other ideas—say, love of one's work, or joy in it—that you feel are important. Use what you can of the dictionary's differentia to form your own logical definition, adding your own ideas to reflect what *professional* really means to you.

Formulate Your Own Definition

To formulate your own definition, you may use examples. In this instance, perhaps you would think of a variety of people who seem to be professionals. Muhammed Ali; your high school English teacher, Ms. Katherine Smith; the best mechanic in town, Gilbert Jones. You may also have looked in the dictionary to find *synonyms* (dedicated, hard-working, expert, specialist, etc.) or thought of other, similar words on your own. All this groundwork, then, could lead to the following logical definition (which could be one of the first sentences in your extended definition):

> A professional is a
> *person* who   (Classification)
> displays skill and dedication to his or her work that places him
> or her well above average.
> In addition, a professional displays loyalty to that   (Differentia)
> work and a love of it that all can see.

Naturally, each writer's definition of *professional* could be different; your job as a writer is to capture *your* idea of what a professional is as accurately as you can. You exclude anything that does not match your idea and include everything that does.

Dismiss Alternate Definitions

Your next step is to show why your definition is more exact than any of the others your audience may know of, that it states the nature of professionalism more precisely. The dictionary is a good indicator of what different meanings are current. But be sure you consider *other* meanings your audience may be aware of in the case of a controversial or emotionally loaded word.

Show that each of the definitions you wish to dismiss is either too broad or too narrow to apply to all professionals as you define them. Explain how alternative definitions do not include enough of the characteristics of the professional to distinguish him or her from other people (too broad). Also explain how still other definitions include characteristics that enable you to identify only some professionals (too narrow). For example, you can easily show that the idea of professionals as graduates of "professional schools" (doctors, lawyers, and so on) is too narrow, since it excludes not only all sports professionals but also characteristics like dedication and skill. Similarly, the idea that a professional is simply someone who gets paid is too broad. Not all professional ballplayers, for example, exhibit the characteristics we've identified as "professional" in the logical definition above—yet all get paid for what they do.

The writer's goal is to convince the reader that the definition really is a useful way of considering the word in question and to show that *other* commonly accepted or important definitions do not come as close to the true meaning of the word. To do this, show that these other definitions are either too *broad* (they don't discriminate finely enough between similar things) or too *narrow* (they discriminate too finely, and exclude valid examples of the thing you're defining).

Support Your Own Definition with Evidence

We have discussed above how to show what a professional is *not* by dismissing alternate definitions. Now, return to the subject of what a professional actually *is*. First, restate your own definition and then develop and support it with evidence in one or more of the following ways:

Examples. If the idea you're defining is, like *professional,* one that is embodied by certain people, use those people as examples. For a definition of *professional,* sports figures abound. Discussing figures such as Ali, Mickey Mantle, Wilt Chamberlain, or John Havlicek could give you lots of support for your definition and lots of ammunition to use against definitions that seem too broad or too narrow. Examples from fiction, TV, or movies are often useful too.

Once you have dismissed competing definitions, try to use positive examples (Ali is a true professional, rather than so-and-so who is *un*professional) to support your definition. Obviously, it's to your advantage to tell your reader what a professional really *is*. If an idea is particularly hard to define, you can sometimes clarify it with negative examples, each one narrowing the field of possibilities by showing what the object, idea, or thing in question is *not*. A neutron, for example, is not an electron or proton; a fugue is not a sonata or concerto.

Etymology. Most dictionaries give the source (Latin, Greek, other) of the word you're investigating, and this "ancestry" of the word is called its etymology. Such information may help by showing another side of the word, or confirming that it has always been used in a certain way. *Profession,* for example, comes from the Latin *professio,* meaning to confess or declare. You can use this etymology to support your view that the professional displays his or her dedication publicly, or that he or she is deeply committed to a profession in some spiritual sense. Note that etymologies offer good support for your definition but are probably less effective than examples and other information about the way the word is used *now*.

Analogies. If you find a definition, particularly of an abstract quality, difficult to pin down, try an analogy. An analogy is a comparison of two things that are usually thought of as being quite different. In our culture, two favorite sources of analogies are animals and sports. Imagine, for example, how many times you've heard *loyalty* described in terms of a lioness and her cubs, or *fidelity* in terms of the family dog. Similarly, *strategy* is often described in terms of a "game plan"; *success* in terms of a "touchdown" or a "home run," etc. For our definition of *professional*, we might take the analogy of the sheepdog, whose tireless loyalty and great skill make him one of the most "professional" of animals.

Synonyms and Antonyms. Another way to define a difficult or abstract word is to use synonyms or antonyms. The former are words that are similar in meaning to the word in question; the latter are words that mean the exact opposite of your word. Synonyms and antonyms are especially useful in distinguishing shades of meaning. For instance, if you're having trouble defining *anger*, you might point out that it lies somewhere between "rage" and "annoyance." Similarly, *fear* is a stronger emotion than "uneasiness" but less strong than "terror."

It might be difficult to find a single synonym for *professional*, given the definition we've worked on above. But you can find antonyms ranging from *amateur* to *dilettante*. Discussion of these antonyms and why people with these qualities are not professionals can help you to get closer to a coherent definition of *professional* and can lend support to your definition when you've formulated it.

Summary

A logical definition is the heart of an extended definition. To formulate a logical definition, look in the dictionary, or at examples from your own life, reading, sports, and so on. Also, look at what the idea or object in question is *not*. State your logical definition so that it includes all examples of what you think the idea, object, or quality in question really is (all the professionals in the world, for example, or all the 747s). At the same time, make sure your definition *excludes* examples that really do not fit your view (amateur, dilettante, expert, specialist), without inadvertently excluding any that really *do* fit. In other words, formulate a logical definition that will include all the world's professionals, not leave any of them out, and not include any nonprofessionals.

After you've stated your logical definition, show why other definitions are either too narrow or too broad to fit the object or idea as you see it. Check the dictionary to find all the possible meanings that may occur to your audience. Then, as you dismiss possible definitions, be sure to cover every one.

Finally, support your definition with examples, etymology, analogies, synonyms, and antonyms. Use as much of this kind of evidence as seems appropriate to illustrate what your definition really means, and how it applies more precisely to the idea, object, etc., in question than other possible definitions.

COMPARISON AND CONTRAST

Comparison and contrast are really two aspects of the same process. When you compare, you take two objects, people, ideas, or whatever, and discuss their *similarities.* When you contrast, you discuss the *differences* between two objects, people, ideas, or whatever.

Comparison/contrast, like the other processes we've been discussing in this book, is not really difficult to use. We all do it every day, in fact, as you'll realize when you recall how many times you've compared teachers, sports figures, or friends. However, to use comparison/contrast effectively, you need to consider when a discussion of similarities or differences would be most appropriate. Also, you have to pay special attention to *organization* when you are comparing or contrasting, so you will be able to state your thesis without confusing your reader.

Comparison or Contrast?

The answer to this question depends on the answer to another: what is the point of the paragraph or essay? Many times, people use comparison/contrast simply to inform and explain. For example, a news reporter might be assigned a piece on two presidential contenders, a piece designed to inform the reader without taking a stand. The reporter might conclude that the candidates have certain similarities (stand on civil rights, attitude toward communism), and certain differences (attitude toward "big" government, stand on inflation). The article would use both comparison and contrast, since the reporter would want to show both sides of the topic.

On the other hand, the reporter might decide to write a column demonstrating that, in reality, there is really very little difference between the candidates. In this instance, he or she would use comparison heavily, and would treat contrast very briefly, if at all. The point, or thesis, of the article would be something like this: "It is true that candidates X and Y differ on the issue of tax reform, but their attitudes toward inflation and government spending are so similar that they really don't offer the voter much choice."

Of course, the reporter might go the other way and decide to write the column on the differences between the candidates. The article would emphasize *contrasts* and minimize comparisons. The thesis of such a discussion would be something like this: "In their attitudes toward economics, X and Y share one similarity, but their different attitudes toward disarmament and foreign policy show that X is the better choice."

What Is the Thesis?

Clearly, then, you would use comparison primarily if you wanted to discuss similarities and use contrast primarily for differences. But our example suggests another point too. Outside of informative pieces, in which you might want to bring out all the differences and similarities between two objects, you'll use comparison/contrast most frequently in support of an *argument*. In other words, you won't just be comparing your own college with another one, or one artist with another; you'll be using the comparison to make a persuasive statement. Generally, this statement will be more than the merely informative thesis many beginning students use to set up a comparison/contrast essay. The informative thesis usually looks like this:

"Candidates X and Y share certain similarities and certain dissimilarities." This statement is true no matter what X and Y stand for; therefore, it really doesn't say much. A better thesis might be that the similarities and differences between the two candidates add up to something significant or interesting:

Candidates X and Y share certain similarities, but the differences between them indicate that X would make a much better president.

Or:

Candidates X and Y are dissimilar in several ways, but both would be highly capable of guiding our nation's economy.

The point is that, in all but the most routine kind of writing, comparison/contrast is a form of argument. Don't be content with simply saying that two people or two things are different and similar. Before writing, decide what those differences and similarities *mean,* and use the comparison/contrast to illustrate that meaning.

Organization

The difficulty with organizing a discussion of comparison/contrast is the number of variables. You have two things to compare and contrast, for example, and you also have all the similarities and differences between them. Let's say that your preliminary sketch for a paper comparing state and private colleges looks like this:

Tentative Thesis: "While the quality of education is reasonably good in both types of schools, the quality of life at private schools is superior."

State School
Education: Large faculty, good library, federally aided, lots of internships and enrichment available.
Quality of Life: Huge student population, large apartment-house style dorms, located miles from the city, big football team, sports school, lots of big, wealthy fraternities.

Private School
Education: Small but versatile faculty—highly respected, good library, small student body makes faculty easy to reach, federal aid and internship programs within everybody's reach.
Quality of Life: Small number of students, small, ivy-covered dorms with suites and kitchenettes, located just outside major city (public transit), football, but mostly individual sports like singles rowing, cross-country skiing, a few clubs, but no fraternities.

You've obviously got some information, but how can you organize it effectively? The information under "education" is mainly made up of similarities, while the "quality of life" information is mainly dissimilar. You have a couple of choices. First, do you want to give comparison *and* contrast equal weight, or should one receive more emphasis than the other? Second, do you want to deal with each school in turn, or with all the similarities first, then all the differences (or vice versa)?

Here are two possible organizations out of many you could use. We'll say right away that the second of these is preferable. Study them and see if you agree.

Organization I
Thesis _____
State Schools
Education

_____
_____
_____
_____
_____

Quality of Life
_____
_____
_____
_____

Private Schools
Education _____

_____
_____

Organization II
Thesis _____
Education
State _____

_____
_____

Private _____
_____

Quality of Life
State _____
_____

Private _____
_____

If you decided that the second organization is preferable, you probably noticed that it gathers together and emphasizes the *meanings* of comparison and contrast rather than the things being compared and contrasted. That is, the major headings of the argument are "education" and "quality of life," and not the types of schools. If you look back to the thesis, you'll notice that Organization II contains an argument—that the discussion should be structured to support. Organization I is really structured to support a different thesis—the general one, which says that X and Y are different, but similar. The repetition in Organization I would tend to produce a very balanced essay, not one that stressed the *differences* the thesis demands.

Summary

As a general rule of thumb, try to structure comparison/contrast essays to avoid too much switching back and forth between the two things being compared, and between the differences and similarities. In most cases, gathering *all* the similarities together in one part of the essay, and all the differences in another, is economical and effective. If your essay is one of comparison, discuss the *differences* first, briefly, to get them over with. If your essay is one of contrast, get the similarities over with first, in a brief paragraph or two. Use a *balance* of comparison and contrast only if your essay is explanatory or does not have an argument about the meaning of the differences and similarities in your discussion.

Finally, to guide you in structuring your discussion of comparison and contrast, here is a summary list of the organizations we've been discussing:

(1) If your argument stresses the comparison between objects, people, or other:

    a. Thesis: X and Y are different in some respects, but the similarities are the most significant.

    b. Differences (a brief paragraph or two).

    c. Similarities (a paragraph or so *on each*).

(2) If your argument stresses contrast:

    a. Thesis: X and Y are sometimes similar, but the differences between them are significant.

    b. Similarities (a brief paragraph or two).

    c. Differences (one difference per paragraph).

(3) If your discussion is intended simply to demonstrate that there are similarities and differences:

    a. Thesis: X and Y are similar in some ways, different in others.

    b. X—things similar to Y
        things that differ
      Y—things similar to X
        things that differ

CAUSE AND EFFECT

The process of examining causes, effects, and the logical links between the two can seem very simple. For instance, when you watch a silent film in which a slapstick comedian takes a pratfall after slipping on a banana peel, you probably imagine the cause-and-effect relationship this way:

          Cause   *Effect*
      Banana Peel   ⟶   Pratfall

But translating this situation into real-life terms might lead you to form a more complex idea of the cause in this case, and the effects. You might ask, for example, who put the banana peel there, or why the person who slipped on it didn't see it in time. For effects, you might discover that the pratfall itself led to a bruised or broken limb. Outside the theater, your view of the cause-and-effect relationship involved might look like this:

Cause(s)		*Effect(s)*
Banana Peel	————	Pratfall; Broken Arm
Person Who Dropped It	————	
Victim's Inattention	————	
Lack of Street Cleaning	————	

And this complication, in fact, can be extended even further.

For example, if you were a lawyer and the victim had asked you to prepare a case suing the city for negligence in allowing the banana peel to remain on the sidewalk, your chain of reasoning might look like this:

Cause(s)

City's lack of → No money in → No streetsweeper → Banana Peel →
emphasis on   streetcleaning   on duty
public safety   budget

Effect(s)

Pratfall ——————→   Broken Arm ———→ Doctor Bills
                                      ———→ Lost Time from
                                            Work

Note that this example doesn't even consider the person who dropped the peel. Also, the chain itself could be extended by several links in either direction—back to discover the causes of the causes above, or forward to discover the effects of the effects we've mentioned.

Obviously, causation is complex, difficult to pin down, and often controversial. There is no way to avoid the difficulties inherent in isolating the real cause of a phenomenon such as inflation, for example—especially when you consider that, according to some philosophers, there is no *one* cause for anything. You can, however, overcome as much of the difficulty as possible by keeping the following steps in mind as you prepare and write your own discussions of cause-and-effect relationships.

(1) Base your discussions of cause and effect on *logic* and *solid evidence*, so that even if people disagree, they will respect your argument and listen to it.

(2) *Order* your discussions clearly, so cause is not mixed with effect and can't be confused with it; choose an order that is easy to grasp and interesting to your reader.

To help you use these steps in your own writing, the rest of this chapter will explain them more fully.

Use Logic and Solid Evidence

To be sure that your discussion of a cause-and-effect relationship is as strong and convincing as possible, answer the following questions before writing:

Have You Isolated the Most Significant Effect or Effects?
Sometimes an effect is obvious—when your car's engine is tuned up, for example, it runs more efficiently. At other times, as with our banana peel example earlier, a cause may have multiple effects, and the most obvious may not be the most important. A doctor, for example, might notice an accident victim's broken leg *first* but would consider internal bleeding a far more serious effect of the accident.

When you examine effects, try to find as many as possible and rank them in the order of their significance. You may not want to write about all of them or even more than one. However, if you examine and order all effects carefully, you won't discover later on that you omitted a crucial one. Mention all the significant effects in your discussion, and explain why you chose one as the *most* significant.

Have You Examined All Reasonable Causes and Isolated the Most Significant One(s)?
We started with effects because they are often more obvious than causes, but be sure to examine causes as thoroughly as you do effects. Listing all the reasonable causes for the effects you are considering will help you to avoid falling into the common trap of mistaking *symptoms* for causes. A doctor would prescribe a painkiller to eliminate the pain of a broken arm, but a doctor would not consider the treatment over when the shot was given. The painkiller would numb the nerve endings in a broken arm—it would eliminate symptoms—but it would do nothing to heal the broken bone. The most significant cause of the patient's pain is the break itself; the effect cannot be wholly eliminated until the break is

repaired. An easy way to choose the most significant cause of the effect you're interested in is to strip away the causes one at a time, and see if the effect remains. Here's a simple example:

Causes	Effect
1. Got good night's sleep	
2. Wore lucky sweater	Got A on test
3. Studied hard all week	
4. Felt relaxed at exam	

You might believe that all of these "causes" had something to do with your A, but chances are that you would have done well on the test even if causes 1, 2, and 4 were absent. If cause 3 were absent, however, you probably would not have received the A.

Obviously, you don't need elaborate logic to explain this cause-and-effect relationship. But if your assignment was a discussion of the causes of World War II, you'd have to consider possible causes very carefully indeed. Test causes for significance by removing them; if you remove a cause and the effect disappears, that cause is highly significant in creating the effect. One caution: the cause you identify and select may not be the *one and only* cause. It takes oxygen *and* a spark to create fire.

Is the Relationship Between the Cause and the Effect Real or Assumed? If you've tested the causes for significance, as we discussed above, you've answered this question. But the question is worth stressing here because your assumptions can often get in the way of sound, logical analysis of cause and effect. Untested assumptions can lead to statements like these—familiar to all of us:

"After Bittendorf took over, the team started to win. He's the cause of the improvement."

"After (some racial or ethnic group) started to move in, the neighborhood began to decline."

"Since I started using X-12 mouthwash, my career has skyrocketed."

Each of these statements is based on a fallacy, an error in logic. Logicians call this particular fallacy *post hoc ergo propter hoc:* "After this, therefore on account of this." Simply put, each statement assumes that events that occur after other events are caused by the preceding events. Sometimes such statements contain a grain of truth, as in the first example above. But in every case, such an assumption opens you to the risk of ignoring far more significant causes. Test statements like these by eliminating the cause in question, and ask which of the remaining causes might have produced the effect.

Use a Clear, Appealing Order

As we've seen, causation can be a very complicated issue and is potentially confusing. Your job, as you write about cause and effect, will be much easier if you use an order of ideas that will be easy to follow. In addition, you'll find it easier to make your point if the way you order your ideas is keyed to the reader's interests.

Order Your Ideas Clearly

Use an outline and arrange your ideas logically so that you move from cause to effect or from effect to cause. You may choose to move either way, as long as you do not shift between causes and effects and then back again. Deal with *all* causes and *all* effects first; then move to all effects or all causes. A simple discussion of *one* cause and *one* effect may look like this:

1. Introduction
2. Cause
3. Effect
4. Conclusion

Or, paragraphs 2 and 3 might be reversed. A more complex paper might look like this:

1. Introduction
2. Cause I
3. Cause II
4. Cause III
5. Effect I
6. Effect II
7. Conclusion

Just as above, the paragraphs on effects could come before those on causes.

Use Transitions Carefully

Be sure to use transitions to link causes ("*Another* cause of inflation is said to be . . .") with other causes and to link effects ("The second effect of Hitler's rise to power was . . .") with effects. In your transitions, as in those above, remind the reader of the cause-and-effect relationship by repeating the *effect* of the causes you're considering ("inflation") or the *cause* of the effects ("Hitler's rise to power"). Consider transitions as signposts to clarify the complexities of causation for your reader.

Use the Most Convenient, Appealing Order

Remember that your paper or discussion should argue for your own particular view of a cause-and-effect relationship. Therefore, don't feel that you have to write a narrative and begin at the beginning. A TV news reporter, for example, could begin a story of a devastating fire with pictures of that fire—a gripping, tragic scene that grabs the viewer. Only after the reporter was sure of your attention would he or she move on to the *causes* of the tragedy.

Similarly, a discussion of the causes of inflation might be easier for the reader to grasp and would certainly be more compelling if it began with a comparison between prices for bread and milk in 1968 (28¢ a loaf, 55¢ a half gallon), and today's prices. The real substance of your paper might be a discussion of the money supply, bank credit, or interest rates. But the *effect* (inflation itself) is the most appealing point for your reader.

Our point here is to show that you have a choice. Move from effect to cause if doing so enables you to dramatize or excite when you need to. On the other hand, move from cause to effect in a discussion where, for example, your audience expects clinical accuracy instead of excitement. Whichever choice you make, be sure that you move consistently in *one* direction and do not jump confusingly from effect to cause and back again.

Summary

To sum up, make your discussions of causation as effective as possible by:
1. Weighing *all* effects and isolating the significant ones,
2. Discovering all reasonable causes and finding the most significant ones,
3. Testing all assumptions,
4. Ordering your ideas with care and moving in one direction only,
5. Using transitions carefully, and by
6. Keeping the reader in mind.

Making Adobes

When Cindy Chou got back from her summer vacation, she reported to her boss, Doug Fowler, editor of the *Living* section of a small weekly newspaper that was published in a suburb of Los Angeles. She wanted to get her next assignment from Doug and catch up on what had been going on since she left.

"Not much's happened," he said. "What did you do on your vacation?"

Cindy told him a little bit about it and added, "Would you believe I watched a bunch of men make mud pies—adobes they call them. I even made some myself."

"That's it," Doug said.

"What's it?"

"That's your next assignment. What a great idea! 'Making adobes' or 'Adobe Making' or how to make them, or something. A lot of people around here might even want to do it, and even just as a human interest piece it'll be good. Let me see it when you get done."

Cindy started to say, "Wait a minute . . ." but Doug said, "Gotta run," and left her standing there with her mouth slightly open.

The trouble was, Cindy thought, I wasn't paying all that much attention to exactly what they were doing. I thought I was on my vacation, not on an assignment. She went back to her desk, sat there, and tried to remember everything.

THE VACATION

Her flight had gone smoothly, the plane landing in the dazzling sun-white heat of the Albuquerque International Airport. Maria, her longtime friend whose family had moved to New Mexico from L.A., had driven her out to the Garcias' house in one of the family's pickups.

The Garcias' house was located on fourteen acres of land on the edge of Belen, a small town near Albuquerque. When they arrived, Maria told Cindy that everyone except her mother would be down at the field making adobes.

Cindy said, "What's an adobe?" and Maria laughed and said, "It's New Mexican concrete; it's a mud brick, cured in the sun."

After they put Cindy's suitcase in the house and Cindy said hello to Mrs. Garcia, Maria took Cindy down to see the operation, saying, "You can see how much they've done already today. The darker-colored ones are today's adobes—they're still wet."

Cindy saw the adobes, lying on the ground in groups of four, each adobe about a foot long and a foot wide and maybe five inches deep. No, that wasn't the measurement exactly, she learned. Maria's brother, Marcus, told her they were 10″ by 14″ by 4½″, and some people, he said, made them half-width so they were 5″ by 14″ by 4½″. But almost nobody did that anymore. When you laid adobes in the wall, Marcus said, most people put them in lengthwise so the wall was 10″ thick, or some people even made a double wall. But Cindy had learned all of that later.

She was looking at the adobes lying on the ground in neat rows, some of them tipped up on edge so they looked like tombstones, when Maria started pointing out how they already had a few hundred stacked on edge in rows of three.

Cindy said, "How come they're all tipped up on edge like that?" and Maria explained that the adobes had to dry for two or three days. After the first day the adobes were turned on edge so the center would dry faster. Then, after a couple more days, they were stacked on edge so they would dry inside—it took at least two weeks, three if you wanted to be sure they were ready to go into a wall.

At that point Marcus yelled, "Hey, Cindy, how're you?" Then Mr. Garcia and Maria's older brother, Albert, saw her and said, "Hi," before they went back to work. Albert and Marcus were shoveling dirt out of the back of a pickup truck and into a trough while Mr. Garcia walked around the trough spreading the dirt out with a hoe.

That was all Cindy saw just then because Mrs. Garcia rang the lunch bell, and they all went in to eat. Over lunch Cindy asked them why the adobes didn't just melt when it rained, and Mr. Garcia said they kept them covered with tarps until they were ready to lay them in the wall. Then the walls were plastered to protect the adobes.

Albert explained that some people added asphalt to the mix to make the adobes pretty much waterproof, but since the Garcias were going to plaster the walls, the asphalt wasn't necessary. Besides, it was expensive and required more work.

After lunch Cindy and Maria went to work with Marcus, Albert, and Mr. Garcia. Mr. Garcia stuck his hoe in the trough, mixed the mud slightly, and pulled the hoe out.

"When the mud slides off the hoe cleanly like that," he said pointing, "it's ready."

Marcus and Albert loaded the wheelbarrows with the mud and brought it over to Mr. Garcia in one row and to Cindy and Maria in the other. Maria showed Cindy how to pull the mud out of the barrow as Albert tipped it down on top of the frame. Then they started pushing the mud down into the frame as Albert went back for another load.

Maria said, "Be sure to push the stuff down into all four spaces evenly (the frame made four adobes) so the adobes will be the same size. And be sure to pack it into the corners firmly."

Cindy thought it was just like making mud pies. After she and Maria had smoothed the tops of the four adobes off evenly, Maria let her lift the frame off, telling her to be sure to pull it straight up. The frame was made of one-inch pine, and the insides were lined with galvanized steel to make the adobes slip off easily, which they did. While Albert was finishing filling the wheelbarrow with another load, Maria and Cindy rinsed the frame in a fifty-gallon drum filled with water.

"It makes the adobes slip out of the frame more easily," Maria explained.

After the next batch, Maria told Albert the mud was really perfect. She told Cindy, "If the mud is too watery, the adobes run together, and you have one big sloshy adobe you can't use. If it's too dry, then they break up when they dry."

After a while Cindy got so lost in the work that she was surprised when Maria said, "That's it." Marcus and Albert had to go get a new load of dirt. Meanwhile, Maria and Cindy counted the adobes they had made, wrote the number on the top of the last one, and washed up the forms. At the same time, Mr. Garcia was spraying water into the two troughs and wiping the sweat off his forehead. Cindy heard him mutter, "I still say this is a crazy way for a dentist to spend his vacation."

When Marcus and Albert got back, each of them began filling one of the troughs. Mr. Garcia told Cindy and Maria they could be the ones to make sure the dirt was spread evenly. When the dirt was spread about three or four inches deep, Mr. Garcia turned on the hose and began spraying it while everyone else rested. He sprayed until little puddles of water formed all over the dirt, and said, "This way we don't have to mix it much. Mixing's terrible work. That mud is unbelievably heavy."

They continued the fill-and-spray process until the troughs were full. That took a long time because each trough was about 4' by 8' by 3'. Then, after letting the mud sit for a few minutes, Cindy and Maria took their turns at the heavy work of shoveling the mud into the wheelbarrow and wheeling it over to the frames.

Cindy thought shoveling the mud was the worst part—it sucked at her shovel and nearly pulled it out of her hands.

She said, "What's the trick to shoveling this stuff?"

Marcus and Albert laughed and said there wasn't one, that it was just a pain in the back, and why else did she think they'd told Maria to invite her to spend her vacation with them?

THE TRIP HOME

Cindy almost felt tired just thinking about adobe making. She remembered leaving for L.A. On the way out to the front gate she and Maria had passed Marcus and Albert. Maria's brothers had one of the pickups backed up next to an embankment, and they were shoveling dirt down from the top.

Maria told her, "You have to be careful about where you get your dirt. If it has too much clay in it, then the adobes crack open and split apart. If it has too much sand, they just don't stick together. The guys tried a bunch of batches before they decided that the dirt there was okay."

SUGGESTED DISCUSSION QUESTIONS

1. What are the major parts of the process of making adobes?
2. How are the different parts of the process sequenced?
3. Does Cindy have all the information she needs?
4. What should Cindy do first, second, third?

SUGGESTED ASSIGNMENTS

1. You are Cindy Chou. Write a process essay about making adobes. (Audience: your newspaper's readers)
2. Write a process essay about making adobes. Address it to someone you know (for example, a friend who lives in the country, an uncle who lives in a house in Albuquerque with a backyard large enough for adobe making). Tell this specific reader how to make adobes in his or her backyard or at some place nearby that you both know about.
3. Select a process you know particularly well (for example, framing pictures, developing black-and-white film, making a bedspread). Be sure to select a process your reader would not be likely to find described in a textbook or magazine article. Write a process essay for a general, unknown audience.

The Lincoln-Head Penny

The letter arrived yesterday. It was from your nephew, Manuel. Manuel's mother told him you once collected coins. Now he wants to. "Mom says you could tell me how to get started," he writes. That's just like your sister. She knows Manuel might not stick with it, so instead of going out and buying a bunch of books on the subject, she tells Manuel to write you for advice.

When you were thirteen, Manuel's age, you had a pretty good coin collection. Manuel didn't say what kinds of coins he wanted to collect, but you guess maybe pennies are still the best, the easiest. That's what you collected, mostly. Quarters were too expensive to keep, and you had to have too much money to get enough unwrapped ones from the bank to bother to search through. Besides, silver collectors had ruined quarter and dime collecting forever by taking all the silver quarters and dimes out of circulation. They were easy to spot, had a nice silvery look to them, unlike the coppery quarters and dimes that were newer, so people spotted them easily and kept them.

Pennies, on the other hand, had certain advantages. With only fifty dollars to start with, Manuel could get 5,000 unwrapped pennies in a bag from the bank, search through them, keep the ones he didn't have unless they were duplicates of valuable ones, and add enough change to get another fifty-dollar bag. Of course, his mother would have to provide the initial fifty dollars. But she could always get it back. Yes, Lincoln pennies were no doubt the most economical place to begin. That's what you did. That's why you know the most about them. Now you wonder what to tell Manuel about collecting them. Since you can't decide what to say in your letter to him, or how to say it, you decide to try brainstorming, just randomly listing everything you remember about collecting pennies. Here is your list (for your own convenience, you decide to number each item on the list):

1. The Lincoln Memorial penny was first produced in 1959.

2. This penny has a picture of Lincoln's head on one side and a picture of the Lincoln Memorial on the other.

3. Before 1959 the Lincoln penny had wheat ears enclosing the One Cent notation on the reverse side.

4. The lines behind the wheat ears can be used to determine the coin's condition.

5. A shiny, uncirculated coin, without any sign of wear is in "excellent" condition.

6. In good condition the wheat ears are missing.

7. In very good condition the lines are partially worn off.

8. In fine condition the lines are visible.

9. All Lincoln pennies are copper except the steel pennies, which were made in 1943.

10. A few steel pennies were accidentally made in 1944; these are especially valuable.

11. Any penny dated before 1940 is sure to be worth keeping (worth more than a penny).

12. The 1909 "S" VDB is one of the rarest, most valuable pennies.

13. The "VDB" stands for the sculptor's initials and is located on the back, bottom edge of the coin.

14. An "S" on the penny means it was minted in San Francisco; "D" means Denver, and no mark means Philadelphia.

15. The first Lincoln pennies were made in 1909.

16. Before 1909 there was an Indian head on the penny.

17. "S" pennies are often especially valuable.

18. The mint mark can be found below the date; the date is on the front of each penny.

19. The 1954 "P" and the 1955 "S" are two of the youngest pennies that used to be worth saving.

20. It's fun to try to save one of each type, even for the ones that are only worth a penny.

21. After 1955, no more "S" pennies were made until 1968.

22. Banks usually require you to wrap the pennies in coin wrappers; fifty pennies fill a wrapper.

23. Banks make you put your name, address, and phone number on the wrapper.

24. You may want to get a rubber stamp with your name, address, and phone number on it if you really get involved in collecting pennies.

25. Cleaning pennies isn't a good idea unless you have to in order to read the date.

26. Be sure to use a strong light when you are searching through the pennies.

27. My eyes used to hurt after I'd looked at 5,000 pennies.

28. You might actually have a valuable collection if you work hard at it and keep it a long time.

29. Most people never sell their penny collections because they like them too much, but I sold mine.

30. It helps if you can find a friendly banker who is willing to let you continually buy fifty-dollar bags of pennies.

31. You can buy some of the pennies from other collectors if you want to fill in your own collection.

32. Spread the pennies out on a big table.

33. You can put them in books you can buy in hobby stores or you can save them in plastic coin tubes.

34. For right now, you might just want to save ones minted before 1940, ones you don't already have one of, and the 1954 "P" and the 1955 "S."

35. You can also try to improve your collection by saving the pennies that are in the best condition.

36. Be careful not to cut your fingers on the coin wrappers.

37. Later on you can buy a book that tells you how much the rare pennies are worth.

38. Saving pennies now might be discouraging because all the old ones might be out of circulation.

39. Hobby shops carry books on coin collecting and inexpensive coin folders, which contain an empty space for each type of penny made.

SUGGESTED DISCUSSION QUESTIONS

1. Is there enough information in the list and in the paragraphs to write Manuel a letter explaining how to collect coins?

2. What does Manuel need to know first? Last?

3. Is there any information you need that you don't have?

4. Should all the information given in the case be included in the letter?

5. How many different ways can this information be put into related groups?

6. How many different ways can related groups of information be sequenced?

SUGGESTED ASSIGNMENTS

1. Assume you are going to write Manuel a letter about how to collect pennies.
   a. place related information in groups
   b. for each group, state a main idea
   c. make a list of your main ideas
   d. decide on a sequence for those main ideas
   e. state a thesis for the letter

2. Write a paragraph in which you explain how you would organize the letter to Manuel. Explain what each of your paragraphs would include and why you would sequence them in a particular way.

3. Write a letter to Manuel in which you tell him how to collect pennies.

4. Assume that you are interested in freelance writing. Your sister's letter about Manuel's interest in coins gives you an idea that other children might be interested in reading a magazine article about collecting pennies. Perhaps *Boys' Life* or *World* or *Dynamite* would be interested in such an article. How will broadening your audience and changing your format from letter to essay alter your style and organization? Write the article.

Hillcrest Manor Nursing Home

Last Friday was your last day of work as the gardener at Hillcrest Manor. As you completed the last chore of the day—washing off the front sidewalk and the dock area and driveway with a hose—you felt good about leaving.

The job had been kind of depressing, such as the time you saw the lady in the window, and then didn't see her.

It happened when you were walking along the side of the building, looking for trash to pick up. There wasn't any really, but your boss, Mr. Bugsby, wanted it checked every day. Since that part of the job was boring, you sometimes looked in the windows at the patients. That's when you saw the lady, stretched out on the bed, the doctor beside her looking disinterestedly at his watch and a priest sitting on the other side of the bed. Her eyes caught yours for a second as you passed by, and you felt her desperate, scared, hurt look before you moved on past the window. The next day when you looked in the window again the lady was gone and the mattress was stripped, rolled up, and placed sideways on the bed. You thought of how you'd seen some patients arrive at the place, but you'd never once seen one leave.

But that Friday when you were finishing up you just shrugged to get the chill off your back that remembering the lady gave you, and then you decided to take one last look around. In front you saw that the lawn looked good, would need watering the day after tomorrow, and since this was the end of the summer, mowing in another three days. During the summer you had to mow once every five days, in the fall and spring, once every week.

You saw that the shrubs looked good—you'd pruned them just the way Bugsby had wanted them done—but then you noticed that some slob had dumped his car ashtray out in the parking lot, so you got the whisk broom and dustpan out of the shed and cleaned up the mess. They did that sometimes, the nervous visitors waiting in cars, usually men, sitting there smoking nervously and wondering what was taking the wife or sister or whoever it was so long to talk to the friend or relative inside.

In back you made sure the patio chairs were stacked in threes and placed under the porch in case it rained; you checked the side gates to make sure they were locked; and you put the dustpan and broom back in the shed and locked it up.

The last stop, forever, you hoped, was Bugsby's office. He said, "I almost forgot. Can you come in one more time, on Monday, to show your replacement what to do? It'll just take you half an hour but I'll pay you for the full afternoon." (The job was supposed to take sixteen hours a week, including lawn mowing, leaf raking, and snow shoveling and blowing.)

You said, "Sure," and when Monday came you gave your replacement, a nice fifteen-year-old guy, a tour of the place. You told him what the basics were and added some advice, such as "If you don't know for sure about pruning a tree or trimming a shrub, ask Bugsby. He's a kind of amateur gardener," and, "Be especially sure the front sidewalk and parking lot are clean because that's where most of the trash ends up, and that's just about the only place Bugsby ever goes."

Richard said, "Okay," didn't ask any questions, and you left.

Today, Wednesday, you got a call from Bugsby. He said, "Listen, what did you tell this guy Richard about washing down the sidewalk out front?"

"I just told him where to get the hose and nozzle and where to attach it. What do you mean?"

"Well, the first thing was he couldn't remember the combination to the shed, so I opened it for him, and now, believe it or not, he's out there washing down the whole parking lot. It's going to take him the whole four hours and he's going to cost me a fortune in water. How about coming out here and straightening him out?"

When you got back out to Hillcrest, Richard didn't seem to remember anything you told him before. He seems like a nice guy though, maybe not too smart, but then this is his first job; he's never worked before.

"It seems like there's so much you gotta do around here," Richard said. "How do you ever remember it all? Do I water those evergreens along the side of the building once or twice a week? And what about the rose bushes in front?"

"Once a week on the evergreens *in back*," you said, "and the roses twice a week."

You took him through the building to get to the shed in back to make sure he remembered the combination; on the way he saw the architect's drawing that Bugsby had proudly hung on the wall five years ago. The map looks like this:

The map gave you an idea. You pointed to places on it and said, "This is where you keep the trash picked up, this is where you mow, and this is where you put all your clippings—Bugsby's got a compost pit there and he wants to build it up for his garden at home . . ."

But Richard started to look more and more unsure of himself, and just then Bugsby came up to the two of you and said, "Now, Richard, you be sure to learn all this today because I can't afford to keep the two of you on the payroll, and I won't be around for the rest of the week to check up on you."

Then Bugsby left you with Richard, who said, "What did you say I do with the chairs?"

SUGGESTED DISCUSSION QUESTIONS

1. How can you best help Richard?
2. What kinds of questions do you have to ask yourself in order to help Richard?
3. What does Richard need to know?
4. Does the order in which you tell Richard what parts of the job to do matter?
5. Have you ever misunderstood anyone's directions? Why?

SUGGESTED ASSIGNMENTS

1. Write a set of directions for Richard. Be sure to make them clear and complete so he won't leave anything undone.
2. Write a set of directions for a job or part of a job that you now have or that you once had. Before you complete this assignment your instructor may want to know what your subject will be and who your audience will be.

The Student Housing Office

Unlike so many other universities whose enrollments were beginning to decline after 1975, State University began to grow. The growth was expected to peak in 1980 or 1981, however, so while the university hired more teachers to handle the increased course demand, the administration did not build any new dormitories. Even in 1975 the existing dormitories could not handle demand; a considerable number of students had to find housing off campus. Each year since, that number has grown.

The number of students forced to live off campus was in the thousands. Even some freshmen, if they registered late for classes, had to rent apartments off campus. The Student Housing Office was responsible for helping these students. Yet because the problem was relatively new, there were few procedures for guiding students. Thus, in the late summer of 1979, when Betty Hirsh was hired as an assistant housing director, one of her primary responsibilities was to upgrade the assistance given to students seeking off-campus housing.

BETTY HIRSH

Betty was, according to A. O. Morgan, her boss, especially suited for the job since she had just graduated from State University and was familiar with the town in which it was located. College Town was a large town of fifty thousand people who were friendly toward the students and appreciative of their business. Without State, A. O. told Betty, College Town would have withered up and blown away.

Betty immediately began looking into the problem of off-campus housing. She found that the SHO (Student Housing Office) had a bulletin board on which was posted information about rooms and apartments for rent. An adjacent bulletin board was also available for off-campus students looking for roommates. Neither bulletin board, however, seemed to have a great number of listings. Upon checking the local newspaper, Betty found that all the apartments listed for the For Rent board were advertised; the board carried no exclusive listings. Moreover, there were about four times as many apartments advertised as were listed on the board.

THE LANDLORDS

It seemed to Betty that her first step should be to contact the eight or nine major real estate agencies in town and encourage them to use SHO services. The other landlords could be reminded about SHO through an ad or two in the paper and/or some public service announcements over the radio. SHO had a small advertising budget, but Morgan had warned Betty that the office was short of funds in general; whatever plans she came up with would have to be low-cost solutions.

When Betty began calling landlords to encourage them to advertise their vacancies at SHO, *without charge,* the reaction she got was mixed.

"We'll try to remember to call you when we call the newspaper," one said.

"I hate to rent to students," another said. "Most of my units are pretty nice and students tend to tear things up and break the lease."

"Students definitely don't understand about leases," still another said. "I'll rent to students if they come to me and if I can't find anybody else, but to be honest with you, I'd rather get a married couple who works full-time."

As Betty talked to more landlords and explained her responsibilities at SHO, they unloaded dozens of stories on her about students. They told her how students brought dogs and cats in that weren't housebroken and so the animals ruined the carpets. They told her how many students left between semesters, and by then they had done so much damage that the last month's rent didn't begin to cover the repair bills. They told her that students didn't clean the apartments, and how often they did things such as nailing a fishnet to the ceiling with two hundred tenpenny nails, gluing corkboard to the walls of an entire room, and painting ceilings purple, green, and orange. The list went on and on as Betty sought suggestions for helping students successfully locate and rent apartments.

Some of the landlords were friendlier than others. By the time Betty finished telephoning she felt sure that three of the landlords would call in their vacancies, three more probably would, and three others might. None would give SHO exclusive listings. Most of them mentioned the students' ignorance about leases and about the general need to obey the lease once it was signed.

THE OFFICE

That much accomplished, Betty went around the office and talked to the receptionist and a couple of staff members who assisted students. She asked them what problems they had run into in helping students find acceptable off-campus housing.

Irene pointed out that most of the students at State University came from small towns, rural areas, and suburbs. These students just didn't have any experience in looking for apartments. They had no idea what a reasonable rent was, how to decide what they could really afford, what utilities and a phone might cost, and what a lease normally included or excluded.

Jacob said he thought the problem with finding suitable roommates was just as important. On campus, he said, the university randomly assigned incoming freshmen a roommate, but if a student had problems with his or her roommate, the R.A. (resident assistant) on the dormitory floor could always help out. If the problem wasn't solved, a fairly painless room switch could be made. The point was that the university did offer students guidance in learning to live with a roommate and help if it didn't work out.

Off campus, Jacob said, the students were completely on their own. Most of them had no experience in selecting a roommate and no help was available to them if the choice didn't work out.

"I've known students," Jacob said, "who have lived in three different apartments in one year because they couldn't find a roommate they could get along with. That kind of shuffling around can't be any good for a student's academic performance."

The last person Betty talked with was Will Lowry. Will agreed with Jacob about the roommate problem. The cards on the bulletin board only gave the name, address, phone, and then a small space for a description

of what the student was looking for. Will said students needed more guidance in how to select a roommate. Were they looking for a smoker or non-
smoker? A party-goer or a quiet type? That kind of thing.

Betty knew from her own experience that roommates often argued over
the use of each other's possessions—stereo, hairdryer, typewriter—and
over such things as having male and/or female friends visit. In an apartment, of course, that argument could be over whether the friend could stay
overnight.

Most students who chose off-campus housing had to find a roommate.
Some single rooms and one-bedroom apartments were available. The
rooms were furnished; the apartments usually were not. There were many
more two- and three-bedroom apartments than singles available. Nearly all
apartments required a lease and included water and trash pickup in the
rent.

LEASES

To learn more about leases Betty obtained a standard lease from a real
estate agent. The language was understandable, but the provisions were
fairly extensive so the lease was fairly long. The major sections of the lease
included the following:

maintenance by landlord	terms (always 12 months)
maintenance by tenant	noncompliance
security deposit	nonpayment of rent
utilities and services	written notice
additional provisions	fixtures and improvements
rules	fire or casualty damage
access	failure to maintain
subletting	abandonment
sale of property	

Most of the provisions were commonsensical things that anyone would
agree with, Betty thought, but some students might find the sections on
noise levels (rules), pets, and water beds particularly worth noting. Upon
checking with landlords Betty found that most of them said they were willing
to make reasonable changes in the lease before the student(s) moved in,
but the important point was for students not to move in first and then ask
for permission, say, to have a pet.

Subletting an apartment was permitted in the standard lease, but the
drawback was that in June nearly twenty thousand students left College
Town and it was usually difficult, though not impossible, to sublease an
apartment. Legally, the lessee was expected to pay the full twelve months'
rent regardless of when he or she left the apartment. Even those who broke
the lease generally lost one or two months' rent—their security deposit.

Betty knew of no standard way for students to calculate the cost of heat and electricity, but she did know the familiar guideline that an individual's rent should be no more than one-quarter to one-third of his or her total net monthly income. Utilities were important to take into account because heat and electricity in some apartments could run as high as $75 or even $100 a month.

The last bit of research Betty did involved average rents. She acquired several weeks' worth of real estate listings and calculated the average rent for a one-, two-, and three-bedroom apartment. She also calculated the rent for single rooms, but so few of these were listed that she wasn't confident about her results. The averages looked like this:

single room (per month)	$105
one-bedroom apartment	$195
two-bedroom apartment	$275
three-bedroom apartment	$310
houses (2–4 bedrooms)	$325

Since College Town had a good transportation system, Betty made no effort to look into the locations of various groups of apartments. After all the other research she'd done, she thought it was time to decide what kind of help the Student Housing Office could and should start offering students.

SUGGESTED DISCUSSION QUESTIONS

1. What kind of help should SHO offer its students?
2. Is State University obligated to help students find apartments or roommates?
3. Are there other sources of information Betty should check?
4. What problems do students have in finding apartments? In finding roommates?

SUGGESTED ASSIGNMENTS

1. Write a flyer (of essay length) for State University students to tell them how to find a suitable apartment.
2. Write a flyer (of essay length) for State University students to tell them how to find a suitable roommate.
3. You are Betty Hirsh. Write a report to your boss in which you define the problems you have discovered and state what action you plan to take.
4. Consider this assignment only if your school has dormitories. Review the local newspapers, including the school newspaper if there is one, to find a list of the types and costs of apartments available in your college area. Make estimates of costs for food and utilities. Write an article for the school's students in which you argue which is cheaper: dorm or apartment living.

United Gear Works

Edward Williams, Executive Vice-President for Operations at United Gear Works, was proud of his thirty years with the firm. In 1950, when he'd first arrived, he'd had to deal with some tough problems. Now, as Ed turned fifty and the company turned 100, he decided maybe one way to introduce new employees and student interns to UGW was to give them a historical problem to consider. Perhaps, Ed thought, the new people could better understand how he and the company dealt with problems now if they had an idea of what kinds of problems United had faced in the past.

Such a problem was one that Ed had noticed during his first year on the job at United. He now sat back and recorded the events so that his secretary could type them up for his new student interns.

ED'S FIRST PROBLEM

During that first year, Ed called in a group of top executives and told them United was having too many on-the-job accidents. Just last week there had been three: an employee down in Shop A lost a finger in a power press; a woman crossing a loading dock was hit by a forklift; and a machine operator in Shop C was badly burned with some hot metal. The situation was clearly serious. National headquarters of two unions had called about it and United's insurance company was going to raise rates and keep raising them. United needed to do something about the accident problem.

THE COMPANY

United Gear had been founded in 1880 by two Quincy, Massachusetts, engineers, and the company had prospered for many years by supplying gears and hardware to the New England elevator and firearms industries, to local and government shipyards, and to other industries. In 1945 the small but profitable company had been taken over by a conglomerate and had expanded considerably. United now operated three large manufacturing shops and had a research laboratory on and around its original Quincy site.

THE ACCIDENT PROBLEM

Company safety officers (employees who had risen through the ranks—under the control of the Operations Division) thought they had a clear idea of how the accident problem had arisen. The recent expansion had been rushed because United was trying to meet several new and very profitable contracts. New personnel and equipment had been brought in too quickly, and there had not been enough care in training the new people and setting up the new machinery. The officers felt that a careful posting of hazards, a day or two of training for some personnel, and the repositioning of one or two of the new machines would turn things around—they had already begun to do this, in fact. In their view, the most recent accidents were the result of the rush to expand; they had told Williams that they were beginning to see "light at the end of the tunnel."

THE MEETING

Ed Williams considered United's problems with accidents serious enough for the company to adopt, and make public, a coherent attitude toward accidents and their prevention in order to deal with the unions and insurance companies effectively. But other executives at United did not believe there was a problem.

Tom Raymond, chief of Plant Design, said that the so-called accidents were just plain human error—mistakes—and had nothing to do with United. The man who had lost his finger wasn't paying attention—he was listening to the ball game or something. Tom had run that machine himself. To Raymond, an accident was something that happened to a worker despite his complete concentration and best efforts to do his job and look out for himself.

Jim Boswell, Williams's deputy in Operations, disagreed. He said Raymond couldn't say that the woman who got hit by the forklift was at fault. It was her job to take charge slips to Purchasing every day; that was the only way to get there. She was walking inside the lines when a driver with an oversized load hit her. That walkway across the dock just wasn't safe.

Raymond argued that everyone accepted a certain amount of risk. United evaluated hazards and attempted to control them. When the risk associated with the hazard seemed acceptable, United had to stop spending time and money on reducing it. From then on it was up to the employee. United already posted signs and educated the employees as well as possible, but it was the employee's decision from then on whether to accept the job and the risk that went with it. It was their decision to stick their fingers in power presses or grab a handful of hot steel. "Besides," Raymond concluded, "the driver says he didn't think he crossed the line."

Jim Boswell argued that an accident occurred when a worker exchanged energy with his environment beyond some acceptable level that could not have been reasonably prevented. Simply put, that meant that United had to know what temperature, pressure, or force would be excessive and take steps to be sure that workers weren't exposed to those excesses.

Boswell told Raymond that many entry-level workers didn't have the knowledge or experience to *run* the machines in complete safety, let alone understand them. The forklift had dropped its cargo all over the marked lines. It was true the worker running the power press had a radio, but he didn't have it on at the time. He couldn't have heard it with the racket the press made. As for the worker down in Shop C, no one had been able to determine how he spilled the hot metal, but it was a tricky job.

Raymond looked as if he was about to explode so, to keep things on an even keel, Williams interposed. He asked Boswell what he wanted to do.

Boswell glanced at his notes and said first they'd have to hire somebody just to do systems safety work. The new safety officer was going to have to do a detailed survey of the whole plant, and he'd need one or more assistants skilled in hazard analysis.

The group had begun groaning when Boswell mentioned "hiring," and their reactions had increased to roars as the costly details of his plan unfolded.

The meeting dissolved into an argument as Boswell finished. Ed Williams had wondered what to do. It was clear to him that United's top management was deeply split on what an "accident" really was, and what United's position should be in regard to safety. It seemed to Williams that they'd have to agree on what these terms really meant. Williams wished they could get away from these abstract ideas and come up with some practical examples.

SUGGESTED DISCUSSION QUESTIONS

Assume you are a student intern who is going to work for Ed Williams and has read the problem Williams described.

1. What are the executives arguing about?
2. How do the terms they use, and their definitions of them, contribute to the argument?
3. What terms do the executives define differently?
4. What methods for defining those terms would be most effective? Why?

SUGGESTED ASSIGNMENTS

1. Assume you are Ed Williams's student intern. Ed's just told you, "Write a short (500–750 words) memo for me in which you define the term or terms these guys are really arguing about. Come up with something reasonable, something that would seem to apply then or now."
2. Using your own personal experience, define the term *accident*, or *safety*. (Audience: the other students in your class)

Who's a Good Teacher?

Doug Jones, President of the Student Body, leaned back in his chair and felt a headache coming on. Instead of reaching for the aspirin, though, he reached for the letter that had started the whole thing. A check for $5,000 had come enclosed in the letter. The letter stipulated how the check was to be used. The donation was to be used to establish a trust fund that would enable the Student Senate to award annually a $250 prize for teaching excellence. The teacher receiving the award was to be from the College of Arts and Sciences. The Student Senate was to seek nominations from the student body, and based upon those nominations, make the award. In short, it was up to the students to decide who deserved to be rewarded for excellent teaching. The writer of the letter and donator of the money chose to remain anonymous, saying only that "Students should think more seriously about what good teaching is, and they should have the opportunity to reward it."

THE SENATE MEETING

Doug announced the provisions of the letter at the next Senate meeting. Everyone was interested enough, but the surprising part came when he leaned back in his chair, looked at the twelve Senators, and said, "As I see it, the first thing we have to do, besides publicizing the award and encouraging nominations, is to agree on a way for us to evaluate the nominations. We've gotta decide how we're going to judge who is an excellent teacher."

That's when it all started, he thought. He wasn't even sure who had said what, but he remembered the first part of the discussion, all right.

It was Anthony Martinez who spoke first, but that figured; he was a senior, a speech major, and he always had something to say.

Anthony said he didn't think this was going to be so hard. A good teacher was one who was exciting, knew how to get up there and get people's attention and keep it, knew how to put on a good show, make the subject interesting. Nobody ever fell asleep in a good teacher's class.

Barb Henkel didn't agree. She said that a teacher wasn't some kind of salesman. A teacher was many things, but not that. The main question the Senate should ask was how much did students learn from the guy?

Jill Benson pointed out that "A teacher has to be somebody you liked, or you aren't going to learn anything from him."

"But personality shouldn't even come into it, really," Danny Roller said before Jill was even through, "because nobody likes everybody. How're you going to decide that? This isn't some kind of popularity contest, is it?"

At that point lots of people had lots of things to say, and Doug couldn't really remember who said what. Somebody said that you couldn't say who was really excellent because it was all a matter of taste. Somebody else said that the kinds of grades the professor gave should be considered, because professors who gave all As and Bs would be more likely to be popular, and somebody else said that the subject matter should be considered because some subjects were easier to teach than others. Then there was the guy who said it was all how much the professor knew and could tell you; and the guy who said it was how fair they were in their grading, along with whether they knew what they were doing. Barb Henkel ended up saying again that it was just according to how much you learned, and then somebody pointed out that you could learn from somebody but learn to hate the subject matter because you were forced to learn. Then Barb said she didn't think students should be spoon-fed an education. Doug sighed. He had pointed out to them that besides deciding upon criteria, they had to decide how to apply them. Should teacher-evaluation forms, to be completed by students, be used? Clearly they should, Doug thought, but he wondered whether teachers shouldn't also recommend and evaluate one another for the award.

SUGGESTED DISCUSSION QUESTIONS

1. What are the major problems in this case?
2. What methods would be most useful in defining "teaching excellence"?
3. What should Doug do? Why?
4. Why are the Senators defining the word differently?

SUGGESTED ASSIGNMENTS

1. You are a member of the Student Senate. Doug has asked you to write a definition essay on "teaching excellence." Your fellow Senators will be your immediate audience. If they approve it, your essay will be presented to the student body.*

2. Write an essay in which you define teaching excellence by showing how a teacher you had in the past was or was not excellent.

3. Do some investigation and determine how teachers are presently evaluated at your college or university. Write an essay in which you (a) report on the teacher-evaluation process or (b) analyze what this process means about how teaching excellence is defined at your college or university.

4. Select a word your friends frequently use, perhaps slang, and define that word so that your parents and teachers understand what it means.

---

*Remember that your audience's diversity of opinion on the subject as well as the way your essay will be used require you to define your criteria by showing "why" you think these criteria are sound. Also, in deciding on criteria, realize that they must be ones that can be used in evaluating award candidates.

To Whom It May Concern

Sonny D. Ance was the editor of the weekly campus newsmagazine, *Focus,* at Monasco State University. Monasco State, with a student enrollment of 23,000 undergraduates and graduates, was one of the state's largest universities. Graduate programs at Monasco State included law and medicine as well as a wide variety of doctoral programs in the sciences, humanities, and arts. Although Sonny and the *Focus* staff of student writers had never been particularly sensitive to the wide variety of perspectives present on campus, a recent letter to the editor had illustrated that variety and stirred up an unexpected controversy. Sonny had printed it in *Focus,* and the letter and his response to it read as follows:

To Whom It May Concern:
The editor of *Focus* and the entire staff display a lack of sensitivity and discrimination by continually referring to those holders of Ph.D.'s as "Mr." or "Ms." or "Mrs." (or sometimes as "Professor") while always referring to our M.D.'s at the med school as "Dr." You should realize that most professors (all Ph.D.'s) are "doctors" as well and therefore should be given the same respect as are M.D.'s.

Alexander J. Arven,
Department of History

Editor's response: It seems to us that "Dr.'s" are medical doctors, physicians.

The day after the letter and Sonny's response were printed, he received a number of letters on the subject. A couple of representative ones follow:

Historically, the Ph.D. is the most respected and the most academically sound degree. The M.D. is much newer. Therefore, holders of the Ph.D. deserve the same treatment as do M.D.'s. The Ph.D. is a doctoral degree, so unless you are going to refer to M.D.'s as Mr., Mrs., and so on, you should certainly recognize the Ph.D. for what it is.

Marlis C. Koedt
Department of Sociology

The Oxford English Dictionary defines the term *doctor* as follows: "A teacher, instructor; one who, by reason of his skill in any branch of knowledge, is competent to teach it; certain early fathers distinguished by their eminent learning; one who, in any faculty or branch of learning, has attained to the highest degree conferred by a university; one who is proficient in theology . . . one who is proficient in the knowledge of law; a doctor of medicine; in popular use, applied to any medical practitioner."

The term is derived from the Latin *docere,* which means "to teach." Surely all of this will clearly show the editor of *Focus* that Ph.D.'s have as much right, in fact more, to be called "Doctor" as those who have M.D.'s.

Kenneth Hunter
Department of English

At this point Sonny decided to withhold comment until other readers of *Focus* had an opportunity to read these last two letters and respond to them. The next day his mail included an additional twenty-two letters on the subject, including the two he selected as the most intelligent and representative:

To the Editor:
Of course it makes sense to call Ph.D.'s "Doctor" but what does the editor propose to do about all the other degrees that are now granted at various colleges, teaching institutes, and universities across the nation? There are D.E.D.'s, D.V.M.'s, and D.F.A.'s—just to name a few. And what about the holder of an honorary doctoral degree? Should that person be called "Dr." or should the right be reserved only for those who have earned their "doctoral" status? To end the confusion I propose that you simply refer to everyone by their department and let it go at that, M.D.'s included.

Marc K. Simons
Secondary Education

To the Editor:
The recent letters to the editor make me think of the very real problem students face in the classroom all the time—what to call our teachers. Some teachers don't tell us what to call them; others say, "Call me Professor so-and-so"; and still others introduce themselves as "Doctor so-and-so." I had one teacher who objected when I called him "Professor" because, he said, he didn't have a Ph.D. and was only an instructor in terms of academic rank. On the other hand, I called another of my teachers, a full professor, "Doctor," and she said "Not Doctor, I don't have a Ph.D." What are students supposed to do? Do we have to research each teacher and find out what degrees each one holds and what rank they are?

May B. Dearin
Premed

THE STAFF

Sonny called his staff together to gather their opinions on what policy, if any, *Focus* should adopt in light of the rash of letters received about titles, academic rank, and degrees held. Sonny's twelve staff writers seemed to share his own surprise at the response—thirty-nine letters in all. They discussed why people were getting so excited about the subject, and they agreed something should be done. Collectively the letters represented no clear mandate as to what *Focus* policy should be.

The majority of Sonny's staff agreed that having to look up the degree's possessed by each source *Focus* quoted or referred to would be a nuisance at best, a difficult and time-consuming process at worst. Then there were the administrators. Of course *Focus* would refer to the president as President Harrington, but some administrators did not have titles that could be conveniently placed before their names. Were they to be referred to by the Mr., Mrs., or Ms. guidelines used in the past or did the *Focus* staff have to look up their degree status as well? One staff member pointed out that forms of address are questions of manners and custom. Many dictionaries included an appendix that guided writers through these issues.

Sonny thought that ideally *Focus* would refer to each person in whatever manner that person wished—if the holder of a Ph.D. wanted to be called "Professor" or "Mister" or "Doctor" or "Ms." or "Mrs.," that was fine. In practice, however, such a procedure might, he thought, seem inconsistent to the readers of *Focus*. Determining each individual's preference, moreover, might well be too much work for reporters.

At the same time, Sonny thought that the writer of the student letter, May B. Dearin, had also raised an interesting issue that deserved some attention. He wondered whether he should assign someone to do a report on that subject. Perhaps several teachers could be interviewed and some general guidelines developed, or perhaps a survey could be taken.

SUGGESTED DISCUSSION QUESTIONS

1. Why was the volume of mail Sonny received so large?
2. Why do people care about the title by which they are referred to?
3. What, exactly, is the problem that *Focus* must solve?
4. What possible solutions should Sonny consider?
5. Why do teachers not always tell students how to address them?
6. What is academic rank?
7. How is academic rank different from degrees held?

SUGGESTED ASSIGNMENTS

1. You are a staff writer for *Focus*. Sonny has asked you to write him a memo in which you recommend what titles *Focus* should use in referring to professional teachers and other degree holders.
2. You are a staff writer for *Focus*. Sonny has asked you to draft an editorial in which you define and defend the magazine's policy.

3. You are a staff writer for *Focus*. Based on your own experience and information you may want to gather from interviews or surveys, write a feature article in which you argue whether it is important that teachers clearly state how
they wish to be addressed, and if so, how they should communicate their
wishes to students. You may also want to discuss how a student should tell
teachers how he or she would like to be addressed in the classroom.

Freshman Initiation

Despite what the students believed, Dean Ross reflected, he did his best to
remain fairly well informed about student activity in the dormitories. His son
and his daughter both attended the college, and Anthony Maratheftis, a
sophomore at the college, was a part-time assistant who talked to the dean
often and openly. Among the normal channels of communication, and his
talk with his children and Anthony, the dean felt that he managed to maintain a fairly complete, accurate picture of what was going on in the dormitories. As Dean of Student Life, that was his job.

However, the dean didn't like the rumors that were circulating and wondered what would be the most effective action to take.

Freshman initiation seemed to be the problem. An unofficially recognized tradition at the college almost since its founding in 1868, freshman
initiation took many forms. While most initiations in the past seemed harm-
less and friendly, Anthony had recently mentioned hearing of some practices that troubled the dean. Dean Ross asked Tony to do a little
investigating.

THE RESIDENT ASSISTANTS

The dean told Tony that of course any kind of regulation of initiation ceremonies would have to start with the resident assistants. One each floor and
wing of each dormitory, an upperclassman or -woman was responsible for
supervising the activities on that floor. The college could write policy forever, but if the resident assistants were not told to enforce it, those policies
would be useless, perhaps worse than useless. But where did friendly initiation ceremonies end and dangerous hazing begin? Sometimes it was difficult to believe, the Dean thought, that these were the 1980s and not the
1950s.

INITIATION

Tony knew that the kinds of initiation freshman students were made to go
through varied from floor to floor. Some floors simply had no kind of initia-

tion ceremony. Other floors (like Tony's) supposedly had no ceremony until, on the spur of the moment, an upperclassman said, "Initiation," and threw a frosh into the showers. Then the whole floor might erupt as struggling freshmen were carried down the hallways, sprayed with shaving cream, and thrown into the showers.

Both Tony and the dean knew that just last week a student had broken his arm in a struggle on the wet, slippery tile floor of the bathroom.

There were other types of initiation. On one floor Tony knew that each freshman was made to drink a pint of well-blended goldfish. Another group was made to go over to what they were told was a women's floor and steal the women's floor sign where it hung in a window. When the freshmen arrived, they were greeted not by women, but by a floor of upperclassmen, mostly football players, all of whom were equipped with cans of shaving cream and Neet hair remover. In another incident the freshmen were told to gather up all their own underwear and throw it out a seventh-floor window.

The women, on the other hand, didn't seem to have as many initiations or as much variety in them. Tony's girlfriend, Clare, had been given a card to have filled out. On the card were spaces for seven signatures, one for each dorm floor. The card read "I'm an Alabama Angel: Put a little devil into me—with a kiss." Tony's girlfriend and the other first-year women on her floor were expected to get a kiss from one male on each floor of a particular dormitory.

When Tony asked Clare why she agreed to do it, she said, "Tony, I'm lucky. At another house the girls had to get five guys on each floor to sign the card." The only other practice on women's floors, so far as Tony knew, was to tie each first-year female up outside with a sign on her that read "Kiss me. I'm a frosh." Only after the female had talked twenty males into kissing her would she be untied. While Tony knew a completely accurate survey would be impossible to take since students were reluctant to talk about it, his calls to 10 percent of the male and female dorm floors on campus revealed that one-third had initiations of some sort. The majority—65 percent—of these were activities such as doing other students' laundry, giving a car wash, or putting on a variety show.

Then there was a whole different approach on one men's floor. Tony could not find out which floor this was, but three sources told him the same story. Four men had raced into the middle of a women's floor meeting. The four, all wearing ski masks, were carrying a fifth man. This young man had absolutely nothing on but a ski mask and a tiny sign that said, "I'm a frosh." He was unceremoniously dumped in the middle of the group of females. Then all five men raced out of the room. Tony shuddered at the image of the four men stripping off that freshman's clothes and then carrying him into the room. He knew Dean Ross had been unable to determine who was responsible for this act.

In an informal meeting with a group representing freshmen, Tony had tried to discuss the matter with them and learn more about their experiences and feelings, but they seemed extremely ill at ease. Tony had the impression that some were amused, but the majority were anxiously wondering whether they were going to have to go through initiation of some sort, and how difficult and embarrassing it might be.

COLLEGE POLICY

Tony underlined the pertinent college policy on initiation ceremonies in the student information handbook. The policy stated:

Hazing is defined as any action intentionally taken that leads directly or indirectly to an individual's physical or mental discomfort or pain. Holding or transporting an individual under physical restraint, whether done in a friendly or unfriendly way, is prohibited. Hazing, on or off campus, by groups or individuals, is prohibited.

A student committing an act of misconduct may be subject to disciplinary action. Sanctions may vary from a written warning to suspension.

Clearly the policy was being violated, but what should be done to correct the situation? Should the resident assistants simply be reminded of the policy? Should they be sent a letter with the relevant policy stated clearly? Should "cream and shower" initiations simply be banned as clearly in violation of college policy? If so, should the resident assistants be warned that they were responsible for enforcing the ban?

SUGGESTED DISCUSSION QUESTIONS

1. Should initiation ceremonies be more tightly regulated?
2. Should they be banned?
3. What kind of ceremony is not in violation of policy? What kind is?
4. How do you identify initiation ceremonies in terms of being acceptable or unacceptable?

SUGGESTED ASSIGNMENTS

1. You are Anthony Maratheftis. Write the dean a memo in which you make your recommendation about what should be done.
2. Suppose the dean agrees with your recommendation. Write a letter to the resident assistants in which you define the college's policy specifically in terms of dormitory initiation ceremonies, and persuade them to enforce it.
3. Write a research paper on initiation ceremonies. You might want to investigate the accidents or even the deaths on college campuses that have occurred because of them.

Getting Out, Not Dropping Out

Dean Hayes hung up the phone and wondered what to do. Being the Dean of Students at Ryerson, a small, four-year college, wasn't, he thought, the easiest or most pleasant job in the world. He'd just finished talking to Martin Wulf about his son Phillip. Phillip had just flunked out of Ryerson.

The dean remembered Wulf's last words. "Tell me why this happened," he'd said. "He did so well in prep school but he's already flunked out of one college and now he's wasted it all. Why did he do it? You know I even told him I'd never pay his way through college again if he didn't make it this time. What did you do to him down there?"

The dean sighed. Phillip Wulf didn't have an easy life ahead of him with a father like that and with his own academic track record.

PHIL'S RECORD

Phillip Wulf had come to Ryerson on a special admissions basis after he'd flunked out after one year at an Ivy League college. His college entrance exam scores showed he had plenty of potential though he wasn't exceptionally intelligent. His background was strong enough. His father had sent him to a well-known prep school on the East Coast; Phillip had played hockey there. The school's reputation, his school grade-point average, and his test scores had been enough to get him into the Ivy League college. But Hayes remembered looking over Phil's transcript.

During his first semester Phil had taken five courses and flunked them all. The second semester he'd taken five more courses and had shown little improvement—one D and four F's. That was enough. The Ivy League college flunked him out.

Ryerson College, on the other hand, had a special admissions program for students like Phil. They began all over again, as if they were freshmen, but they were required to achieve a C average their first semester. Ironically, Phil had taken a course that semester that was taught by the dean. Dean Hayes liked to teach one course per semester because he enjoyed it. The course, Principles of Accounting, went well enough, but Phil was a disappointment.

After giving him a D on the first test, the dean called Phil into his office.

"I admit I didn't study," Phil said. "I did fairly well on the questions over your lectures but," he grinned, "you gave us problems that covered the book pretty thoroughly. I guess I haven't really opened it yet."

Dean Hayes was impressed with Phil's honesty. He seemed like an intelligent young man. He dressed well, was probably good-looking by anyone's standards, and seemed at ease talking about himself and his father.

"My dad is really big on me getting an excellent education. But I feel burned out. You know, I can do the work—I proved that in prep school. But I wanted to stay out for a year after high school graduation. My dad said I'd get behind everyone else my age and I had to go. But I just couldn't get interested in studying and I wasted the whole year. Then my dad had a long talk with me and said I had to try again. We argued a lot but he always wins. He's very persuasive. No matter what I think of, he's always got a better argument, or two, or three."

After a long talk with the dean, Phil agreed that what he needed to do was get to work and start completing assignments. The dean felt that Phil was sincere in promising to make a real effort to get the work done. He continued to attend class, though less regularly.

At the semester's end, however, Phil had managed only a D+ average in his course work at Ryerson. The dean suspected that Phil was well educated enough and intelligent enough to get a D+ average without even studying for five minutes. With regret he notified Phil and Mr. Wulf that Phil would not be allowed to attend Ryerson in the spring.

The day—it must have been the very minute—Wulf got the letter he called the dean long-distance. Wulf was furious, whether at the college or with his son, Hayes wasn't sure.

"I thought you told me you had a talk with my son," Wulf said.

"I did. He doesn't seem at all interested in going to college, Mr. Wulf. He told me he wanted to stay out for a year."

"That's ridiculous," Wulf said.

Dean Hayes tried to calm Wulf down but didn't get very far. The dean suggested counseling for both the son and his father but Wulf rejected the idea with a laugh. After a long argument, Wulf persuaded the dean to give Phil one last chance. Wulf said Phillip had finally made up his mind to work hard.

THE SPECIAL SESSION

Ryerson offered a special, four-week session in the month of January. Any academically eligible student could enroll, but all students were allowed to take just one course. The dean agreed that Phil would be allowed to enroll in the session. If he got a C or better in his class, then he would be allowed to continue at Ryerson in the spring semester (which began the first week of February). At Hayes's suggestion, Mr. Wulf agreed to allow Phil to choose the course. Phil chose freshman English. When Phil returned to campus, he met with Dean Hayes and said freshman composition ought to be easy enough because he'd already taken the course three times.

Phil flunked the course. Since the dean learned about it before Mr. Wulf did, he took the opportunity to call the English Department to talk with Phil's instructor. The report he got wasn't surprising. The instructor had called Phil in for a special conference after the first week (the equivalent of the first four weeks during a semester of normal length). Phil hadn't completed any of the assignments given. To force Phil into action, the instructor told him that if he didn't complete all the short assignments and the first essay by the next day, Phil would flunk the course automatically. The two of them had a long talk and the next day Phil turned in all the work, including the first essay. He got an A on the essay.

"It was quite well written," the instructor told the dean. "He's definitely got plenty of ability."

For the next three weeks, however, Phil turned in absolutely nothing and frequently failed to attend class. He did come in one more time for a conference. It was to tell the instructor that he was thinking of dropping out of school. A friend wanted him to become the assistant manager of a new stereo store that was part of a rapidly growing chain. Phil liked the idea of earning his own money but didn't know how he was going to convince his father that it was the right thing to do.

"I'm sorry I couldn't pass him," the instructor said, "but he only completed 20 percent of the work in the course. It doesn't matter how good the work was—all I ever saw was 20 percent of what I was supposed to get. He talked a lot about his father. I told him to go see you."

The dean had had one last talk with Phil. Phil had just come in to thank him for all his help, to apologize for not making it, and to say good-bye.

"What're you going to do?" Dean Hayes asked him.

"Right now I've got to go home. Then I was thinking of taking this job. College just isn't for me right now. Prep school was like a military academy and I had to do it. But I'm getting out of college. I've got this good chance to start in business, but it's a long story. Right now I've got to go home and try to talk to my father."

MR. WULF

Dean Hayes looked again at the phone he had just hung up and shook his head. Well, he thought, at this point I guess all I can do is write Mr. Wulf a letter explaining our position. Bits of his last conversation with Wulf floated through his mind.

"Why did this happen?" Wulf had said. "With an A on that first paper you can see he can do the work. Why not give him another chance? And he did so well in prep school."

SUGGESTED DISCUSSION QUESTIONS

1. How would you describe the relationship between Mr. Wulf and Phil?
2. Why did Phil do so much better in prep school?
3. Why did the dean let Phil enroll in Ryerson to begin with?

4. Why did he readmit Phil?
5. Why did he refuse to allow Phil to enroll in Ryerson for spring semester?
6. What kind of letter should the dean send to Mr. Wulf?

SUGGESTED ASSIGNMENTS

1. Assume you are Dean Hayes. Write a letter to Mr. Wulf in which you explain your action and in which you tell him anything else you think he ought to know.
2. Assume you are Dean Hayes. Write a memo for Phillip's academic file in which you describe Phil's academic career at Ryerson.
3. Based on this case and your own experience, write an article for high school guidance counselors or for parents about the need to understand a student's motivation and interest in going to college.

Neighborhood Youth Corps

It's late in the summer, and you are into your last month as a group leader for the Neighborhood Youth Corps, a city-sponsored clean-up and fix-up program that employs several hundred inner-city junior high and high school students. Things have been going well. But you have to admit you'll be glad to get back to school and away from the routine of cleaning empty lots, fixing up playgrounds, painting fences, and such.

This morning, as you report for work, you find the following note from your boss, Roy Grimes, Program Coordinator for the area you're working in:

I'm worried about your group. I've been getting reports about a couple of your kids getting into trouble after work, and three people have complained to me about the quality of the work you've been doing lately.

As you know, our funding for next year depends on how well we do *this* year. So I don't want any more complaints for the rest of the month. Come and see me at 9:30. Let me know what the problem is and how you intend to handle it.

THE YOUTH CORPS

The NYC is a program designed to benefit the kids and the community. Part of the program's purpose is to clean up the city and shape it up for the winter. Another major aim is to give participants something to do during the summer, keep them out of trouble, and provide them with some income.

One reason you got into the program was to get some supervisory experience on your resume, but you also believed you could do some good in the combination boss/counselor role the job seemed to require.

You have done some good, too. Several of the kids seem more willing to cooperate, assume responsibility, and follow through on things than they did earlier in the summer. Naturally, you didn't reach everybody, but the group has been running pretty smoothly in general. Or at least that's what you thought until this morning, when you got Grimes's note.

You'll be meeting with Grimes in one hour, so you decide to go over the notes in the file you've accumulated this summer as part of your job. Grimes's letter doesn't give any specific details, but you feel sure your notes will help you get some idea of what he's upset about. You pull out the file and begin leafing through the notes you've made on the kids in your group.

THE GROUP

WILL EVERS

Bright, capable, sixteen years old. People say he has a "bad attitude" but you don't buy this completely. Late for work twice last month, absent five times.

Evers is good at leading small groups of workers when he feels the job is interesting or important. He is not easy to motivate, however. He's just as apt to skip out if you're not watching, except on projects he's really excited about. You've been told that Evers was arrested for drunk driving several weeks ago; he's admitted that he steals cars for joy rides on occasion.

SKIP WHITE

Fourteen years old. A problem, in your view. Very sweet to your face, and a terror if left alone. Skip is in and out of trouble every day. He stole a case of Coke from a delivery truck during his first week at work. With some difficulty you and Grimes managed to smooth that event over.

Skip does not seem interested in the job, and his attitude often affects the other kids. He was absent six times last month and late almost every other day. You finally had to dock his pay, a disciplinary action you and Grimes feel should be a "last resort."

THE OTHERS

The other notes on your remaining workers (eight in all) are fairly routine. They are generally a nice group but are not interested in much except parties, an occasional ball game, and "hanging out" on the corner at night. You find it a chore to lead them because they seem to require so much guidance. They have to be taken every step of the way on almost every job you give them.

THE SUMMER PROJECTS

Your notes also include records of all the projects your group has worked on this summer. Again, the notes give you a few clues about the problems Grimes mentioned in his note.

COLUMBIA PARK

The park is more than a mile square and filthy. The boys picked up trash for a couple of hours without making noticeable headway. Finally, Skip White just sat down and said he wasn't going to do any more. You tried to keep the others going, but it was a losing battle. You ended up giving them an early lunch and going on to another project afterward.

The boys covered all of the park eventually, but the job had to be done a little at a time; a few hours of that work a day is all they could take. By the time your crew had worked over the whole park, however, the place where they'd started was filthy again.

FIFTH STREET BASKETBALL COURTS

They worked hard all one Monday to set up a new backboard and paint white lines. You had some help from the City Park Department, but your crew really did most of the work.

You left Evers in charge of the crew for a while because an emergency came up and you had to leave. Grimes had sent you to help out with an accident at a project nearby. A twelve-year-old boy had broken his arm and his group leader had gone with him to the hospital. When you got back, White and another crew member were playing basketball against the new backboard; Evers and the rest were watching the game.

The Park Department worker was complaining, even though the job was finished. He said the kids were no good, the program was a waste of tax money, and he didn't see why the city bothered. You expected him to file a complaint with Grimes.

EXPRESSWAY MURALS

With the help of an artist, the kids are to design and paint (by numbers) their own murals on the massive concrete wall supporting the Midtown Expressway. Evers seems excited about all this, as are two or three others. You still have not received the final go-ahead on this project from Grimes, who feels it could be very risky.

You feel the risk too. You'll have to be downtown at staff meetings during one of the days the kids will be doing the murals. Grimes agrees that there is no danger of accidents because of a chain-link fence and concrete abutments, but there could be a real public foul-up: everybody can see the mural site from the housing project across the expressway.

The boys, however, really want to do the murals; they are a lot more enthusiastic about this project than they have been about anything else this summer. Everybody's excited except White; he's constantly shooting the project down and making the shyer kids afraid to admit they want to take part or to contribute any of their ideas.

Evers seems eager and willing to help plan and supervise. You've had several good talks with him about the murals.

THE PROBLEM

As you read this last section of your notes, you realize that you've got to convince Grimes that you have a handle on the problem within the group and you know how to solve it. If you can't convince him of this, he'll never approve the mural. You feel that the mural might be the key to the whole summer. Without it, the kids could lose interest, and the ground you've gained with some of them could be lost.

SUGGESTED DISCUSSION QUESTIONS

1. What should the group do for the rest of the summer? Why?
2. What does Grimes seem to think the problem is with the group?
3. What do you think the problem is?
4. How can you persuade Grimes to let you do what you want?

SUGGESTED ASSIGNMENTS

1. You arrive for the meeting with Grimes, but he has been called away to City Hall. His secretary says he wants you to write him a memo telling him (1) exactly what the problem is within your group, and (2) how you intend to correct it.

2. You talk with Grimes, and he tells you that Evers and White are troublemakers, and the solution is to fire them. He says he doesn't have time to argue with you now and tells you to leave him a short report by the end of the day. The report should explain (1) what the real problem is, and (2) why firing Evers and White is or is not a real solution to it.

3. Grimes meets with you and tells you that the real problem is giving the kids jobs they're not mature enough to handle. He wants you to solve the problem by keeping a low profile for the rest of the month—by cleaning up a few big parks and empty lots and keeping the kids out of sight. You mention the murals, but he cuts you off quickly—"No way."

    That night you decide to write Grimes, defend the idea of the murals, and show how a project such as the murals might help solve other problems. Your report should identify the *real* problem as you see it and should show why the mural project might constitute a solution to that problem.

White Bones and Indian Bones

In late spring Cordall Construction Company began work on a new state highway between Maloof and Durman, two large towns in the southern part of the state. Since the terrain was essentially flat, and because the right-of-way cut across farmlands, the construction proceeded as planned. By June, Cordall was actually ahead of schedule with more than half of the work finished.

On June 2nd, however, a bulldozer operator who was clearing land about fifteen miles east of Durman made a discovery that temporarily halted work in that area. The operator had been cutting into a slight rise in the ground when the bulldozer's blade suddenly unearthed a group of bones, including a human skull. Cordall Construction, it turned out, had unearthed part of an unmarked cemetery.

In questioning people in the very small (population 146) nearby, unincorporated town of Kemps, John Lubbock, one of Cordall's project supervisors, learned that the cemetery had evidently been used in the mid-1800s for a short time. No one had any idea as to how many bodies might be interred, but one man, aged 85, seemed to think that only a couple of dozen people had been buried there.

STATE LAW

According to state law as specified in the state code, Cordall and the State Highway Commission had two options. If the cemetery was held to have sufficient historical interest, then new plans could be made and the highway could be rerouted. If not, the remains would be properly reinterred elsewhere and construction would continue. The "historical significance" of a place or thing was determined by the State Historical Society and by the state-appointed archeologist. The state code specified that the state archeologist had to be given sufficient time to excavate and examine any site of potential historical significance.

A preliminary investigation by the state archeologist, Ernest Smith, led to his recommendation that the bones be reinterred. Smith was an experienced and qualified archeologist. He had been appointed by the governor eight years ago. In his investigation, Smith found that no graves were marked. No surviving descendants were known; the cemetery and its contents seemed unknown and uncared for. Or at least that seemed to be the case at the time.

THE STATE HISTORICAL SOCIETY

The State Historical Society was composed of twelve members who were appointed to four-year terms by the governor. The members met on a regular basis and were paid an honorarium and traveling expenses. The members represented a wide variety of occupations and came from every major geographic area in the state. Although they were not necessarily historical experts, they shared the concern of protecting the state's antiquities, the state's history. Upon reading Smith's report, the society approved his recommendation unanimously.

THE CEMETERY

Under the state archeologist's supervision, workers immediately began removing the bones and placing them in a nearby municipal cemetery. Upon excavating the fourteenth grave, however, Smith made an unexpected discovery. While all the previously excavated graves had clearly held the remains of pioneers of one sort or another, this grave was different. Scattered around the bones was an assortment of American Indian artifacts—over a hundred beads, two clay pots, two ax heads, and a half-dozen pieces of small jewelry.

Smith reported his discovery to the press, and several state newspapers carried the story. Although this grave site was from the same general period as the others, he felt it might be slightly older. The burial had been quite elaborate and was obviously traditional, Smith said. It was similar to a few burial sites dating from as early as 1800. Moreover, the unusually complete range of artifacts gave more complete information about this particular tribe's culture than had previously been available to archeologists. These Indian remains, Smith said, carried special historical significance and should be preserved. The Indian bones and artifacts were carefully packed up and shipped off to the state museum where Smith was curator. There he planned to examine, catalogue, and display his findings.

THE YANQUI INDIANS

Darlene Lightfoot, a member of the Yanqui Indian tribe, which was located near Maloof, read about Smith's plan and promptly protested his action in short letters to the governor, Smith himself, and the State Historical Society. The Yanqui tribe (with 173 members on its tribal roll) supported her protest. Why, Ms. Lightfoot asked, were these Indian bones to be put on display when the twenty-one sets of "white" bones (the last seven graves contained only bones and the kinds of jewelry and personal artifacts that midninteenth century pioneers posessed) had all been carefully reinterred in a white, municipal cemetery. Ms. Lightfoot pointed out that state burial laws did not discriminate against Indians. Even Smith agreed to this. Yet, she said, Smith was allowed to discriminate against Indians. Ms. Lightfoot argued that the Indian bones were most likely Yanqui (Smith himself had said so in one newspaper account). She wanted the bones and artifacts returned to her for proper burial in the Yanqui way.

SMITH'S RESPONSE

Smith's response was a simple "No." He wasn't, he said, going to go giving away something of historical significance to a woman just because she asked for it. The bones and artifacts were already scheduled to go on display in the state university's well-respected Museum of Anthropology. The governor and the State Historical Society both initially responded by saying that they would have to wait for Smith's full report before considering any course of action. Meanwhile, one big-city newspaper carried an account of Lightfoot's protest and Smith announced that while he wouldn't put the Indian bones on display, he still planned to display the artifacts found with them. Ms. Lightfoot said that only a return of both the bones and the artifacts would allow for proper Yanqui burial.

SUGGESTED DISCUSSION QUESTIONS

1. What is the conflict in this case?
2. How are the bones that went to the municipal cemetery different from those that Smith took to the museum?
3. What can Ms. Lightfoot do? Does she have a valid protest?
4. What are Smith's options?

SUGGESTED ASSIGNMENTS

1. You are Darlene Lightfoot. Write letters to one or more of the following individuals or groups (persuade your reader that your request is reasonable): Ernest Smith, the governor, the State Historical Society.
2. You are Ernest Smith. (1) Write a report in which you defend your decision. Your audience is the State Historical Society and the governor. (2) Write Darlene Lightfoot and defend your position.
3. You are an interested citizen who has read about this situation. Write an essay in which you state your opinion about what should be done with the Indian bones. Select one or more of the following audiences: Ernest Smith, Darlene Lightfoot, the State Historical Society, the governor, the readers of a major newspaper's letters to the editor page.

Howard House Road Race

It's early spring at Rosner College, and Howard House is planning its first annual minimarathon—a 10.6-mile run out to the lake, around the Howard statue, then back to the house. As a member of the race committee and an avid runner, you've been looking forward to the race all winter. But you and the other members of the race committee have recently become alarmed over a potential clash with the college administration—a clash that may end the race before the starting gun is fired.

HOWARD HOUSE

Howard House is named after Anthony Howard, a Rosner College student who died in the invasion of Normandy in World War II. Howard had been an excellent athlete—a terrific miler and almost an All-American in football. He had also been a brilliant student and had already been accepted by Harvard Law School before he left college for the Air Corps in 1942.

Howard House was founded after the war as a co-op residence for Rosner College students who were planning a legal or other professional career—one of the "special interest" houses that attracted many students to Rosner in the first place. Howard House attracted its share of athletes too. In the 1960s, however, many students had been turned off by its reputation as a "jock house." But times had changed and now the waiting list for space at Howard House was nearly always full.

Despite its popularity, Howard House has nevertheless nearly always been on shaky financial ground. As a co-op house, it is allowed to charge students only a modest rental—people are expected to work out the rest of their room and board by keeping the place clean, cooking meals, and so on. Rising food and eating costs have, however, outstripped the modest savings provided by the students' free labor. Now the house is on the verge of financial collapse, and bills are coming due for which no funds are available. The college administration is sympathetic but can offer no substantial assistance.

THE RACE

You and other house members have tried to get emergency funding from the college and from the alumni association, but the amount raised hasn't made much of a dent. Things looked pretty bleak until Mark Drake, a junior in chemistry, suggested the race. "It's simple," he explained, "people around here are really into running, but most of them never get the chance to run a real road race—you know, like the Boston Marathon."

You asked Drake how a road race would raise money.

"So we *give* them the chance," Drake said. "We'll put on a shorter race—say ten miles or so on and around the campus. We'll attract a lot of so-so runners, a few good ones too. We'll make them all pay ten bucks to enter. Then we'll print up programs and get some local stores to take ads. We can't miss. I'll bet we could clear a couple of thousand bucks on this."

At first you and the others were skeptical, but Drake turned out to have a real flair for organizing this sort of thing. He was able to get the college to sanction the race and to provide a little money to help with logistics. Drake and other house members were able to use the Howard name to get the town to back the race too. The chief of police had been especially help-ful in choosing the route, getting permission from the Town Council to close certain roads, and assigning police to help with the crowds and traffic on race day. People were signing up fast. By April 15th, two weeks before the race, the field was up to over four hundred people, largely or partly because of some well-known runners who had entered. "And at ten bucks a head entry fee, and the money we've gotten from the ads, that means we're going to be able to pay our bills," Drake crowed.

At one point, race committee members had even managed to get a lo-cal soft-drink bottler to sponsor the event. The bottler had agreed to pay Howard House $2,500 in return for having the runners wear numbers with "Dover Cola" printed on them. The same name was to be strung on a ban-ner across the finish line, and the program was to have a "Dover Cola" logo printed on its cover.

However, Dean Simpson had quickly moved to squash this commercial tie-in, saying that the race was a college-sanctioned event, and could not be associated with a business enterprise. "No cola," he told the race com-mittee, "or the race is off.' You had all agreed, though reluctantly. It looked as if the house would still make more than enough money from entry fees and program ads to pay its debts.

THE PROBLEM

It's the last Monday before the race and you and the other committee mem-bers now face a new and unexpected problem. Dean Simpson called Mark Drake in this afternoon and threatened to cancel the race unless three run-ners were removed from the line-up. The dean said that the three are professionals, and that college rules allow only amateurs to participate in college-sanctioned events. As he did on the cola issue, the dean has threatened to cancel the race unless the three runners are withdrawn.

Drake meets with you and the other race committee members and ex-plains that the three runners are not considered professionals by AAU standards and two out of the three have even participated in Olympic tryouts. "But Rosner College has its own rules, Simpson told me; and it's either go along, or else."

The trouble is, you learn as the discussion progresses, that many of the area's sporting-goods shops and businesses had agreed to place ads and put up posters only after they discovered that some big-name runners were entering.

"If we kick these three out," Drake explained, "some of our advertisers might decide to pull out, or the race might be a flop. If we lose our big program ads, we'll lose most of our profits. It could be a real bad scene."

In any case, Dean Simpson has given you twenty-four hours to decide what to do. You, Drake, and the rest of the race committee are to meet with him tomorrow to resolve the problem. You decide to do a little research before the meeting.

YOUR RESEARCH

For the program, Drake has prepared brief biographies of some of the top runners, including the three in question. You decide to look these over, to find out how "professional" these people really are:

Terry Melville: One of the top women athletes of the year, according to *Sportsworld* magazine. Terry has run the Boston Marathon in 2:30:20 and is considered a real contender in this year's Bonne Bell series. She has been running actively for six years now. When she's not training, Terry spends her time as a representative of TRAK Running Shoes, Inc., and as an advisor to Diana Athletic Wear Co.

Kirk Walters: Runner-up for a spot on the U.S. Men's squad at Montreal in '76, Kirk is one of the strongest distance runners in this area. His best marathon has been 2:15:54, but he hopes to challenge Rodgers in New York this year. Kirk's other claim to fame is as an actor. At least he can say that his feet and legs are "actors." He stood in as double for Michael Williams in his recent film, *The Marathoner* (a Cinemetro Production).

Barry Gordon: Rosner's own "Marathon Man," Barry owns the local Superstar running store. But he's even more than a good businessman. Barry has run the Boston Marathon four times. Last year he finished New York in the sensational time of 2:22:34. Barry's dream, aside from owning a chain of Superstars around the country, is to break 2:20 at Boston next year.

In addition to the biographies, you also dig out a copy of the college's *Athletic Guidelines,* the book containing the school's policy on amateurism. The policy reads this way:

This college believes strongly in the value of amateur sports, and asserts that professionalism and money have no place on the college athletic field. Therefore, only amateur athletes may take part in college sports events, or engage in athletic activity on the Rosner Campus. No student, or any other person, who has ever received money in connection with any sport shall be allowed to participate. In addition, NO student or other person who has ever received money for discussing sports on television or radio, or in newspapers or magazines, or for endorsing any product or service on the basis of his or her sports experience, or from representing a manufacturer or business on the basis of his or her sports experience, shall be allowed to participate in any athletic activity sponsored by the college.

As Drake pointed out, AAU rules are much less strict than this school policy. Top-ranked athletes are now allowed to receive money from manufacturers, magazines, and so on, as long as they do not get paid *directly* for engaging in their sport. NCAA rules on the other hand, are strict—much more like Rosner's.

The trouble, you reason, is that the college's rules were made to cover *collegiate* athletics—to prevent unfair advantages, "fixing," and other irregularities in sporting events. Howard's race, however, includes people from all over the area and all over the country. You are expecting people of all ages and occupations, not just students. Is it fair to limit participation in the race with rules that are meant to apply to, say, school football or basketball teams?

If Howard House has to follow the college's rules, it might as well give up the race now. At best, the house may not earn all of the money it really needs, and the race will lose a lot of credibility as a serious event for local and area runners.

SUGGESTED DISCUSSION QUESTIONS

1. What is the conflict in this case?
2. Why would the college choose to define "amateur" the way it has?
3. What is the difference between an amateur and a professional?
4. Should the college make an exception to its rule in this situation? Why or why not?

SUGGESTED ASSIGNMENTS

1. The committee asks you to convince the dean that the athletes in question are really amateurs and that their presence poses no threat to the amateurism of the rest of the school's athletics. To do this, you'll need a solid definition of "amateur" as you see the word and a strong argument showing that the college's stricter definition should not apply in this case.
2. You try to convince the dean and fail. It's *no* "pros," or no race. Reluctantly, you agree. You're worried, of course, because you realize that most of the merchants who paid for ads and helped out did so mainly because of the "name" runners you'd promised. You decide that you'd better explain the situation to the merchants right away to try to keep as many with you as possible. Write a letter to Jeanette Morrison, President of the local Chamber of Commerce, explaining your situation and asking her to help you keep the business support the race now has. You know little about Morrison; she is, you're told, the most influential member of the local business community.
3. You succeed in persuading the dean to let the three "outside" athletes run, but only because you made it very clear that none of the three will receive a penny from Howard House or from the college. You're relieved, but when

you get back to the house you get a phone call from Terry Melville. She's in Maine and wonders if you intend to pay her expenses out to Rosner College and back. She explains that it's customary for race organizers to do this when they invite a top athlete to run.

You discuss the issue with her and find out that she wants about $300— a small sum, really, and one that could easily come out of the race budget. You consider going back to Simpson and asking for an exception to the ruling he's just given you. But you're afraid that raising the money issue with him now will put the whole race in jeopardy. You try to reach Melville by phone to discuss your decision but find that she will be away until the end of the week. Write her a letter explaining why you can't offer her the money, persuading her to come anyway.

Too Many Summer Jobs

It's early in the spring of your sophomore year at Eastern University, and you're giving a lot of thought to what you'll do this summer. You have two goals. The first is to save some money. Your parents say that they'll be able to help you get by with tuition again next year, but you hope to earn enough money this summer to take some of the pressure off them.

Your second goal is to try and gain some experience that will help you to get ahead later. At this point in your life, you have not yet decided exactly what you'd like to do after college. But you know that you'll be aiming at some kind of a professional career, and you hope to pick up some "pre-professional" experience (as they call it at the Placement Office) this summer.

THE LETTERS

Now, sitting in the library studying for a psychology exam, you wonder if you're going to be able to accomplish both goals this year. You open your looseleaf and pull out two letters you received recently. Taken together, they seem to symbolize your dilemma.

The first letter is from your father, and the last couple of paragraphs read as follows:

Oh, by the way, Stuart was by the other night and gave us some exciting news. He says that you can have your job at Wilton Corp. again this summer, and that he's arranged for you to come back as acting supervisor!!!

It's not just that Stuart's your uncle, either. He says old man Wilton was really impressed with you last year and asked for you back himself. Best news yet—you'll be making $205 a week—not bad. That's over $10,000 a year.

Be sure to write to Stuart and thank him. He'll give you the details.

Your job at Wilton last year had involved packing tools into crates for shipping. You imagine that your job this summer will involve the same part of the plant since you lack the skills to handle the manufacturing and machining jobs the plant offers. In one sense, your father's letter was great news. You'd be making good money for a summer job and, living at home, you'd be able to save a lot. You could end up with a couple of thousand dollars for next year and still have some summer spending money.

However, the news didn't make you as happy as it might have—primarily because of a letter you'd received just two days before your father's. This letter was from Jim O'Donnell, Creative Director at O'Donnell Associates, an ad agency located near the state capitol. O'Donnell is a university alumnus and had been on campus a few weeks ago recruiting applicants for a summer job in his agency. His letter reads, in part:

So, I'm glad to offer you a job as an advertising intern this summer. We think you've got the brains and the people skills we need to start with, and we'll teach you the rest.

The down side, of course, is money, just as I said when we met. We can offer an intern $125 a week, and I can only guarantee you eight weeks of work, though I'm pretty sure we'll be able to offer you three or four more weeks when the time comes.

Let me know if you'll accept, and please do so soon, as we have another candidate in mind if you turn us down. But we hope you'll come, and we're looking forward to seeing you this summer.

This job really appeals to you—both because you think that advertising is an exciting profession and because you were really impressed with O'Donnell during the interview. You're certain, too, that you'd get some really solid experience if you take the job. O'Donnell has promised that you'd be involved in copywriting, media selection, ad production, and client contact. The job seems to fit your goal of preparing for a professional career very well; the experience would be valuable in any profession you selected later.

Of course, the salary at O'Donnell Associates is not good and you'd have to spend the summer in the state capital, close to the job. Even though your roommate will be able to put you up for part of the summer, there's no chance you'd be able to save much money. You'd be lucky if you reached the end of the summer without owing anybody.

THE CHOICE

You sit back in the library carrel and put the letters away. It's funny—you've got everything you want, in a sense. It's too bad you can't handle both jobs. However, you've obviously got to choose between them or else keep looking for another job that meets both your need for money and your need to get some experience. Clearly, you've got to do some hard thinking about what you really want.

Another thought strikes you, too. If you accept the job with O'Donnell, you're going to need a good explanation for your dad and your Uncle Stuart. You don't expect that they'll be overjoyed at your going to O'Donnell, but you'd like them to *understand* what you're doing.

On the other hand, you really like Jim O'Donnell a lot. Even if you don't go to work for him this summer, he may be able to give you a lot of help next year or even after college. If you choose to go to the Wilton plant, you'll want to have a sound argument to present to O'Donnell. You want to leave him with the impression, if you choose not to accept his offer, that you're a careful thinker and a rational person—the kind he might like to employ some time in the future.

SUGGESTED DISCUSSION QUESTIONS

1. What are the conflicts in this case?
2. What are the advantages of the Wilton job?
3. What are the advantages of the O'Donnell job?
4. What kinds of choices have you made in the past about summer jobs?
5. Have you been happy with those choices?

SUGGESTED ASSIGNMENTS

1. You decide to accept O'Donnell's offer.
   a. Write to your father and explain to him your reasons for rejecting the Wilton job.
   b. Write to Uncle Stuart and explain your decision.
2. You decide to reject O'Donnell's offer and go back to Wilton for the summer. Write to O'Donnell and explain your decision. Your letter should reject the offer but retain O'Donnell's good opinion of you.

Research Assistant Wanted

You answered the ad on the bulletin board on a whim; it read:

WANTED: Research Assistant for Prof. Higgins. Work 10–12 hrs./wk. $2.90/hr. Business majors preferred, but all interested students invited to apply. #5546, Student Employment Service.

You really didn't expect to get the job—mainly because your major was "distributed studies," and the ad indicated that business majors had the inside track. But your interview with Professor Higgins went very well. He seemed to appreciate your interest in research and your openness in stating that you are not declaring a specialized major. In any case, he called you the next day with the good news.

As he described the job to you, it sounded interesting, even exciting. He was working on a textbook and a couple of articles. The subject concerned inflation and the effects of the growth of consumer credit—credit cards, loans, that sort of thing. What he really needed, he said, was someone to read, digest, and think about a lot of jumbled information—everything from magazine articles to federal reserve reports. The research assistant wouldn't have to know much about business, but he or she would have to be a clear thinker and a hard worker. Higgins added that a small part of the time would be devoted to helping him with administrative details such as getting permissions to quote people in the text, helping with the manuscript, and so on. But he made it clear that he wasn't hiring you as a secretary or gofer. The administrative work would be a *small* part of the job.

WORKING FOR HIGGINS

The first two months on the job lived up to your expectations. Your work consisted mainly of looking through the *Wall Street Journal* and business magazines like *Fortune* and *Forbes*. You had to collect articles on topics that seemed to be relevant to Higgins's work and make summaries of any that looked especially useful.

In addition, you occasionally had to go to the library and do some real digging. Sometimes you had to find, read, and summarize an important or hard-to-find article in a journal of economics or history. At other times Higgins sent you out to investigate broader topics such as the effects of inflation in Germany in the 1920s or the increased use of credit cards in the U.S. since 1970.

All in all, you found the first two months exciting and useful. The work taught you a lot and helped you to narrow down the fields you might work in after college. You're really quite satisfied with the job, or at least you were until a few weeks ago. Things started to change when Higgins called you in to tell you that his publisher had moved up the deadline for completion of the textbook.

"It's going to be tough," Higgins told you. "But I think we can make it. I hope you'll bear with me until I get this thing finished—I'll probably be a little disorganized until then."

THE PROBLEM

You expected that the increased pressure Higgins was feeling would result in an increased work load for you—rush jobs, last-minute visits to the library, and so on. But the "extra work" did not turn out to be research at all. One day, for example, you walked into Higgins's office and found this note:

I hate to ask you to do this, but would you mind straightening out the office for me today? It's getting so I can't find things when I need them, and you know how important it is for me to work as quickly and efficiently as possible these days.

Thanks.

PS—Go by the supply room, too. I've attached a list of things I need.

As you worked on the office, replacing books in the case, sorting papers and rearranging files, it struck you that this wasn't really what you believed your job should be. However, Higgins was under a lot of pressure, and he probably needed the "assistant" part of your job more than the "research" part right now.

As the next few weeks went by, however, you found that tasks such as straightening the office, copying letters, and answering the phone were becoming more time-consuming parts of your job, and the research was becoming less important. Once, for example, Higgins asked you to call some students to cancel appointments they'd made with him. He was just too busy, he said. Another time, he asked you to make some travel reservations for him since he had to leave town in a hurry and the department's secretary was ill.

You'd done all these things because you wanted to be helpful and because the job itself still seemed ultimately worthwhile—if you could ever get it back to the way it had been before. Higgins wasn't paying you, however, to clean up his office and you weren't learning anything by doing it. You wanted to speak to him about it but decided to wait until this week, when the textbook would finally be finished.

You intended, in fact, to bring up the subject when you met with him this morning. Instead, however, you found the following note:

It sure is good to be finished—I'll bet you're glad too. I couldn't take the office anymore, so I went home for the day. I'm out for the rest of the week. A conference at State University. To keep you busy for today, though, please do the following:

—get rid of all the old bluebooks and folders in my briefcase
—mail the letters on the shelf by the door
—pick up a couple of ribbons for my typewriter
—call Maintenance and get my window fixed

PS—Next week is vacation—Happy Spring! See you in two weeks.

You'd been hoping that Higgins would leave you some research to start on while he was away, or at least tell you that you could go back to the research part of your job now that the crunch was over. So the note leaves you somewhat let down. For a while Higgins had treated you almost as a junior colleague, someone who could be trusted to help with important pieces of his work. Now, it appears that what he really wanted was somebody to do his chores for him, some kind of servant.

As you mull the situation over, you decide you've got to do something. Things can't go on as they are.

SUGGESTED DISCUSSION QUESTIONS

1. What is the problem in this case?
2. What possible solutions exist?
3. Is Higgins right to expect what he does? Why or why not?
4. What should a student expect from this kind of job?

SUGGESTED ASSIGNMENTS

1. You try to call Higgins that weekend but find that he's gone on vacation already. Since you'll be away all the next week, you decide to write to him and explain your feelings. Write him a letter explaining your dissatisfaction.
2. You reach Higgins by phone the next week and begin to explain your position. However, he interrupts you and says that he thought you were willing to give him a hand during a difficult time, and that he didn't know the "chores" bothered you. He concludes by saying that if you're really that dissatisfied with the job, he will give it to someone else. Then he hangs up before you can say anything.
   a. Write Higgins and get your job back if you want it.
   b. You resign from the position, but you get a confidential questionnaire from the Student Placement Office. The questionnaire guarantees you confidentiality and anonymity and asks you to "describe whether you thought your research assistantship was successful."

On Patrol with the City P.D.

Chief Humke of the Rierdon Police Department needed a response to a letter he had just received from John B. Toth, an assistant professor of sociology at Fairfield University. The Chief reread the letter:

Dear Chief Humke:

At present I'm working on an article about college-town law enforcement and how our citizens view their police departments.

Before I came to Fairfield I did research in Bloomington, Indiana. There the police chief was most helpful, particularly by allowing me to interview officers and ride in a patrol car on a day and night shift.

When would be a convenient time for me to visit with you and members of your force? I'm particularly interested in a few more nights on the beat, especially since homecoming is coming up.

Sincerely yours,

John B. Toth

The letter troubled the chief because it represented another example in a trend he'd seen developing in his two years as Chief of Police. More and more people wanted to ride on patrol to do research, it seemed, and the Department had no particular policy established for dealing with these requests.

BACKGROUND

Rierdon was a city of forty thousand, a kind of bedroom suburb of a nearby large city. Many of the citizens were professionals of one sort or another. Many were students; Fairfield University enrolled a total of 9,245 undergraduate and graduate students. It was important to the Chief to maintain goodwill with the college community. Of course he was also the chief law enforcement official for the city and therefore responsible for every citizen's safety.

HUMKE

Chief Humke regularly spoke to individuals and community groups about the police department, so he was ready to visit with Roth in the station. Moreover, Humke was proud of his well-trained police force and was quite willing to have anyone speak with his officers about their work.

However, Humke had not decided exactly what to do about requests such as Toth's. Just the previous semester Humke had received a similar persuasive request from an undergraduate in journalism at Iowa State. Humke found the young woman's arguments for being allowed to go on assignment and ride in a patrol car quite convincing. Humke was always eager to maintain goodwill with the student population, and this young woman happened to be active in many social organizations on campus.

As a precaution, Humke asked the city attorney whether the city would be liable if, and this seemed extremely unlikely, the young woman were to be injured while on patrol. The city attorney responded by saying, in summary, that while the Department could have her sign a waiver, there was no way to eliminate the possibility that she would sue. The argument went something like this: Even though she might waive her rights, she could still sue, whether she had a good claim or not. Moreover, the waiver itself could be challenged in court and found not binding. However, the city attorney felt reasonably certain that a well-written waiver would give the city, the department, and the officer a great deal of protection. The Chief asked the city attorney to draft such a waiver; Humke received it a week later.

GOOD NEWS IN THE DAILY

The Chief consulted with his shift commanders and found an officer who was willing to take on a civilian observer. The watch was chosen for its relative safety, and all other officers on duty were appraised of the situation. When the student, Emily Bonfils, arrived, she willingly signed the waiver, and off she went with the officer.

The result of her patrol was an article in the *Fairfield Daily,* the student newspaper. The article pleased Humke because it was accurate and because it clearly made the police officer sound like a good guy—that night he'd helped an 85-year-old woman get her car started, he'd put out a brush fire behind a restaurant, and he'd told some good stories to his passenger. The Chief felt pleased with his decision and felt the Department had gained some goodwill and positive exposure.

The next day, however, the Chief began to change his mind. A journalism professor, the very professor who had given Mary Bonfils the assignment, called the Chief and demanded that the professor's other twenty-nine students be given the same opportunity. It wasn't fair, the professor argued, to let one student ride one particular semester and not let other students ride. Humke also got a call from a student in the English department at Fairfield. This student wanted to ride so he could write a short story based on the experience. Over the next few weeks the calls continued to come in.

It was impractical, of course, to try to schedule rides for everyone who asked. Humke felt he could not require officers to take along civilians. And while he was taking a tiny risk by allowing one rider, he wasn't prepared to increase that risk by allowing ten or twenty each semester. Then, of course, there was the actual efficiency of his officers to consider. Finally, the Chief solved the problem by saying the Department just didn't have time, that semester, to allow any more riders. But Humke knew he needed a long-term solution. Some sort of guidelines and procedures were what the Chief had in mind.

DISCUSSION QUESTIONS

1. What are the advantages to the Department of allowing people to interview officers and ride on patrol with them?

2. What are the disadvantages?

3. What policy should the Chief adopt?

4. Should Toth be made an exception to this policy? Or is he an example of the kind of rider who *should* be allowed?

SUGGESTED ASSIGNMENTS

1. Suppose you are an assistant to the Chief. Write him a memo in which you argue in favor of a particular policy.

2. Suppose you are an assistant to the Chief. Write Professor Toth and explain what the Department can and cannot offer him and why.

3. Try calling your own police department to determine what policy, if any, it has regarding civilians riding on patrol. Is the policy in writing? Write a letter to the Department and persuade it to allow you to visit the Department and discuss its policies. If you really want to write about your police department, persuade it to let you ride on patrol with an officer.

Chapter 7

Judgment and Opinion

Every time you tell a friend that *Gone With the Wind* is a great movie, or that so-and-so is an excellent ball player, you're making a judgment. Or, rather, you are expressing a judgment you have already made—either just now or much earlier. Making and expressing judgments, in fact, is something that all of us begin to do very early in our lives: even babies do it as they enthusiastically react to, say, applesauce, and just as strongly reject strained peaches. Judgments are not important because we start making them early. Their real significance lies in the fact that we make them *all the time*—"It's a beautiful day"—and at all key times in our lives—"He or she is the perfect mate"; "This is a great job."

One problem with judgments, though, is that we make them so automatically it's often difficult to talk about them. One of the first things people notice about college life, for example, is the importance placed on having opinions, on having something to say. People at college constantly ask you what you think. But if you tell someone that capital punishment is evil, then he or she will usually want to know *why*; it's not always easy to answer.

Everybody has seen or been in an argument in which one of the two participants tries to defend an assertion like "The Yankees are the best team in baseball" with repetition instead of logic: *"Because* they are the best, that's why!" The point is that you have opinions you're expected to express, but it's not always clear how you got your opinions or how you can best explain them.

Learning the Process

At times people make judgments without thinking, as you can see when a friend wrinkles up his or her nose at the smell of sour milk or an overly spicy soup. But making judgments is an identifiable process just the same—a process that can be slowed down, examined, and learned. It's important to learn this process mainly because your gut feelings, valid as they are, are not persuasive arguments for people who don't share them. It's important to know how you make judgments in another way as well—to make them more skillfully and accurately. Making good judgments is important since you have to make so many of them, some that are especially important in your life.

You'll find, too, that if you can explain the reasons behind your opinion coherently, you'll be much more convincing, especially to people who haven't examined their own opinions clearly. Even if you can't convince others with very different opinions to adopt yours, you can at least establish yourself as a reasonable person and open up the channels of communication between you and your audience.

The process of making a judgment, then, is worth investigating. It's simple enough in the abstract but, like riding a bike or hitting a golf ball, you have to learn it by doing it. Here are the steps involved in the process; note that they can form the outline of an essay that explains the judgment as they explain what you did to make the judgment.

Judgment: X is an excellent Y.

Step One: Decide on the criteria for judgment, the standards that an X must meet to be "excellent."

Step Two: Rank the criteria in order of importance.

Step Three: Determine how the object, person, and such being judged fits or does not fit the criteria.

Looking at an Example

Criteria are simply *standards;* you use them every time you say "smooth as silk," or "light as a feather." Here's an example to show you how to develop criteria.

Suppose your brother or sister is ready for college and has been accepted by both a big midwestern state university and a small private college in New England. The judgment he or she must make is "X is the best college for me."

If you were asked for advice you'd probably ask what was really wanted out of college, or what kind of place he or she wanted to spend the next four years in. You'd be asking for *criteria*, for a list of standards that, for your sibling, a college must meet to be a good one. If you asked a number of questions, you might uncover four or five criteria that look like this:

—good social life
—near a big city
—strong athletics department
—good _____ program
—excellent academic reputation

Next, you'd have to determine the relative importance of each of the criteria, the value of each. One way to determine value is to rank criteria from most to least important. Suppose that a "good social life" was really the most important criterion on the list, as it is for some students, and that the rest of the list is ranked in the same order as above, with an "excellent academic reputation" lowest in terms of importance.

Ranking the judgments this way makes it easier to make a judgment that's as close as possible to what is really wanted. You can make the judgment more easily by getting even more specific about the relative value of each criterion. Suppose, for example, that a "good social life" was so important that your brother or sister said, "If the college doesn't have a good social life, I'm not going." If that were the case, then either college—the one in the midwest or the one in New England—that didn't have a good social life would be ruled out automatically. It wouldn't matter if the college fulfilled the other criteria. You can decide on the relative importance of criteria by ranking them and also by deciding, as much as possible, how much weight each one carries.

Once you and your brother or sister defined the criteria for a good college and decided on the relative value of each criterion, you could examine each of the schools and check its characteristics off against the list. You might find, for example, that the state school has a reputation as a very social campus, while the small school was considered a haven for individualists. If you checked off each school against the list, you'd probably see that one college would fit the criteria that seemed most important. If your list was exhaustive, if it really reflected all the important things that made a college "good" for your brother or sister, then you could determine which of the schools was better and be fairly sure that the judgment would hold up.

Being Reasonable: Communicating

The criteria discussed above might show what, for your brother or sister, are the standards a good college must meet. Remember that any judgment is personal. Your standards will not necessarily match those of your parents or your roommate or the person sitting next to you in English class. Your parents' list of criteria, for example, might place much importance on "cost" with almost as much importance placed on "excellent academic reputation." And a "good social life" might not even be on their list. Since people disagree in so many judgments, the purpose of analyzing them in the step-by-step process outlined in this chapter is to allow you to explain your opinion to others.

Many people defend assertions simply by saying, "It's my opinion, and I have a right to it." They're right, of course, but they're also not communicating. To convince people that *your* judgment is reasonable, explain your standards clearly, show why they're reasonable, and realize that others will see things differently. If you show that your opinions are *reasonable*, that they're based on logical application of consistent, clear standards, your opinions will be respected. You will have communicated with your audience and left the door open for further communication.

Summary

The process of making a judgment and of explaining how you made it has three basic steps:

1. Decide on the criteria for judgment.
2. Rank them; determine their relative importance.
3. Show how the object, person, or thing being judged fits or does not fit the criteria.

People will listen to you and understand you and your opinions according to how well you make and explain the many judgments you make throughout your college career and your life.

Museum of Technology

It's late June, and you're really enjoying your summer job as coordinator of the museum's tour program for inner-city kids. You're planning to handle about 3,550 kids this summer—by far the most ever—and you expect to have plenty of federal money to pay for buses, lunches for the kids, and program expenses. At this point, you're the program's only full-time staff member. You have a secretary to answer the phone and type things up for you, of course, but the secretary works only part-time. The real work force, essential to the success of the program, is a group of ten to twelve volunteers. They are mostly retired people and suburban housewives, with a few college students thrown in.

YOUR JOB

Each day the program provides seventy innercity kids with a tour of the museum, a lecture-demonstration, a free lunch, and a round-trip bus ride. The kids come from schools, Y's, and day camp programs, range in age from eight to thirteen, and are of all ethnic backgrounds. Your job is to confirm the schedule (set up last fall by your predecessor) with the schools and the bus company weekly; recruit, schedule, and train volunteers; represent the program and the museum at outside activities; and be an on-the-scene troubleshooter during the five hours the kids are at the museum every day.

You've found running the program to be rewarding, but an awful lot of work. The schedule is always breaking down; schools back out, forget when they're to come, and come with twice as many kids as they'd agreed to. Buses are rarely on time—sometimes they don't show up at all. The pool of volunteers is always shifting, so you've got to keep getting new ones through ads and word of mouth; you end up training several new volunteers almost every week and covering for those who forget to come. And the combination of representing your program at the museum and at outside functions in the evening and finding kids' sweaters and tying their shoes in the daytime is confusing, as much as you like it.

After three tough weeks, you decide that the job is too big and too widely diversified for one person. You explain the situation to your boss, the museum's director of education, and she agrees. After a meeting with *her* boss, she tells you that you now have a budget of $150 a week for an assistant, and that you're to go out and hire somebody.

THE PROBLEM

You're excited by the responsibility, but a little uneasy. You've never had to hire anyone before and don't know how to begin. There really isn't time to advertise widely, so you simply call a few college placement offices and put up a sign in the volunteer's lounge:

> Assistant to Coordinator wanted. 40 hours/wk.
> $600 a month until August 31. See me to apply.
> Position open immediately.

Immediately nine or ten volunteers apply, plus a few other people you've never heard of. They are mostly students who've heard about the job through their placement offices. As you interview these people (it takes two days), you realize that you're not sure what the "ideal" candidate for the job should be like. You've been so busy trying to do your own job that you haven't had time to decide what parts of it an assistant could take over. In short, you're not sure what you're looking for. After the interviews you're left with four candidates—all of whom impressed you. As you sit down at your desk late one afternoon, you notice a message from your boss.

"Must know the decision on your asst. by 9 A.M. tomorrow. Get going!"

You pick up the notes you made during and after the interviews with the four finalists and try to make a decision.

THE FINALISTS

Erica Castell: Age 32, a mother and housewife from Weston, Massachusetts. Graduated from Wellesley College in '68, B.A. in History of Science. One of your best volunteers, she's able to explain the museum's exhibits better than anyone else and has assisted you in training volunteers. Desires responsibilities and challenge, not money. Erica told you she felt certain that she could handle all the scheduling and training of volunteers and probably could even improve the quality of the tour you give the kids. She hopes she can bring in a lot more volunteers, too, if she gets the job.

Chuck Cole: A junior at Boston University's School of Management. Has worked in sales and marketing in past summers; wants this job because he's changed his plans to go to summer school at the last minute. Dresses better than you do and explains that he'd be most useful handling the public relations part of the job and "outside" contacts such as the schools and bus company. Says he's a good fund raiser and a whiz at scheduling. Chuck would like more than $150 a week if he could get it. Not a volunteer.

Ray Manitelli: Late 60s. Recently retired manager of a large supermarket in the suburbs. Ray wants the job because volunteering's not enough for him; he's afraid retirement will kill him unless he stays busy. An expert schedule maker and troubleshooter, he feels he could "hold down the office" for you, make calls, find lost kids, fill in for missing volunteers, etc. "It would leave you ample time for the more professional duties you have," Ray said, "like training volunteers and representing the program."

Kelly Jacobs: A senior in education at State College. A warm, friendly person, Kelly cares for the kids, and they know it: by the end of the day they are following her around everywhere. She frankly admits that she's not tough, hates facing the public, and wants to leave the business details to you. But she knows she can help with the day-to-day "kid problems" and with the volunteers. She's sure that this experience will lead to her landing a full-time job after she graduates next spring, if you'll just give her the chance. "It would be ideal for my resume," she says.

SUGGESTED DISCUSSION QUESTIONS

1. How are you going to decide whom to hire?
2. Why is deciding difficult?
3. Are all the candidates qualified in certain ways? How?
4. How would you define your job as coordinator of the museum?
5. How would you define your assistant's job?

SUGGESTED ASSIGNMENTS

1. Make a list of the criteria you would use in deciding whom to hire. Judge each candidate according to your list. If possible, rank the candidates in order of qualification, from most to least qualified.
2. Your boss just called you on the phone and said, "I don't know why you decided to hire X, but you'd better send me a memo explaining why. One of the candidates that didn't get hired knows some influential people here and has complained about your decision."
3. Suppose you were deciding whom to hire for a job (cashier in the cafeteria, dorm floor supervisor, manager of the bookstore). State the specific job you have in mind, and list the criteria by which you would judge applicants.

Brenda Green

Your mail today included a letter from a friend, Brenda Green, who is attending a private, four-year college in the East. When you recognized her handwriting on the envelope, you felt good because you've written Brenda about once a month since school started (this is the first year of college for both of you), but she hasn't written you for some three months. You had been afraid that she'd stopped writing altogether. Here's the part of the letter that explains why Brenda is writing to you now:

. . . So since I don't know what to do, and you've always been such a close friend, I thought I'd write and ask your advice. Since you're not here, you can be more objective. Bob thinks I should go ahead and have the baby—we'd get married right away—and then he says next year I can come back to school and we'll figure out some way of taking care of the baby.

But then he says if I want to, it's okay with him if I get an abortion, but if I do, I have to do it right away since I'm already nearly three months pregnant. I think I love Bob, but this doesn't seem like the right time for us to be getting married, or the right reason either, but then when I think about having the baby I get excited because it seems like it would be a good thing and you know I've always wanted to have children. Sometimes it seems like the more I think about it the less I can make up my mind. And you know I'm supposed to be the hot-shot student going to law school.

Of course my parents don't know, nobody else knows yet except you, and I won't have to tell them, at least maybe not until it's over, if I decide to get an abortion. Money is no problem since I have plenty of my own savings and there is a medical center nearby where they'll do it. I've already seen a doctor there. I don't know what else to tell you except write me back today.

The Green Family

Brenda's father is the owner of a local hardware store in your hometown. He seems like a nice enough guy, though he's almost never home, or so Brenda's always said. Her mother works for the phone company, but you have never been able to figure out exactly what it is that she does. Because Brenda's two brothers are quite a few years older than she is, the family seems to treat her as if she were the "baby." You can imagine how concerned they'd be if they knew she was pregnant. And you're not too sure how her father would react, although your guess is that her mother would probably support her in whatever she decided to do. You've always thought of the Green family as "good people." They are involved in community affairs but don't belong to any particular church.

Brenda is paying for her college education partly with her own savings, partly with a loan/grant, and partly with help from her parents. You suppose anyone would call the Greens middle-class, but inflation has hurt them too. They have never seemed to have any money to spare, but they have always had enough.

BOB REMINGTON

From a previous letter you already know that Bob Remington, Brenda's boyfriend, is somebody she met at college and fell for in a hurry. The last letter she wrote talked about nothing but what she and Bob were busy with, and she told you that, like herself, he is a political science major who hopes to go on to law school after he obtains his undergraduate degree.

Of course Brenda's letter now makes you want to know more about Bob, so you dig out two letters in which she mentioned him. (You are one of those people who keeps every letter you receive.) In one letter, Brenda mentions that Bob is from a big family—six children—and that he is the youngest of four boys. Both of his parents are teachers. With so many children to put through college, Brenda wrote, although Bob's parents encouraged him to go to college, they expect him to make his own way. He was awarded a partial scholarship and borrowed the rest of the money he needed for tuition.

"The family really hopes Bob will do well," Brenda wrote. "They are proud of how well he did in high school."

SUGGESTED DISCUSSION QUESTIONS

1. What are the problems in this case?
2. Who has to make a decision?
3. What is Bob Remington like?
4. What does Brenda's letter tell you about her?
5. What should Brenda do? Why?

SUGGESTED ASSIGNMENTS*

1. Write a letter to Brenda. Tell her what you think she should do.
2. Write a letter to Bob. Tell him what you think he should do.
3. Write an opinion essay in which you state what you think Brenda should do. (Audience: a student who has read the case)

*For each of these assignments make a list of criteria to determine what Brenda should do and why. (Your instructor may ask you to turn in this list along with your letter or essay.)

The Red Key Society

You are president of the Red Key Society, a prestigious campus service club. The Red Key was formed over fifty years ago to function as a group of student representatives for the university. Uniformly bright and articulate, Red Key members provide guided tours of the campus for visiting VIPs, speak at alumni and admissions office functions, and act as advisors on student affairs to the deans and the university president.

Competition is fierce when it comes to getting into Red Key. Traditionally, its members go on to success in graduate school and academic and professional careers, and it has always provided the core of the university's loyal and generous alumni club. Most students view Red Key as something like an insurance policy for success at the university, so naturally people want to get in and try their best to do so.

Of course, it's difficult to get into Red Key, too—primarily because the society is so small. There are always just twenty-four members: no freshmen, eight people from each of the upper three classes. Like the campus fraternities and sororities, Red Key holds a "rush week" every fall when prospective sophomore members are interviewed. For the eight openings in the society this year, you and your fellow members received 275 applications, and interviewed thirty sophomores.

You recall all the hard work of sorting through the applications and trying to make faces and papers match in the interviews. Many of the decisions you and the others had to make were difficult. The responsibility was heavy because you realized that your decision to accept or reject each applicant could have an effect on that person's career. Therefore, you made the best decisions you could; naturally you were relieved when rush week was over.

DAVE EDWARDS

Now, in the last few weeks of the fall semester, you're pleased with the group of people accepted this year. They've learned the ropes quickly, and you have received good reports about several of them from the alumni and from the dean of admissions. Unfortunately, your satisfaction has just been shattered by a letter you found in the society's mailbox this afternoon. The letter is from Gary Wright, Secretary of the Associated Alumni club, and it concerns a potentially difficult situation. The letter concludes this way:

So, to put it in a nutshell, I need to know why you didn't admit Dave Edwards into the society. As you know, his father is one of our major contributors, and he is absolutely furious that his son didn't make it.

As far as I know, David is doing well in his courses, and his father claims he's bright and personable—"perfect Key material."

I hate to put pressure on you or the others, but we've got to keep Edward's father happy if we can. What do you suggest?

You saw Dave Edwards at the rush week interviews and recall that he hadn't impressed you very much. You're not really sure why he was rejected, so you go back to the applications and interview notes in your file to find out.

Edwards was doing well in school, that was true. The minimum GPA needed to apply for the Red Key was 3.0. Edwards had a 3.31, so his grades were competitive. It was equally clear, however, that the other members of Red Key hadn't reacted very favorably to Edwards.

Rita Mooney, senior, wrote: "David's a nice enough person—dresses well, seems friendly. But he's terribly nervous—painfully shy too. Saw him in a group of three other sophs. He couldn't get a word in edgewise. Too bad, really, because I think he's a bright guy. But I vote no."

Bob Adretti, junior: "This guy's a zero. Didn't say 'boo' the whole time I was with him. Like trying to talk to a brick wall. Doesn't look like a turkey, but imagine him trying to guide some big alum around campus. NO WAY."

Sam Harris, senior: "Not sure. I thought he was pretty weak for most of the time I spent with him. He's awfully quiet. But we got to talking about movies and he really opened up. *Annie Hall, Citizen Kane, The Big Sleep*—he's really an expert, lots of fun to listen to. I think he really wants to join us, and he might develop into a dynamite member IF we help him. I'll take a risk and vote yes."

Kay Tyler, junior: "I hate to say it, but NO. I like this candidate a lot—he looks like a Key member. But he's very quiet and self-conscious. Also, I don't think he's really committed to doing all the work the Key requires.

"I know Dave personally, at least a little. He's got a lot of extracurricular stuff on his shoulders already. He said he needs the Key to get into law school but feels a little put off by the kind of time it would demand from him."

After looking at the material, you're sure that you and the rest made the right decision. Competition is so keen, for example, that this year all but one of those who gained admission did so with unanimous support from Key members. It is clear that you must stick by the decision not to admit Edwards; neither letting a current member go to make room for Edwards nor adding him as an unprecedented twenty-fifth member is acceptable to you, the society, or the university.

SUGGESTED DISCUSSION QUESTIONS

1. What kinds of activities do Red Key members participate in?
2. What kinds of skills and abilities do these activities require?
3. What sort of criteria would be useful in judging whether Red Key applicants should be accepted?
4. How does Dave Edwards meet or fail to meet these criteria?
5. What should you do to convince Edwards that the decision not to admit him was a fair one?

SUGGESTED ASSIGNMENTS

1. Write Gary Wright and explain why Dave Edwards was not admitted. Consider how much you need to say about the society's criteria for admission and provide evidence that Edwards does not meet them.
2. You talk to Wright on the phone, and he's pleased with your explanation. The best way out of the situation, he says, might be for you to write Edwards a formal letter explaining the society's admissions criteria and telling why you could not accept him. Wright asks you to bear in mind that Edwards's father may have access to the letter. Wright adds that he hopes you'll be honest without offending anyone.
3. You meet Wright and discuss the situation. He seems satisfied with your decision. As you leave, he asks you to provide him with a clearer idea of how

people actually get chosen for the Key. Let him have a list of at least three of the criteria being applied in the Edwards case. Explain why each one is a valid standard by which to judge applicants.

The Presidential Election (A)

With a student enrollment of just 9,000, Cisco State College, located in Central California, had never done particularly well in football, but its basketball team was a great source of pride. In fact, the previous year Cisco State had gone so far as to win its game against the University of New Mexico in the first round of the NCAA men's basketball championship. Basketball wasn't just the most popular sport at Cisco State; it was the *only* sport that consistently drew large crowds. These crowds had caused the administration and the Athletic Department at Cisco State to begin planning the construction of a new basketball arena.

TINGLEY FIELD HOUSE

Tingley Field House, the present home of the Cisco Warriors, was in need of renovation and seated only 4,000. The Athletic Department, basing its estimates on preseason ticket demand, felt that Cisco State could easily fill a 12,000-seat arena on a regular basis. Once completed, the arena would provide additional capacity that would add a significant amount of income to the athletic program since the Warriors played at least ten games at home every year. But the proposed construction of the new arena had caused considerable controversy on campus, and this controversy had spilled over into the election for a student body president.

FUNDING AND USE

The administration planned to use the new $5.7 million arena for men's basketball, wrestling, and gymnastics. The new arena would be located on university-owned land about two miles from central campus. An additional $100,000 was to be set aside to partially renovate Tingley Field House for women's basketball and gymnastics. An important part of the financing for the construction and renovation was to come from a five-dollar-per semester increase in tuition that would have to be approved by the California State Board of Regents. The student activity fee was also to be increased five dollars each year for five years. But when the administration and the Athletic Department unveiled their plans, many students protested vigorously.

PROTESTS

A large group of feminists announced that they would oppose any increase in tuition or activity fee because the administration was obviously giving women second-rate treatment. Only after deciding that the Tingley Field House was a potential fire hazard and had a worn-out hardwood floor (the feminists pointed out), did the administration condescend to allow women its exclusive use. The majority of women's games and workouts had previously been held in Peterson Gymnasium—the women's physical education building. Under the federal government's Title IX provision, the feminists argued, the administration had to give women equal time in the new arena.

The administration responded to the criticism by saying it hadn't meant to exclude women from the arena, but that the men's teams, which consistently drew much larger crowds, should certainly be given priority in its use. (The arena was to include a weight room, sauna, and whirlpool, all with the most up-to-date equipment.)

ROBERT J. KELLY

Robert Kelly, who was already considering a run for the presidency of the student government, remained unconvinced of the administration's good intentions. Kelly was a senior in business administration, an excellent student academically, and possibly the most active student on campus. He had previously worked with the administration enough to understand its financial point of view, but he thought perhaps Tingley, which was located right on the main campus, should be *fully* renovated and then turned over to the students for intramural and recreational use. In a letter to the editor of the school newspaper, Kelly said he wasn't sure whether he completely agreed with the feminists, but he pointed out that expecting women to use Tingley exclusively or primarily would leave little time for intramural and recreational use of the building. Kelly pointed out that even the administration had agreed that the students were already short on recreational facilities.

Intramural games had to be scheduled at noon and dinner times to accommodate all the teams. During intramurals, the basketball, handball, and racketball courts were seldom, if ever, available for recreational use. In fact, even intramurals had to be limited due to a lack of space, and students had shown an increasing interest in recreational sports. Kelly also pointed out that the women's basketball team played only a sixteen-game schedule, with just eight home games. Previously they had played all eight in Tingley. Now they could play all eight in the new arena. He wondered whether eighteen-to-twenty men's and women's basketball games would really keep the arena so busy that the women couldn't be allowed to use it for gymnastics meets as well.

THE PRESIDENTIAL ELECTION

Many students admired Kelly's aggressiveness in questioning the administration, and before long he was nominated and running for student body president. Kelly was well known on campus because he was an active member of many clubs and campus organizations. People who knew him, in fact, were amazed at how much he accomplished. It was no surprise that he had little time for partying and no girlfriend on campus (though he was said to have a girlfriend down at U.C.L.A.). Between maintaining his high grade-point average, working part-time as a bookkeeper, and participating in a plethora of campus activities, Kelly must have been busy seventy to eighty hours a week. In his initial campaign speech, Kelly pledged to question the increase in the activity fee, *which had to be approved by the student body president.* Since Kelly was still privately undecided about forcing the administration to guarantee women's teams equal access to the new arena (and therefore all students' increased access to Tingley), Kelly made no specific promises about these issues.

MARK SHANNON

Mark Shannon, quarterback of Cisco State's football team, was Kelly's sole opponent. Shannon said men should have top priority in use of the new arena because men's basketball had created the need for it *and* because men's basketball would pay for it. If the women could conveniently be allowed to play a few games there, fine, but their presence shouldn't inconvenience the men in any way. It wasn't practical, Shannon added, to put a women's basketball game in a 12,000-seat arena when a crowd of only a thousand or two would be all that would attend. When women had earned their way and had proven their popularity in sports, Shannon argued, then they could be given equal use of the arena.

THE STUDENT VOTERS

The vast majority—95 percent—of Cisco State's students came from California; most of them came from middle-class families in northern and central California. Normally these students, who were generally more liberal than students in southern California, were apathetic about student government. In the last election, for example, although 8,756 students were eligible to vote, only 1,016 had bothered to do so. The number of males and females attending Cisco State was about the same; the percentage of minority students who attended the college was representative of the area.

JANETTE RASHAD AND MITCH HUDNELL

As political science majors, Janette Rashad and Mitch Hudnell had a special interest in joining Robert Kelly's campaign staff. Janette immediately completed what she and Mitch believed to be a fairly accurate pool of the student voters. Kelly led in the pool with 42 percent, Shannon had 40 percent, and 18 percent were undecided. The election was a tough one to predict because of traditional student apathy. Who would the students who bothered to vote support?

Janette and Mitch really thought Kelly was a winner. Robert was generally considered to be a good-looking guy, though not quite handsome; he knew many more people across the campus than Shannon did, and he could honestly say that his business background would make him a more effective president. Shannon's major was physical education. There was clearly a block of student voters who wanted to use Tingley for intramural and recreational purposes, and an even larger block of voters who wanted women to have equal access to the arena. Also, there was a group who would obviously vote for Kelly just because they liked him personally.

Mitch and Janette discussed exactly what position Kelly should take about the new arena and about the renovation of Tingley Field House. Mitch pointed out that the administration had admitted that the $100,000 would only pay for renovation of the basketball court itself, yet it was common knowledge that the bench seats in Tingley were clearly in need of replacement, the lighting for all the courts was antiquated and inadequate, and the adjacent racketball courts badly needed refinishing.

One option was that Kelly could campaign on the promise that he would absolutely oppose *any* construction using student fees unless women's teams were guaranteed full access—all home basketball games and gymnastic tournaments as well as work-out times—to the new arena. Another option was some sort of compromise between Shannon and the feminists. Because the issue was a hot one on campus, Janette and Mitch agreed that Kelly would definitely have to formulate a clearly stated opinion.

SUGGESTED DISCUSSION QUESTIONS

1. Should Cisco State give women equal access to the new arena?
2. What is Cisco State's student population like?
3. What rights do women have in the funding and support of college sports competition?
4. What should Kelly do?

SUGGESTED ASSIGNMENTS

1. You are Mark Shannon's campaign manager. Write a position paper about the new arena and state Shannon's opinion.

2. You are Janette Rashad or Mitch Hudnell. Write a position paper for Kelly that states (what you think) Kelly's position should be on the new arena.

3. You are Janette Rashad or Mitch Hudnell. Write Robert Kelly a memo in which you tell him what you think his position should be. Show him that your opinion on this issue is reasonable and consistent.

4. Write an article for publication in your own school newspaper. Explain Title IX (you may have to do quite a bit of research), and state your opinion about whether women's sports deserve funding equal to the funding allocated for men's sports.

The Presidential Election (B)

Robert Kelly carefully considered the opinions of his campaign managers, Janette Rashad and Mitch Hudnell, and decided upon his position. He announced that he strongly believed the administration should guarantee women's teams equal access to the new arena and give all students interested in intramurals and/or recreation increased access to a fully renovated Tingley Field House. The administration had recently disclosed that full renovation would cost $400,000, and that was why the plan had been abandoned.

Shannon continued to call for preference to men. Since the complete renovation of Tingley would force the administration to raise student fees an additional two or three dollars a year, Shannon was opposed to it. He agreed that students needed better facilities, but he said that Cisco State's students couldn't afford both better facilities *and* a new arena. He also said they wouldn't support both. The new arena was more important. Perhaps, in a couple of years, Tingley renovation could be continued.

Kelly said that Tingley renovation and nonsexist resource allocation were more important. If students had to pay a bit more, they should and would.

THE ANONYMOUS NOTE

In the final week before election day, the contest continued to pan out as Janette and Mitch had predicted, though their latest pool put Kelly at 53 percent, Shannon at 46 percent, and one percent undecided. Obviously Kelly's strong stance on the new arena had polarized the vote.

The first day of the last week, as Kelly was talking to the Accounting and Marketing Clubs and telling them that women would draw better crowds if given the chance to do so, Janette and Mitch received a note in the intercampus mail. It read:

You ever wonder why Kelly never goes out with girls? It isn't because he's got a girlfriend at U.C.L.A., like he says. It's because he's got a boyfriend there. If you don't believe it, ask him. If he doesn't drop out of the race by the end of the week, the whole college will know that Kelly is a homosexual.

Janette's first impulse was to throw the note away, but Mitch stopped her and said, "Let's think this over. What if they did spread the rumor? We'd lose votes, wouldn't we? Maybe just a few, but it's a close race."

Before Janette could reply she got a phone call from the editor of the school paper. "I got the message that you called," he said. "Something about a story you have on Kelly, about his friend at U.C.L.A.?"

Janette told the editor to never mind. They had no story. She and Mitch had agreed that they couldn't exactly take a poll to find out students' views on having a gay president. They couldn't think of anything else, so they went off to find Robert. He was in the library up on the fourth floor at a carrel he always used. Janette looked around uneasily, but no one else seemed to be on the floor. Only Kelly would climb way up there to study late on a Friday afternoon, she thought. She and Mitch sat down and she handed Robert the note. He read it, blushed slightly, and looked down at the table as if to concentrate. After a few seconds he handed her back the note, looked her in the eyes, and said, "Well, it's true. What do we do now?"

SUGGESTED DISCUSSION QUESTIONS

1. Should Kelly do anything about the note?
2. What options does Kelly have in dealing with the note?
3. Would students vote against him if he announced that he was gay?
4. What is Cisco State's student population like?

SUGGESTED ASSIGNMENTS

1. You are Janette Rashad or Mitch Hudnell. Write Robert Kelly a confidential memo recommending what action he should take.
2. You are Janette Rashad or Mitch Hudnell. Write a statement (for publication in the school paper) in which Kelly announces that he is gay or which deals with the expected rumors in some other way.
3. You are Mark Shannon's campaign manager. You have just received a copy

of the anonymous note that Janette received. Write a memo to Mark recommending what action, if any, he should take.

4. The campus newspaper announces that Kelly has admitted he is gay but that he feels that fact is irrelevant to this or any other campaign. Write an essay for the *Cisco State Warrior* in which you give your opinion about Kelly's position that his sexual preferences are irrelevant.

To Build or Not to Build (A)

In the fall of 1982 Jack Trice, head of the city of Trinidad's Recreation Program, met with the Trinidad Softball Association officers and the head of Trinidad's Parks and Recreation Department, Marvin Bell. The problem was obvious, but the solution wasn't. During the prior three softball seasons participation in the city's fast-pitch and slow-pitch softball leagues had increased from 12 teams in 1980 to 122 teams in 1982. And yet the city simply didn't have enough softball diamonds for all the teams to play at convenient hours. In fact, several team applications had to be denied in 1982 because there was no time available to schedule enough games. The only solution seemed to be to build more softball diamonds.

The Trinidad Softball Association—an independent organization representing the interests of the city's softball teams—strongly favored building more and better diamonds. Presently Trinidad was not competitive with other cities the same size, and there were too few diamonds to permit the holding of statewide or even large regional tournaments. These tournaments, the Association argued, could bring money to the Association itself (through tournament fees and vending profits), to the Parks and Recreation Department (through diamond and vendor rental fees), and to the city of Trinidad (through the commerce created by visiting teams and their fans).

JACK TRICE

Jack Trice favored building new diamonds, as did Marvin Bell, his boss. However, there were two obstacles that Trice and Bell faced: cost and location. The city code required that large expenses, such as would be incurred by building the proposed four-diamond complex, had to be approved by either the City Council or by voter referendum. The City Council routinely declined to approve similar kinds of expenditures. For example, the Council had referred for referendum the Parks and Recreation Department's request for a new city swimming pool—presently the city had no outdoor pool. However, the voters had not approved the referendum on the proposed pool, even though many argued the pool was much needed. Trice and Bell felt certain, therefore, that a softball diamond referendum would *never* be approved. In Bell's words, "If the voters don't even want their kids to have the chance to swim in an outdoor pool in the summertime, they sure aren't going to spend money so a bunch of jocks can play softball."

Trice suggested that the players themselves pay for the diamond construction. By charging the players a ten-dollar user fee for each year for the next five years, Trice and Bell estimated they could raise $85,000, enough to build four new diamonds, fence them, and light them. Proper fences and lights were especially important because both were required by the American Softball Association for Association-sanctioned tournaments.

LEAGUE FEES

At the end of the 1982 season the softball leagues were organized as follows. There were seven men's slow-pitch leagues comprising a total of ninety-two teams. There were two women's slow-pitch leagues with eight teams each, and there were fast-pitch teams for men and women, each of the two leagues having seven teams. Each team admitted to a league was required to pay a league fee averaging, in 1982, $250. The fee paid for all the upkeep required on the diamonds as well as for umpires for the games and for additional supervisory staff hired on a seasonal basis. Most teams wore uniforms, but uniforms were not required. Most teams had sponsors—local businesses—that paid the league fees and bought uniforms as well as equipment. Many teams, however, were forced to rely upon team players to pay all expenses. Other expenses the teams and/or their team members incurred included diamond rental fees for practices and entry fees for tournaments. Membership in the Trinidad Softball Association was voluntary for city-league teams, but 90 percent of the teams paid the twenty-dollar-per year fee.

YES AND NO

Trice thought the players would be willing to pay the ten-dollar user fee if they were promised four excellent softball diamonds as a return on their investment. Bell agreed. The four-diamond complex would take five years to complete, but all four unlit, unfenced diamonds could be used during the second year the fee was charged. Some preliminary studies by a landscape architect showed that the city could get the job done for about $85,000, excluding the purchase of any new land. The required ten acres of land could cost as much as a quarter of a million dollars or even more. Trice, Bell, and the officers of the Association agreed that team players would not be able to pay for the land as well—fees would be too high and have to be collected over too long a period of time.

THE CITY COUNCIL

The next step was for Bell and Trice to go to the City Council and ask for its approval for the Department to pay for a study to determine where to locate the new diamonds. The Council approved the idea of a study. Bell asked the Parks and Recreation Commission—a group of volunteers from the community—to study the problem of site location and make a recommendation to the City Council. The Commission studied seventeen possible sites and concluded that the four-diamond complex should be located in a city park on the western edge of town, right next to the three best softball diamonds the city had to offer.

FERGUSON PARK

Ferguson Park, located in a river valley right on the city's western edge, seemed like the obvious choice. Composed of 160 acres, the park was largely a wooded area, with the exception of one large area used for flag football and one area used for Little League Baseball. Due to size and other differences, the Little League area was not suitable for softball. This area bordered directly on the backyards of houses in the areas, and some of those residents already complained about the temporary snow fences that were erected during the Little League Season. The flat football area, however, was further away from nearby houses and the Parks and Recreation Department could relocate those games elsewhere.

From the city's standpoint the location was ideal because the Parks and Recreation Department's maintenance facility was already located at Ferguson Park. Thus diamond maintenance would involve a minimum of time and travel. The Trinidad Softball Association also favored the site because three excellent diamonds were already located there; softball tournaments could be easily managed in one central location, and some vending facilities were already available.

The Commission also took other factors into consideration—the availability of water and power lines, the prohibitive cost of buying land anywhere, and so on. The Commission held two public meetings, which were attended only by enthusiastic softball players. Finally, the Commission made its recommendation to the City Council, in the winter of 1982. The Council discussed the plan at one public meeting and approved it at the next. The Council gave the Parks and Rec Department the power to collect the fees and approved the construction, provided that no city funds were used.

THE PLAYERS VOTE

Early the following spring, in 1983, Trice and Bell called a meeting of all 125 managers of the 1983 softball teams. The proposed five-year plan, including the ten-dollar-per-player,-per-year, fee was discussed in detail. A few team managers argued that scheduling games was indeed a problem—nobody could play before 5:30 because players worked and no one wanted to play any later than 10:00 P.M.—but players from unsponsored teams already had to pay a lot of money to play softball. These team managers felt that a ten-dollar-per-player user fee was too much, and they argued that just the competitive, tournament-oriented teams would benefit. Trice countered by promising that all teams would share equal time on all diamonds, new or old. After much discussion, a paper ballot was distributed to each team manager. The results: 76 percent of the managers present (just five managers were missing) endorsed the plan. Trice and Bell were pleased with the results, and they went to work collecting the fees and planning the construction.

THE FIRST-YEAR FEES

That first year the fees raised a total of $17,450 (teams could register as few as ten or as many as twenty players). That was enough money for Bell and Trice to complete, in the fall, the planning, grading, and seeding of the new complex. In early 1984 backstops would be erected and other basic work would be completed. The following year, in early 1985, two of the diamonds would be fenced and lit. In the fourth year, the other two diamonds would be fenced and lit. In the fifth year final touches would be added, including an additional concession stand, bleachers, gates to control crowds and allow tickets to be sold, and so on. It was an ambitious plan, but the architects (two softball players who had volunteered their time and were experienced professional architects) assured Bell and Trice all the work could be done given the projected budget. Of course if more teams could be added to the leagues as more diamond time was made available, then more money would be raised. Trice was eager to get more diamond time because he planned one league, popular in other cities, that Trinidad had been unable to offer in the past—a corecreational slow-pitch league. Trice estimated the new league would produce another eight to ten teams and bring with it at least one or two dozen new league members.

THE FALL OF 1983

Thus in the fall of 1983 Bell and Trice were pleased about finally getting construction underway. The players had had to pay extra money and hadn't seen anything except plans for several months. But now the graders were out working in Ferguson Park, and if all went reasonably well the city would have four more softball diamonds, albeit unfenced and unlit, in the spring or early summer.

THE NEIGHBORHOOD ASSOCIATION REACTS

Then the unexpected happened. Ferguson Park bordered on one of the best neighborhoods in Trinidad—houses worth an average of ninety-five thousand dollars or more. The day after the first grader arrived at the park, the neighborhood began to organize itself to stop construction. Ralph Marquand, who lived one block from the park, organized a petition drive and a letter-to-the-editor campaign. The petition, eventually signed by 324 registered voters, stated that the neighborhood had not been adequately informed of these plans and that it should be allowed to argue its case before the City Council. Meanwhile, construction should cease immediately.

The letters varied, but many of them began to appear in the *Trinidad Daily,* as did a few letters supporting the diamond construction. Two sample letters appear below:

Residents of Trinidad are probably unaware that the softball diamond project currently under construction at Ferguson Park will take ten acres of beautiful park land and ruin the aesthetic appearance of Ferguson Park to visitors of our city. The fenced-in diamonds will render the park useless for jogging, touch football, kite flying, bicycle riding, soccer, and cross-country skiing. What will remain of the park will be a small picnic area on one side of the river and a narrow strip of land already taken up by Little League diamonds.

There is no question that the city needs new diamonds, but the diamonds should be built somewhere else. Residents of this neighborhood were not adequately informed of these plans. Moreover, Ferguson Park is designated as multipurpose, yet the new diamonds will rule out many purposes while bringing more traffic, noise, and congestion than the neighborhood can handle.

The City Council and the Parks and Recreation Department should go back to the drawing board and find a new place to put the softball diamonds.

John Dunahee, 1930 Ferguson Park Road

We were appalled to learn about the plan of the Parks and Recreation Department to ruin Ferguson Park by inserting a ten-acre chain-link fenced softball diamond complex in the heart of the park. The proposed plan will include massive lights and ugly fences. These players have no regard for the neighbors of the park—and the day after the games, their low regard for the park itself is reflected in the number of beer cans littering the grounds.

When this plan is utilized there will be no open ground left, and these changes will require the removal of some twenty-five mature trees. The Council has the power to halt this project. We urge all citizens to contact their council members at once and get this plan stopped.

Mich and Thelma Rooters, 1735 Bluebay Road

SUGGESTED DISCUSSION QUESTIONS

1. What are the different criteria that each group is using to judge what the best use for the park is?
2. What caused this sudden opposition to the planned construction?
3. What solutions are available to Trice and Bell?

SUGGESTED ASSIGNMENTS

1. You are the manager of one of the softball teams. You voted in favor of the player user fee, and you have learned about the background of the plan by talking to Bell and Trice. Now you see the above two letters to the editor in the paper, and a few more like them. Write your own letter to the editor.

2. You are a citizen of Trinidad who neither lives near Ferguson Park nor plays softball. However, you have come to know the facts of the case by talking with a neighbor who does play softball. Write a letter to the editor in which you express your own opinion about the situation.

3. You are a resident of the Ferguson Park neighborhood. Your house borders on the park. You have nothing against softball players, but your kids, ages four and seven, have trouble getting to sleep at night in the summer because the crowds make a lot of noise *and* because the bright lights from the three present softball diamonds make it hard for the kids to think it is nighttime. Write a letter to the editor and oppose construction. Before you do, do a little research into the situation by reading the case.

4. You are Jack Trice. Write a memo to Marvin Bell in which you tell him what you think Parks and Rec ought to do, given the latest developments in the softball diamond plans.

Chapter 8

Persuasion

Persuasion is the process of getting your audience to accept a controversial statement or to take some particular action, a statement or an action they may not favor. There are probably as many opinions on *how* to persuade effectively as there are persuaders. Imagine how many advertisements you've heard and seen in the past year, and how varied are their techniques at getting you to buy, sell, do or not do certain things, and you'll see just how complex the question of persuasion can be.

In this chapter, we want to approach persuasion in a way that is manageable and most appropriate to the kind of writing you'll be doing in school and at work. Our aim is to help you to work toward solid arguments based on clear logic and sufficient evidence. We want you to be able to *explain* your position, *support* it with evidence, and refute counterarguments, not dazzle your readers with super-subtle logic or fancy footwork.

To help you work toward effective persuasion, we'll deal with three issues: structuring a positive paper, choosing your evidence and making effective use of it, and avoiding logical errors.

Structuring a Persuasive Paper

Start with the basic premise that a well-organized essay has already gone more than halfway toward your goal of persuading the reader. In other words, assume that an essay with a clear introduction and statement of purpose, smooth and clean transitions, and logically sequenced paragraphs is really going to tell your reader what you want to say. Such an essay eliminates confusion that can cause doubt and misunderstanding to begin with.

With this basic need for clarity in mind, how else can you structure your essay to make it more persuasive? For one thing, you need to allow sufficient space to deal with potential objections to your argument. As in any writing situation, you will assess your audience's feelings on your topic and your own position on it *before* writing. In many cases, you'll find that the audience probably views the issue or problem you are dealing with differently from the way you do. The audience might choose another candidate, favor a different solution, or buy another product than the one you are going to propose.

In a persuasive essay, you must deal with such alternatives. Your writing will never be sufficiently persuasive if you simply show that candidate X is best for the job, back up your position with a lot of evidence, and stop there. People who oppose your view, remember, will have done exactly the same thing in support of candidates Y or Z. Therefore, bolster your arguments in favor of X with a paragraph or more of *refutation*, a discussion demonstrating that Y and Z are not as suitable for the job. Your point here would be not to show that Y and Z are *bad* in themselves, as this would reflect on those who believe in them, the people you are trying to persuade. Instead, your emphasis would be on showing that your choice is *better*. With this strategy, you fill up the space with your own choice and remove all possible alternatives.

An outline of the strategy we've been discussing might look like this:

X is the best candidate for 3
   reasons.
     paragraph 1—reason
     paragraph 2—reason
     paragraph 3—reason   Argument: place most of your
                                    emphasis here.
X is better than Y.
   —reasons, evidence   Refutation: write one or two
X is better than Z.   paragraphs at most.
   —reasons, evidence

An important question for you to decide, based on your knowledge of the situation and audience, is whether to put your solution, candidate, product—your argument—before or after your refutation. If you put your preferred choice first, you immediately emphasize its positive aspects. You will not, however, receive a full measure of your audience's attention because they will be partially focused on their own choices, and how they can refute the things you're saying. On the other hand, if you refute or eliminate the other alternatives first, you cut the ground out from under your audience and almost force them to accept your final choice. Your argument, however, is essentially negative. It immediately focuses on the *defects* of the alternatives rather than the virtues of your choice.

These orders have advantages and disadvantages. In writing situations in which many alternatives are possible and you sense that at least some of your audience is open-minded or wavering, try the first approach above. Put your argument first, your refutation second. Your emphasis will be positive, and your recommendation, your thesis, will not seem to be the lesser of several evils. On the other hand, in situations in which only a couple of alternatives exist, and in which you sense that the audience has *already* made up its mind, use the second approach. Your emphasis may be negative, but in this situation perhaps no one would have listened open-mindedly to a positive presentation anyway.

Here are two final suggestions about structuring your paper persuasively. First, strike a balance on the amount of space you devote to refuting alternative arguments. Don't ignore them or attempt to dismiss them with a contemptuous line or two—unless they really are empty or obviously foolish. On the other hand, don't devote more space to refuting them than to *supporting* your own position. Try to keep your refutation as short as possible, while dealing with all the main counterarguments.

Also, don't be afraid to be assertive. State flatly that "We should elect candidate X, or adopt procedure Y." Such a straightforward tone suggests that you are confident. Saying what you really mean, instead of trying to imply it or hint at it, also ensures the kind of clarity we discussed earlier.

With all this in mind, here is an outline of the structure of a persuasive paper; bear in mind that this is only one version, and that your outline will depend on your subject, your thesis, your audience, and yourself:

Introduction: what is the problem, situation, etc? Why is it worth discussing? What are the choices to be made, or the positions to be taken?

Your position: explain it clearly, support it with evidence. (Your argument here may take the form of a definition, a judgment, a classification, or more than one of the other structures we discuss in this book.)

Refutation: show why your position is better (more consistent with evidence and logic) than others that could be adopted. Focus on showing the advantages of your position, not on showing that the others are bad in themselves.

Sum up: restate main ideas, reemphasize that your position is the strongest one possible.

Selecting and Using Your Evidence

Often in this book we have mentioned *supporting* your views with evidence. By now you should know how important it is to back up each of your assertions with evidence. Even so, it may be useful here to make some general points on using evidence effectively in persuasive writing.

First, choose your evidence with care. If you have really looked into the question at hand, you've probably got more facts than you really need. Once you have all the facts, use only those that relate directly to your thesis or supporting ideas. For instance, imagine you're writing an essay on the effects of exercise on the cardiovascular system. Here is one assertion you might want to make, and four facts you've uncovered to back it up:

Assertion: Running for 60 minutes a day helps eliminate the risk of heart attack.

Fact 1. Men run a higher risk of heart attack than women.

Fact 2. Studies show that only one marathon runner in a hundred develops heart disease.

Fact 3. Clarence Demar (a great marathoner) had a stronger heart at age 62 than most 25-year-old males have.

Fact 4. More than 20 million pairs of running shoes were sold in 1978.

Strictly speaking, none of these facts is irrelevant in your essay. But facts 1 and 4, interesting as they may be, do not support your assertion as well as facts 2 and 3, which are directly related to the link between running and reductions of heart disease. Fact 1 diverts the reader to the question of the relationship between sex and heart disease, a relationship that you may consider later in your essay but are not considering now. Fact 4 is not related to the heart disease issue at all and is irrelevant at this point in your essay.

Such misapplied evidence can distract your reader from the actual point and can weaken your essay by allowing the reader to question your research process. The same sort of problem appears when you use *too much* evidence, even when it is of the right kind. Support your point fully, but avoid belaboring the point with item after item of evidence that adds nothing to your argument (e.g., details of ten simple, identical laboratory tests, or several redundant accounts of a meeting). Indicate that you *have* such evidence if you need to, but don't feel that you have to produce every single bit of it in an essay.

Finally, *never* let your evidence speak for itself. Most of us, having dug up what we feel is convincing evidence to support our thesis, feel a natural tendency to place supporting ideas and evidence side by side and feel our job is done. We forget, however, that the reader did not participate in the fact-gathering process, and so may not be able to see exactly *how* the evidence supports the point.

Consider the following example:

Assertion: There is no oxygen in this chamber.
Fact: A match will not burn in the chamber.

For most of us, the link here is obvious—fire needs oxygen to burn. But if you didn't know about that relationship, the evidence wouldn't have much impact. The point is that you must explain the link between your point and the evidence you're using to support it. Take the time to interpret the evidence so that the reader can understand the extent to which it supports your assertion.

Our example, then, ought to look like this:

Assertion: There is no oxygen in this chamber.
Fact: A match will not burn in the chamber.
Interpretation: Fire requires oxygen; if the match is not defective, it's
  failing to burn because oxygen is not present.

Before we leave the topic of evidence, let's examine some of the different types of evidence you might want to use in a persuasive essay and appropriate ways to use each type:

Anecdote

Anecdotes are stories, examples, accounts by people who have "been there." Anecdotal evidence does not provide you with a broad or structured view of what you are investigating. Instead, anecdotal evidence provides you with a vivid but spotty and subjective account—your own or others'. The danger is· that this kind of evidence will only give you a partial look at your topic—an unreliable basis on which to form your conclusion.

Authority

Quotations and testimony of experts in the field you're discussing, derived most often from books and articles, are sources of authority. Generally, authority is *secondary* evidence, uncovered by others' investigations. This type of evidence is useful, especially in technical or specialized fields, as *support* for your thesis. It is, however, no substitute for *primary* evidence. Authority is probably the most common kind of evidence; it is basically an expert's interpretation of data, however, and so it is often less convincing than data itself.

Data

Facts and statistics you uncover, perhaps through research, can be good evidence. *Facts* might include interviews you conduct for a sociology paper or old town records you consult to establish geneology. This kind of evidence is *primary*—directly related to what you are investigating—and is powerful. *Statistics* are often very powerful *primary* evidence, too. Many people place more trust in numbers than words as definitive indications of reality. Of course, numbers can be misleading and as easily manipulated as words. Statistics are convincing, but they require careful interpretation so your reader does not get lost or misled.

All of these kinds of evidence have their uses; certainly an essay relying on anecdote would run the risk of ignoring important aspects of the subject, just as an essay using only statistics would be boring and difficult to read. Try to investigate your topic from enough angles so you can *blend* different types of evidence and provide yourself with the fullest support possible.

Avoiding Logical Errors

We've discussed several rhetorical methods or logical structures to use in constructing arguments. As you have probably noticed, persuading others to accept your logic, no matter how good it is, is a process that can become emotional very quickly. Emotion can lead to errors in even the most careful logic.

If you've participated in more than one or two late-night discussion sessions in your home, apartment, or dorm, you've probably heard people using arguments like these:

A. "It's got to be a good coffee-maker if Joe DiMaggio endorses it."

B. "That can't be a very good solution; after all, the Soviets thought of it first."

C. "He was seen leaving the building earlier, so he *had* to be the one who did it."

Actually, all of these statements involve errors in logic—errors that can destroy your credibility in a persuasive essay. Joe DiMaggio, for example, is not an electronics or cooking expert, so his endorsement doesn't mean very much. Similarly, you may or may not like the Soviets, but that does not mean they can't have a good idea. Finally, just because one thing happens before another is insufficient reason to connect them logically.

As you can see, these errors can be easy to fall into. They may sound good at the time you write them, but an alert reader will pounce on them and use them to discredit even the logically valid parts of your argument. To help you avoid such errors in logic, here's a list of some common ones and some ideas on how to recognize and eliminate them.

Fallacies Stemming From Insufficient Evidence

The Post Hoc, Ergo Propter Hoc Fallacy. This fallacy assumes that be cause one thing happens before another, the first must be the cause of the other. A good example of this fallacy occurs in Mark Twain's *A Connecticut Yankee in King Arthur's Court* when the hero seems to "cause" an eclipse simply because he predicted it.

Appeal to Ignorance. This fallacy occurs when one asserts that something is true because it cannot be proven false. The fallacy rests on a groundless assumption—that the absence of proof that something cannot happen is the same as actual proof that it can happen. You can see the fallacy in all this when you consider that, since there is no medical proof that humans cannot live to be two or three hundred years old, the appeal to ignorance would have us believe that we really could live that long. Here, common sense comes to the rescue. But in more complicated arguments this fallacy is often taken for truth.

Generalization without Sufficient Evidence. "When you've seen one, you've seen 'em all" is rarely true when it comes to people, countries, novels, or other complex things. Yet people constantly generalize on the basis of one or two contacts with other people, things, and so on, instead of waiting for more of the evidence to come in. Examples would include the tired fallacies that all Irish people love beer, all black people love to dance, and all Arabs are wealthy oil barons.

Each of the above fallacies reflects an assumption based on insufficient evidence. If you find yourself committing any of them, go back to your facts and test your assumptions. Get more information if necessary, so that you can be sure your assumptions are as close as possible to reality.

Fallacies of Irrelevance

Ad Populum. Going along with the crowd is not bad in itself but can be fallacious when you use the crowd's actions as evidence for one of your assertions. This is the "everybody's doing it, so it's got to be good" fallacy. *Ad Populum*, or "appeal to the masses," fallacy involves going along with the beliefs or prejudices of the crowd, using them as evidence.

Ad Hominem. "Against the Man" in Latin, *Ad Hominem* involves an attack on the person presenting the opposing arguments, instead of on the arguments themselves. Here is an example: a famous politician with a well-known scandal in his past is against arms control. His opponents attack him by bringing up the scandal again and again rather than refuting his position on the real issue: arms control.

Opposition. This fallacy involves discrediting an idea because of the people who support it. Back in the 1950s, when the anti-Communist mania was at its height, some people tried to condemn the use of fluoride in drinking water by trying to link this dental treatment with Communism. Remember that the real issue is usually the idea itself, not who is for or against it.

Appeal to Inappropriate Authority. Linked with the above fallacy of opposition is the appeal to inappropriate authority. An example of this type of fallacy was given earlier: "It's got to be a good coffee-maker if Joe DiMaggio endorses it." Perhaps the most widely used of the fallacies, this one uses the irrelevant authority of some public figure to cast a false lustre on some product, service, or idea.

Appeal to Pity. This fallacy uses the emotion generated by misfortunes as "evidence" for one's assertion or viewpoints. Examples are the lawyer who uses a condemned man's wife and children to soften the judge's sentence, or the professor who passes a failing student with personal problems. In both cases, the pity may be justified, but it's important to realize that the factors that create the feeling of pity have nothing, logically, to do with the decision.

Each of these fallacies is based on irrelevant factors or "evidence," as we've seen. The key to avoiding them is to test each element of evidence you use and examine each step that goes into your decisions. Be sure you are not being influenced by anything not critically and directly related to the decision at hand. In particular, try to pinpoint areas where your own emotions, or that of others, may be leading you astray. Test your logic and evidence particularly hard in those areas.

These are not the only possible fallacies, or errors in logic, of course. Consult a logic handbook for others and examples of them. The ones we have described are some of the most common. If you're aware of them and work to avoid them in your writing, you will lessen the risk of making mistakes that could hurt your essay's credibility and thereby make the essay less persuasive than it deserves to be.

Summary

Remember the following guidelines as you work on making your persuasive writing as effective as possible. First, structure your essay to make it more persuasive. Decide where to put your refutation, how much space to devote to it, and how to order your supporting ideas. As you write your paragraphs, choose relevant evidence and use enough of it to be convincing without being boring or repetitive. Use varying kinds of evidence and interpret that evidence for the reader—never let it speak for itself. Finally, avoid logical fallacies, especially those involving insufficient evidence or the use of irrelevant material in the place of evidence.

Logical Arguments?

As a second-year Teaching Assistant at SMG, you're used to students' complaints about grades. You've taught a section of macroeconomics twice now, and feel that you're generally successful in the classroom, and that your grading practices are firm but fair. Certainly, you're not as tough as Prof. Smith, the Course Head; she has a reputation as the most ruthless grader on the management faculty. But you know your subject, and are sure that you can provide a convincing reason for every grade you give.

GRADING

Exams in this course consist mostly of essay questions, though of course each answer must be supported with clear and convincing calculations. You're good with numbers, and have received very few complaints about the way you handle students' calculations; but the essays are really the most important parts of the tests, and this semester you're receiving more complaints and comments on your harsh essay grades than ever before.

YOUR PROBLEMS

You've just had four conferences with unhappy students this afternoon, and you're depressed and tired. None of the students convinced you that you were wrong, of course; you took time in grading and made sure of your position. But you failed to convince them that you are right, and you're upset because they remain dissatisfied. You think back over each conference, wondering how to improve communication with your students.

Your first conference was with Al Reardon, a very bright and articulate guy who is a star soccer player. "I can't understand this grade at all," he said. When you asked him why, he replied, "Because my answers are always as good as anybody else's. They're good. This subject is so subjective, anyway." As the conversation developed, it became apparent to you that Al was not really listening to your discussion of his mistakes. He became openly angry after a while. "Look," he said, "these answers are as good as anything else you've got. You said yourself my numbers are OK— what more do you want? You've got a thing against Jocks, I've heard, and now I believe it." Then he stormed out of the office.

The next conference was very different, but no better. Dick Marshall, an older student, married, with two kids, came in very upset. "I know I screwed up, Professor," he began, "but this grade is going to ruin me. If I don't raise it to at least a C, I'll flunk the course and lose my financial aid. Then I'll be prevented from graduating in June, and I'll lose the job I've just been offered at Textron." He'd taken the course before and failed it, he adds. "It must be a mental block. I'm doing real well in my other subjects. Anyway, this course has nothing to do with my real goals in life. I *have* to take it, that's all. Please don't fail me. I don't know what I'll do if I lose this job." You try to discuss the exam with him, but he's not listening. When he leaves, you feel even worse than before, if that's possible.

Lori Watson came in next. "Look at these," she said, plopping four or five blue books down on your desk. "Same exam as we had. My friends are taking the course with Ms. White and Mr. Harrington," (two other TA's) "and just look at *their* grades. Look at this one," she urged. "It's no better than mine—as far as *I* can see, but it's a B+ and you gave me a C−." You explain that *Lori's* exam is what you need to talk about, but don't get far. "All the other TA's seem to be easier than you. They can't *all* be wrong. You're just trying to be like Prof. Smith. She doesn't even have tenure, so her grading system can't be all that great."

Finally, Michelle Larson comes in. You're relieved to see her smiling and friendly, and you make small talk for a while. She very reasonably suggests that perhaps you might reconsider her grade, since she's obviously trying very hard and *is* improving, though slowly. You tell her that you'll try to reward her effort at the end of the semester, but that the exam had to be graded solely on its own merits. "That's not fair," she responds. "Jim Wright got a better grade than me, and he hardly ever comes to class. Anyway, that's not the way a teacher is supposed to be. You're supposed to *nurture* us, not just measure our achievements like a computer or a robot. To me, a teacher is somebody like Mr. Chips or Gabe Kaplan—somebody who helps you and brings you along. You're not a teacher—you're more like a drill sergeant or a cop. You expect too much from us."

After they've all gone, you sit trying to figure out what to do. There's too much discontent, you feel, to ignore the situation. You disagree with each of the students you've talked to today, but can't seem to make it clear why. You decide to try to figure out what's wrong in what they said, and to speak to them or drop them each a note. You're wondering, too, whether or not a note to all of your students—among whom these complaints are said to be common—might not be a good idea.

SUGGESTED DISCUSSION QUESTIONS

1. What errors in logic are these students making?
2. Would a memo from the teaching assistant be a good idea?
3. How much should teachers and students discuss grades?

SUGGESTED ASSIGNMENTS

1. Suppose you are the TA in the case above. Make a list of the errors in logic you note in student arguments. Identify by type each error.
2. Select a current subject of controversy, either on the local or national scene. Read the letters-to-the-editor section of your local newspaper, for example, and see what concerns people. Then note the logical arguments involved and those that are not logical. Make a list.
3. After completing assignment 2 above, use your list to generate your own persuasive essay on the subject you've chosen. Remember to both argue your own position and to refute counterarguments.

An Ecological Disaster

When Peter Lopez came home from college for Thanksgiving vacation, he headed for the ponds the first chance he got. He left his fishing gear behind but took his camera. With images of cattails swaying softly in the wind and redwing blackbirds darting from tree to tree, Peter walked quickly out into the morning air.

The ponds, as Peter and others from the tiny town of Baja called them, were a pair of small natural pools located about two miles outside town and hidden just off the paved two-lane highway. Many of the townspeople valued the ponds because Baja, as did much of New Mexico, got less than twelve inches of rain per year. So having two clean, clear ponds anywhere nearby was quite unusual.

It was true that no one from the town owned the ponds or the land around them, but that didn't seem to matter. The rumor was that a rich man from Hollywood or Los Angeles had inherited them and was just keeping them as an investment. No one in Baja was rich or even close to it. The joke was that half the townspeople were on welfare and the other half would have been, only they couldn't afford it.

The ponds were unique—two deep, clear patches of blue in a dry land. Peter loved the small piñon and juniper trees that were scattered across the land—"bushes" he remembered hearing more than one Easterner call them—and the bunch grass, sage brush, rabbit bush. He loved the landscape, but the ponds were special. They actually had fish in them, although they were usually pretty well fished out. That's why Peter was walking along now in the hot morning sun with nothing but his camera to carry.

There would be plenty to see. Chipmunks and squirrels and rabbits, too, enjoyed the lush grass that grew thickly both above the ponds where the spring trickled out and below where the ponds' dams held in the precious water. In the early morning, Peter knew, if one were quiet and lucky, one could sneak up the side of the dam and sometimes see a couple of deer getting a drink before they vanished back into the rolling hills and jagged sandstone formations that defined the terrain.

That morning Peter felt like whistling as he walked along, but he moved as quietly as he could. The sun felt friendly as it shone down on him through pristine air. A breeze blew gently, the countryside quietly awoke and began the day. The quietness was a special kind one could find only outside a very small town located way out in the country by itself. But then, as Peter got nearer to the ponds, he heard a sound that first annoyed him because it disrupted the morning's tranquility; then, as he walked along, it worried him because he couldn't figure out what it was.

Instinctively, he walked faster, listening, worrying. Then, when he realized he was listening to the sound of a diesel tractor or bulldozer, he broke into a run. He ran up the arroyo (a dry steam bed), climbed out of it, raced up the last hill, and stood at its top, gasping, out of breath.

What he saw wrenched at his stomach. A man in a bulldozer had just finished wiping out the earth dam that held back one pond's water, and the water was streaming down the usually dry arroyo—that once-clean water all muddy now, cattails floating off, birds chattering nervously in the trees and overhead.

Peter didn't want to believe what he saw; the man had deliberately destroyed the pond, wiping it out so that the water was rushing away, vanishing down the arroyo. Without thinking about what he was going to do, Peter raced down the hill. He slipped on loose rocks, but didn't fall or slow down because he was determined not to waste another second.

Below the broken dam everything was an impossible, muddy night-mare. The grass was gone, two or three fish wiggled in the mud as they began to die, a frog sat dazed and unmoving among the fallen cattails, and muddy water trickled down through them.

It was such a shock Peter could only stand there in the mud and won-der if he was going to get sick to his stomach, maybe even cry, or get wildly angry. He couldn't move; he felt paralyzed and dazed like the frog. He was paralyzed, that is, until he saw that the bulldozer was heading for the sec-ond pond's dam.

Then suddenly he was all action, leaping forward and yelling, "Stop it! Stop it!" at the bulldozer man. The diesel made such a racket the man couldn't hear him, hadn't even seen him yet. So Peter, in a crazy, desper-ate dash, ran out in front of the bulldozer and stood in the path of its steel blade. He screamed and shook his fist, waved, jumped up and down.

The man jerked forward in his seat as if someone had rudely awak-ened him, and the bulldozer came to an abrupt halt. The man cranked the engine down to a surprisingly quiet idle as Peter yelled, "What the heck are you doing? Are you crazy? You can't do this!"

The man stared at Peter for a moment and then beckoned to him.

Peter tramped through the mud and said, as he looked up at the man, "You're killing everything."

The man seemed to wince. He threw his cigarette down into the mud and took off his cap to wipe the sweat from his forehead. He did all these things as if he had to in order to speak.

"Look, kid," he said. "I don't like doing this, but it isn't my land, and I don't guess it's yours, either. The owner hired us to come down here from Santa Fe and take out the two ponds. He's the owner."

The man's sunburned neck was sweaty. His eyes looked tired.

"But why?" Peter said, "It's crazy. It doesn't make any sense."

The man spit and shook his head. "He said it was because of the hip-pies. You know, the ones in Baja. They were coming out here and skinny-dipping all summer and he didn't like it when he heard about it."

"The hippies?" Peter asked blankly. Some new people had moved into town over the past few years—jewelry makers, potters, painters, some peo-ple just on welfare, maybe fifty of them—a good many, since Baja's popu-lation was only 327. But nobody called them hippies anymore. Or probably no one did. That went out in the 1960s after the first few of them moved in.

"Yeah, you know," the man said. The diesel idled so quietly it was hard to believe it could do something such as wipe out the ponds.

"Well," the man said as if he had to get back to an unpleasant task. "I gotta get moving. Look, I grew up near here. I know about these ponds. But the owner's the boss. It's his land."

"Wait a minute," Peter said. He argued with the man, pleaded with him, said he had to have some time to talk to the owner or something, to think about what to do. Finally the man sighed, wiped the sweat off his forehead once again, and told Peter what he could do. He said it was getting close to lunch time, so he could stop and have lunch. Then, if he concentrated on just cleaning out the one pond, he could use up the rest of the day. Peter pleaded for as much time as he could possibly get. It turned out that the man—his name was Dick Anderson—had a job to complete in Galisteo. That work was going to take him all of next week. Since he didn't work on Sundays and today was Saturday, Peter had a week to do something about the second pond. Anderson's employer was Joe Montoya, owner and manager of Montoya Construction Company in Santa Fe, New Mexico. Anderson said Peter could call Montoya and find out more about the owner of the ponds.

When Peter got home, he told his parents what happened. Mr. Lopez shook his head and said it didn't make sense to take out the ponds. People in the area drilled wells 150 feet deep to get water and this man was wiping out two springfed ponds. It obviously lowered the value of his land. Mr. Lopez said the complaint about the swimmers didn't make much sense, either. It was true that some of the old-timers called some of the young people who swam there "hippies," and the rumor was that sometimes they didn't have any clothes on, but the place was pretty secluded. So far as Mr. Lopez knew, nobody really cared.

Peter's first step was to call Montoya Construction. He talked briefly with Mr. Montoya, who said, "Oh sure, that was Cal Davies who hired us to doze out the ponds. Said he was tired of hippies skinny-dipping there and didn't see what was so special about two little ponds. Said, 'We've got the whole Pacific Ocean in L.A.' " Mr. Montoya went on to tell Peter that Davies had paid the construction company half the estimated bill in cash and had told them to bill him for the rest. He had said he was planning to spend two weeks or more in Sante Fe at 2314 Camino Real. He was visiting some friends there but he hadn't given their name or the phone number where he could be reached. Peter knew Santa Fe, a city of over forty thousand, fairly well; Camino Real was one of those streets lined with estates, big houses hidden way back from the road and sometimes protected by a locked wrought-iron gate.

THE SANTA FEAN

Peter considered his options. He decided that his next move should be to call some people in Baja and get their opinions about what had happened. There were sixty-seven residential numbers listed in the Baja telephone book; he began by calling ten randomly selected numbers. Six of the numbers called answered. Peter asked two questions. The first was whether they approved of the ponds' being destroyed. One person said he was new in town and didn't know anything about the ponds so he didn't have an opinion; the other five said they were opposed to it. Peter's second question was whether they had heard of people skinny-dipping in the ponds and, if so, what did they think about it. All five had heard the rumor, but only one person said she thought it was wrong. The others either laughed or said something like, "What difference does it make?"

Encouraged by these responses, Peter next considered taking the problem to a newspaper. Baja didn't have its own town newspaper, but most of the townspeople subscribed to the *Santa Fean,* a weekly newspaper that came out on Tuesdays. So Peter called the offices of the *Santa Fean.* Since it was Saturday, he was surprised to find anyone there, but the city editor answered the phone. He told Peter that the story sounded interesting and suggested that Peter write a letter to the editor about the matter. They would try to print the letter if Peter got it to them by Monday morning. He went on to say that they might be able to put a reporter onto the story, but Peter had to remember that the paper served Sante Fe primarily and, although dozens of small communities like Baja were of interest to the editors as well as to the readers of the *Santa Fean,* the staff was extremely small and Monday was a late day to try to work in another story.

SUGGESTED DISCUSSION QUESTIONS

1. What should Peter do about communicating with Mr. Davies?
2. Does Mr. Davies have the right to do whatever he wants with his own property?
3. What should Peter do to communicate further with members of his community?
4. What should Peter do about the *Santa Fean?*
5. Why is Mr. Davies eliminating the two ponds?
6. Do you agree with Mr. Davies's actions? Why or why not?

SUGGESTED ASSIGNMENTS

1. Write a letter to the editor of the *Santa Fean.* Motivate all concerned citizens to write to the landowner in support of your own opinion about the ponds.
2. Write a letter to the owner in which you attack or defend his action.
3. Write a letter to the Montoya Construction Company and persuade the company to leave the second pond alone until you have communicated with Cal Davies.
4. Write a letter to the editor of the *Santa Fean.* Persuade him that the story about the ponds is sufficiently important to warrant the assignment of a reporter to cover it.
5. Write an essay about an ecological problem in your own community. Address the essay to those responsible for the problem and suggest ways they could solve it.

John Giorgino

John Giorgino put down the phone, stared out the window, and wondered what he was going to do. His father had just called long distance and asked him to drop out of school—in the middle of his sixth semester in college—and come back home to help run the family business. John was afraid that once his father got him involved in the family business John would never really get a chance to return to college.

GIORGINO'S STATIONERY SUPPLY COMPANY, INC.

When John's father, Ricardo Giorgino, immigrated to the United States in 1936, he was just a young guy who was willing to work hard and who had one thing a lot of other immigrants didn't have—some savings that he brought with him. After arriving in the United States, he moved into what was then a small town in Rhode Island. He decided, after looking around for a month or two, to buy a little card shop that was for sale.

Ricardo and his wife didn't have any children then, so both of them were able to work in the shop. They worked long, hard hours, were careful with their money, had some luck as the business district around them grew, and their business grew rapidly. By the late 1950s, Giorgino's was one of the larger stationers in the state, and by 1970 Ricardo had opened two more stores to serve customers who had moved into different sections of what was now the second largest city in the state.

By this time the Giorginos had three children—John was the oldest—and Mrs. Giorgino no longer waited on customers. Instead, she divided her time between doing the company's bookkeeping and taking care of the work at home. Mr. Giorgino had hired several sales clerks to work in each of the stores, as well as three store managers, one for each store. He had recently found the work load too great (he'd had a heart attack in 1974 and was supposed to be working less), so he had hired a general manager to supervise the three stores and to help with the complex process of ordering the thousands of items that make up the stock of any well-supplied stationery store.

Ricardo had always said that he wanted John to go to college, get a degree in business administration, and eventually take over the family business.

"I know you could make the stores much more profitable than I ever dreamed," he said. "All Momma and I ever did was work hard and pinch pennies. Now you can go to college and learn all the things that can make this the most efficient business in the state. Maybe we can start stocking different items or open up some other kind of store here or in Massachusetts. Anything is possible for a man when he has a son like you."

JOHN'S COLLEGE CAREER

For practically as long as he could remember, John had worked in his father's store. As he got older, he assumed more and more responsibility. By the time he was in high school, he spent his summers taking turns managing one of the three stores as each manager took his or her summer vacation. He'd even helped his father order merchandise and manage the overall operation of the stores when the general manager, Ben Whittier, took his summer vacation.

All of his experience had given John a clear idea of what it would be like to have a career as a stationer. He generally enjoyed the work and he liked working for his father. It was true that Ricardo always demanded that everything be done in a certain way and that he frequently became unreasonably angry when even small mistakes were made in ordering merchandise or in serving customers, but John admired how much his father knew about the business.

When John went off to college, then, he fully expected to get the degree in business administration that his father had so frequently talked about. John planned to learn all there was to know about managing a business and then come back and apply it all, maybe even show his father a few things he didn't know yet. It seemed like the right thing to do as he began his college career.

After taking a few courses, however, John began to be interested in some subjects other than first-year accounting. As a first-term freshman he had taken an introductory psychology course that he had enjoyed, and he had received an A. He took psychology as an elective the following term and found that he did his psychology homework first, and everything else second.

In the fourth semester of his second year, John began thinking about changing his major to psychology, with a minor in business administration, but he didn't want to tell his parents about it, so he put off deciding. He had all A's in his psychology courses—he'd kept taking one each semester until his junior year and then he'd upped it to two—and he was sure he'd get an A in psychology this current semester.

In business administration, on the other hand, he had all B's except for two C's in accounting. He had hesitated about telling his parents anything even when, after he'd come back from Christmas vacation, he had finally changed his major to psychology. He hadn't told them yet, he told his friends, because he hadn't thought of a good way of explaining it. He knew Ricardo would be hurt and disappointed when he found out and kept imagining him saying, "But what about business? How are you going to use psychology in the business?"

That was the biggest problem of all. Just working in the store part-time and during the summer was one thing, John thought, but taking business courses and applying them was something else. Some of the course work was boring and most of it he just didn't enjoy. What he did enjoy was psychology, so much so that he'd begun to think about going on to graduate-school after obtaining his bachelor's degree. His advisor had encouraged him in this, but he suggested that John drop the business administration minor since it was lowering his overall grade-point average.

"You've done much better in English," his advisor said. "Why not minor in it? You said you enjoyed the English courses you've taken thus far, and improving your writing could be useful if you go on to grad school."

BEN WHITTIER

When his father called, he said it was an emergency situation at home because he'd just fired Ben Whittier. Whittier had been doing a poor job, Ricardo had explained, and last week had made his last mistake. Ben over-ordered on a special offer from a wholesaler so that he could get a free movie camera in the deal. Ricardo had learned about the camera when the wholesaler had accidently mailed it to the store rather than to Whittier's home. By that time it was too late to cancel the order, which was for some cheap merchandise that Ricardo thought would take years to get rid of. Meanwhile, it would take up space and inventory, and besides, he said, it just wasn't ethical for a buyer like Ben to accept gifts, no matter what kind of deal he was offered.

Firing Ben wasn't the only problem, however, because when the manager of the main store found out about it, she quit. The other two managers also liked Ben and were clearly displeased. So with his general manager and main store manager gone and with the other two angry, Ricardo said he was desperate. Easter was coming up and with it, a special sale and then storewide inventory. Things were a mess and he just had to have John come home to help out. John's two sisters worked in the stores, but at twelve and fifteen they were too young to help manage them.

Ricardo had suggested that perhaps John shouldn't go back to school at all. John hadn't done all that well in his course work, Ricardo said, but he could still take over the general manager's job right now and have a bright future ahead of him. "I can pay you $15,500 a year to start," Ricardo said. "Look at me. You don't need a college degree to make money. You'll do well without the degree."

Ricardo hung up shortly after that, telling John that he had already made reservations for the trip home the next day.

SUGGESTED DISCUSSION QUESTIONS

1. Did Ben Whittier do anything wrong?
2. Should Ricardo try to get him to come back to work?

3. What is John's problem?

4. Does Ricardo really need John?

5. Is John obligated to go back and help the family? Why or why not?

6. If John returns, how long should he stay? Forever?

SUGGESTED ASSIGNMENTS

1. You are John Giorgino. To make sure you get all your thoughts organized and explained, you decide to write your father a letter. Persuade him that your decision to help out with the current crisis but to return to school afterward is valid. Decide for yourself whether you want to mention the change in your major.

2. You are John Giorgino's roommate or friend. John has just told you all that has happened at home, and he wants you to help him decide what to do about his father by trying to persuade him to take one course of action or another. John says if you argue with him about it he can better understand what he really needs to do. The problem is that your schedules don't leave you any time together, especially since John is so busy talking to administrators and instructors about his withdrawal from the university. Write a letter to John and persuade him to take some particular course of action.

3. You are Mrs. Giorgino. Three days before Mr. Giorgino's call to John, on the day your husband fires Ben Whittier, you sit down to write John a letter. You sense that your husband is getting ready to ask John to come home and take over the business, but he hasn't done so yet. Unlike your husband, you have been able to guess from John's grades and conversations with you that he is much more interested in psychology than in business administration. You know that John wants very much to finish college; you suspect he is changing or has changed his major; but you realize that the family business needs some help. Write John a letter and persuade him to act in his own and the family's best interests.

The Place Department Store (B)

When Pat McMurphy got back to her desk that morning, she expected to find a memo from Grace Montgomery explaining her involvement in the recently reported security violations at The Hotel Place. (The Hotel Place, a department of The Place Department Store, was located in the lobby of a downtown high-rise building.)

Ms. McMurphy was concerned about Grace for a number of reasons. Pat had known all along that the Security Department did not like the way Ryan White managed The Hotel Place. Recently she had heard that the new head of security, Frank Ranklin, was even more opposed to Ryan's "change box," a way Ryan avoided having to make multiple small sales, than was Ranklin's predecessor. Ranklin was also upset with Ryan's and Grace's performance on the new computer terminal-cash register that had been installed in the store.

"On days that Ryan is off," Ranklin had told Pat, "Grace and her floater balance out even, or at least are a hell of a lot closer to it than they ever get with Ryan on the job."

Pat McMurphy was also concerned about Grace because she knew that working with Ryan in that little store wasn't easy. Ryan had a higher-than-average turnover rate for assistants. The new terminal, which Pat knew Ryan had trouble operating (she had trained him in its use), made things even harder on Grace. But that was partly why Pat had sent Grace over there. She wanted someone there who would be efficient enough, and tactful enough about it, to compensate for Ryan's shortcomings.

RYAN WHITE

Ryan White had come to The Place fifteen years ago as an assistant department manager. George Koury, who was then general manager of The Place, and was now president of the corporation and chairman of the board of directors, had met Ryan at that time and had liked him immensely. Koury had gotten Ryan the manager's job at The Hotel Place; Koury thought Ryan had a marvelous way of pleasing the customers there, many of whom were Koury's business friends and associates. But Ryan had never excelled at The Hotel Place; sales increased only marginally every year. But this was where Ryan would be until he retired in another ten years.

GRACE'S MEMO

Pat found the memo from Grace on her desk. It was unexpectedly short:

I resign from The Place Department Store in protest over my treatment in connection with the security check at The Hotel Place. I cannot build a career on a record ruined by false charges. I feel I've been treated unfairly. Please mail me my check.

Grace Montgomery

cc: Allen Licht, General Manager

Pat could hardly believe it. She knew that Grace, a sensitive, quiet young woman, was anxious about developing her career, but she had never imagined that Grace would resign over the incident. As she thought over Grace's note, she shuffled through the rest of her in-box material. There was a memo there from Allen Licht. It read:

I just got my copy of Grace Montgomery's resignation. What's going on over there? I thought you told me just last week that she was one of our most promising young people. And Ryan White's called Koury, who called me to ask why Ryan's "favorite girl" quit. What happened?

THE SECURITY REPORT

The security report didn't tell Pat much that she didn't already know. It reported that Grace, according to "shoppers" hired by the store to observe and report on cashiers, had violated store policy by failing to give receipts to customers, by failing to record each sale, and by recording nonexistent sales. Grace had signed the report in acknowledgment that she had read the charges, but she added a note to the effect that she had only been following her boss's instructions.

Since Pat had been counting on Grace's report to give her a more accurate picture of what happened, she didn't know exactly what to do next. So she called Ryan.

Ryan was his usual happy, talkative self until Pat mentioned Grace. "Oh, that was a bad thing," he said. "We were very busy you know, and then the shoppers came in just after I went on break and she said she put their receipts on the counter, but security said she had to hand them to the customers, and I miss her, Pat. I called George Koury to tell him because I miss her, and I didn't like the security man's behavior. I think Grace cried after he left."

Pat didn't say much, but she thought to herself that one of Ryan's bad habits was to yell and complain to Koury when he wanted something, and the worst part of it was that Koury let him.

THE CALL TO GRACE

Pat still didn't feel comfortable with her information, so she called Grace. Grace's roommate told her that Grace had left town for the rest of the week, that she was angry and upset, and that she was trying to decide what to do next. But she had apparently made up her mind not to return to The Place.

WAYNE BOTEN

Later on, as Pat was going down the hall and thinking about Grace, she saw Wayne Boten, record buyer. She knew Wayne and Grace were good friends, so she asked Wayne if he knew anything about why Grace had resigned.

Wayne looked uneasily at her—she knew the look, it meant that he didn't like a superior asking him to talk about a fellow employee—and said, "Yeah, she talked about it some."

After working on Wayne for a while, Pat got the whole story out of him (see "The Place Department Store" (A), p. 128), although she had to tell him quite a bit in exchange. Wayne had listened to Grace during the whole lunch hour the day it happened, had listened to her more than an hour, in fact. When Wayne finished, Pat thanked him and promised he wouldn't be sorry he'd been so open with her. Then she went back to her office to decide what to do about the situation.

SUGGESTED DISCUSSION QUESTIONS

1. Did Grace have a valid reason for resigning?
2. Should Pat try to get her back?
3. What should Pat do? Why?
4. What caused this situation to exist?
5. If you were Grace, what would you have done?

SUGGESTED ASSIGNMENTS

1. You are Pat McMurphy. Write a memo to Allen Licht. Explain your view of the situation, what you plan to do about it, and why.
2. You are Pat McMurphy. Assume you do not plan to ask Grace to return to work. Write a report of her resignation and the reasons for it (to be placed in her file).
3. You are Wayne Boten. What Pat McMurphy didn't tell you about the situation you already knew from what Grace had told you and from store gossip. Write Pat a letter in which you urge her to persuade Grace to come back to work. (You know that Grace has been treated unfairly; you know that she could be a success at The Place, and besides, you miss her.)
4. You are Pat McMurphy. Assume you decide to ask Grace to come back to work. Write her a letter in which you persuade her to return to The Place.
5. Assume it is the beginning of a new term in the collegiate school year. You are enrolled in a class in management practices. On the first day, the instructor gives the class the case and asks for a written analysis on Grace Montgomery's problems. The instructor's purpose in making this assignment is to start you thinking about the subject of handling employees and to enable him or her to get a feeling for the attitudes and ideas you and your classmates bring to the subject. This instructor also wants to see how well you write. Eager to make a good impression, you begin to analyze the subject, audience (your instructor and classmates), and purpose. After you complete your analysis, write your essay.

Child Abuse Investigation

Lynn Stoddard reviewed the events over the last few days that had led to the report she had to write. As a social worker, her assignment was to write an abuse report that would determine if an incident of child abuse had occurred. Physical abuse was defined by state law as "any *nonaccidental injury* caused by the *acts or omissions* of a *parent* or other person responsible for the care of the child." Lynn Stoddard mentally underlined the key words of the definition. She knew that to establish child abuse, all these elements had to be present. She also knew that the definition was quite broad, so she had to apply it carefully in every situation. With this definition in mind, Lynn began to review the facts of the case.

THE SCHOOL PRINCIPAL

The principal of a local junior high school had called the social services office to report the suspected physical abuse of Jane Meyers, an eighth grader. Jane's parents were Joe and Doris Meyers, both aged thirty-five. They lived at 555 Fifth Street. The Meyers also had a younger child, Fred, who was seven.

The principal said that Jane had forgotten her gym clothes one day and had requested permission to go home during a study hall to get them (she lived only four blocks from school). Permission was granted. When Jane got back to school she seemed upset and started to cry when her teacher asked her what was wrong. The teacher sent her to see Dick Reed, the guidance counselor.

Jane told the counselor that when she went home to get her gym clothes, both her parents were there and they were arguing about money. Joe Meyers recently got laid off from John Deere, and the mother's income from working at a manufacturing plant was not enough. When Jane came in the door they both started to yell at her for forgetting her clothes, not being responsible, causing them trouble, and so on. Jane yelled back and her father hit her across the arm and neck. Jane said her dad hit her often and it upset her when he did.

The guidance counselor arranged to call the social services office to report the suspected case of child abuse. According to policy, Lynn began the investigation within an hour by going to the school to see Jane and the guidance counselor.

JANE MEYERS

This time Jane told her story to Lynn Stoddard. Jane was a nice-looking girl with long, straight, dark hair and a trim, nicely developed figure. She was dressed neatly in jeans and a wool sweater and she wore no makeup. An examination showed that her upper left shoulder was tender but showed no signs of bruising. The left side of her neck had two small light-purple bruises, each about an inch in diameter.

　　Jane was fidgety throughout the interview, but she looked Lynn right in the eyes as they talked. Several times Jane started to cry, but she was able to regain her composure and keep talking. When pressed as to whether she herself might have started the argument or whether her dad had hit her unintentionally or in self-defense, she said "no" without hesitation and stuck to her story. When Lynn explained that she would need to talk with Jane's parents, Jane was unhappy—whether out of fear or simple nervousness Lynn couldn't tell. Jane said she was afraid of causing another fight at home by having told Lynn what happened.

MR. AND MRS. MEYERS

Lynn next went to the Meyers's home and found both Mr. and Mrs. Meyers in. After introducing herself, Lynn explained that Jane had gone back to school upset and worried because there had been a fight and she had been hit. Lynn asked the Meyers if the three of them could talk about it. Mr. and Mrs. Meyers glanced at each other, hesitated, and seemed to tense up, but they welcomed Lynn inside. Both were dressed casually but were neat in appearance. Their home was an older house in a middle-class neighborhood and was neatly kept.

　　Mrs. Meyers did most of the talking throughout the interview. She said there had been an argument when Jane came home. Jane wasn't very responsible and did not show much respect for her things. She was not helpful around the house and was often rebellious whenever they set limits. Sometimes she got "mouthy" and talked back—that upset both parents. Although Mrs. Meyers agreed there had been a verbal argument between them and Jane, she said that Mr. Meyers had not hit Jane. Jane had left the house crying because they told her she was "grounded" for a week and could not have any phone privileges. They hoped that would force her to be more responsible and remember things better. It seemed to Lynn that the punishment was excessive, but she decided to leave that issue for a later discussion.

　　Lynn readily observed that Mrs. Meyers got more comfortable as she talked. Mrs. Meyers was warm and openly expressed concern about being a parent. She seemed perplexed by how rebellious Jane was becoming. Mrs. Meyers talked rapidly and gestured frequently with her hands. Mr. Meyers was quiet throughout the interview. Except for chain-smoking cigarettes, he did not really move. He simply sat in a chair and looked down at the carpet. When Lynn directly asked him questions, his wife almost always answered for him. The only time he spoke was to say that Jane had to stop talking back and how he had toed the line when he was growing up. Neither parent admitted to having any problems with their seven-year-old son.

Lynn decided not to interview anyone else, such as the neighbors or the Meyers's son Fred, for two reasons. First, to do so would be a violation of confidentiality laws, and second, no one had first-hand knowledge of the incident. Lynn thought that both Jane and her mother generally seemed to talk openly and honestly, but if Mrs. Meyers was telling the truth, then how did Jane get the bruises on her neck?

THE SECOND DAY

On the second day of her investigation, Lynn again visited Jane at school. Jane immediately apologized for making up stories and said her mom took off from work last night so she and her husband and Jane could talk. Jane said her dad hadn't hit her, but she refused to offer an explanation for the cause of the bruises. She was composed and apologetic but she did not once make eye contact. She seemed to consider her words carefully, and she sat rigidly in the chair. Upon returning to her office, Lynn received a call from Mrs. Meyers. She said she had called the Mental Health Center to make an appointment for Jane. Lynn took advantage of Mrs. Meyers's call by asking if Mr. Meyers would come to the office to talk with her. He said he couldn't that day but would come the next.

THE THIRD DAY

Although Lynn had asked only Mr. Meyers, both Mr. and Mrs. Meyers came to the office the next day. Lynn spoke with Mr. Meyers alone first. He chain-smoked and had a hard time making eye contact. He sat slumped down in a chair and answered slowly. His voice was steady but his shoulders were tight and his face looked strained. Lynn went over the incident again. Mr. Meyers admitted to having a temper and sometimes hitting objects when he got mad. He said that at present he was under a lot of stress because he was out of a job. He thought he might have swung in the air with his right arm when they were arguing (Jane was facing him, so that would match up with bruises on her left side), but he did not remember hitting Jane even accidentally. He said he used to spank her when she was smaller but now he just "put her on restriction."

Lynn next talked to Mrs. Meyers alone. Mrs. Meyers immediately leaned forward in the chair and wanted to know what her husband had said, but Lynn would not tell her. Instead, Lynn simply asked her to go over the incident again. Upon questioning, Mrs. Meyers said she had no recollection of her husband swinging in the air during the argument. However, she said he did hit Jane occasionally when Jane did not do what he said. Lynn asked Mrs. Meyers to define "occasionally," but Mrs. Meyers wouldn't. She repeated that Mr. Meyers had not hit Jane that day. She said she did not feel that she or her husband had any problems. She sat on the edge of her chair; her hands clenched her knees and she spoke assertively, her eyes nervously darting about the room.

Lynn wondered whose version of the story was right. Neither parents had offered an explanation for Jane's bruises. Lynn had waited to see if they would.

THE FOURTH DAY

Lynn called the guidance counselor, Dick Reed, and asked him to talk to Jane again. She wanted to see if Jane might tell Dick a different story. Dick called back to report that Jane said she was sorry she had caused so much trouble and had repeated that her dad had not hit her. Dick said, "I'm worried that maybe she's been threatened not to talk to us anymore. I asked her where she got the bruises, but she seemed to get upset, then recover and just not say anything."

Lynn stopped at the Meyers's home, but no one was there. She wanted to try to pin down Mr. Meyers a bit more, so she called later in the day. He agreed to come back to the office the following day.

THE FIFTH DAY

Mr. Meyers did not keep his appointment. Since the law requires that a report be filed within ninety-six hours, Lynn had no choice but to write the abuse report with the facts she had. Keeping the state law's definition of physical abuse in mind, she outlined five possible conclusions she could reach:

1. No injury was thought to have occurred.
2. An injury was substantiated, but it was not a result of abuse.
3. The injury was not substantiated, but abuse was suspected.
4. The injury was substantiated, and abuse was suspected.
5. The injury was substantiated, and abuse was verified.

THE REPORT

Lynn knew her report would be read by both a judge and the county attorney, who would take whatever legal action, if any, was required. In addition, a copy of the report would be sent to the state's Central Registry. If Lynn found that there was no injury and no abuse, the report would be kept temporarily on file and then destroyed, as would all copies. If Lynn found abuse verified, Central Registry would carefully review her report to determine whether such a finding seemed justified. If Central Registry determined that the facts presented led to a conclusion of substantiated abuse, the report would be placed on file. If not, the report would be returned. Returned reports could be rewritten. Although Lynn *had to* write the report with the facts she had, she could *also* call or write the judge and request a ten-day extension so that she could continue her investigation once the *initial report* was completed.

SUGGESTED DISCUSSION QUESTIONS

1. What kinds of information does Lynn Stoddard find potentially useful? (Testimony? Nonverbal communication? Appearance? Why?)

2. Who are the major sources of Lynn's information?

3. How do you rate the quality of Jane's testimony? Of Mrs. Meyers's? Of Mr. Meyers's? Of Dick Reed's? Of the principal's? Of Jane's teachers'?

5. In what ways does the testimony conflict?

6. What are the *causes* of the conflicts in testimony?

SUGGESTED ASSIGNMENTS

1. You are in your first day of class in Social Work 203. Your instructor realizes you have no experience or education in the field but wants you to complete the following assignment anyway: write Lynn's initial report on the Meyers case.

2. You are Lynn Stoddard. In a letter appended to the report, persuade the judge to grant you a ten-day extension of your investigation.

3. Suppose the judge grants you the extension. You arrange to see Mr. Meyers in your office at the beginning of the following week, and once again he fails to come in for his appointment. When you finally reach him at home, he is abrupt. He says he is working full-time again and doesn't want to be late to work. He doesn't have time, he says, to come in and see you. Mrs. Meyers comes on the line and says she doesn't have time to talk either because she is working overtime to earn extra money.

   When you stop by the Meyers's home, Mrs. Meyers does not invite you in. "We don't have any problems," she says. "My husband is working again and we're trying to help Jane be more mature." Strangely enough, Mrs. Meyers smiles nicely as she closes the door in your face. At school, Jane studies the floor, clenches and unclenches her hands, and says, "Please don't ask me any more questions. I'm sorry I made up the story. I can't tell you anything else."

   It's already time to write your second report. Based on these events, write the report.

To Build or Not to Build (B)

Janey Hunkee, a citizen of Trinidad, decided to study the softball-diamond complex controversy. The Parks and Recreation Department, along with the Parks and Recreation Commission, had scheduled a public meeting for further discussion and explanation of the plans for the softball diamonds.

Janey's first task, as she saw it, was to get the background information on the controversy. She did so by interviewing Trice and Bell (read "To Build or Not to Build" (A), p. 269.) She also read a couple of the letters to the editor in the paper.

In an interview with Trice, Janey learned that the Parks and Recreation Department had scheduled the fall flag football games for another location. Trice also made a special point of telling Janey that it was true that twenty-five mature trees were in the way of the new diamonds, but only five of them had actually been cut down. Already fifteen had been moved—at considerable expense—to other areas of the park. In the next week the remaining five would also be safely transplanted.

Janey also called the President of the Trinidad Softball Association, Bob Phelps. Phelps said that the Association felt that over fifteen hundred softball players were entitled to their diamonds after all the study and planning had been completed; Phelps also said the three-hundred-plus residents opposed were a vocal but small minority of uninformed but influential citizens. Phelps said he still assumed the plan would continue, but he'd been told by Trice and others that the City Council did have the power to cancel the plan simply by not allowing the collection of any more fees in the future. Phelps said that if this happened the Association would sue, on behalf of the players, and force the city to return the seventeen thousand dollars it had already collected.

Clearly, Phelps argued, the city would be guilty of a breach of contract if it collected $17,540 as the first step in constructing four diamonds and then did not build the diamonds. Phelps said his attorney assured him the Association would have an excellent case. Phelps also said he thought the players were frustrated—most of them were fairly young, many of them were students at the local community college and/or hard-working types without a lot of money, and they felt like they might get treated unfairly.

THE PARKS AND RECREATION DEPARTMENT MEETING

Although Janey arrived forty-five minutes early for the 7:00 P.M. meeting at the Parks and Recreation Department's large conference room, she could hardly get inside. Already the room was overflowing, with the legal limit, according to fire regulations posted on the wall, surely exceeded. Janey counted ninety-three people in the room. Later, as it turned out, about sixty people had been unable to find a place to squeeze in. Nearly all of them had left, many of them angry at the city for holding the meeting in a room designed to hold only eighty people. Nearly a dozen or so had stayed out in the hallway and tried to listen to the meeting from there.

Janey used her tape recorder at the meeting, but she also took notes, both to highlight places where she felt the discussion was particularly important and to record impressions that couldn't be recorded on tape. The meeting lasted two hours and could have gone on for a couple more, she thought, but another meeting was scheduled in the room for 9:00 P.M., and so the discussion was simply terminated. Janey did her best to make accurate and perceptive observations and judgments as she took notes.

JANEY'S NOTES

Meeting begins by Bell and Trice making summary remarks covering the history of the diamond development and the need for the diamonds.

Commission Chair Al Longirn briefly summarizes how the Commission studied 17 sites and concluded that Ferguson Park was the best.

Crowd grumbles. Bell calls for discussion. Recognizes Marquand.

Marquand speaks for a long time. Marquand is the President of the First National Bank of Trinidad. Dressed in suit. Waves new petition around. Repeats need for many activities such as touch football, frisbee throwing, picnics, pickup softball games—people would be locked out of these diamonds, he says—jogging, kite flying. Calls for the city to look at buying land elsewhere. Says he has nothing against softball. He states that earlier that evening he attended the City Council meeting and stayed long enough to get the diamond issue put on the agenda for one week from today. Says he has 373 signatures of registered voters who call for suspension of construction until a new study can be done.

Bob Phelps is recognized from the floor. He speaks of the need for the diamonds and praises the players' willingness to pay for the development. Phelps repeats that nobody can afford the land required. Phelps is the owner of a small bar in downtown Trinidad. He doesn't talk long and is obviously uncomfortable in front of this group.

Woman is recognized. She says the noise and lights are already a major imposition on the neighborhood from the three present diamonds. Games last until eleven at night. Her children can't get to sleep because the lights bother them. And just because these softball players have the money doesn't mean they can come in and buy up the park. People cheer and applaud her. Then some boo. A guy in the back says, "Screw you, lady," under his breath, but lots of people hear.

The Dean of the local community college gets up and speaks for five minutes about the importance of maintaining the aesthetic value of the park. He supports softball and wishes the College could help, but it can't. He states that the diamonds would ruin the park aesthetically.

A guy with a John Deere cap on, sweat shirt, and blue jeans gets up and says he is tired of being insulted by people in the neighborhood who think all softball players do is drink beer and scream too loud. He says he works full-time and sometimes sixty hours a week, and he pays his taxes, and sometimes he has cleaned up more trash, before games, in that park than the local neighbors ever have. In fact, they probably left the damn trash there, he says, or their kids on their mopeds did. He's tired of getting insulted by a bunch of people who don't know what they're talking about.

Some people cheer loudly and applaud; lots of people look angry and insulted.

The discussion heats up. The antidiamond people seem to be present in greater numbers and are more willing to volunteer to comment. They talk longer and seem better organized somehow.

"I don't like even five trees getting cut down," one woman says.

"I like softball," a man says, "but the park is already burdened with lots of Little League games and traffic. I don't think the streets and the parking lots can handle any more such traffic."

" I wonder," a man in a business suit says, "whether the city has done a traffic study to determine whether the main streets can handle the traffic if we start having these huge softball tournaments."

A softball player—he has his jersey on (ALLIGATORS)—says, "Where were all of you when the Commission had its first two meetings? They were announced in the paper just like all public meetings. And don't you read the paper? These plans were reported twice on the front page of the Saturday paper." He pulls out two newspaper clippings from his pocket and reads the headlines and the dates.

Marquand gains the floor and says, "I admit we may have been a little remiss in not having realized the full extent of this development when it was announced in the paper last spring. However, the articles were short, and there was no illustration provided by the Commission to show the extent of the plans."

Longirn responds to that by saying, "I guess we could've provided an illustration, and we still can, but I thought the articles did a good enough job describing the plans, and the *Daily* didn't ask us for an illustration of any sort. Nor did anybody call us and ask for one."

Marquand is still standing. He says, "Even so, it's still in the best interest of this city to fully research every possibility before ruining Ferguson Park. It's not too late to build the diamonds elsewhere."

A guy in the back yells, "Yes it is. We already spent seventeen thousand dollars."

The meeting heats up. People look angry and comment to one another as the discussion goes on. Woman says, "I can't believe anyone in Trinidad could be so rude, but then just *look* at these people." Guy says to his friend, "We're getting screwed over by a bunch of squealing rich jerks."

A man gets up and says he is a softball team manager. He begins strongly by saying, "The issue here isn't over frisbees and touch football. Not if you look at the facts. And the issue isn't over kite flying and cross-country skiing. Or Jogging. Not if you look at the facts. People can still jog in the park . . ." He starts to talk about how people can still jog and then he doubles back to cross-country skiing; he seems to get lost, and he never does say what the issue is. Finally he sits down, embarrassed.

Lots of people from the neighborhood speak out. A few more softball players do.

AFTER THE MEETING

When Janey left the meeting she was grateful she'd taken a tape recorder. She had many excellent impressions of the conflict itself—of how the softball players had seemed surprised and angry at the opposition and how in many cases they hadn't argued well. In contrast, the neighborhood group seemed better organized—more of them seemed to be present and different people made different arguments about everything from trees and kites to parking and traffic. As for most of the precise quotes, Janey had a few in writing but all, of course, on tape. Now she just had to figure out what to do with all that information.

SUGGESTED DISCUSSION QUESTIONS

1. What are the most basic conflicts evident during the meeting?
2. What are the best arguments each side has to offer?
3. What are some ways each of these arguments can be refuted?
4. What errors in fact or logic are people making?
5. What should the Softball Association do to prepare for the City Council meeting?
6. What should the Neighborhood Association do to prepare for the City Council meeting?

SUGGESTED ASSIGNMENTS

1. You are Janey Hunkee. Suppose your English instructor has told you to write an argument in which you state what you think ought to be done about the softball diamond complex. Write an argument based on cases A and B.

2. You are Janey Hunkee. Suppose your sociology professor has sent you to this meeting as a way for you to study Trinidad society. Use your material and impressions to make an argument about the societal conflicts you see here.

3. You are Janey Hunkee. Suppose your political science professor has sent you to this meeting to study city politics and how government works at the local level. Study the material in the two cases and write an essay in which you

discuss what caused these problems. You may also want to analyze whether this conflict could have been avoided and/or discuss ways it can be resolved, for example, through some sort of task force or through more meetings.

4. You are Janey Hunkee, a concerned citizen of Trinidad. Now that you have attended the meeting, write a letter to the *Trinidad Daily* in which you argue some particular point about this controversy. Alternatively, address your argument to Marquand, Phelps, Trice, or Longirn.

5. You are Janey Hunkee. Suppose you decide to write a feature article on the softball diamond controversy. Write the article and then write a cover letter that persuades the editor of the *Trinidad Daily* to publish your article and give you a by-line. Alternatively, submit the article, with cover letter, to the daily paper for Trinidad Junior College, *The Trinidad J.C. Daily News*.

Part III

Beyond Cases

The case approach you've experienced in either or both of the first two parts of this book should have taught you some essential writing habits *and* left you restless to do a lot more discovering on your own. The essential habits are these: to establish a specific purpose for your writing to achieve; to identify and write to a particular audience; and to use a variety of inventive and organizational techniques to develop, structure, and revise your material.

Part Three assumes you are beginning to practice these essentials. We also assume here that writing within and about cases has left you eager to look for your own problems to solve and your own subjects to explore and write about. The purpose of Part Three is to help you continue to develop your writing skills as you write on subjects beyond cases. That's a big subject, almost a book in itself. Part Three takes a quick look at some of the basics as well as some of the most exciting possibilities of writing beyond cases. This portion of the text is an appetizer, not a whole meal; it's a quick set of directions, not an entire atlas. Still, you should find some useful beginnings here: your endings are all out there.

Beyond Cases

The Right Subject

Suppose, then, that instead of working with a case you've been told to select your own subject for an essay (and perhaps your own audience as well). Of course you can brainstorm, make lists, and try freewriting, and so on (see Chapter 2), but here are three steps you must take in order to do well.

Care About Your Subject

If you don't care about your subject, you probably won't care about your writing, and your reader won't care about it either. So don't choose a subject unless you have a genuine interest in it, or better yet, an emotional investment. You may be angry or sad, excited or scared to death, amused or depressed. What do you talk about over coffee or a Coke with your best friend? What part of the newspaper do you read? What books? What television shows do you watch? What movies? A gripe or a conviction, a sarcastic or critical view may be a rich source of material for your subject.

Limit Your Subject

One way to decide whether you really care about a subject and are properly limiting it is to check your pulse. Consider this subject: football. Do you feel much of a reaction? Probably not. The subject is so general it's likely that nobody, including your readers and yourself, is going to get excited. "Monday Night Football," however, is specific enough to offer a writer some promise. If your subject is "Howard Cosell: The Man People Love to Hate" *and* you write about Monday Night Football, then you've probably got your hands on a promising subject.

If your subject is "Drunk Drivers," then you've chosen to write about something with built-in or intrinsic interest, but *what about* drunk drivers? There could be a hundred subjects hidden in those two words. Find yours by limiting your subject *and* by committing yourself somehow. Perhaps you can title your essay "Dear Drunk Driver: You Could Have Saved My Brother's Life." Now you've got an emotional stake all right— a drunk driver killed your brother when that driver could have taken a taxi home from the bar.

Of course the length of your essay matters tremendously when you are trying to decide how much to limit your subject. If you've got just one paragraph to write, no more, no less, then an essay on Howard Cosell might be limited to "Instant Replays on Monday Night Football" or "How Howard Ad-Libs Half-time Highlights." If your general subject is drunk drivers, then perhaps one paragraph might be about how Breathalyzers could be used in bars. In general, as you limit your subject you increase the possibilities for rich detail; you also increase the readers' interest. Only practice will teach you how a 500-word subject differs in size from a 2000-word subject. For a first draft, writers typically begin with a subject that's too large. Ultimately it's probably true of subjects that "small is beautiful."

Know Your Subject

The last step you must take in selecting a subject is to know it well. Write about only those subjects you either know well or come to know well as you research them. Readers distrust and dislike ignorant writers. A writer who makes an argument about motorcycles will lose credibility with knowledgeable readers if he or she writes, "Harley-Davidson's are all-American bikes—they're the only motorcycles made in the United States." That's simply not true—Honda also manufactures motorcycles in the U.S.; any reader who knows about Hondas will therefore immediately discount *everything* the Harley-Davidson writer has to say.

Basically, readers read what you've written for two reasons: to learn new information and to listen to your ideas. Therefore, you must know at least as much—and preferably far more—about the subject than does your reader. Otherwise you have nothing to teach. Remember, especially for a writer, knowledge is power.

The Right Research

The library, therefore, is one of a writer's greatest sources of power. Personal experience and personal knowledge are great sources of material for writers, but even the most experienced and best writers may end up in the library, where they dig out new facts and double check information for accuracy. So even if you think you're an expert on your chosen subject, a trip to the library may be essential. There's no room here, however, to write a complete guide on library research (and sometimes partial guides are worse than no guide at all). Instead, here are two tips to using the library: try a "quick fix" and then really dig in.

Try A Quick Fix

If you do venture to the library, don't begin with the card catalogue if your goal is a quick check to see just how knowledgeable you are. Remember: information in books is two to five years old the day it *arrives* in a library. Another initial problem with beginning with books is that their sheer bulk may overwhelm you.

One source of a "quick fix" is the Magazine Index. The Magazine Index is a wonder of modern technology. It's a microform index of all the articles more than a hundred magazines have published during the past five years or so. In other words, it's a listing, by topic, of hundreds of thousands of essay titles. If you can push two buttons, turn a knob, and read, then you can operate the Magazine Index without further instruction. If your subject is Drunk Driving, run the Magazine Index to the *d*'s and see what's listed there. Chances are that your library has some or even all of these publications available within minutes of where you sit. Select five of the most relevant and interesting-looking articles and go look them up. Skim the articles quickly and see if all the information they contain seems like obvious fact to you. If you already know this stuff, great—you're on the right track in selecting a subject in that you seem to know it. If you discover you don't know nearly as much about the subject as you thought you did, that's okay—now's the time to learn what you don't know. Alternatively, you can always choose another subject.

Really Dig In

Library research is simpler than most of us admit. Beyond the Magazine Index and a similar index for business periodicals called the Business Index, there are other indices, such as the *Reader's Guide to Periodicals*, which can be excellent resources. Then, too, abstracts—summaries of articles or books—are also available in many subject areas, as are other sources of information. If you aren't confident about your ability to use these sources efficiently—to go to the right sources and find what you want in minutes or hours and not days—then you may want to buy a book (or borrow one from the library) that will tell you what to do. Another option is simply to go to the library's reference desk and ask for help—that's what the librarians are there for. At the end of Part Three there's a list of suitable books that give guidance on library research and documentation. You may also want to ask your instructor for advice.

Outside the Library

The library is an excellent source of information, but it's not the only source. Another approach you can try is to interview experts on your subject. Suppose you are writing an essay about why the bookstore doesn't seem to pay students a fair price for their used textbooks. An obvious person to interview would be the bookstore manager or the textbook manager at the bookstore. These people are experts, or should be. They have the knowledge that can give your essay muscle, so go get it.

Phone interviews are acceptable if you must call someone long distance—the President of the National Association of College Bookstores, for example. Personal interviews are better yet. In either case, know what questions you want to ask before you begin the interview. Have at least some questions written down. Consider using a tape recorder to get a complete record of each answer. If you use a tape recorder, of course it's courteous to ask for permission to do so. If you don't use a tape recorder, or even if you do, take notes, lots of notes. Later on you'll have to credit the information you've gained to the source, and you want to be accurate.

Taking a survey is another way to acquire information outside a library. The kind of surveys George Gallup took involve random samples and technology you simply don't have and can't afford. Even so, a few basics are required if your survey is going to be worth mentioning. If all you write in your essay, for example, is that, "According to the students I asked, Howard Cosell is hated by football fans," then your reader won't consider your survey to be reliable. *What* students did you ask? *How* did you select them? *What* exactly did you ask? These are a few of the things readers need to know. Your instructor may have specific requirements for any survey you take, but here are some basic guidelines you should follow:

1. Write out the questions. If you ask them orally, repeat the question exactly the same way each time.

2. If you provide possible answers (agree, disagree), usually it's best to allow for a "no opinion" option or an "undecided."

3. Attach a copy of the survey itself to your essay so your readers may examine your questions.

4. Make the questions neutral in tone: "Do you favor requiring all convicted first-time, drunk-driving offenders to be jailed for at least three days?" (Not, "Don't you think every drunk driver ought to be thrown in jail and justly punished if he's caught?")

5. Make your sample broad and large enough to be meaningful. Don't just ask your friends at work or six people in your English class. If you are researching student opinion about, for example, the prices the bookstore pays for used textbooks, then you could stand at the front of the bookstore for an hour and ask as many students as you can what they think.

For additional guidance on using surveys, ask your instructor or consult with your librarian.

The Right Documentation

Wherever you gather your information, once you use it in your essay, you must document your source. Doing so is more than a courtesy to the reader: it's an ethical responsibility of the writer. However, the need to document sources produces at least two challenging problems for the writer. One is the question of what kind of documentation is appropriate. A second is the nearly unlimited variations in form in which information is presented.

To solve the first problem—what kind of documentation is required— you must ask your instructor or your boss. The *MLA Style Sheet* is just one possibility. To solve your second problem—how to do the job right given all the different kinds of sources you have—the solution is to use the best guide: either a highly recommended handbook or a textbook on writing research papers. Some dictionaries and many writing texts come with some examples of how to document your sources properly, but those few examples can be frustrating for the beginner if his or her source doesn't match up perfectly to the text. In short, a partial list is sometimes worse than none. Either try one of the texts listed at the end of Part Three or ask your instructor for his or her recommendation.

As soon as you go beyond cases, you have to be concerned with properly documenting your sources. Part of that challenge is properly footnoting your information and properly providing a bibliography. At first, it may seem to you that the technicalities of footnoting and bibliography are overwhelming. If you already know these techniques, great. In either case, the greatest challenge is still ahead: that is, to usefully and fairly quote or paraphrase information you have acquired. Again, there's no space here for a thorough discussion of writing a research paper, but whenever you write beyond cases, you should be familiar with three basic terms or concepts: common knowledge, paraphrasing, and plagiarism.

Anything that is common knowledge requires no footnoting, no documentation. So what's common knowledge and what isn't? Many sources will tell you that a football field is a hundred yards long, that Jim Brown was one of the greatest rushers in the history of professional football, that artificial turf and indoor stadiums have changed the nature of the game. All this is common knowledge and requires no documentation. If, however, you hear Don Meredith say, on *Monday Night Football*, that he thinks X rule should be changed because the players obviously can't play without violating the rule on nearly every punt return, then you should give Meredith credit for his opinion. Not doing so would be a form of plagiarism—the theft of an opinion (or a fact or an idea). Paraphrasing Don Meredith, as we've done above, is acceptable, even preferable in some cases. Paraphrasing simply involves repeating information or ideas with altered phrasing.

A good paraphrase saves space and expresses someone else's idea in the writer's own language and style. But even paraphrasing requires that credit be given to Meredith, or to whomever your information belongs.

For some practical experience in documentation, you and your class may want to examine the case ("The Case of the Plagiarized Paper") which follows this section of Part Three.

Sources for Subjects: Research Cases

The sources for subjects discussed and given below can keep you busy for an entire semester by themselves. If you follow the guidelines you've been given for choosing a subject, you should be able to choose well, given any of the following options.

A "research case" is actually just an extended writing assignment; it's an assignment that establishes a writing situation for you—a scenario, an audience, a purpose. Yet these extended writing assignments *require* you to go out and do research—to gather your own information, even to select your own subject in most cases. Here are ten such assignments.

The Case of the Plagiarized Paper

By the time Julie got back to her dorm she had managed to stop crying, but just barely. She sat down on her bed and looked at the essay she held in her trembling hand. The cover sheet read:

"Wife-Beating: Not a Low-Class Act"
by Julie Burke
March 1, 1978
Professor Jacks
English 102-3F

Across the top of the cover sheet there was a big red F followed by the word *PLAGIARIZED!*

She said aloud to herself "I don't know what to do." She thought about what had happened to her.

PROFESSOR JACKS

When Professor Jacks didn't return her essay, but did give her a note that said "Please come to my office this afternoon," Julie didn't know what to think, except that maybe something was wrong. Just how wrong things were she had no idea. She had thought the essay she had written was all right. Maybe, in fact, it was pretty good.

In Professor Jacks's office she sat by the side of his metal desk and looked at all his books on the bookcases instead of looking at him. She was wondering whether he'd read all those books when he said, "I asked you to come in here today, Julie, because your essay disturbed me."

He held up a copy of *Newsweek* magazine and said "Does this look familiar to you?"

She didn't know what to say. Of course she recognized *Newsweek* magazine—who wouldn't, it was on every newsstand in the country—but so what?

"Yeah," she said. "I mean, of course, I know what it is. Everybody reads it." At the same time, she started to feel sick to her stomach.

Professor Jacks's face changed from a stern, tired look to one of exasperation and anger. He opened up the page to an article and put the magazine down in front of her. Various portions of the article were underlined with red ink.

Julie just said "I've never read it. Why?"

"If you've never read the article," Jacks said, "then how do you explain the fact that you've copied sentences and practically whole paragraphs right out of it?"

That was when Jacks put her essay down on the desk with the big F on the cover sheet. It seemed to Julie that the F practically glowed like a neon sign. For a while all she could think was that he was wrong, that it just wasn't true, that she had never read the article, that she had never even looked at the magazine, and that she had written her essay without any help from anyone at all.

But Professor Jacks was sure of himself. When he showed her two examples, Julie suddenly remembered the note cards. They were Sue Rahlson's note cards. The night before the essay was due she was down in the rec room buying a Coke and candy bar when Sue came in.

Julie had told Sue she was worried because this English essay was due tomorrow and she didn't have any ideas about what to say. Then Sue had told her about the cards. Sue said she'd had to write on the same topic, more or less, last term, and she hadn't known what to say either, so she had asked around and this guy gave her all these note cards. It turned out he'd done a lot of research on the subject. Sue said she thought she still had most of them. What Julie needed to do, she said, was read through them and maybe get some ideas from them.

So Julie told Professor Jacks she'd done just that—read through the note cards—and then she'd written her paper. She used some of the ideas, but she didn't think there was anything wrong with that because she had some of her own too, and besides, she didn't know what else she was supposed to do.

Professor Jacks said it was just like stealing. "You can't just steal from other people. If somebody said, "Here, take this color TV set, this guy gave it to me and he said he didn't want it and neither do I," would you just take the color TV, no questions asked? If you want to keep me from having to report this to the Dean, here's what you'll have to do. Take your essay and compare it to the article it's plagiarized from. It's the February 2, 1976, issue of *Newsweek*. The article is by Linda Bird Francke. It's entitled "Battered Women." You'll have to properly document every quote or paraphrase, and you'll have to make sure *your* ideas control each paragraph, not somebody else's."

Before Julie left Professor Jacks's office, he added that the essay would be weak even if she hadn't plagiarized it since it was so poorly organized and expressed. If she expected him to accept it, he said, she'd have to completely revise the essay. Even then she'd get an F on it as a penalty for stealing someone else's work. Professor Jacks had spent two class sessions on plagiarism, paraphrasing, and documentation, and Julie had been present at both.

Here is what Julie's original essay looked like:

Wife-Beating: Not a Low-Class Act

The plight of battered women is a problem that demands an increasing amount of attention from law enforcement officers, attorneys, judges, and the general public. The incidence of wife-beating is not necessarily on the rise, but the protests of the women are starting to attract attention to the problem and stir some change in its treatment. As more cases are reported, numerous government and social agencies are developing programs to help the victims of this previously ignored crime.

Because wife-beating, like sexual assault, is often not reported, it is almost impossible to document since it is listed under "assault and battery" or "disputes." Another difficulty in dealing with cases involving battered women is the fact that wife-beating is not a crime limited to the bottom level of society. As one police officer notes, wife-beating has been categorized as a lower-class crime, but that's wrong. A lot of men are under the same frustrations whether they're rich or poor.

Perhaps the biggest obstacle to a reasonable handling of the wife-beating situation is the problem of defining what really constitutes an infringement of the law. In any fight between members of a particular family, the line between family squabble and criminal act is hard to draw. The police don't seem able to differentiate between a woman in danger and a woman just trying to put a scare into her spouse. One divorce attorney estimates that about 40 percent of her seven hundred low-income clients have been beaten.

To make a bad situation even worse, battered women have very little recourse against their male antagonists, even if they seek legal aid. State laws vary widely and women find themselves shunted between civil, criminal, and family court—and often advised not to bring a complaint at all. To alleviate this situation, a number of groups have opened shelter houses both in the U.S. and abroad to give battered women refuge against their assailants. Also, police in some areas are working on new methods to deal with both victims and offenders. In Atlanta, cops are taught, through role-playing, to defuse family fights by projecting a calm, mediating force rather than the aggressive posture of an arresting officer. In Hayward, Calif., three-year-old Project Outreach has teamed family counselors with police, thereby reducing the recurrence of domestic-quarrel complaints from 50 percent to 20 percent.

Though the picture for victims of wife-beating is anything but rosy, the fact that more and more women are willing to come forward and demand attention is encouraging. As this problem is brought into the public eye it becomes something to be dealt with, and not a shameful family secret to be concealed or ignored. The tremendous need for just legislation and prompt attention is obvious when we consider a few statistics. In Washington, D.C., seventy women recently called a referral number broadcast on a local television show on wife-beating. That was on a Saturday night. Monday morning, the hot line picked up a hundred more calls from women who had memorized the number—then waited to call until their husbands were safely off to work.

SUGGESTED DISCUSSION QUESTIONS

1. What is plagiarism?

2. What does *paraphrase* mean?

3. How could Julie have avoided her problem?

4. Exactly what should Julie do now? Why?

5. Do you know whether Sue Rahlson plagiarized?

6. Suppose that rather than copying from the *Newsweek* article, Julie had copied, in a similar way, from another student's paper (one from a different class). Would Julie then be guilty of plagiarism? Does it matter whether the "borrowed" but not credited material is in print?

SUGGESTED ASSIGNMENTS

1. Write a brief definition, including your own example, of *plagiarism*.
2. Write a brief definition, including your own example, of *paraphrasing*.
3. Rewrite Julie's essay so that it contains no plagiarism.
4. Select one paragraph from Julie's essay that contains plagiarized material. Reconstruct the paragraph so that it properly uses the material to support a point you want to make.
5. In an essay called "Stealing Made Easy," or some such inventive and ironic title, illustrate techniques for "creative plagiarism." The point, of course, is to educate students and to discourage them from plagiarizing by showing how it denies the student writer's own creative and intellectual powers.

Martin Luther King, Jr.: The Writer, the National Day of Recognition

As a writer for your school's literary magazine, you are asked to look into doing some kind of analytical piece about Martin Luther King, Jr. You know a little about King—that he was a civil rights leader, that he believed, as did Gandhi, in peaceful civil disobedience. You do a little checking by grabbing hold of *Reader's Guide to Periodicals* and you find, in the first volume you happen to lay your hands on, reference to the national holiday established in recognition of King.

The October 31, 1983, issues of *Time, Newsweek,* and *U.S. News and World Report* fill you in on some background about the holiday itself. You learn that in August, 1983, the House of Representatives voted 338 to 90 for the holiday, and then on October 19 the Senate followed the House with a vote of 78 to 22. Shortly thereafter, President Reagan signed the legislation, which specifies that beginning in 1986 the third Monday in January will be a national holiday commemorating King's birth (King was born on January 15, 1929). George Washington's birthday is the only other birthday so commemorated. You also learn, incidentally, that local and state governments may choose to stay open on this day, though all federal offices will be closed. Seventeen states already close their offices on this day, it so happens.

Learning all this makes you wonder a bit more about King. A quick look in the card catalogue tells you that King published many books, among them *Why We Can't Wait*. In the stacks you find the book and decide to see what kind of a writer King is. You begin by reading King's "Letter From Birmingham Jail—April 16, 1963." The letter interests you because of its premise: it's written by someone on the inside of a jail cell, by someone who's done something wrong by societal standards. You're also curious about the letter because it begins, "My Dear Fellow Clergymen." You've read enough of *Casebook Rhetoric* by now to know the usefulness of identifying the intended readers for a particular piece of writing. You also know that King is actually writing to a much broader audience than just these clergymen.

In fact, as you read the "letter" you realize it isn't a letter at all, at least not in the rhetorical sense. King's writing here is really an essay, a persuasive argument with a thesis, which is developed in various ways. As you read the "letter," you begin to use what you know about effective writing to analyze the quality of King's prose.

SUGGESTED DISCUSSION QUESTIONS

1. What do you and your classmates know about Martin Luther King, Jr.?
2. How many people in the class have previously read anything written by King?
3. What methods of development does King use in his letter to develop his argument?
4. What is the thesis of King's letter?

SUGGESTED ASSIGNMENTS

(Note: For each of the assignments below you may want your instructor's guidance in deciding whether you can expect your audience to have read "Letter From Birmingham Jail.")

1. Write a critical analysis of King's letter. Be specific in your thesis and state what, exactly, makes the letter an effective persuasion essay.
2. Using King's thesis in his letter as your subject, agree or disagree with King's position. Explain and develop your position by using your own examples and other kinds of evidence.
3. Using King's thesis as your starting point, examine some specific social or economic issue of interest to you. You may wish to compare, for example, King's point of view with the approach taken by those groups who oppose the construction and operation of nuclear power plants.
4. Do some further reading about King and write an essay in which you explain how King's actions have (or have not) changed your own life.

Wanted: Literary Critic (Reward Offered)

You don't necessarily think of yourself as an excellent writer *or* as a literary critic, but as you are reading the school newspaper one day you notice the following announcement:

The English Department announces a critical writing contest with cash awards for the winner in each category. Carl J. and Matilda M. Peterson, both alumni, have created the awards, which total $1200 annually.

Contestants should choose their own literature for analysis, or may do so in consultation with a member of the English Department. Separate awards will be given to freshmen, sophomores, and so on.

The Petersons chose to make the awards to freshmen the highest amounts: $150, $100, and $50 to the first-, second-, and third-place winners, respectively. Freshmen who are non-English majors (or undecided) will compete in a separate category with awards of the same amount specified above.

Minimum essay length is 500 words. Essays may be longer. Applicants are encouraged to consult with a member of the English faculty. Applicants may write an analysis of poetry, fiction, drama, or nonfiction, but each essay must show the applicant's ability to evaluate the literature chosen.

You start thinking about the odds and decide that it might actually be worthwhile to enter this contest. The competition *is* limited and, besides, you might be able to earn credit for your work in your present English course. You know enough by now, however, to wonder who your audience will be: are you writing to the Petersons or everyone who teaches English or to whom?

You call the English Department and learn the following. The awards committee is comprised of one undergraduate English major, one teacher of English, and one journalist from the local newspaper—you aren't told which journalist (the Petersons were both newspaper writers). You are told that you should assume the panel is familiar with whatever piece of literature you decide to analyze. If one or more panel members is not familiar with that work, then they will read it before making a final decision about the effectiveness of your essay.

You are encouraged to select the highest-quality literature to analyze, be it contemporary or classical. Of course you know yourself that you'll have to find something you can truly appreciate or you won't have the emotional commitment to do well. So, knowing all this, you start to look around for a possible source and subject. You also decide to ask your English instructor for some guidance.

SUGGESTED DISCUSSION QUESTIONS

1. How do the guidelines given for selecting the right subject apply to this situation?
2. What are three possible topics you might choose?
3. What kind of literature do you most like to read? Why?
4. Would this kind of literature be suitable for a critical analysis? Why or why not?

SUGGESTED ASSIGNMENTS

1. Make a list of five possible topics for your critical analysis. You may want to discuss these possibilities with your instructor or share some of them with your classmates.
2. Write a critical analysis of a selected piece of literature.

Orwell Other Than 1984

Now that "the year" is over, your editor on the school's literary magazine decides someone should do a retrospective piece on George Orwell, whose novel *1984* made the year so noteworthy for generations. Your job, your editor says, is to write something about Orwell, not necessarily having anything to do with the famous novel.

"In fact," your editor said, "it'd better if you didn't write about the novel. Why not remind people that Orwell wrote *other* books?"

The other books you don't know about, so you do a little investigating and find that Orwell was both a novelist and an essayist. Surprisingly, you find that while *1984* got all the publicity, Orwell is probably most often studied as an essayist. In fact, your English teacher tells you that three of Orwell's essays—"Shooting an Elephant," "A Hanging," and "Politics and the English Language"—are three of the most frequently studied essays in college English courses. If there was such a thing as an English essay pop chart, these three essays would all be platinum best sellers.

Interestingly enough, all three come from a single book, *Shooting an Elephant and Other Essays*. This book, you notice, is copyrighted 1950, but some further study indicates that these essays were previously published in magazines or journals and then collected and published in book form. After reading one of the essays as a sampler, you decide to write your retrospective not about *1984,* the novel *or* the year, but about Orwell's skill as an essayist.

SUGGESTED DISCUSSION QUESTIONS

1. What other facts do you and your classmates know about George Orwell?
2. What kinds of subjects did Orwell write about?
3. Why are Orwell's essays so widely used in English classes?

SUGGESTED ASSIGNMENTS

1. You decide to write a critical analysis about some aspect of one of Orwell's essays. Remembering what you've read in *Casebook Rhetoric*, you decide to use a particular writing principle the text emphasizes as a way to analyze Orwell's effectiveness as an essayist (e.g., the organization of vivid detail in narration).
2. You decide to write a critical analysis based on one highly specific aspect of writing present in *all three* of these essays.
3. You do some additional research and begin to wonder about Orwell's original audience. Obviously when he wrote these essays he wasn't writing for you— you weren't even born yet. To whom was he writing then? You decide to select *one* of the three essays, discover the original source of its publication, analyze who read that magazine or journal, and then write an essay about how effective Orwell was in writing to his original audience—the readers of his day.

Where'd It Come From?
Where'd It Go?

In 1976 the *County Shopper* merged with *The County Times* to produce a weekly paper that was an odd kind of hybrid. The *County Shopper* had, in the past, been just that, a shopper, a newspaper devoted strictly to advertising and distributed to nearly every household in the county free of charge. *The County Times* had previously been a small weekly newspaper with a heavy emphasis on local news and a couple of local columns written by local journalists. *The County Shopper-Times,* the new paper, was distributed weekly free of charge to every household in the county, and 95 percent of its space was devoted to advertising, but because it now included a small amount of news and two weekly columns, its advertising rates were higher.

One of the two columns retained in the new paper was entitled "Where'd It Come From? Where'd It Go?" Written by Gene Bibbons, the column was kept on after the merger because it was popular and because the owners of the *Shopper Times* liked Gene and the work he did. Gene was not a journalist professionally, and he was paid just twenty dollars a week for his column, but he enjoyed writing.

Gene dreamed up the column, you vaguely remember him telling you once, because he got to wondering where certain technological wonders had come from, and what happened to the duds.

"Like the Edsel," Gene said. "You know why the Edsel failed? Do you?"

Just plain curiosity was one reason why people read Gene's column. Gene's idea was that if he kept his column fresh people would keep reading, and he could keep getting paid to satisfy his personal curiosity about things.

"Like those solar batteries on calculators," Gene said. Gene thought it was amazing that those calculators could operate on room light. So he'd done some research and written about how Sanyo of Japan had developed solar electricity and had ended up producing those little photovoltaic cells. "Now they're putting them on transistor radios in Japan," Gene said.

Actually you don't have any copies of Gene's column on hand, but you do remember one other column he wrote—about microwave ovens. But you can't remember the details of the column—something about Raytheon. Now you wish you could remember more because you've just been asked by Gene for a favor. Gene's just called and explained he's going on vacation for two weeks—to Hawaii—and he wants someone to write the column for him while he's gone.

"I'm all out of ideas anyway," Gene said. "Why don't you write one? We usually have space for something between 500 and 750 words. You can't really go much longer than 750 because we can't afford to give up the space. And be sure to make it tight since every inch you don't use we can sell to an advertiser. Okay?"

Before you could really say much of anything Gene was thanking you for volunteering and telling you he'd see you in a couple of weeks. You are expected to turn your column in to Alice Hidder, Gene's editor.

"Don't provide formal footnotes," Gene said, "but be sure to credit your sources for the specific information you get from them. Alice'll give you help with that part if you ask her."

SUGGESTED DISCUSSION QUESTIONS

1. What other subjects might be interesting sources for an essay with a "where'd it come from?" point of view?

2. What other titles for this column are possible?

3. What other subjects might be suitable for an essay with a "where'd it go?" point of view?

SUGGESTED ASSIGNMENTS

1. Write a column for the *Shopper-Times* entitled "Where'd It Come From?" Microwave ovens and photovoltaic cells are the only two subjects Gene has already covered.

2. Write a column for the *Shopper-Times* entitled "Where'd It Go?" The only topic you know Gene wrote about is the Edsel, but just jotting down an initial list of possibilities yourself, you produce the following: hoola-hoops, boomerangs, The Dave Clark Five, the Studebaker, knickers, saddle shoes, the slide rule, and the topless bathing suit. Check with Alice about a specific topic selection.

Write Your Own

You are sitting there staring at this textbook when you suddenly decide you should try writing your own case. What a great idea! You have enjoyed reading some of the cases in this book, but now it's time for a change.

Maybe reading the cases made you think of a problem-centered writing situation you know about, one you yourself were really in or someone you know was in. Or maybe you just suddenly feel especially creative and you want to write a case that is realistic, but one that you have made up from scratch, out of your own imagination.

Will your instructor allow you to write your own case? What do instructors need to know about assignments when students do something different? You will probably be told you may do it if your request is persuasive. But what will the instructor need to know about your case? Should you do a quick audience analysis of your instructor before going any further?

THE ESSENTIAL INGREDIENTS

Of course any instructor's first question would be, "What, *exactly,* do you want to do?" There are at least two options. One is to write a case other students could use. Another is to write both a case *and* an essay, letter, memo, or report based on that case. Let's consider each in turn.

If you plan to focus exclusively on writing a case rather than writing, for example, an essay the rest of the class has been assigned, then one of your first considerations is to determine how to persuade the instructor that you have a good idea for a case *and* that writing one will be just as difficult as completing the assignment other students have been given. So, what do you know about cases? You know that they are self-contained; are problem-centered; involve realistic, purposeful writing assignments; and describe one or more potential audiences for the writer.

Consider these elements when outlining and writing your case. The reader of the case needs all the information necessary to define and solve the problems the case describes. Therefore, to persuade your instructor to let you write a case, you will have to show that you have the *kind* of information, and enough of it, to write a self-contained case. The case should be centered on a problem that someone could solve or help to solve by writing an essay, letter, memo, or report. That means the case should give the student reader the sense that there is a real purpose to completing a written assignment based on the case. Lastly, the case must provide the student reader with someone to whom to write. In other words, the case should include some mention of a potential audience. Some details about that audience should be included so that the instructor has some way of judging whether a student writer who completes an assignment effectively addresses a particular reader. To summarize, you need to persuade the instructor that the case you are planning will be self-contained, problem-centered, purposeful, realistic, and will describe a potential audience.

Ideally, of course, your case would be as complete and as useful as are the ones in this book. If you plan to write the case, but not to write anything based on it, then the instructor may expect your case to be as nearly complete and useful as any student could possibly make one. On the other hand, if you plan both to write the "case" and to write an essay based on it, then your instructor may be willing to settle for less detail in the case. In fact, you might be allowed to write not a complete case but an extended, detailed assignment.

If you choose to write your own extended assignment, then your instructor should not expect you to write one that is self-contained. The two of you should be able to agree that your essay will be much longer and more detailed than the extended assignment upon which it is based. Even so, in order for your instructor to evaluate your work fairly and objectively, you will need to include some of the basic elements of a case in it.

Including these elements should help persuade the instructor that your alternative assignment is acceptable. First, describe the problem that you want to write about. In other words, write a paragraph or two in which you define the subject about which you are going to write. Second, indicate what the purpose or goal of your essay will be. Are you trying simply to inform the audience about, for example, the problem of bikes on campus, or are you trying to persuade the audience that the administration needs to provide faculty, staff, and students with more bike racks? Third, in a paragraph or two, describe the reader to whom you will write. Keep in mind that the instructor will have to "become" this person in order to evaluate the essay objectively, fairly, and completely. To summarize, if you are going to write both an extended assignment and an essay related to it, then write your instructor several paragraphs in which you describe your subject and the problem you are writing about, the purpose of your essay, and the reader to whom you are writing.

SUGGESTED DISCUSSION QUESTIONS

1. What are two options you have if you decide to "write your own"?
2. What are some examples of "problems" on campus, in the community, or in one of the essays, stories, poems, plays, or novels you have read for this class?
3. What would be the purpose in writing about one of these "problems"?
4. What elements should be included in every case?
5. What elements should be included in an extended assignment?
6. What is the difference between an extended writing assignment and a case?

SUGGESTED ASSIGNMENTS

1. Write a short essay to your instructor. Persuade him or her to let you write your own case. You may want to include an outline of your proposed case.
2. Write your own case. Write one or more assignments based on it.
3. Write a short essay to your instructor. Persuade him or her to let you write an essay based on an extended assignment you propose to write.
4. Write an extended assignment.
5. Exchange cases or extended assignments with another student. Evaluate the strengths and weaknesses of what you have received. Suggest alternative approaches to eliminate the weaknesses in the case or the extended assignment. Present this evaluation to your instructor in the form of an essay. Your audience is the student who wrote the case.
6. Instead of choosing to assess another student's case, draft a letter to the authors of this textbook, in care of the English Editor, Holt, Rinehart and Winston, 383 Madison Avenue, New York, NY 10017. Point out weaknesses and strengths in one or more of the cases you have read. Be as specific as possible, particularly in your suggestions for strengthening the cases.

The Mayoral Primary

When Michael Apodaca decided to run for mayor, Diana Garcia joined the campaign staff. Michael's first goal was to win the primary. Diana had volunteered to work for Apodaca's election because she believed he would be a good mayor and because his political views were quite similar to hers.

Even so, as she drove to headquarters, she wasn't sure she could really be all that much help. She didn't really have any political experience.

At headquarters she was surprised by what she was asked to do. None of the candidates in the primaries, the campaign manager explained, were well known. Apodaca was perhaps even less well known than were the others. Furthermore, none of the candidates had a lot of money to spend. Therefore, the campaign would be won not on the basis of flashy Madison Avenue techniques, but on the issues. The questions were: What were the issues? What bothered the people in the city? What problems did they have? What did they care about?

Diana and several other college students were assigned the task of defining one problem or issue facing the city. To avoid duplication, each student volunteer was to check with the campaign manager once he or she had selected a problem. The next step was to write up a problem definition. The purpose of the definition was to convince the campaign manager and Apodaca that the "problem" selected was a genuine one, one of general concern to the city's populace, or at least to a large segment of it.

Once the problem definition was accepted by Apodaca and his manager, a position paper, an argument based on the problem, was to be written by the volunteer. Naturally Apodaca couldn't make any wild or expensive-sounding proposals, but showing a thorough understanding of the problem and proposing common-sense solutions were two abilities any good politician should have. Diana and the others were told to use common sense in arguing for a particular solution or set of solutions. If the argument was persuasive enough, it would become part of Apodaca's campaign platform and copies of the essay would be distributed to the press and the public. If the argument was not persuasive, the volunteer might be asked to reformulate the paper.

Diana and the others immediately had questions about how they were supposed to identify problems. What did they know? they asked. They were just college students. Some of them didn't ever get involved or pay attention to politics. How were they supposed to know what the issues were? The campaign manager had some suggestions. First, they could try reading the local newspaper and looking for newspaper articles that would give them leads. Second, they might try randomly interviewing a dozen people in the city or maybe a lot more. Third, they could read the "letters to the editor" column in the newspaper of the past several weeks and see what was bothering people, what people were responding to. Another technique would be to interview city employees who provided services to the community—the police department, the fire department, the animal control center—and see what these city employees had to say about the city and its problems. Obviously, the manager concluded, some research was required here.

Diana went out the door wondering where to start.

SUGGESTED DISCUSSION QUESTIONS

1. What are the current issues of importance in your community?
2. Where can you discover which topics might be of interest to voters?
3. How can you discover which topics might be of interest to voters?

SUGGESTED ASSIGNMENTS

1. You are Diana Garcia. Select an issue and write a memorandum persuading Apodaca to take a particular position or stance.
2. You are Diana Garcia. Your instructor is Apodaca's campaign manager. Go through the steps involved in writing a position paper and write the paper. Choose a real problem in your city or town.
3. You are Diana Garcia. Write a speech for Apodaca based on an issue you believe is important. Select an appropriate audience.

The Campus Task Force

With a grant from the federal government, your university (or college) has established a task force that is expected to investigate problems on campus and propose solutions for them. The task force is composed of thirty faculty, administrative, and student members and is directed by a chairperson. In the interest of achieving the widest possible perspective, each committee member has been asked to write a short statement that fully defines a problem on campus. To avoid duplication, each member is to clear his or her choice with the chairperson before investigating and defining that problem. In selecting and defining a problem, each writer is encouraged to consider personal experience, to interview people in the campus community, and to review issues of the campus newspaper.

Once each member has submitted a problem definition, the task force will review all problems and select those that seem to be the most serious, to be of the greatest general interest, and to offer some hope of resolution. The task force will then break down into a number of small groups. These groups will complete the investigation of the problem and possible solutions to it. One member of the group will then be selected to write a draft of the group's task force paper on that problem. The paper should fully analyze the problem and argue in favor of a particular solution to it. The group will jointly rewrite and edit the paper until everyone in the group is satisfied with it.

After a general review of all group papers by the entire task force, the papers will be published (with funds provided by the grant) in booklet form and distributed throughout the campus community.

SUGGESTED DISCUSSION QUESTIONS

1. What are some important current issues on your campus?
2. How can you discover what issues concern students? Faculty? Administrators?
3. Where should you look for possible subjects to study?

SUGGESTED ASSIGNMENTS

1. You are a member of the campus task force. Select a problem on campus and clear it with your chairperson (your instructor). Write a problem definition. (Your instructor may want to review this definition with you.) Assume your problem has been selected by the task force. Due to the large number of problems selected and the absence of some task force members, you have to write, rewrite, and edit your own paper for publication in the task force booklet.

2. You are a member of the campus task force. Select a problem on campus and clear it with your chairperson (your instructor). Write a problem definition. (Your instructor may want to review this definition with you.) In a class discussion, the class will select the problems to be investigated by each group. Under your instructor's guidance, organize the class into groups and with your group complete the task force paper on the problem your group has been assigned.

City News and Nuclear Energy

On Wednesday morning, March 28, 1979, the police in Harrisburg, Pennsylvania, reported a general emergency at the nuclear power plant located nearby. The "general emergency" condition at the plant—Three-Mile Island—meant that radiation was escaping beyond its borders. The same day Metropolitan Edison indicated that the emergency situation was under control. By Thursday, representatives of the United States federal government's Nuclear Regulatory Commission (NRC) confirmed Metropolitan Edison's control of the situation.

On Friday, however, two more uncontrolled releases of radiation and the news that a hydrogen bubble had formed inside the reactor shocked Harrisburg residents and the nation as well. On Saturday Metropolitan Edison and the NRC disagreed about the size of the bubble. On Sunday the

Associated Press released a report that the hydrogen bubble could become explosive if enough oxygen entered it. Many residents of the area, already uncertain about whether to leave, were angry and frightened, yet by Monday the situation once again seemed to be under control.

The incident received much attention from the media as dozens of reporters traveled to Harrisburg. These reporters found it difficult to ask questions and get answers, however, not only because they themselves knew little or nothing about nuclear power plants, but also because Met Ed and the NRC did not know how to or did not want to explain the situation fully and clearly.

Even now, the importance of the nuclear accident that occurred at Three-Mile Island is not clear. It has been used by both antinuclear and pronuclear groups to argue their positions. Some people say that the confusion and uncertainty at Three-Mile Island prove just how dangerous nuclear energy is. Others say that the accident proves that the NRC and the utility companies can deal with a situation like this quite successfully.

CITY NEWS

The editor of the City News, Jay Kanowitz, felt that his readers were interested in the dangers of nuclear power plants. Some of the problems the accident illustrated were: the general public's ignorance about how a nuclear power plant operates; reporters' ignorance about the plants' operation and their consequential difficulty in investigating nuclear accident stories; the governor, Governor Thornburgh's, difficulty in getting accurate and consistent information about the accident.

Obviously Three-Mile Island was an important event in a country that was short on petroleum and wary of nuclear power. The President had thought it important enough to visit Three-Mile Island during the crisis. After it was over he appointed the President's Commission on the Accident at Three-Mile Island, otherwise called the "Kemeny Commission," after its chairman. The committee reported its findings and recommendations to the President and the Departments of HEW and DOE.

But what did all this mean to *City News*? Jay Kanowitz resolved to appoint some young reporter to do one or more articles about nuclear power in the area served by *City News* readers. Kanowitz wondered if the *News* might conduct a survey of its readers to determine how much the average person knew about nuclear power plants and how they worked. How, he wondered, could people out there be expected to listen to debates about nuclear power plants if they didn't even know how the things worked? He also wondered whether people even knew whether there was a nuclear power plant near them and what effects a "general emergency" would have on them. Did they know what would happen to them should the nearest plant go into the "China syndrome"? Perhaps, Jay Kanowitz thought, the paper should do a series of articles on nuclear energy.

SUGGESTED DISCUSSION QUESTIONS

1. Where is the nearest nuclear power plant in your area?
2. What do you know about how a nuclear power plant works?
3. As best you are able, describe the process by which a nuclear power plant produces energy.
4. Discuss what you know about the safety devices used and the procedures followed to prevent nuclear accidents.
5. What would happen in your area if a "general emergency" was announced at your nuclear power plant?
6. What would happen in your area if your plant went into the "China Syndrome?"

SUGGESTED ASSIGNMENTS

1. Write an article for the City News in your area. Explain to the readers how a nuclear power plant works.
2. Write an article for the City News in your area. Explain the "China Syndrome."
3. Discuss what, if any, evacuation procedures would be followed.
4. Using the Kemeny report and other research data, argue whether the nuclear power plant nearest you is safe.

The Career of Your Choice

As part of its work in helping students in their growth and development, your Student Counseling Service offers students guidance in selecting a major and a career. Suppose that as a part of that service SCS has a career library. In this library are shelves filled with useful guidance and reference materials.

The shelves in one section are filled with neatly labeled black folders. Each folder contains a researched essay about a highly specific career or occupation. For example, there are essays about careers in equine veterinary medicine, hog confinement management, public accounting, commercial lending, and so on.

Freshmen who are undecided about their majors and *other students* who want to investigate career options come into this room, consult an in-dex, and read these essays. These students are hoping to learn all kinds of things about a career and the kind of personal interests, educational back-ground, and other requirements it entails.

Your job, as a student staff member of SCS, is to write *one* additional research essay for Student Counseling Services. While every student who reads a particular essay will have different questions in mind as he or she reads your essay, collectively your readers may ask you dozens of different questions about the particular career you are describing. You consult with your boss and learn that the only limitation on your subject is that the career must be one toward which a student at your school could conceivably be working. Your boss also gives you the following list of questions student readers may ask, though you may not be able to answer all of them. Here are the questions (in no particular order):

How many people are presently employed in this field?
By the time I graduate and look for a job, how many people will be em-ployed in this field?
What is the average starting salary of someone doing this job?
How difficult is it to get into this occupation?
What kind of financial investment, if any, is necessary?
What kind of funding is available?
What are some of the attractive features of the job?
What's bad about it?
What is a day-in-the-life of an X like?
What advice does an expert in this field have to give students like me?
What kind of major in college is required?
Do I have to go to graduate school?

Obviously, your boss says, this list of questions is incomplete and each subject will have its own unique requirements. Even so, your boss says that acquiring the answers to the above questions, or as many of them as you possibly can, will be a good start in beginning to write this essay.

Your boss says that the exact length of your essay is something that the two of you can work out. Of course the size of your subject and the depth of your research will do much to determine your essay's size. Some initial starting places for your research that your boss recommends include the following:

—*Reader's Guide to Periodicals*
—Magazine Index
—Business Index
—the card catalogue
—an interview with someone in the career of your choice
—at least one journal written for people in the career of your choice

—the classified ads listing of job opportunities in your local area or in a nearby metropolitan area

Your boss concludes by saying, "Remember, you should design your essay so that it's written only for our students—right down to suggesting, perhaps, exactly what courses they should take."

SUGGESTED DISCUSSION QUESTIONS

1. What are some possible careers you could write about?
2. What are the students at your college or university like?
3. How much responsibility should your college or university assume in guiding students in choosing a career?
4. What kinds of materials *are* presently available on your campus?

SUGGESTED ASSIGNMENTS

1. As an initial step to writing a research essay about a career, write a direction-giving essay that guides students through the process of fully researching a career and making the right decision.
2. Write a research essay on a career of your choice.
3. Write an essay that persuades students visiting SCS to take the time to research a career before seeking or accepting a job.

ADDITIONAL SOURCES FOR SUBJECTS

Literature

Literature includes poems and plays, short stories and novels, essays and book-length nonfiction. Two basic options in using literature as a source for your own subject-searching are to use another writer's viewpoint or thesis as a jumping-off point or springboard for your own work OR to write an analysis of another writer's work. Hundreds of books have been written about the art of writing from and about literature; the advice you'll read here is simple and general.

If you choose the springboard approach, then generally you might begin a draft of your essay with a statement like this: "George Orwell's experience of shooting an elephant taught me something about myself and the day I shot a mockingbird." Given this tentative thesis, you could use many methods to develop your point and write your essay. Your instructor can provide you with additional guidance.

If you choose to write a critical analysis of some piece of literature, then the following five tips should help you avoid some common problems and errors inexperienced writers make.

1. Remember to analyze your audience. Simply stated, you have three possible readerships: readers who haven't read the literature under discussion, readers who have, and readers who are a mixture of the first two groups. If your readers haven't read the material, then, *as you make your points* you will have to include brief bits of summary or detail to make sure the reader understands what you are analyzing. But the analysis itself should *always* get more space and attention than background or summary. If your reader *has* read the material, then don't summarize at all—don't retell the story. Doing so insults your reader, who is smart enough to remember all that stuff. If you are writing to both groups at the same time—an extremely difficult task for any writer—you must include enough background to orient some of your readers and yet not so much background that you offend or bore the rest of your readers. That's a tough assignment, perhaps one you should avoid altogether.

2. Analyze, don't summarize. Usually you'll be writing to someone who has already read the material. Don't tell them what they already know: don't summarize the plot. Just analyze. When you analyze, you give meaning to your subject. In other words, you make an argument about your subject—there's no argument in a summary.

3. Make your analysis an argument. A sturdy thesis for a literary analysis states an argument worth making: "Chekhov achieves a special sense of realism in *The Three Sisters* through four key techniques." Stick your neck out. If you don't, you may bore the reader and/or waste his or her time. If you do, your readers may disagree or criticize your point of view, but at least they'll be paying attention.

4. Quote the appropriate evidence. When you write about literature, your supporting evidence, the detail you use to support your argument, comes from the text itself. Some of it you will want to quote to prove your point. Short quotations—those no more than two typed lines long—are the easiest for the reader to follow. If you quote the text precisely, use quotation marks. If you must quote something longer than two lines, then indent five spaces and single space:

> But if you use this method, remember to precede your quote with a colon and end it with a period. Also, it's best not to

quote over five lines. Long quotes make it difficult for your reader to reenter your argument and follow your main idea.

5. Finally, whether you quote briefly or at length, end the quote with a page number provided in parentheses (p. 47).

Movies, Television, and Other Visual Experiences

All the above tips about writing about literature apply here, and then some. Writing about something visual—a movie, a play, a television show—challenges the memory of the writer. Suppose you decide to write an analysis of a play that is being produced in your town. Once you've seen the play, the art is gone—you can't reexamine or study it unless you buy another ticket. Or suppose you decide to write an *analysis* of one or more segments of "M.A.S.H." or "Hill Street Blues." (Remember it must be an analysis—leave the summaries to *TV Guide*). If you have a video recorder you may be able to study the show many times. Otherwise, you've just one opportunity—at least until reruns begin. Here are two ways to cope with your problem, and your readers' problem, of limited availability.

1. Try to see the show more than once. If you can view your subject just once, take notes as fast as you can. A legal pad works well. Keep your eyes glued to the stage or screen and record not just the basics of what you see, but any analytical impressions you get. Write across the page as neatly as you can without looking, leave horizontal space between each sentence, and use lots of paper. One approach to good note taking is to make a note for each scene. Professional writers who are good at this technique may take 40 or more pages of notes in an hour.

2. Excellent notes should solve your own memory problem—they will enable you to visualize your subject many times over—but of course your readers face the same problem. Therefore, even if your reader has seen the work you are analyzing, you may want to include phrases and sentences that set the stage or establish the action. Remember that there's no need to summarize the obvious, however. Your purpose is to make some kind of an argument about what you've seen.

Current Events and Popular Culture

Yet another common approach to essay writing is for the writer to analyze and make an argument about either a current event or some aspect
of popular culture. The current event may range from the latest crisis in
the Middle East to last week's murder of a state highway trooper on the
interstate just outside the city limits; the aspect of popular culture might
be an analysis of why some men have their ears pierced, or why women
in increasing numbers are attending women-only video dance shows and
strip-tease acts.

Of course the word *current* should tip you off to a weakness that's
inherent in this kind of writing: what's current today might not be at all
relevant tomorrow. Thus your essay may quickly become as interesting
to read as yesterday's newspaper. Or last week's, or last month's. For example, a current event of not so long ago (as this text is being written),
was the death of hundreds of Marines in Lebanon after a terrorist attack.
But as you read these words, surely other international events seem
much more relevant to you. In fact, perhaps you only vaguely remember
the bombing in Beirut.

Popular culture subjects carry with them the same kind of weakness.
Consider the student writer who, years ago, wrote an analysis of streak-
ing on college campuses or argued for the death penalty for John Lennon's murderer. These subjects may seem unimportant to readers today.

Even so, a current event or an aspect of popular culture can be a
good choice for an essay topic. If you choose well, you can count on a
high level of interest from your readers, at least initially. And of course
it's always helpful to have readers ready to pay attention to you from
word one. Assuming that you've decided to write such an essay, here are
two dangers you should be aware of.

Beware the Huge Subject

Unless you're the world's expert (and maybe especially then), you should
avoid current events issues that are too large to discuss intelligently in a
short essay. The writer who tries to say in five hundred or even fifteen
hundred words what the United States government should do about inflation, unemployment, or high deficits is probably going to end up with
a string of generalities that bore or anger most readers and convince
none. "The Arms Race" is another subject likely to end even the most
successful writer's winning streak. Specifying the subject—the MX mis-
sile system—may help some, but even then there are dangers aplenty in
tackling such a large, complex issue; so—beware.

Be an Expert

Once you've zeroed in on a specific subject, be sure you're the resident expert on it. As was mentioned in the beginning of Part III, readers will probably reject the ignorant writer more quickly than the sloppy or unskilled one. In other words, nobody will listen to your *ideas* if you don't know all your facts first.

This fact of life for writers—the need to be an expert—is especially crucial when current events or popular culture is the writer's subject. If you've chosen, for example, to analyze punk rock dress and appearance, then you must be an expert on what punkers really look like and why. Your audience may actually include a punker or a close friend of one, and this kind of reader may discount *everything* you have to say the instant you make one mistake in fact.

The same is true for fans—Elvis fans, rock fans, baseball fans—or for experts—comic book collectors, video game players, bikers. For these people, knowledge of their subject is often a deep source of pride; they'll be checking every sentence to see if you know as much as they do. Thus you must be sure you know your subject especially well.

In summary, remember to choose your subject with care, making sure that your subject is concrete and specific and that you know it as well, or preferably much better, than anyone who may read your essay.

APPROACHES TO SUBJECTS

As you select a subject, you may also want to consider some unusual or different ways of approaching it. Below we discuss five ways you can get your reader's attention and, perhaps, increase your own excitement about writing. Because each of these five techniques requires some special creativity, you may find one or more of them useless to you or too difficult. On the other hand, you may find one or more of them richly rewarding. Why not give one a try?

Humor

Suppose you are told to write a process analysis essay about a subject of your choice. Instead of writing the typical "How to Make A Teddy Bear," you may want to try an offbeat, humorous approach. "How to Go Grocery Shopping with Your Wife or Girlfriend" and "How to Get Your Way in a Bureaucracy" are two possibilities. If you want to make fun of people's manners, you might try "How to Offend People in Public." The possibilities are endless. If you try this approach, remember that part of the humor can come from mimicking the typical process paper. One student, for example, began an essay on "How to Catch the Abominable Snowman" with an initial section on required materials: two gallons of Wild Turkey, sixteen pairs of size sixteen double-D snow boots, from L. L. Bean, two tickets to the Super Bowl, and one MacDonald's Restaurant. Sound funny? Chances are that readers like you would read on to see just what *this* writer was up to.

Other subjects and methods of developing a thesis offer equally good opportunities for humorous essays. A humorous classification essay, for example, might classify winter drivers as follows: the-peer-out-the-peephole-lazy-bum, the-drive-ten-times-slower-than-anybody-else-coward, the-drive-ten-times-faster-than-anybody-else-crazy, and the-spin-your-wheels-at-ninety-miles-per-hour-dumbbell. The subject you choose here depends on what group you want to have fun with.

Of course any unusual approach involves the writer in taking risks, and that's a disadvantage. On the plus side, readers like to laugh, and if your approach is unusual, your reader's attention will at least temporarily be heightened. A creative essay may be more likely to fail, but it's also true that readers usually prefer a flawed but original piece of writing to a proper but dull piece of writing.

Persona

Actually you've already had lots of practice adopting a persona. Every time you played the role of a particular person in one of the cases in this textbook you adopted a persona—you were that person. Writers sometimes adopt a persona—write as if they are someone else—to give themselves a different way of achieving their purpose and conveying their main idea.

Suppose, for example, that you want to make a point about how frightening and depressing it is to be unemployed. Your purpose is to persuade those people with jobs to feel compassion for the unemployed, or perhaps your purpose is to persuade your readers to support the extension of unemployment benefits. A typical way to achieve your purpose would be to write a persuasive essay in which you argue several points that support the extension of benefits. Alternatively, you might achieve your purpose by adopting a persona and writing a completely different kind of essay. You might, for example, write as if you were an unemployed steel worker in Pittsburgh. *What* you write would be unlimited in scope. Here are three examples of what you might write, given this persona: (1) a diary, (2) a letter to the President of the United States, (3) a letter to your spouse explaining how difficult it is for you to find a job in Houston.

Obviously when you adopt a persona, you expect your reader to realize, as he or she reads, who you are writing as and to whom you are writing. In your English class your instructor may ask you to identify your persona and audience beforehand so the reader will not have to do any guessing. Or your essay may simply begin "Dear Mr. President: As an unemployed steel worker from Pittsburgh, I'm writing to tell you . . . " There are many ways to make your chosen persona and audience clear to your actual reader; doing so is crucial.

Because adopting a persona may require so much imagination and sensitivity, you may find this approach extremely challenging and difficult. By the same token, the challenge may stimulate you and enable you to say things you could never have expressed any other way.

Audience

Just as you've practiced adopting a persona, you have also practiced writing to particular audiences. Now consider the possibility of selecting your own audience. In doing so you may decide that the best way to convey your main idea is to write not to your class members and instructors *directly* but to some other group. For example, you could write to the president of the United States about unemployment, to a forty-five-year-old unemployed steel worker about the importance of a college education, to Burt Reynolds about his latest movie (you may tell him, for example, that you're sorry to see him doing garbage like that). This list could go on and on.

You have still other alternatives. You may write reflectively by writing to someone from your past—the first girlfriend or boyfriend you ever had, the boy who broke your nose when you were fifteen, or even to someone who's dead (your father or mother, Paul "Bear" Bryant, or John Lennon). Write to the first visitor we have from outer space. The sky isn't the limit here; your imagination is.

As with adopting a persona, designating a special audience for your writing carries as much risk as reward, so be prepared to work extra hard.

A Confessional

Of course a "confessional," strictly speaking, is an acknowledgment of guilt or, if the audience is a priest, an acknowledgment of sin. But for a writer a confessional is simply another approach to a subject, humorous or serious. A humorous confessional, beyond being funny, should teach the readers some truth about a particular subject. For example, you might decide to title your essay, "Confessions of a Soap Opera Addict" and write a humorous description of yourself and your habits for the purpose of showing how and why people become addicted to soap operas. Alternatively, you might write "Confessions of a Video Game Addict" or "Confessions of a Computer Coward." The former essay might explain the virtues and vices of video games. The latter might show how all the media emphasis on computer literacy has one middle-aged car salesman (you) scared to death. A serious confessional also reveals truth about a subject, but with greater depth, perhaps, and with a greater intent to expose the difficult-to-discuss. Consider, for example, an essay entitled "Confessions of an Abused Child" or "Confessions of a Drug Addict."

As with other unusual approaches to a subject, the confessional essay probably increases the reader's attention level initially. The catch is that then you have to deliver—you have to reveal something about yourself (or your persona) that you wouldn't be able to or willing to otherwise. Confessionals give the writer the opportunity to depend on a personal experience, make use of an emotional reaction to a subject, and convey a truth about the writer (or his persona) that might otherwise never be communicated. At the same time, confessionals must meet the readers' raised expectations.

A Dialogue

Quoting what real or imaginary people have said is another way to write an entire essay (as well as simply provide evidence within an essay). There's a story about Calvin Coolidge that goes something like this: A woman has spent most of a dinner trying to get the President, known to be a man of few words, to speak to her, but she's failed completely, so finally, she says, "Mr. President, I made a bet that I could get you to say more than three words this evening." Coolidge smiled at her and said, "Madam, you lose."

This anecdote about Coolidge wouldn't be worth telling without the dialogue. Dialogue can enrich an essay just as it can enrich a short story. Beyond occasional use of dialogue, it's also possible to write nearly an entire essay with dialogue. Whenever you choose to use dialogue, some scene setting is usually necessary. Here's an example from a newspaper column published by one of the authors of this text in the *Ames Tribune*, Thursday, October 22, 1981:

In a lounge just off Lincoln Way in Nevada, the drunk turns on his bar stool and glares at a tall guy, clearly not a farmer or laborer, crouched over a video game screen.

"Ya make any money playin' those machines?" the drunk shouts. Half falling off his bar stool, he wanders over to the machine, an upright model with bright yellow sides, blue-black screen, a single joy stick with a red knob, and select buttons for one- or two-player games. "Then why you playin' 'em?" he shouts in the guy's ear.

Once the scene is set you may devote either a couple of lines or a couple of pages to what the characters say. Writing an entire essay through dialogue may carry high risk, but sometimes taking risks is good for a writer. Certainly the use of dialogue throughout an essay would be one way to get in a lot of practice at using dialogue.

More

There are more approaches out there, and a variety of combinations, as you've already seen, of the approaches discussed here. You can, for example, write in the persona of a fifteen-year-old alcoholic and choose as your audience the teenager's parents. Your essay or letter in this situation could be a confessional or it might be almost all dialogue: "Dear Mom and Dad: You never listen when I talk, so I'm going to write you this letter in the form of a play. I'll say what I have to say and then, to save you the work and since I already know anyway, I'll write down what you'll say." Our point here is simply that there's no limit to what you can try except those limits set by your instructor, your boss, or you yourself.

EPILOGUE

There's no conclusion to BEYOND CASES, just this epilogue. This book has given you writing opportunities ranging from the extremely practical and specific to the highly creative and unrestricted. Practicing both will develop your own writing mind and muscle. Use both—think and sweat like a writer and you'll be one. Your own limits are out there. Look for them.

HANDBOOKS AND RESEARCH-PAPER BOOKS

Corder, Jim W. *Handbook of Current English*, 6th ed. Glenview, Ill.: Scott, Foresman, 1981.

Ferre, John P. *Merrill Guide to the Research Paper*. Columbus, Ohio: Charles E. Merrill, 1983.

Walker, Melissa. *Writing Research Papers: A Norton Guide*. New York: W. W. Norton and Co., 1984.

Weidenborner, Stephen, and Domenick Caruso. *Writing Research Papers*. New York: St. Martin's Press, 1982.

Note: You may want to ask your instructor what book he or she recommends.

Index